eLEARNING – THEORIES, DESIGN, SOFTWARE AND APPLICATIONS

Edited by **Patrizia Ghislandi**

eLearning – Theories, Design, Software and Applications
Edited by Patrizia Ghislandi

Published by InTech
Janeza Trdine 9, 51000 Rijeka, Croatia

Publishing Process Manager Ivona Lovric

Technical Editor Teodora Smiljanic

Cover Designer InTech Design Team

Additional hard copies can be obtained from orders@intechopen.com

eLearning – Theories, Design, Software and Applications, Edited by Patrizia Ghislandi
p. cm.
ISBN 978-953-51-0475-9

For EU product safety concerns:
IN TECH d.o.o., Prolaz Marije Krucifikse Kozulić 3, 51000 Rijeka, Croatia,
info@intechopen.com or visit our website at intechopen.com.

Meet the editor

Patrizia Ghislandi is full professor of "educational technologies" at the Faculty of Cognitive Sciences, Trento University, Italy. Between 1987 and 2000 she was director of the CTU-Centro di Tecnologie per l'Apprendimento, the eLearning Center of the University of Milan, which she had set up in 1976. She initiated, and between 2001 and 2004 coordinated, the Trento's university Online Teaching project, and for that period was pro-rector for distance teaching/learning. She has been carrying out researches and experimentations in the field of training technologies and methodology since 1976. She has been a speaker at over 100 national and international conferences; published more than 150 scientific papers and edited 5 monographs and textbooks. She is member of several editorial boards of scientific journals.

Contents

Preface

eLearning or electronic learning.

The term was coined when electronics, with the personal computer, was very popular and internet was still at its dawn. It is a very successful term, by now firmly in schools, universities, and SMEs education and training. Just to give an example 3.5 millions of students were engaged in some online courses in higher education institutions in 2006 in the USA[1].

Everything started in the seventies with researches and experimentations by Starr Roxanne Hiltz and Murray Turoff at the New Jersey Institute of Technology (Harasim et al, 1995).[2] In the same period the Open University in UK and the University of British Columbia were exploring the possibility for students to discuss and co-build knowledge using a learning network. Linda Harasim was then one of the first authors to publish an important book on the topic, called in those days *online learning* or —when the forum use was particularly intense— *computer conferencing* (Harasim, 1990).[3]

eLearning today refers to the use of the network technologies to design, deliver, select, manage and broaden learning and the possibilities made available by internet to offer to the users synchronous and asynchronous learning, so that they can access the courses content anytime and wherever there is an internet connection (wikipedia, 2012).[4]

The peculiarities of the net allow to design a teaching /learning process that is:

1. interactive, because the student can interact with the networked content;
2. collaborative, as the group give the possibility to everyone to co-build its own knowledge;
3. dynamic, when it allow the student to acquire new specific knowledge *just in time;*
4. modular, when the course content is organized in self-contained modules that can be assembled in several way, according to the different educational goals and user needs;
5. multimedia, because it uses in a sage way all the media: text, audio, still frames, motion sequences;
6. accessible, meaning that " the digital resources and their method of delivery are matched to the needs and preferences of the user" (IMS Global Consortium, 2010).[5]

If these student-centered characteristics are in place, eLearning is today very far away from traditional distance teaching, that delivers the same monolithic contents to all the students.

In "eLearning. Theories, design, software & applications" we investigate the eLearning in its many different facets in four sections and fourteen chapters.

In the section "theories" the main contents are:

1. Characteristics of the emerging eLearning environments, particularly through networked learning and learning in knowledge networks (*New eLearning Environments: e-Merging Networks in the Relational Society*, Blanca C. Garcia, Northern Borderlands Research College, Colef, Mexico);
2. Knowledge building in online learning (*Knowledge Building in eLearning*, Xinyu Zhang and Lu Yuhao; Tsinghua University China);
3. Identity, variety and destiny in productive eLearning, with specific reference to desired learning outcomes (*E-Learning and Desired Learning Outcomes*, Ralph Palliam, American University of Kuwait);

In the section "design":

4. Readiness of SMEs for eLearning and attempts to transfer existing best practice of eLearning solutions to other SMEs. (*Innovative E-Learning Solutions and Environments for Small and Medium Sized Companies (SMEs)*, Ileana Hamburg, Institute for Work and Technology – FH-Gelsenkirchen, Germany);
5. Reciprocal leadership for eLearning instructional designs in distance learning settings (*Reciprocal Leading: Improving Instructional Designs in E-Learning*, Kathleen Scalise and Leanne R. Ketterlin-Geller, University of Oregon, Southern Methodist University USA);
6. Quality in eLearning, analyzed through the identification of good academic online/blended course characteristics and of the most suitable methods to monitor them (*adAstra: A Rubrics' Set for Quality eLearning Design*, Patrizia Ghislandi, University of Trento, Cognitive and Education Sciences Department, Italy);

In the section "software":

7. Learning objects and their applications in physics education (*Learning Objects and Their Applications*, Selahattin Gonen and Bulent Basaran, Dicle University, Turkey);
8. Evolutive platform, a new paradigm with regard to learning processes and educational practices allowing personalization, adapting the behavior of the system according to some specific information related to an individual user (*Evolutive Platform - A Genetic E-Learning Environment*, Jorge Manuel Pires and Manuel Pérez Cota, Universidade de Vigo, Spain);
9. A framework for implementing a content integrated learning management system with specific focus on multimedia enrichment in learning content (*A Multimedia*

Integrated Framework for Learning Management Systems, Nishantha Giguruwa, Danh Hoang Anh and Davar Pishva Ritsumeikan Asia Pacific University, Japan);

10. An algorithm for automatic alignment of ontologies, relating to different fields of knowledge, allowing the exchange of a semantic point of view among many people (*Ontology Alignment OWL-Lite*, Aammou Souhaib, Khaldi Mohamed and El Kadiri Kamal Eddine, LIROSA, Faculté des Sciences, Université Abdelmalek Essaadi, Tétouan, Maroc);

In the section "applications":

11. Creation and testing of the influence of a online/onsite Community of Practice on the teachers' conceptions of the Nature of Science by means of a master's-level graduate course (*Developing a Online/Onsite Community of Practice to Support K-8 Teachers' Improvement in Nature of Science Conceptions*, Valarie L. Akerson[1] , J. Scott Townsend[2] , Ingrid S. Weiland[3] and Vanashri Nargund-Joshi[1], [1] Indiana University, [2] Eastern Kentucky University, [3] University of LouisvilleUSA);
12. eLearning in the development of the modern curriculum of physics (*eLearning in the Modern Curriculum Development*, Robert Repnik, Branko Kaučič and Marjan Krašna, University of Maribor and University of Ljubljana, Faculty of Natural Sciences and Mathematics, Faculty of Education, Faculty of Arts, Slovenia);
13. Virtual Lab, a teaching system which is based on Web and virtual reality technology and consists of virtual experimental workbench, virtual equipment library and open laboratory management system (*Open Web-Based Virtual Lab for Experimental Enhanced Educational Environment*, Fuan Wen, Beijing University of Posts and Telecommunications, China).

I wish you all a very interesting readings.

Dr. Patrizia Ghislandi
University of Trento,
Italy

[1] "E-Learning", Wikipedia, The Free Encyclopedia, http://en.wikipedia.org/wiki/E-learning (accessed March 27, 2012).
[2] Harasim L., S. R. Hiltz, L. Teles e M. Turoff, 1995, "Learning Networks. A field guide to teaching and learning online", Cambridge, Massachusetts, The Mit Press
[3] Harasim L. (ed.), 1990, "Online education. Perspectives on a new environment", New York, Praeger
[4] "E-Learning", Wikipedia, The Free Encyclopedia, http://en.wikipedia.org/wiki/E-learning (accessed March 27, 2012).
[5] IMS Global Learning Consortium, 2010, "Access For All Personal Needs and Preferences for Digital Delivery Information Model v2.0" – Revision: 30 April 2010, http://www.imsglobal.org/community/index.html, date of access: 23 March 2012

Part 1

Theories

New e-Learning Environments: e-Merging Networks in the Relational Society

Blanca C. Garcia
El Colegio de la Frontera Norte, COLEF
Mexico

1. Introduction

It was only a few seasons ago that explorations into the remote frontiers of the e-learning field invited venturing into *blended learning, mobile learning, networked learning* or maybe into *complex adaptable e-learning systems*, if we were really adventurous learning technologists. Web 2.0 culture artefacts and other technology-based options were made available to integrate them into our regular practice: instant messaging and blogging, Yahoo® Groups, professional or social network memberships or Skype® video-conferencing on one hand. Radio chat broadcastings, *SharePoint®* Docs, purpose-built forums within on-line communities, or regular webinars on the other. Any of them would seemingly increase our sense of learning and connectivity. However, just a season later, with *Second Life®* and other like-environments, we joined Manuel Castells (Castells, 2004) and others in witnessing the *Rise of the Network Society*, as well as a relentless shift from the knowledge-based societies into *relational-based economies* and *societies* (Allen, et.al., 2009).

Today, in the realities of the web 3.0, as e-learning practitioners, we seek to actively converge for collaborative learning in groups and organisations that evoke the networked community metaphor in a number of shapes and colours. As learning professionals, we are now dealing with intriguing learning environments: *edupunk*, expanded education, lifelong learning, *edupop*, incidental learning, and ubiquitous learning, seemingly sample versions of emerging environments such as *invisible learning* (Cobo & Moravec, 2011).

In such intriguing context, the first part of this chapter attempts a literature review on how different forms of networks, (linked to knowledge for community development) map out the nature, development and impact of collective knowledge, also known as *societal knowledge* (Tuomi, 2007, Huysman & Wulf, 2005; Huysman & de Witt, 2004; Dvir & Pasher, 2004; Engestrom, 2004). In the second part of the chapter knowledge-creation is highlighted as a knowledge-based development practice in distinct networked settings, such as knowledge networks, networks of practice (NoPs) or even networked virtual cities, in which social knowledge facilitation is fostered. By means of characterizing those emerging actors and territories, this chapter will include exploring spaces for conversations where "there is a convergence between the 'sciences of development' and the 'sciences of knowledge' as together, they refer to the whole domain of human experience and potential". (Carrillo, 2002:384). In the third part of the chapter, this approach will be followed by a deeper inquiry on the role of networked practices, on how they add value to the social capital of members, communities and regions through access negotiation, autonomy and participation (Wasko & Faraj, 2008, Cox, 2007, Monge & Contractor, 2003, Brown & Duguid, 2000, Augier and Vendelo, 1999).

2. Meaning construction and connectivity in e-merging contexts

Indeed, our present societies are powerfully shaped by the presence (and/or absence) of on-line, self-paced development processes. We clearly keep building multi-cultural, multi-ideological information highways. By doing so, we are seemingly shaping our globe into a world of parallel systems of meaning (Toumi, 2004). In this multi-meaning universe, the emerging societies in different parts of our world are increasingly depending on international links and networks to live on: their communication activities become critically important in the social construction of communities that learn (Tuomi, 2004). In these emerging societies, our culture-led communication artefacts and culturally-based arrangements such as technologies, information systems and connection infrastructures are intending to make our communication activities more intense and more relevant to others. At the same time, access to meaningful communication (or the lack of it) is shaping our self-perceptions as individuals; and our perceptions about other humans, cultures, and value systems in many ways. Hence, our unconventional exchanges of information, knowledge and experiences over the Internet are becoming permanent and personal processes of meaning negotiation. Message significance depends on who and where are the users at the moment of interaction. This meaning negotiation is the new reality of e-learning environments and Internet-based interactions happening world-wide on a 24/7 basis: an increasing flow of continuous and creative interaction.

At the core of this complex makeover of the social, economic and technical sub-systems, sits the system of learning on which each of our societies rely on. Our systems of learning are historical societal structures now seemingly developing into systems of meaning creation (Tuomi, 2004). Indeed, the learning systems in our societies appear to be challenged by the power of networked communication with varying levels of intensity. More than an information revolution, the new millennium has openly confronted us with a learning revolution (Sloman, 2001). Intranets, virtual communities and e-learning are seemingly only the tip of a gigantic iceberg in this emerging revolution. Predictably, given the emphasis of communication in meaning-creation processes, information and communication technologies (ICTs) in such models are indeed playing a major role in the system of learning of emerging knowledge-based societies, or k-societies.

On the other hand, a key assumption of (strong) connectivity, knowledge-intensive learning environments is that the more social interactions elicited, the more meaningful the learning experience would be. Therefore communication activities in these environments become critically important in the social construction of communities that learn (Tuomi, 2004a:1). In these emerging models, the support of information and communication technologies (ICTs), information systems and connection infrastructures are required to make our interactions more intense and more relevant to others, beyond the regional frontiers.

Connectivity has been defined by some scholars as: "a process by which individuals are in a continuous flow of communication by means of a networked computer and are able and willing to share information for learning purposes" (Sloman, 2001:4, Wasko & Faraj, 2008,

Cox, 2007, Monge & Contractor, 2003, Brown and Duguid, 2002, Augier & Vendelo, 1999). In this working definition, the connectivity processes are seemingly determined by the intensity of the flow of information coming to and from each practitioners' interactions as part of a network. However, it has been Barabasi's (Barabasi, 2002) seminal *Theory of Networks* that has influenced recent views on networks for research purposes. Barabasi's portrait of Internet as a collection of sub-networks, one of which is the World Wide Web which has been the basis for distributed learning models and the development of network-based learning and knowledge-creation. For Barabasi, a network is a number of nodes (in our case, practitioners able to access a personal computer in the workplace) linked or connected to one or more nodes (other practitioners and/or learners) in order to exchange information, which constitute "the very nature of the fabric of most complex systems" (Barabasi, 2002:222). Some *Theory of Networks* derivations imply that humans act as nodes, or take part of a de-humanised system of knowledge-creation. Although this has been widely critiqued in e-learning circles (Delargy and Lethany,2005; Servage, 2005; Garrison and Anderson, 2003; Salmon, 2000, Paloff & Pratt, 1999), this *Theory of Networks* has brought a common ground for e-learning as a knowledge-creation process, thought not to occur in isolation. Learning is hence perceived as a collective product in a network. And it can thus be defined as the "resulting knowledge created through the interactions with other individuals or groups in an body or organization" (Jones, 2004b). Learning, (although a very personal matter) must never be an individual matter" (…) one learns best by and with others" (Sumner, 2000:272). For this reason, the basis of networked learning is communication, "characterised as the degree of 'noise' accepted by the host institution. The more communication there is with and amongst the learners, the more noise there is in the system: "that noise is the sound of people coming together to learn" (Sumner, 2000:272). Such considerations are critical to shed some light into the practice of learning that is technology-mediated, adult-targeted and delivered in emerging structures generally known as networks.

3. The theory: knowledge-based networks and the relational society

However, research on networks of social nature has been traced out from Henry Fayol's work, a French mining engineer and director of mines who developed a general theory of business administration. In 1916 he published his experience in the book *Administration Industrielle et Générale*, where he promotes a team spirit to build harmony and unity within the organisation. He called it *Esprit de Corps* (body spirit). This principle is thought to have triggered research on organisational network structures. More recently, the discussion of team-based network structures in management literature has been influenced above all by the research of Peter Drucker (Drucker, 1989), Charles Savage (Savage, 1990), and new millennial scholars like Seufert (Seufert, 1999) and Brown & Duguid (Brown & Duguid, 2002).

From this view, the term *network* designates a social relationship between actors. Actors in a social network can be persons, groups, but also collectives in the form of clusters, institutions, communities or even societies (Seufert el al., 1999). Networks are determined by *contents* (e.g., products or services, information, emotions), *form* (e.g., duration and closeness of the relationship) and *intensity* (e.g., communication-frequency). It is thought that form and intensity of network relationships establish the network structure (Burt, 2000). Moreover, the relationships between the actors are founded upon personal-organizational or technical-institutional interconnections on a long-term basis (Seufert el al., 1999). Network members' relationships stem from their individual autonomy and interdependence, their tensions between cooperation and competition as well as reciprocity and stability. Clearly, "boundaries are constructed socially by the network members" (Seufert, et.al., 2003).

Like Barabasi's view of internet, networks of a social nature disregard the usual tacit social norms and boundaries and even change them (Servage, 2005:304). Thus they convey a characteristic of network-based learning experiences, which assume equal power relations amongst participants (Bottrup, 2005:514). From this perspective, active participation in a network is regarded as a learning activity comparable to intense training and development courses at the workplace (Bottrup, 2005:508). These concepts are particularly advantageous when the workplace is a knowledge-intensive environment (from universities and research centres, to innovation clusters or government social projects etc.), where complex learning networks are already an embedded tradition of the workplace, and the analysis of formal and informal networks of learning becomes a complex, multi-layered task.

3.1 Knowledge networks

Indeed, in recent years a number of scholars have attempted to define the elements and characteristics of *Networks*, especially those who add value to the social capital of organisations. For instance, Monge & Contractor (Monge & Contractor, 2003), suggest three kinds of value-adding, on-line networks for learning, of which, for the purposes of this chapter the third category of networks is highlighted:

> *Social Knowledge Networks. Its not who you know, its what they think you know.* These networks are created by relationships between people who discover each other through their own knowledge (content, projects, comments, questions, answers): not just "social" information ("who knows what?" instead of the "who knows who") of the typical online social network services. These networks are also known as user-generated networks.
>
> (Monge & Contractor, 2003).

Seemingly, *Social Knowledge networks* are overcoming typical on-line barriers of meaning construction by generating a common theoretical base and language of exchange amongst its users. Indeed, user-friendly, internet-based networking technologies have accelerated the development of new forms of exchange: open and public technologies have enabled the creation of strong networked communities, and "virtual" networks by underlining the role of shared community repositories (documents, databases, research outputs) that enable the network to generate a common language or practice.

Social Knowledge networks are also defined by different degrees of knowledge transfer capabilities. Hansen (1999) found that weak ties help a sub-network search for useful knowledge in other sub-network, but impede the transfer of tacit knowledge, which requires strong ties between the two parties to an effective transfer (see Figure 1). Strong ties are defined by *bonding, bridging and linking social capital*. Bonding social capital refers to the intra-community ties within relatively homogeneous groups (family and ethnic group, amongst others), in which members can depend on in situations of need. Bonding social capital helps build group cohesiveness and a sense of shared goals Bridging social capital refers to the inter-community ties between individuals and groups, which cross social divides, such as ethnicity, gender and socio-economic status. Although these are unlikely to be as strong as the intra-community ties, it would seem that a combination of both is required for individuals to "transcend their communities and join the economic mainstream" (Granovetter, 1995).

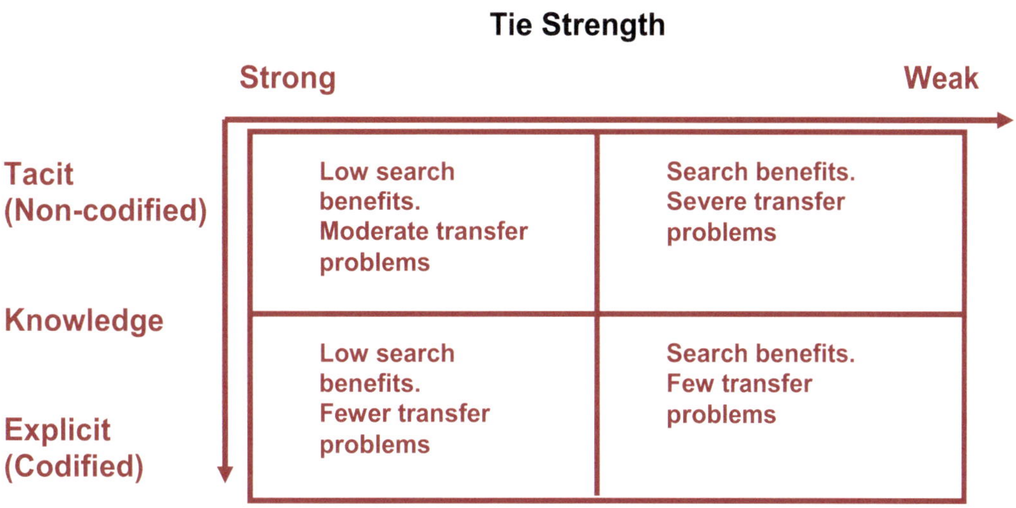

Source: Adapted from Hansen, 1989, in Augier and Vandelo (1999).

Fig. 1. Network Strength

Linking social capital or embeddedness, for some authors (Taylor, et.al. 2004), refers to the nature and extend of the ties connecting the civil and political spheres (Taylor, et.al., 2004:228) and/or the relations between individuals and groups in vertical, hierarchical or power-based relationships (Healy, 2002:79). The concept of embeddedness reflects a relatively horizontal distribution of power relations that fosters mutual trust and cooperative norms between citizens and the state (Wallis and Killerby, 2004:250). Strong ties seemingly allow for face-to-face interaction between the two parties involved in the transfer, and thus the richness of the media used for the knowledge transfer is high and better suited for transfer of tacit knowledge (Augier & Vendelo, 1999).

Nevertheless, according to Hansen, (after Granovetter, 1973) distant and infrequent relationships, i.e. weak ties, are highly efficient for knowledge sharing because they give access to novel information by bridging otherwise disconnected groups and individuals in organizations. Surprisingly enough, opposite strong ties are likely to provide redundant information as they often exist among a small group of actors in which everyone knows what the others know (Hansen, 1999, p. 83).

3.2 Networks of practice

On the other hand, Knowledge-based Development (KBD) and associated disciplines had foreseen the use of networks throughout further different dimensions. The emerging networked forms of people-interaction converge around shared practices as they also share meaning and identity. However, "some of the more prevalent groups of theorists/practitioners are often not linked in concrete daily practices and are rarely physically co-present yet are capable of sharing a great deal of knowledge based on similar experiences" (Kuhn, 2006:106). Brown and Duguid (2002:143) suggest that such groupings be termed "networks of practice" to signify that the relations among members are looser than in communities of practice (Kuhn, 2006:107). Consequently, NoPs appear as on-line systems "distributed in space whose interaction is intermittent, semi-public" (Cox, 2007:766), while a community of practice (CoP) is mostly a face-to-face group with a common sense of purpose nested within a larger network. Such network can take the shape of a *network of practice* (NoP) (Kuhn, 2006) or a *constellation of practice* (Wenger, 1998:126-33). Hence, a working definition for a *Network of Practice* (NoP) as another kind of value-adding, on-line networks has been advanced, since

> *Networks of Practice.* are a community form of fast knowledge diffusion and assimilation over a wide network of Communities of Practice (CoPs) for the creation of new knowledge and meaning. This kind of on-line learning approach also provides a home for the identities of the members through the engagement in the combination of new types of knowledge and the maintenance of a stored body of collective knowledge.
>
> Brown and Duguid, (2000).

In CoPs, learning is generally situated and therefore the local context is essential to construct the meaning of such interactions. While an on-line environment can arguably support situated learning (Lave and Wenger, 1991), the kind of exchange reached within a *Network of Practice* (NoP) is seemingly overcoming typical on-line barriers of meaning construction by generating a common theoretical base and language of exchange. This kind of on-line learning approach also provides a home for the identities of the members through the engagement in the combination of new types of knowledge and the maintenance of a stored body of collective knowledge. NoPs can seemingly overcome the constraints posed by situational learning by establishing ground for common understanding. To this respect, Wenger (1998) has later proposed a learning-in-a-network model within the social community as a *constellation* of interrelated (networked) CoPs, while Brown and Duguid (1991) have introduced notions of *Surrounding Knowledge-ecology systems*. In any case, the Networks of Practice (NoP) are seemingly developing a stronger ability than CoPs that allows the transfer of knowledge and the facilitation of learning through social links.

Molly Wasko and Samer Faraj have also advanced that a NoP is similar to a community of practice (CoP) in that "it is a social space where individuals working on similar problems self-organize to help each other and share perspectives about their practice". However, in a network of practice, "people work within occupations; or having similar interests, they congregate electronically to engage in knowledge exchange about the problems and issues common to their shared practice" regardless of distance and situational spaces. (Wasko & Faraj, 2008:4). Moreover, differences between NoPs and CoPs rest in that most networks of practice rely on electronic communication. NoPs exist beyond a common organizational environment or physical space. In them, NoP members "have the ability to reach everyone in the network, while a CoP is defined by localized tight-knit relationships" (Wasko & Faraj, 2008:4). Clearly, NoPs do not share the material and social context that is typical of CoPs (Brown & Duguid, 2001). In a NoP, "their members do not interact directly and do not share practices per se, and yet they are connected to each other" (Vaast, 2004). Rather, NoPs appear as open systems that emerge spontaneously, "by sheer will of its members and whose eagerness to collaborate, learn and create knowledge together increases with time" (Cox, 2007).

3.3 e-knowledge cities

A third kind of value-adding, on-line networks in the wider social context, (still a matter of debate and contestation) involves the essence of a comprehensive and socially constructed human (individual and collective) capital definition. It is commonly know as Social Capital. Amongst the definitions built around this concept, the OECD Report on *The Well-being of Nations: The Role of Human and Social Capital* has defined human (collective) capital as "the total of social networks together with shared norms, values and understandings that facilitate cooperation within or amongst groups" (OECD Report, 2001, in Healy,2002:78). In this context, social capital is thus "a metaphor about advantage" and the contextual complement of human capital (Burt, 2000:3). Human capital is perceived a close complement of social capital. (Healy, 2002:78).

Yet, *Social Capital* concepts find their conceptual roots in political science and sociology. In their comprehensive literature review on the evolution of social capital conceptualisations, Marleen Huysman and Volker Wulf (2005) propose a working definition for social capital, adopted here for the purposes of this paper:

> *It refers to networked ties of goodwill, mutual support, shared language, shared norms, social trust and a sense of mutual obligation that people can derive from. Social capital is about value gained from being a member of a network. Social capital is often seen as the glue that brings and holds communities together.*

(Huysman and Wulf, 2005:2).

Such definition is the result of years of collective action. The first systematic contemporary analysis of social capital was produced by Pierre Bourdieu, who saw it as a durable network of relationships (1980, in Portes, 1998:3). But it was Granovetter in 1985, (in Huysman and Wulf, 2005) the one who introduced the concept of *embeddedness* of social action, bringing the element of *trust* into the scene. Also, on a theoretical level, Coleman (1988), Burt (1992) and Portes (1998) have provided key contributions to the discussions on human capital and its relation to social capital. Later, it is Putnam (1993) the one who brings social capital to the level of civic engagement, and applies it to cities, regions and whole nations. Social entities, especially cities, are more pre-eminent in the analysis of learning, and we witness the emergence of learning city and knowledge city (KC) knowledge-based models, with integrative and global aspirations. Social capital becomes the prevalence of the network, through which information and knowledge are transmitted more efficiently (Halal, 2005:13).

In this context, cities are taking a leading role as units of analysis, and are re-defined by their history, cities take a leading role and are re-defined by their history, their experience and their level of development. As for individuals, all of these constitute the cities' identity, and the way its citizenship use knowledge to build their infrastructure, their institutions and their future. In the process, most of them are also building knowledge repositories or "depots" of information and "know-how" strategies from which they can withdraw elements of creativity to thrive in challenging times. Seemingly, in a knowledge-based urban community 'people link to form knowledge-based extended networks to achieve strategic goals, cultivate innovation and successfully respond to rapidly changing conditions". (Chatzkel, 2004:62).

In emerging knowledge-based development contexts, a new way of conducting innovation is already operating, quasi-independently of the current money system: its chief requirements are things like time, imagination, knowledge, initiative and trust, with money moving from primary to secondary concern (Paquet, 2010).

Hence, a qualitative change in us as individuals has taken place: we are driven by a fundamental division between the self and the net (Castells, 2004) and is constituted not so much by any notion of identity, but rather of *dividuals*: "we are made up of multiple micro-publics, sharing tele-presence with intimates with whom we are in near-constant contact" (Deleuze in Varnelis, 2010). Not surprisingly, emerging sorts of agents, networks and also cities are progressively finding a place in these new scenarios. For instance, our well known *knowledge worker* (Drucker, 1973) later diversified into prototypes of the *knowledge facilitator* (in Garcia, 2007) has been identified in the relationship economy as a *knowmad*, a type of nomadic knowledge worker (Durrant, 2010, Moravec, 2008). *Knowmads* are thought to be creative, imaginative, and innovative people who can work with almost anybody, anytime, and anywhere, able to instantly reconfigure their social learning environment (Durrant, 2010). They are also active first-rate knowledge network weavers (Paquet, 2010). But most importantly, they take part in networks that are bringing about "emerging cognitive infrastructure, in the shape of multitude of *virtual cities*"; these *cities* will "bring together people with shared values and orientations towards the future, and who are in a position to collaborate to bring something new into the world" (Paquet, 2010). indeed, spaces such as these in which people live, work and learn (Garcia, 2007), are uncharted territories worth exploring in the next paragraphs.

4. Networked practice: new learning environments and actors

At the core of this complex makeover of the social, economic and technical sub-systems, sits the system of learning on which each of our societies rely on. Our systems of learning are historical societal structures now seemingly developing into systems of meaning creation (Tuomi, 2004a:2). A key assumption of (strong) connectivity, knowledge-generating environments is that the more social interactions elicited, the more meaningful the knowledge experience would be. Therefore communication activities in these environments become critically important in the social construction of communities that learn (Tuomi, 2004). For this matter, it can be advanced that a full-color collage of ideas and trends is arising in the e-learning front. Edupunk, expanded education, lifelong learning, edupop, incidental learning, and ubiquitous learning are explored –each of them as an invitation, from very different perspectives, to explore patterns of learning that are more flexible, innovative and creative. Learning is available anytime and anywhere.

4.1 Telecentres as knowledge networks, by Telecentre operators agency

It is only recently that the humble community access points, or *telecentres* have been deemed as the core starting point to develop *Knowledge Hubs* into *Knowledge Networks*.

The first *telecottages* were established in Scandinavia and community technology centres (CTC) were established in the US (Ariyabandu, 2009). According to Molnár and Karvalics (2001), the first community technical centre was opened in Harlem, USA, in 1983, with the primary aim of bridging the growing digital divide between the upper and lower levels of society. CTCs offered free access to technologies and placed great emphasis on training at low cost. This same idea of creating places where the members of a community could access Information and Communication Technologies (ICT) was also followed in 1985 in the villages of Vemdalen and Harjedalen in Sweden (Molnár and Karvalics 2001). From these beginnings, two basic telecentre models can be identified: a) the Scandinavian model with the social aim of connecting the rural and village societies thus supporting their development, and b) the more profit-oriented Anglo-Saxon model, providing long-term access to the ICT devices primarily aiming at profit production (Rega, 2010).

However, since *telecentre* is a generic term which has acquired variety of names depending on the type of use (they could range from Multipurpose Community Telecentres, Community Tele- Services Centres, Community Information Centres, Community Learning Centres Telekiosk, Telecottages, etc.). Hence a working definition of telecentre could be

> *A public ICT access point with value-adding knowledge, training, and services to support its community's economic, social and educational development, reducing isolation, promoting education, employment, health and like services, empowering women and bridging the digital, economic, social and gender divides that polarize our societies*

(adapted from Ariyabandu, 2009:10).

As telecentres are transformed into a more development-oriented version of knowledge networks, their *Knowledge-hub* potential becomes the key intermediate step between common telecentres and *Knowledge networks*, as emerging actors in the regional development scenario. A conventional knowledge hub can be described as:

> *A vibrant public ICT access point which is accessible to communities to gain, share and organize knowledge depending on their needs and environment.*

(adapted from ESCAP 2006, in Ariyabandu, 2009:10).

In a knowledge-based scenario, *Knowledge hubs* can localize knowledge gained from peer ICT-based access points in other regions and serve their community. They could also contribute to creating knowledge by providing experience gained from the local communities to the benefit of the global networks at large. Indeed, knowledge networks, as knowledge hubs, are thought to trigger many other knowledge functions such as education, employment, agriculture and health besides providing conventional ICT facilities to bridge the digital divide. It is thus thought that rural/marginal community empowerment can be attained if the community is provided with access to information and knowledge to improve its livelihood and seek for sustainable development. However, such process involves the emergence of new partnerships, governance structures, participation and business plans. Such partnership dynamics could capture and manage relevant information, and eventually generate more knowledge from the fragmented and otherwise lost collective knowledge of communities.

However, it was deemed important to identify who are the actors behind potentially transforming Telecentres into Knowledge Hubs and Knowledge Networks, focusing on e-Learning elicitation and skill development for Telecentre operators. In the Latin American context, telecentre users' efficiency such as gathering information, managing relevant information, and generating knowledge they can actually apply, are highly intangible issues yet to be explored (Huerta, 2007). Nevertheless, the presence of telecentres in the region since the mid to late nineties left a rich heritage for networking and a form of knowledge-based networks. Some of them have since disappeared; new ones emerge and others continue to work and have become part of an active community fostered and supported by www.telecentre.org (Caicedo, 2009). In Colombia, for instance, the Colombian National Telecentre Network led by Colnodo is "on its way to becoming a sustainable initiative that will offer continuous support to telecentres in Colombia and the region" (Caicedo, 2009). Of a special note amongst such success stories of Colombian telecentres is CINARA's knowledge network dealing with Water Supply, Environmental Sanitation and Water Resources Conservation in hydric stressed areas such as the Alta Guajira near the Atlantic coastal border (Latorre, 2010). This particular group is benefiting from telecentres' networked technologies to facilitate and build permanent focus groups that include local government institutions, private sector and hydric-stressed communities. Also a skills development process was triggered by participatory research within the community, in which the indigenous knowledge was re-valued. Telecentre operators strived to generate a network in which partnerships were built, horizontal relationships were created and participation was the articulating principle of the whole project. As they work in consultation teams, solutions to the communities' acute lack of water emerge as they follow principles of knowledge-based development initiatives that are environment-friendly and people-centred (Latorre, 2009).

From this perspective, it is of extreme importance that Telecentre operators become efficient e-learners and dominate the theoretical aspects of the cognitive e-learning process (learning as knowledge creation), so they are able to lead users to their next level of e-learning capabilities. If operators are not familiarized with learning processes, "they would be unable to support or guide his/her users correctly or will not be able to offer learning options to trigger significant learning amongst the Telecentre users" (Flores, 2005:47). Researchers in the Latin American region perceive Telecentres as an optimal context for well trained promoters, suitably enabled to guide the users in how to take advantage of the digital technology and the learning how to learn frameworks (Flores, 2005:75). Under emerging networked models, it is hoped that telecentre operators can be empowered (through training) to become self-taught, autonomous learners, able to advise on activities and active courses addressed to the different learner groups that telecentres serve. Such kind of knowledge-agent could become a companion who helps others to become aware and sensitive to on-line learning, guiding others to learn on a self-taught and independent basis.

4.2 Networks of practice through network facilitators

While knowledge networks are thought to facilitate development, novel knowledge is deemed to be found in networks consisting of weak ties, which can then link for collaboration with strong-tie networks for transfer of tacit knowledge elicitation. This is were Networks of Practice become a key element of emergent learning environments.

At the macro level, there have been numerous attempts to generate awareness on international networks' social capital. An effective way of creating synergies within such international communities and networks of practice has been the consultation of City benchmarking. By using knowledge-based development frameworks, CoPs and NoPs have started a modern tradition (Beaverstock, et. al., 1998) seeking to gather consensus on KBD practices to identify and recognize best practices in a number of aspects of urban communities: economic competitiveness, entrepreneurial activity, environmental sustainability, freedom of expression, e-government initiatives, or innovation (Kriščiūnas and Daugeliene, 2006). Hence, a stream of awards of different nature are being presented to cities: *Global Location Attractiveness Ranking, Global Competitiveness Report, Best Business Environment, Transparency International, Intellectual Property Rights Protection, Most Globalised Nation in the world, Most Network-Ready City, Most Walkable City in the World,* just to name a few. Such is the case in Networks of Practice such as the MAKCi exercise, in which the multiple weak ties existing within the entire NoP would potentially allow multiple opportunities of knowledge-creation episodes.

Launched in November 2006, the *Most Admired Knowledge City Awards* (MAKCi Awards) is a consensus study that includes an annual consulting exercise established to identify and recognize those communities around the world who are successfully engaging in formal and systematic knowledge-based development processes under the flag of Knowledge Cities (Carrillo, 2007). The MAKCI Awards can be defined as a "knowledge-based initiative whose contribution to innovation depends largely on human imagination and creativity and the knowledge assets available at a point in time and context" (Malhontra, 2003). The MAKCi consultation, as a collaborative research study, represents a community space to build meaningful, collective knowledge that would contribute on an annual basis to the understanding of Knowledge Cities dynamics and transformations.

Clearly, the cornerstone of the MAKCi exercise is a consultation to a Panel of Experts, which is integrated on an annual basis by invitation only. A MAKCi executive committee invites the participation of researchers and practitioners with credentials in Intellectual Capital (IC), Knowledge Management (KM) Knowledge-based development (KBD), and/or Knowledge-based Urban Development (KBUD) practice. As part of such emerging global network, experts are invited to interact on a virtual platform with fellow researchers and practitioners, all of them coming from diverse disciplines, regions, nationalities and ways of life. They converge in this consultation space to discuss and establish the relative future development capacities of worldwide urban communities by assessing their capital value base in a knowledge-based world. In practice, the MAKCi Panel of Experts seemingly acts as a social knowledge network. Even further, as it conglomerates experts from a number of specific KBD regional CoPs, it fits the identified notion that characterizes it as a Network of Practice (NoP). Indeed, in knowledge-generating exercises such as MAKCi, the networked interactions between geographically distant communities of practice (CoPs) within the network are rather complex. According to Kuhn (2006), a possible approach to interaction success is "to create connections within the network by nurturing individuals who can be members of two or more communities simultaneously" (Kuhn, 2006:108). For Kuhn, such connectors or "brokers" are members of the network who "translate, coordinate, and align perspectives through ties to multiple communities" (Kuhn, 2006:109). In the context of the MAKCi exercise, consultation dynamics has relied on a core of active and steady panel members, and some other roles in peripheral participation such as the *Forum Facilitator* and the *MAKCi Technical Secretary*. Such roles would need enough legitimacy to influence the development of the consultation, mobilize attention and address conflicting interests. It also requires the ability to "link practices by facilitating transactions between them and to cause learning by introducing into present practices elements from another community's practice" (Wenger, 1998:109).

In the particular case of the MAKCi NoP, it was observed that most panel members showed scholarly scope, group legitimacy and technical flexibility. Scholarly scope was observed in experts' knowledge and ability to discuss KBD topics on line with informed and authoritative skill. By doing so, their participation has impact and influence on the panellists providing leadership, direction and vision to the exercise; which led them to gain legitimacy amongst participants' different groups. It was also observed that those panel members in their role of connectors or brokers adapted easily to the technical intricacies of participating in a network-based discussion platform, with little or no concern of the environments created through the use of virtual forums. These panellists were already internet-literate as per the demands of their own academic/professional work.

Nevertheless, the MAKCi exercise, as a example of NoP, relies on the full list of Panel participants. Each and every member of the network of experts participating in each successive edition has an echo and contribution to the exercise. Every member of the panel impacts and shapes interactions even if his/her voice is not heard (i.e. the lurkers or observing participants' case). As most experts are somewhat familiar with each other's perspectives and work, (within their sphere of common events and projects, or CoP) they are fully aware of how their contributions can balance exercise outcomes or trigger further discussions. Overall a sense of fellowship, a space to converge with acquaintances and old friends encourage participants to convene as panellists in the exercise (Chase, 2008). As experts agree to participate on a voluntary basis, clearly on a good-will venture, free knowledge sharing is part of the freedom spirit within the MAKCi exercise. Such spirit, and the Delphi methodology that permeates MAKE and MAKCi studies has kept a core experts group fairly consistent over the different editions of the exercises. To that extent, good will and trust are at the core of the MAKCi NoP to function and perform (Chase, 2008).

4.3 e-knowledge cities and network weavers

A lot of the measurable social capital of human communities is triggered by interactions in the marketplace. The internet, extranets, and intranets, are increasing those interactions exponentially (i.e. e-Bay). That's also a promise for knowledge markets (Davis, 2007). This vision of Knowledge Markets is conglomerating notions of e-Learning, social capital and Knowledge Cities, in emerging notions of e-Knowledge Cities, in which networks are the core basic structure and scaffolding of urban reality.

Such networks are part of the city's capital, and it can take different forms. With time, as the city's population grows and diversifies, so does its knowledge, and the channels and networks through which it is distributed. Portes indicates: "whereas economic capital is in people's bank accounts, and human capital is inside their heads, social capital inheres in the structure of their relationships… To possess social capital, a person must be related to others, and it is those others, not himself, who are the actual source of his or her advantage" (Portes,1998). Clearly, in the e-learning realm, social capital concepts like this have triggered swift advancements, with new dynamic and powerful forms of *network weaving*. Some scholars believe that "something ground-breaking is to emerge" with a critical mass of people now "aware of one another and adeptly making use of microblogging — talking *and* listening — to become acquainted with one another and building mutual trust and knowledge". People who purposefully create social capital are thought as first-rate *knowledge network weavers* (Paquet, 2010).

In these emerging e-Knowledge Cities, new intersections of social capital, entrepreneurship, knowledge, innovation, money, and finance are at the forefront. However, innovation is no longer about financial investments. It is more about time, imagination, knowledge, initiative and trust. In these contexts, visionaries such as Sebastien Paquet see "an emerging set of tools and customs -- cognitive infrastructure, when you think about it -- that will give us the necessary scaffolding to grow a multitude of *virtual cities*". These cities will bring together people with shared values and orientations towards the future, and who are in a position to collaborate to bring something new into the world. "They are part and parcel of the emerging Relationship Economy" (Paquet, 2010).

But who are the actors and knowledge agents in this emerging networked world? Several pieces of social Infrastructure, such as Symbionomics, networked tribes, peer production etc join the powerful concept of *Knowmads*, who are the Telecentre operators and the NoP Knowledge-Facilitators of prior network-based Learning enviroments. *Knowmads* are the network weavers of these emerging e-Knowledge Cities.

The Knowmad term was coined by John Moravec, and he defines it as a *nomadic knowledge worker* -that is, a creative, imaginative, and innovative person who can work with almost anybody, anytime, and anywhere. Industrial society is giving way to knowledge and innovation work." (Moravec, 2008). Technologies allow Knowmads to work either at a specific place, virtually, or any blended combination. Knowmads are able to instantly reconfigure and re-contextualize their work environments (Moravec, op. cit.). In fact, the develop a set of peculiar characteristics (see Table 1).

Competences	Knowledge Workers	Knowledge Agents & Knowledge Facilitators	*Knowmads* & other knowledge network weavers
C1. Highly inventive, collaborative & intuitive, able to generate new ideas.	35%	60%	70%
C2. Highly adaptable to new contexts and challenges. Unafraid to failure.	35%	60%	90%
C3. Uses information and generates knowledge to solve unknown challenges in a variety of contexts.	35%	60%	90%
C4. Able to create socially-constructed meaning.	50%	80%	90%
C5. Network generator, always connected to people, ideas, institutions & organizations.	50%	80%	90%
C6. Able to generate horizontal knowledge networks.	50%	80%	90%
C7. Digital Literate, knowledgeable on technology uses and purposes.	70%	80%	90%
C8. Attentive to contexts and information adaptability & usage.	70%	80%	90%

Competences	Knowledge Workers	Knowledge Agents & Knowledge Facilitators	*Knowmads* & other knowledge network weavers
C9. Values and promotes knowledge-sharing and free access to information.	70%	80%	90%
C10. Practices life-long Learning: Able to learn & unlearn quickly, adding new useful knowledge.	70%	80%	90%

Source: Adapted from Cobo, 2009, and Cobo & Moravec (2011)

Table 1. e-Learning Competences Decalogue in the e-Merging Paradigms (estimated)

5. Discussion: New learning environments, new challenges

The identified typologies of networked e-Learning environments and their key knowledge agents, emerged as clearly inscribed in the context of core processes (such as e-learning) eliciting Knowledge-based perspectives. Learning is seemingly part of a global convergence of knowledge systems. However, the frameworks that could bring the analysis into the different levels of networks (Tuomi, 2004b) are yet to be created. Emerging frameworks attempt to highlight the importance of interactions, dialogues and *knowledge moments* for value-based knowledge sharing in multiple and emerging learning spaces of city participation.

Paradigms	Information Society	Knowledge Society	Relational Society
Aim	Tacit knowledge conversion of performing individuals and Archiving Information in purpose-built repositories.	Developing Social Capital in communities, and later Value-driven Capital systems in cities and societies	Developing parallel systems of meaning through relational-based knowledge networks at a global scale.
Some key Authors	Callon **(1991)** Latour **(1987)**, Wiig **(1997)**,	Brown & Duguid **(2002)**, Sassen **(2002)**, Huysman & Wulf **(2005)**, Dvir **(2006)**, Siemens **(2006)**, Gundry **(2006)**, O'Reilly **(2005)**,	Eijkman **(2008)**, Engestrom **(2004)**, Tuomi **(2002, 2010)**, Varnelis **(2010)**, Paquet, **(2010)**, Cobo & Moravec **(2011)**.
Key words	Informatics, knowledge storage and transmission	Connectivity, Network Interaction, Globalization Real-time Dialogues, Fractal Knowledge	Conversations, Meanings, Knowledge Markets & Global Markets for ideas and capital.
Target Agent	*Communities of Practice* and their potential of knowledge sharing	*Knowledge citizens* in cities and regions integrated as performing systems for value-creating knowledge sharing.	Practice-based *knowers* and *knowledge revolutionaries* able to manage social conflict and change.

Paradigms	**Information Society**	**Knowledge Society**	**Relational Society**
Users	Every member of an interconnected city/society, engaged in innovation through technology-based interaction.	Social networks such as Communities of Practice (Wenger's CoPs) engaged in problem-solving activities. This includes emerging virtual CoPs and NoPs.	Every member of a globalised city/society, generating continuous contacts and interactions in meaningful "conversations" and/or *Knowledge moments*
Key Actors/ Core Knowledge Agents	**Knowledge Workers**	**Knowledge Facilitators**	**Knowmads** (First-rate knowledge network weavers)
e-Learning Sample Practices	* e-Training * Computer-Aided Instruction * Computer-based Training * Simulation-Based Training * On-Line Learning * Computer Assisted Learning	* Distributed Learning * Web-based Distance Learning * Networked Learning * Blended Learning * Interactive Computer-Aided Learning * Computer-Supported * Collaborative Learning * Interactive Learning Environments	* Socially Distributed Thinking * Intelligent/Virtual Learning Environments. * Invisible Learning
Web Affordances	**Web 1.0** DoubleClick Ofoto Akamai mp3.com Britannica Online personal websites Evite Domain name speculation Page views Screen scraping Publishing Content management systems Directories (taxonomy) stickiness	**Web 2.0** Google AdSense Flickr BitTorrent Napster Wikipedia Blogging upcoming.org and EVDB search engine optimization cost per click views web services participation wikis tagging ("Folksonomy") syndication	**Web 3.0** * Drupal /Jumla (Personal Webpage management) * Microblogging * UTube Message creation, communication & Learning * Yahoo, *Ask Jeeves* interactive Questions * LinkedIn , Yahoo & Google Networked Groups. * Symbionomics * Regional & National scale synchronization through FaceBook and Twitter.

Source: Adapted from Huysman, M.H. and Wulf, V. (2005); Tuomi, I (2002), Gundry (2006), O'Reilly,(2005), Cobo & Moravec (2011).

Table 2. e-Learning practice in emerging Social Paradigms

The types of networks identified during the building up of the present research work seem to have triggered the emergence of a clearer path for networked knowledge-generating strategies, and attempted to highlight that knowledge facilitation is at the core of network-development processes. The chapter has advanced the importance and role of a skilful knowledge facilitator within the three types of network presented, that actually correspond to the historical, socio-cultural and technological progressions depicted as the Information, Knowledge and Relational Societies displayed in Table 2.

Indeed, the wide variety of networked learning models and approaches reviewed during this chapter could be seen with contrasting degrees of culture, technology, innovation through the social determinants of three historical moments. Viewed from a social capital perspective, those three moments of Society are determined by people's degree and capabilities for relationships.

Most approaches observed during research responded to the generic reference of networked learning, a dominant phase of e-learning, although they convey different learning and development purposes. These network-based learning processes emphasize different degrees of social interaction and thus produce different social learning processes and outputs. Since for the purposes of this piece of research work connectivity has been defined as the process by which individuals are linked by means of a computer and can share information in a network (Sloman, 2001:4), the intensity of knowledge creation is critical. Clearly, these principles have determined the kind of facilitator skills that have emerged for each of the facilitator types identified through the three network frameworks (Telecentres, NoPs and e-Knowledge Networks.

Such findings in terms of networking possibilities within the different networked e-learning approaches observed in three international contexts attempted to bring about a multidisciplinary view of networked facilitation strategies at the practitioners' level, then within the e-learning arena so different levels of interaction could be appreciated following the same basic notion of a network.

6. Final thoughts

This Chapter has aimed to contribute to the existing e-learning, and networked knowledge-creation bodies of knowledge from the social facilitation role perspective. By developing a comprehensive review of Network notions and examples, an exploration of e-learning as a knowledge-generative process was carried out, using a novel approach that adds to uncharted areas of e-learning territories.

The chapter has sought to include a review of the state of the art in Knowledge Networks and parallel notions, in which technology-mediated learning processes in institutions and regions have been deemed paramount. Such extensive literature concepts have been presented along with a metaphor of *meaning-negotiation* and *connectivity*, as well as some knowledge network and knowledge agent typologies that clearly characterize new Learning Environments. The Chapter has sought to combine a multi-disciplinary perspective of e-learning, Networked Learning and *Knowledge-based Development (KBD)* core processes (notably those of social capital development). The present study has thus attempted to bring and original and fresh understanding of networked e-Learning processes in different settings. It can be affirmed that the KM angle assumed for the chapter is not frequently found in recent specialised literature. Because the research was a response to an existing gap in specialised literature of network facilitation strategies, the chapter eventually included wider knowledge-based development schemes that have opened a new window into interpreting the e-learning realities in emerging knowledge-intensive contexts.

Indeed, as notions of *network-based learning* continue to be the dominant discourse in e-learning practice, further theoretical aspirations could develop the network forms here presented. The gap in the literature in regards of the understanding of social skill development processes in on-line facilitation is still wide, and additional research awaits. As the challenges and findings of this research are on the table of discussions, further advancements of e-learning in theory and practice is warmly expected.

7. References

Allen, S. Deragon, J.T. Orem, M. and Smith, C.F. (2009). 'The Emergence of the Relationship Economy: The New Order of Things to Come', see general information at: http://www.happyabout.com/RelationshipEconomy.php with book preview at: http://www.happyabout.com/bookinfo/EmergenceOfTheRelationshipEconomy-WP.pdf

Ariyabandu, R. (2009). "Role of Telecentres as Knowledge Networks: Successes and Challenges", for Information and Communication Technology and Disaster Risk Reduction Division, United Nations ESCAP, United Nations Building, Rajdamnern Nok Avenue, Bangkok 10200, Thailand. Accessed on 6 February 2010, from: http://www.unescap.org/idd/working%20papers/IDD_TP_09_06_of_WP_7_2_905.pdf

Augier, M.; Vandelo, M.T. (1999). 'Networks, cognition and management of tacit knowledge' in *Journal of Knowledge Management*, Vol. 3 No. 4, pp. 252-261.

Barabasi, A-L. (2002). *Linked: the new science of networks*. Cambridge, MA: Perseus Publishing.

Brown J. S. and Duguid P. (2000) *The Social Life of Information*, Boston, MA: Harvard Business School Press.

Brown, J. S. and Duguid, P. (1991). "Organizational learning and communities of practice: toward a unified view of working, learning and innovation", in *Organizational Science*, Vol. 2 No. 1, pp. 40-57.

Bottrup, P. (2005). "Learning in a network: a 'third way' between school learning and workplace learning?", in *Journal of Workplace Learning*. Vol. 17 No. 8, Special Issue Workplace Learning; pp. 508-520.

Burt, R. (2000). "The network structure of social capital" in Sutton, I and Staw, B.M., *Research in Organisational Behaviour*. Vol. 22. Greenwich, Connecticut: JAI Press.

Carrillo, F. J. (2002). "Capital systems: implications for a global knowledge agenda" in *Journal of Knowledge Management,* Special issue on Knowledge-based development Vol. 6, no.4.

Carrillo, F.J. (2007). Introduction to the *Most Admired Knowledge City (MAKCi) Report*. World Capital Institute & Teleos. Available from: http://www.worldcapitalinstitute.org/makci

Castells, M. (2004). *The Network Society: A Cross-Cultural Perspective*. Cheltenham, UK; Northampton, MA,: Edward Elgar Publishers.

Chase, R. (2008). Personal communication at the MAKCi Executive Committee Meeting in the context of 2008 ADIAT Conference (Acapulco, Mexico) on Knowledge Management & Innovation. 6th March 2008.

Chatzkel, J. (2004). "Greater Phoenix as a knowledge capital". in *Journal of Knowledge Management,* Special issue on Knowledge-based development II: knowledge cities Vol. 8, no.5, pp. 28-46.

Cobo, C., and Pardo H. (2007). *Web 2.0. Planet. Collective Intelligence or fast food media.* Published as an *e-Book*. Mexico City (Mexico), and Barcelona (Spain): Creative Commons. ISBN 978-84-934995-8-7. Retrieved on 10 Feb 2008 from http://www.planetaweb2.net/

Cobo, C. (2009) "Strategies to promote the development of e-competences in the next generation of professionals: European and International trends". SKOPE Issues Paper Series. Published at the *ESRC Centre on Skills, Knowledge and Organisational Performance, Department of Education*, Oxford University & the *School of Social Sciences*, Cardiff University. N°13, September 2009. ISSN 1466-1535. Retrieved on 15 Aug 2011 from http://e-competencies.org/

Cobo, C. and Moravec, J. (2011). *Invisible Learning. Toward a New Ecology of Education.* Barcelona: Laboratori de Mitjans Interactius (University of Barcelona) and Andalucia: International University of Andalucía. http://www.invisiblelearning.com/en/ Retrieved on 17 September 2011 from: http://www.aprendizajeinvisible.com/download/AprendizajeInvisible.pdf

Cothrel, J. and Williams, R. (1999). 'On-line communities: helping them form and grow' in *Journal of Knowledge Management*,. Vol. 3, no.3 pp.54-60.

Cox A. (2007). *Beyond Information. Factors in participation in Networks of Practice*, in Journal of Documentation. Vol. 68, No. 5 . pp. 765-787

Davis, B. E. (2007). Harnessing knowledge market innovations for business advantage. Wealth Creation & Knowledge Value Innovation in the New Economy. Toronto: Kaieteur Institute for Knowledge Management. Retrieved on 3 October 2011 from: http://www.kikm.org/downloads/LeveragingKnowledgeMarketsStudy.pdf

Delargy, K. and Leteney, F. (2005)."Just the tip of the Iceberg!" *e-Learning Age*.Issue: May 2005, Available from: *http://www.feenix.co.uk/docs/iceberg.pdf* (Accessed on 25th February 2006).

Drucker, P. F. (1989). *The new realities*. New York: Harper Business.

Durrant, D. (2010). 'Knowmads: Nomadic Knowledge Workers', on 20th Nov 2010, at: http://openintelligence.amplify.com/2010/05/03/knowmads-nomadic-knowledge-workers-20nov08/ and http://spacecollective.org/Wildcat/5803/Hybrid-futures-Knowmads-and-the-Notion-state

Dvir, R. and Pasher, E (2004). "Innovation engines for knowledge cities: an innovation ecology perspective" in *Journal of Knowledge Management*, Special issue on Knowledge-Based Development II: Knowledge Cities. Vol. 8, no.5, pp.16-27.

Engeström, Y. (2004). "New forms of learning in Co-configuration work", in *Journal of Workplace Learning*. Vol. 16 No. 1/2, 2004 pp. 11-21.

ESCAP (2006). "Knowledge Networks though ICT Access Points for Disadvantaged Communities" Bangkok, Thailand: *United Nations Development Account Project*.

Flores, A.D. (2005). "Promotors of CCAs as Users' knowledge-facilitators", Educational Technology MSc dissertation. Monterrey: ITESM (2005).

Garcia, B. (2007). "Working and Learning in a Knowledge City: a Framework for Knowledge Workers". *Journal of Knowledge Management*, October 2007 Vol. 11, No.5 pp: 18-30. Annual Special Issue on Knowledge Cities.

Garrison, D.R. and Anderson, T (2003). *E-learning in the 21st Century*. A Framework for Research and Practice. London: Routledge Falmer.

Granovetter, M.S. (1973). *The strength of weak ties*, in *American Journal of Sociology*, Vol. 78 No. 6, pp. 1360-80

Gundry, J. (2006). *Web 0.0 Social Media.* Paper from *Knowledge Ability Ltd,* Malmesbury UK. Published at www.knowab.co.uk/socialmedia.html . September 2006.

Halal, W. E. (2005). *Making sense of knowledge.* Bradford (UK): Emerald publishing.

Healy, T. (2002). "From Human Capital to Social Capital" in Instance, D.; Schuetze, H.G. and Schuller T. (2002). *International Perspectives on Lifelong Learning. From Recurrent Education to the Knowledge Society.* Milton Keynes: SRHE and Open University Press.

Huerta E. and Sandoval, R. (2007). "Digital Literacy: Problems Faced by Telecentre Users in Mexico" in *Information Technology for Development.* Volume 13, No.3, April 2007 p. 217-232 (2007).

Huysman, M.H. and de Wit, D. (2004). "Practices in Knowledge sharing: Towards a second generation of Knowledge Management", in *Knowledge and Process Management.* Vol 11 No. 2 pp 81-92.

Huysman M.H. and Wulf D. (2005). "The role of Information Technology in building and sustaining the relational base of communities", in *The Information Society,* Special issue No. 21, pp 81-89

Jones, C. (2004). "Theory and the Practices of Learning Technology" in *Networked Learning Conference 2004.*September, 2004, in Sheffield, UK.in NLC 2004. Research Proceedings of the Networked Learning Conference (Sheffield 2004). Available at: *http://www.networkedlearningconference.org.uk/past/nlc2004/proceedings/symposia/symposium1/jones.htm* (Accessed 18th October 2005).

Kriščiūnas, K. and Daugeliene, R. (2006) 'The assessment models of knowledge-based economy penetration', *Engineering Economics,* Vol. 50, No. 5, pp.36-46.

Kuhn, T. (2006), *Negotiating boundaries between scholars and practitioners: CoPs and NoPs,* in *Management Communication Quarterly,* Vol. 16, No. 1, August 2002 pp. 106-112.

Lave J. and Wenger E. (1991) *Situated Learning. Legitimate Peripheral Participation* Cambridge University Press.

Latorre, J. (2010). "Water Supply, Environmental Sanitation and Water Resources Conservation in Hydric Stressed areas: Colombia Alta Guajira's case.". Key Note Presentation in *2nd International Simposium, CAALCA 2010.* ITESM, Monterrey, México. 7th May 2010. CINARA Research Centre: http://cinara.univalle.edu.co/english/; in partnership with http://www.fundacionescerrejon.org

Malhotra, Y. (2003). "Measuring Knowledge Assets of a Nation: Knowledge Systems for Development" Research paper prepared for the Invited Keynote presentation delivered at the *United Nations Advisory Meeting, Department of Economic and Social Affairs.* New York City, New York, 4-5 September 2003.

Molnar, S and Karvalics, L. (2001). "Two models and six types of telecentres: a typological experiment", in Papers of Information Society and Trend Research Institute, Technical University. Budapest, Hungary. Accessed on 8 April 2010, from www.ittk.hu/english/docs/two_models_six_type.pdf

Monge, P. R. & Contractor, N. S. (2003). *Theories of Communication Networks.* New York: Oxford University Press. See summary: www.uiuc.edu/ph/www/nosh

Moravec, J. (2008). 'Knowmads in Web 3.0', 20th November 2008, in http://www.educationfutures.com/2008/11/20/knowmads-in-society-30/

O'Reilly, T. (2005). *What is Web 2.0: Design Patterns and Business Models for the next generation of software.* O'Reilly website, 30th September 2005. O'Reilly Media Inc. Available online at: http://www.oreillynet.com/pub/a/oreilly/tim/news/2005/09/30/what-is-web-20.html Last accessed 12/06/09.

Pallof, R. and Pratt K. (1999). *Building Learning Communities in Cyberspace*. Strategies for the On-line classroom. San Francisco: Jossey Bass.

Paquet, Sebastien (2011). *What are Emergent Cities?*, Accessed on 3 Nov 2010, from: http://emergentcities.sebpaquet.net/what-are-emergent-cities

Rega, I (2010). "What do local people think about telecentres? A key issue for sustainability". A dissertation Submitted to the Faculty of Communication Sciences University of Lugano for the degree of Ph.D. in Communication Sciences. February 2010. Accessed 26 July 2010 from: http://doc.rero.ch/lm.php?url=1000,40,6,20100413103342-GI/2010COM001.pdf

Salmon, G. (2000). *E-moderating: The Key to Teaching and learning on line*. London: Kogan Page.

Servage, L. (2005). "Strategizing for workplace e-learning: some critical considerations", in *Journal of Workplace Learning*. Vol. 17 No. 5/6, 2005 pp. 304-317. Special Issue: e-Learning at the Workplace.

Seufert, A. and Seufert S. (1998): 'Knowledge Creation and Transfer in Knowledge Networks', in *IO Management*, 67, pp. 77-84.

Seufert, A., Krogh, G. von and Back, A. (1999) 'Towards knowledge networking'. *Journal of Knowledge Management*, Vol. 3, No. 3, pp. 180-190. Retrieved on 3 October 2011 from: http://citeseerx.ist.psu.edu/viewdoc/download?doi=10.1.1.116.9649&rep=rep1&type=pdf

Seufert, A., Krogh, G. von and Back, A. (2003) 'Unleashing the power of networks for knowledge management: putting knowledge networks into action', in *Knowledge management and networked environments*. Amacom New York, NY, USA. ISBN:0-8144-0742-0.

Siemens, G. (2006). *Knowing Knowledge*. eBook released on 4th Nov 2006. Retrieved on 21st Nov 2006, from: http://www.elearnspace.org/KnowingKnowledge_LowRes.pdf

Sloman, M. (2001). *The e-learning revolution*. London: Chartered Institute of Personnel and Development (CIPD).

Sumner, J. (2000). "A Critical History of Distance education", in *Open Learning*. Vol. 15, No. 1, pp. 267-285. Available at: ABI Inform Global Database (Accessed 5 February 2006).

Taylor, D.W. Jones, O. and Boles, K. (2004). "Building social capital through action learning: an insight into the entrepreneur" in *Education and Training*. Vol. 46, Number 5, pp. 226-235.

Tuomi, I. (2004). "Knowledge sharing and the idea of Public Domain" Paper presented at the Unesco 21st Century Dialogue on *Building Knowledge Societies*. Seoul, 28 July 2004. A conference organized in the occasion of the 50th anniversary of the Korean National Commission for UNESCO. Accessed 3rd March 2006. Available from: http://www.meaningprocessing.com/personalPages/tuomi/articles/KnowledgeSharingAndTheIdeaOfPublicDomain.pdf

Tuomi, I. (2007) Learning in the Age of Networked Intelligence. *European Journal of Education*, 42(2), pp. 235-54.

Varnelis, K. (2010) 'The meaning of network culture', Retrieved on 14th January 2010, from: http://www.eurozine.com/articles/2010-01-14-varnelis-en.html

Wallis, J.; Killerby, P. and Dollery, B. (2004). "Social economics and social capital", in *International Journal of Social Economics*. Vol. 31, no.3, pp. 239-258.

Wasko, M. and Faraj, S. (2008). The Web of Knowledge: An Investigation of Knowledge Exchange in Networks of Practice, in *Academy of Management Journal* 2008.

Wenger E. (1998) *Communities of Practice: Learning, Meaning and Identity*. CUP.

2

Knowledge Building in E-Learning

Xinyu Zhang and Lu Yuhao
Tsinghua University
China

1. Introduction

With the rapid development of information society and wide spread of life-long learning, the needs for knowledge are growing dramatically. With the fast pace of modern life, most people cannot afford to take formal courses in the classroom. Therefore, more and more people turn to distance learning for its flexibility in time and space. Different from face to face learning, both the learners and tutors can resort to information technology to facilitate communication and information transfer. As PCs become popular and the bandwidth increases, e-Learning has gained major popularity among the learners. Consequently, a well-designed and sophisticated online learning environment can stimulate learners to learn, simplify the learning process, facilitate deeper comprehension and increase collaboration, which can contribute not only to the growth of learners' knowledge, but also to the improvement of learning and communication capability. The annual report of Online Education in the United States demonstrates that 29.3% of the students at colleges or universities in the United States chose online education. Accordingly, the attention by the scholars to the changes in the learning modes, resource building and sharing, platform design and maintenance and instructional or curriculum reform that the internet brings forth is constantly increasing. However, the studies concerning the influence of new technology environment on knowledge building is relatively weak. What are the changes in knowledge acquisition, representation and application in the web environment taking place? How to conduct knowledge service in on-line learning with remarkable performance? How would cloud computing and cloud services affect learners' knowledge building? This paper made efforts to analyze knowledge building in on-line learning regarding four aspects including knowledge engineering, knowledge services, cloud computing and cloud services against the background of developing theories of knowledge in order to provide guidance promoting online education.

The remainder of this paper is organized as follows. Section 2 describes the development of knowledge theories; Section 3 discusses the knowledge engineering and knowledge building in on-line learning; Section 4 describes knowledge services and knowledge building in on-line learning; at the last section we presents our future work directions.

2. The development of knowledge theories

The theories of knowledge, as the basic opinions from people on knowledge are related to the whole understanding and basic views of knowledge including hypotheses and beliefs of the nature, attribute, value, standard, paradigm and validity of knowledge. The theories of knowledge are not knowledge itself but people's ideas and retrospection of knowledge during the process of gaining, enriching and growing knowledge. Considering the development of contemporary theories of knowledge, the evolution of the theories comprises of Rationalism, Empiricism, Pragmatism, Constructivism and Post modernism among which the first four types of theories belong to modern views of knowledge while the later refer to "Post-modernism".

2.1 The modern theories of knowledge

In view of the modern theories of knowledge, knowledge is "the understanding of property and relations, which is shown as psychological patterns including perceptions, presentations, definitions and rules" (Shi Zhongying, 2001).This view is created in 17 century with philosophical bases including Rationalism, Empiricism and Pragmatism.

Rationalism regards knowledge as objective existence independent of subjects without any link to the object of knowing. In addition, knowledge can only be acquired through people's rational activities. Opposed to Rationalism to a certain extent, Empiricism holds that knowledge originates in sense experience. All knowledge is empirical, which in essence emphasizes the psychological level of the individual's sense experience. This view affected American Pragmatism substantially. However, Pragmatism differs from Empiricism on the point that Pragmatism attaches emphases to the behavioral level of individual's behavior, believing that knowledge is the tool of behaviors. Knowledge should be examined through experiments to be known as truth or fiction (Thomas • E • Hill, 1989). The essence of instruction does not lie in the knowledge injection but in rebuilding experience.

Although a great number of differences found among the three theories, they all bear the characteristics of objectivity, universality and neutrality. The objectivity of modern knowledge refers to that knowledge correctively reflects the nature of objects or the essential and necessary link between objects. Universality means that the objective statements of knowledge can be accepted beyond various social and individual limitations. Neutrality indicates that knowledge is the product of pure experience and reason. Knowledge is "culture-free" or "value-free" since it is only related to the property and ability of objects' knowing.

2.2 Post-modern theories of knowledge

Dating back to 1960s, the development of information technology brought about profound changes in modes of production, styles of life and concepts of culture. The industrialized society has transferred into the information society moving towards the knowledge society which encourages knowledge innovation and aims to cultivate innovative and creative elites. During the process mentioned above, people have introspected the objectivity, universality and neutrality pursued by modernists. Criticism that inheriting the modern theories of knowledge from Rationalism and Empiricism, the pursuit of objectivity and certainty leads to authoritarian and hierarchicality of knowledge and partial understanding and abuse of reason ending with superstition and desperation of scientific knowledge were raised. Constructive theory of knowledge and post-modern theories of knowledge have pointed out critical comments on the issues mentioned.

Constructivists with broad views of knowledge regard sociability, contextuality, constructivity, complexity and implicity as central elements of knowledge. The main views of constructivism are mainly divided into individual constructivism and social constructivism.

The Swiss cognitive psychologist Jean Piaget is the founder of individual constructivist theory of knowledge. In his view, knowledge is generated neither from objects nor subjects but from the interactions between objects and subjects— —"activities" . Children construct their knowledge about the external world through the process of interacting with the environment in means of assimilation and accommodation, which develops their cognitive structure. In addition, Piaget opposes the idea that knowledge is "input" with his view that the new and old experience of children colliding with each other initiates changes in concepts and reconstruction in frameworks with a process of assimilation and accommodation.

The Social Constructivism represented by the Soviet psychologist L.S.Vy-gotsky emphasizes the crucial rule "interpersonal communication" and "social-cultural environment" play in knowledge construction. Learners' interaction and communication with society are valued. Furthermore, the theories and practice of social constructivism are displayed by Ontario Institute for Studies in Education, University of Toronto. Scardamalia and Bereiter(1994) maintain that knowledge is not the truths stored in human brains. It is created collectively through group discussion, which is not just as an assemblage of individuals' knowledge. The process of building knowledge is modifying and updating the collective knowledge. The aim of knowledge building is to form public knowledge of certain value for the learning community rather than simply increasing the content of individual's brain. Given the core of learning is how to facilitate learners to be knowledge builders, the increase of content in individuals' brain is one of the byproducts of learning.

The constructivism generated new meaning experiencing the wave of post-modern education. Doll (Doll, W.) at the *Louisiana* State *University, USA* pointed out that knowledge is not absolute, objective but uncertain. Knowledge is not universal but contextual. Knowledge is not neutral but valuable. Knowledge is not unique but diverse. Based on his thoughts, a new post-modern theory of knowledge has been built. Doll opposes the idea of the modern theories of knowledge that knowledge is a meaning system that could be investigated from the outside for the reason that it is the objective reflection to reality, closed and stable in his book A *Post - Modern* Perspective on Curriculum. In his view, knowledge is the interpretation of the dynamic, open self-adjustment system which is within the system (William E. Doll, 1993).

Above all, the Post-modern views of knowledge mainly demonstrate the cultural, contextual, valuable, diverse elements of knowledge. Highlights have been made that knowledge is the information and its construction through interaction between individuals and environment. Knowledge encompasses the storage and retrieval means of knowledge as well as the application and transmission routes. The Post-modern views of knowledge reveal the independent relation between individuals and the environment and the nature of knowledge as information. They further point out openness as the characteristic and value of application and transmission, which meets the trend and goal of economy and science development as updates based on retrospection and critics on modern views of knowledge.

2.3 Knowledge building in on-line environments

Knowledge building refers to a process of creating and improving valuable thoughts for the community as an integral part of spreading cultural advancement through increasing the possibility of the situation that what the community has realized is larger than assemblage of individual contribution. The concept was raised by Marlene Scardamalia and Carl Bereiter from the Ontario Institute for Studies in Education, University of Toronto, in 1987. They maintain that knowledge is not the truth stored in individual's brain but collective knowledge that is created collectively through learners' group discussion. The collective knowledge is larger than the assemblage of individual's knowledge. Moreover, the process of knowledge building is modifying and improving the collective knowledge. What distinguishes knowledge building and the traditional instructional practices significantly is that traditional instruction normally focuses on how an individual acquires knowledge while knowledge building pays more attention to students' spiritual state of learning and collective knowledge's proceeding.

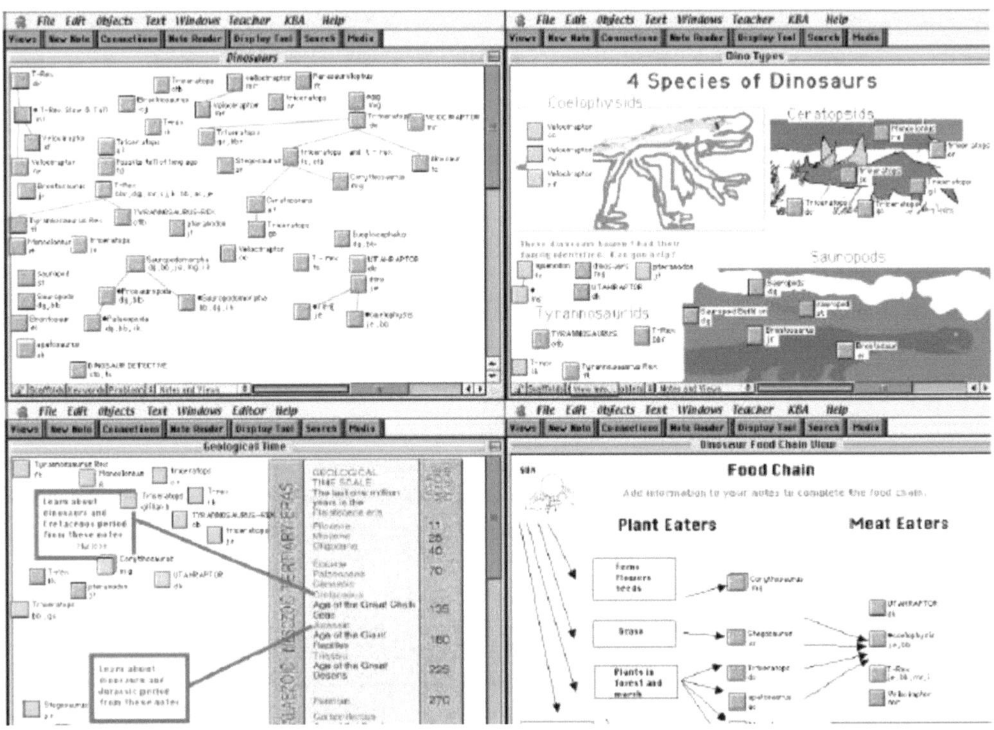

Fig.1. User Interfaces of Knowledge Forum

In order to support knowledge building, Marlene Scardamalia and Cal Bereiter along with their team designed Knowledge Forum previously called CSILE (Computer Supported International Learning Environment) before 1996. CSILE was aimed to provide external support for objective-oriented learning and knowledge construction via information technologies helping communities transfer from the task-oriented type to the knowledge construction type. The core concepts of Knowledge Forum are composed of objective-oriented learning, expertise process and knowledge construction communities. As an environment for activities, knowledge forum converts knowledge into an objective-based activity through supporting presentation, expression and transformation of information and opinions with learners writing "note"s to express themselves.

Learners can offer an "opinion" to integrate all existing notes to form a more complete and more systematic opinion as the upper level. Knowledge forum provides six types of tools to support collaborative knowledge building. The first type is "based on" which can allow learners to build their own opinions on the basis of others' opinions. The second is "quote" which can allow learners to quote an existing note in the system knowledge base. The third is "annotate" which helps learners comment on others' opinions. The fourth is "collaborative creating" with which learners can modify text, images of others if authorized to edit records by writers. The fifth is "published status". When the writers think their opinions worth publishing they can set the "published status"up of the opinions. The last tool "refine" is the most powerful tool allowing users to refine the theories or opinions through collaboration and integration by users to form new theories or opinions. After refinement, the former theories or opinions will disappear from the knowledge base.

Knowledge Forum is tried and promoted over several districts of the world currently in an effort to make a clear objective-based learning process to guide students to bear more responsibilities of helping others learn and to support organizing a knowledge building community with technology. As a new theory of learning, knowledge building looking forward to the prospect to some extent complies with requirements for learning and instruction from time.

3. Knowledge engineering and knowledge building in e-learning

3.1 General view of knowledge engineering

The phrase Knowledge Engineering originates from artificial intelligence. On the fifth International Joint Conference on Artificial Intelligence the professor Feigenbaum at the computer department of Standford University introduced the name "knowledge engineering", which is the landmark for knowledge operability.

As for the history of knowledge engineering, it is created while "expert system" building was under investigation. In truth, the focal point of knowledge engineering is knowledge. The research directions of Knowledge engineering encompass knowledge acquisition, knowledge representation, knowledge reasoning and so on. Knowledge engineering is aimed to dig and extract human knowledge and to represent this knowledge with certain form which can be subject to computer processing so that computers can possess certain intelligence. The knowledge engineering on the basis mentioned above is a discipline that involves human intelligence and human knowledge and how to use computers to simulate human intelligence to develop human knowledge.

3.2 The relationship between knowledge engineering and knowledge building

Considering the evolution of theories of knowledge, modern constructivism emphasizes sociality, context, constructively, complexity and implicity while knowledge engineering as key means of knowledge building in on-line learning is influenced by artificial intelligence, database technology, mathematical logic, cognitive science, psychology and so on, moving towards intelligentization and openness. The relationship between knowledge engineering and knowledge building is illustrated in terms of three factors of knowledge engineering: knowledge acquisition, knowledge representation and knowledge application.

3.2.1 Knowledge acquisition

Constructivists attach great importance to the origin and acquisition of knowledge, which is opposed to rationalists' theories. The Swiss psychologist Piage points out that knowledge is gradually built during the process of interaction between subjects and environment by means of assimilation and accommodation so that the cognitive structure can be developed. Vy-gotsky maintains that knowledge is acquired through interaction between individuals and society and transformation from external, expanding, collective activities to internal, concise, individual form in a certain socio-cultural background. Scardamalia and Bereiter hold that knowledge is not the truth stored in individuals' brain but collective knowledge created in a collective effort through group discussion. Above all, constructivism regards sociability and contextuality as central elements in knowledge acquisition, which is well displayed in knowledge acquisition of knowledge engineering. The acquisition of knowledge is expanding from the unidirectional communicator-to-communicator pattern of transmission to the multidirectional and interactional human-to-computer pattern in the online environment. Everyone is in the link of the knowledge web and can act as an expert to use their power of knowledge, accept knowledge, consume knowledge, retail knowledge and create knowledge, which completely demonstrates diversity and universality of knowledge acquisition in the eyes of post-modern theories of knowledge.

In the knowledge engineering domain, means of acquiring explicit knowledge include Distributed Searching and date mining. Distributed Searching means to create distributed index server on the standards of districts, topics and so on. The index servers can exchange medium information and a query can be redirected. If a searching server fails to satisfy a query, it can send the requirements of the query to a searching server which contains related information. The Distributed searching engine is a searching strategy which can be used in knowledge query and retrieval in relation database, Special-purpose document internet searching site, web and so on, which can help acquire explicit knowledge in the related domains broadly.

Data mining refers to a high-level process of extracting reliable, new, effective information from a huge amount of data in an understandable pattern. Data mining is not just simple searching, inquiring and transferring towards special database but also conducting statistics, analyses, synthesizing and reasoning in micro, middle and macro ways to receive solutions to actual problems, to discover relations between events or even to predict future activities in use of existing data. It discovers and acquires knowledge through data extraction, preprocessing, transferring, pattern extraction, knowledge evaluation and process optimization by means of applying statistical methods including discriminant analysis , cluster analysis and exploratory analysis.

The way of acquiring tacit knowledge is non-automatic knowledge acquisition (manual acquisition), semi-automatic knowledge acquisition and automatic knowledge acquisition. Non-automatic knowledge acquisition refers to complete manual work while semi-automatic knowledge acquisition means that the work is finished through joint efforts of knowledge engineers and knowledge acquisition institutions in expert systems. Knowledge engineers are responsible for extracting knowledge and representing the knowledge in proper patterns while knowledge acquisition institutions in the expert system are responsible for transferring knowledge into internal forms which can be stored in computers and putting them into knowledge base. Automatic knowledge acquisition means that the system can automatically modify and perfect knowledge base with users' responses to results and can automatically accumulate and form various kinds of useful knowledge during solving process.

3.2.2 Knowledge representation

Knowledge representation can be viewed as a set of rules on objects used to represent human knowledge as data structures. The process of representing knowledge is to encode knowledge into certain data structures. Knowledge representation breaks down into two types including declarative knowledge representation and procedural knowledge representation. Declarative knowledge representation refers to processing separately knowledge representation and knowledge application. When representing knowledge, how to apply the knowledge is hardly involved, which is a static way of describing. Procedural knowledge representation is to combine knowledge representation and knowledge application. The knowledge is in the programme, which is an active descriptive way. The ways of knowledge representation commonly seen are:

The first-order predicate logic representation: this is an important way of knowledge representation based on logic. It has been the most accurate formal language to represent human mind and reasoning until now. The way of representation is considerably close to human natural language and the representation can be accurately reasoned by computers.

The Production Representation which is also called The Production Rule Representation enjoys the same computing ability of Turing machines. Recently, production representation has become one of the mostly used forms of knowledge representations in the artificial intelligence applications. The production representation normally is used to represent knowledge of causal link with the basic form that $P \rightarrow Q$ or IF P THEN Q where p is the premise or condition of the production while Q is a set of conclusions or movements. P is used to point out whether the production is a usable condition while Q is to display what conclusion or operation should be made when the premise p is satisfied. P and Q can be a or a set of mathematical expressions or natural languages.

Frame representation: it is a structuralized knowledge representation based on frame theory suitable for representing various types of knowledge. The basic views of framing theory: human brains have stored abundant typical scenarios. When facing new scenarios, people can select a basic knowledge structure named a frame from their memory. The specific content of a frame changes from new scenarios, forming knowledge on new scenarios and store that in human mind.

Semantic networks representation: a Semantic network is a structuralized graphic formed by nodes and arcs or links which represent knowledge. A semantic network representation consists of four related parts: (1) The lexical part involving each nod or arc determines what symbols are allowed to appear in the representation vocabulary list. (2)The structure part appointing the nod pairs connecting arcs describes the limits on the order of symbols. (3)The process part states the access process which can be used to build and modify the description and answer related questions. (4)The semantic part ascertains the ways of describing associated meaning namely ascertains the sequence of related nods and the possession and corresponding arcs. The semantic networks have already become a mostly applicable form of knowledge representation especially in the natural language processing.

Object-oriented representation: in recent years, when designating and constructing the intelligent systems, people have started to utilize object-oriented thoughts, means and development technologies in knowledge representation, organization and management of a knowledge base, expert systems design, which accomplishes rapid growth.

Therefore, knowledge representation can organize the content into a number of reusable smaller parts and build meaningful, direct links among them so that users can swiftly locate all the relative knowledge, which makes it convenient for users to build knowledge. It can be discovered that knowledge representation is spreading information origins on the basis of a great amount of denotation and connotation of explicit knowledge, reorganizing and processing information itself and excavating implicit and deeper layer information and knowledge from relational data base. The process mentioned is consistent with the evolution of human theories of knowledge. Human's attention transfers from objective explicit knowledge gradually into subjective, individual, contextual tacit knowledge, which accompanies knowledge representation changing from standardization, hierarchicality into conceptualization, cognitive maps, problem solving.

3.2.3 Knowledge application and management

Objectivistic theories of knowledge suggest that objects exist objectively and knowledge is the presentation of objects. Scientific definitions are corresponding to various objects. Scientific propositions, theorems are the only correct and true interpretation of objects which experience scientific examinations. The application and management in the knowledge engineering is not the process or method of studying specific knowledge applications but possible ways or patterns that could be used in various concrete knowledge applications including reasoning, searching, knowledge management and maintenance, matching and identifying. Reasoning refers to studies concerning various ways or patterns of reasoning including various logical relations between premises and conclusions, the transfer rule of truth degree or the confidence level. Search refers to studies related to all kinds of searching means and methods. It is to search or explore a certain object which can satisfy given conditions or requirements in the myriad object (including knowledge itself) space. Knowledge management and maintenance include all kinds of operations (retrieval, adding, modifying or deleting) of the knowledge base to assure the consistency and completeness of knowledge in the knowledge base. Matching and identifying refer to various principles and methods of finding one datum or more data or object matching the given template and identify various objects in the environment consisting of solely incomplete information or knowledge.

Above all, knowledge engineering aimed at realizing the order and organization of knowledge pays more attention to practical engineering operations of knowledge, through proper exchange of matter, energy and information between systems and external world, negative entropy increase, cooperation and competition of nonlinear systems to realize self-organizing and hetero-organizing activities. During the process, information, knowledge and intelligence appear alternatively and interconvert into each other. The position of Information, knowledge and intelligence in the entire information process and the relationship among them fit the process of information creating knowledge and knowledge activates intelligence in the activities of human building the perception of the world and improving the world. However, the current studies of knowledge engineering has hardly involved and solved the theoretical problems of knowledge itself nor have they revealed the essential relations among "information-knowledge-intelligence". Revealing the knowledge building process will enhance exploration of the relations among the three factors and realize the shift from knowledge to intelligence in actual practices.

4. Knowledge services and knowledge building in e-learning

4.1 Overview of knowledge services

As for definitions of knowledge service, three major views are listed below: solutions to users' problems are emphasized. This type of concepts focus on providing users with knowledge products or service during problem solving process through the serving staff's own knowledge and abilities. (2)this type of view displays the concept of knowledge management employing the transformation between explicit knowledge and implicit knowledge, which emphasizes the value of exploiting tacit knowledge (3)distinguish knowledge service in a broad view from knowledge service in a narrowed view, which emphasizes layers of knowledge service.

Knowledge service is a type of comprehensive knowledge-intensive and procedural service. It realizes the combination of knowledge service experts, related research group, various distributed information resources and computer technologies along with the combination of various theories of information knowledge, human experience and knowledge. It is knowledge content oriented. The value and core competitive strength of knowledge service mainly lie in the amount of knowledge and the density of knowledge content. It can provide users with the product and service at different layers because of different amount of knowledge to different types of knowledge requirements. In addition, knowledge service itself is an iterative process of knowledge acquisition, knowledge absorption, knowledge innovation and knowledge application, adjusting and optimizing knowledge service products and solution plans in the entire science research process.

Studies on the knowledge service aboard fall into theoretical and practical aspects. In the theoretical studies, the experts on the Canadian knowledge service programs proposed knowledge service system models and theory frame based on knowledge service process (Simard A, 2007). N. F. Abernethy explored frame-based knowledge service system on database management system (DBMS) (Abernethy, N. F. et al, 1999). The E-service project funded by Danish Research Agency systematically studied the development of knowledge service theories and created the roles and related products through case studies of service institutions and clients. UNDP (United National Development Program) identified the connotation, task and range of knowledge services.

A majority of studies focusing on the semantic Web technologies as to knowledge service applications for example York Sure hold that semantic Web technologies play a core role in the knowledge base of digital libraries and object semantic description (Sure Y. & Studer R,

2007). A.Sheth published research results concerning ontology-driven information retrieval, analysis and integration of application systems (Sheth A & Ramakrishnan C, 2003). Based on the studies, some scholars build ontological knowledge service frames pointing out that ontological representation technologies can transfer complex information resources into information that could be understood and processed easily by machines. Additionally, a number of institutions have made creative attempts on knowledge service applications for instance, LMC provides computer technologies based on knowledge Byte to produce customized multimedia knowledge transmission experience, which makes knowledge shared in a building or over the world.

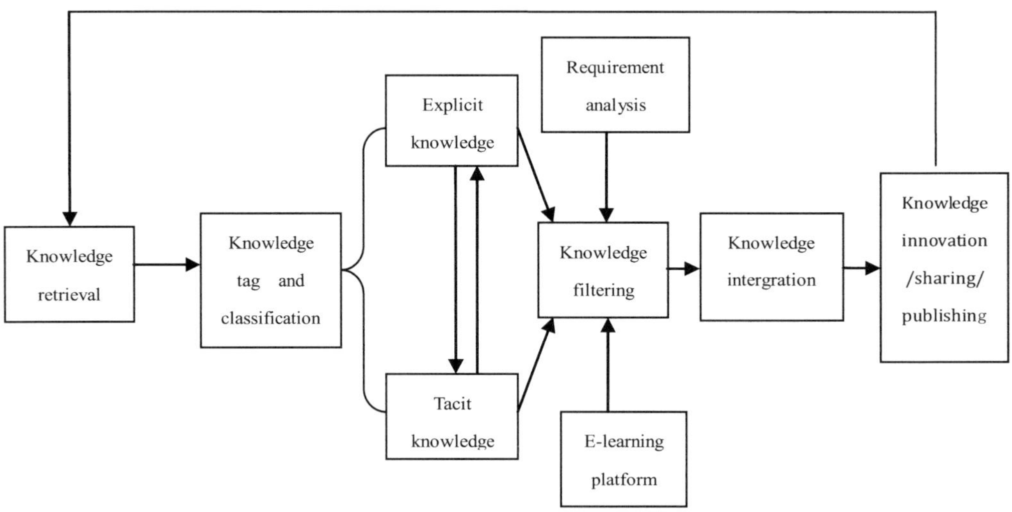

Fig. 2. the knowledge services model based on the on-line knowledge building

4.2 The knowledge services model based on the on-line knowledge building

After the overview of knowledge building, knowledge engineering and knowledge services combined with on-line learning features, the knowledge services model for on-line knowledge building are developed as shown below:

4.2.1 Knowledge retrieval

The knowledge retrieval consists of explicit knowledge and tacit knowledge. Traditional knowledge retrieval can access to abundant data and information with low retrieval rate and small amount of knowledge. In contrast, knowledge retrieval in the knowledge services draws on the advanced theories and technologies in various disciplines including information technology, artificial intelligence, cognitive science and linguistics. It serves as a advanced information retrieval means to fully represent and optimize users' requirements extracting all media type knowledge sources(text, image, video, sound etc) and selecting accurately the result users required. This type of knowledge retrieval emphasizes reveal of knowledge unit and knowledge connection as a match of knowledge and semantics based on Web page information. It can be regarded as an advanced information retrieval way to realize intelligent query based on understanding of the information semantic content on the premise that a nonlinear knowledge organization of the knowledge retrieval is conducted. The realization of knowledge retrieval can hardly succeed without the support of artificial intelligence and knowledge engineering.

Normally, the knowledge building systems can provide knowledge retrieval function in the actual practices. The major objective is to solve the problem of retrieval of structured data and non-structured data. For instance, apart from queries of some characteristics of elites, queries of the content of the resumes are of more importance. In the mean time, it can provide semi-structured content retrieval and intelligent knowledge retrieval based on XML as well, for example, if the word "computer" is be searched, all the information contains "computer" will be retrieved, which is the primary stage of intelligent retrieval. Intelligent retrieval should pay more attention to the text extraction function. On the knowledge interface provided, a guidance tool for users is called for in order to increase the utilization efficiency and provide convenience for knowledge organization and sharing of internal and external tacit knowledge of enterprises.

4.2.2 Knowledge tag and classification

After searching, knowledge can be classified and tagged. Classification mainly means to divide knowledge into explicit knowledge and tacit knowledge. Tacit knowledge refers to experience judgment and behavior tendency of a subject based on their instinct and perception of objective events in their working and living practices. The formation of tacit knowledge is a process of learning accumulation and innovation during which different subjects affect each other. Tacit knowledge is hard to be formalized. It can hardly articulated existing deeply in personal experience, decisions, associations, innovation and sub-consciousness. In addition, hard to be standardized and transmitted to others, implicit knowledge demonstrates as experience, skills, abilities or know-how. Fixed and visual, different from the former type of knowledge, explicit knowledge can be transmitted in standard and systematic languages. Any kind of knowledge that can be defined, written or put in computers can become explicit knowledge. According to related studies, explicit knowledge appears in a small amount in a majority number of organizations. The majority of knowledge exists in human as tacit knowledge.

The chief use of tagging is to offer every categories a proper name which can comply with people's habits and include all items of the type while distinguish from items of other types.

The way of tagging is to pick up a series of key information which can cover the content property and be used as the access of user's searching from the documents. Using the information to tag the document can help gain access to the knowledge of the document by putting in keywords. Methods and technologies of ontology can be used to create knowledge structures and conduct tagging for the reason that ontology provides standard ways of specifically describing a certain field and store the data collected to meta-data base according to regulated structure.

4.2.3 The platform for knowledge exchange –tacit knowledge transferring into explicit knowledge

After explicit knowledge and tacit knowledge being indentified, a platform for knowledge exchange is provided to promote transferring from tacit knowledge into explicit knowledge. Knowledge map is regarded as a favorable tool for the transformation. It can assist users to find knowledge points in a short time through accurate expression and classification of concepts and knowledge relations and can return to related knowledge sources so that organizations can assemble intelligent sources of the entire organization in the fast speed with easiest operations when crucial decisions are expected to be made. In the mean time, the knowledge community as a platform for knowledge exchange can be introduced so that staff of the organizations or cooperative partners can log in the knowledge portal and communicate and leave a message to realize transmission of tacit knowledge.

4.2.4 Knowledge filtering

After fully investigating users' requirements, knowledge acquired should be filtered through the on-line instructional platform. Various forms of knowledge should be assembled. First, compatibility of knowledge should be taken into consideration. Compatibility is the basis and rules that decide whether knowledge in various fields can build up collective relations and form collective system judgments and choices. Second, the organizational absorption of the target knowledge should be analyzed. Knowledge integration is built on the full understanding and absorption of knowledge. Third, the quality of knowledge source should be assessed since only knowledge of high quality can realize excellent service effect. Last, integration of knowledge application and user requirements should be analyzed considering that the ultimate goal of knowledge services is to satisfy clients' requirements and create value, which makes it a vital link.

4.2.5 Knowledge integration

Knowledge integration refers to a series of orderly and systematic activities including organizing, processing, revealing, controlling on knowledge objects employing certain organizing tools, methods and standards based on the inner logical relations of knowledge. The aim of the knowledge integration is not simply to order knowledge storage and provide knowledge but to realize knowledge representation of knowledge mining by means of integration analysis, induction, reasoning and so on. As a high form of knowledge organization, it embodies the characteristics of automation, integration, and intelligentization. The knowledge organization methods adopted consist of knowledge reorganization, knowledge clustering, knowledge storage, knowledge editing, knowledge layout, knowledge monitoring and so on. The knowledge organization technologies are composed of super-text technologies, expert systems, data warehouse and knowledge mining.

4.2.6 Knowledge innovation, sharing, publishing

Eventually knowledge integration results in knowledge innovation, sharing and publishing. On one aspect, the knowledge is shared by members of organizations in the form of explicit knowledge. On the other aspect, the knowledge is digested by members after members learning of the explicit knowledge, which constructs major sources for knowledge searching for the reason that the knowledge is fixed into individuals and the organization and gradually becomes their implicit knowledge. In the end, each member can contribute to collective knowledge creating new knowledge in the formed knowledge building communities. In addition, knowledge sharing in the organization brings out knowledge innovation and growth.

5. Conclusion and future research

The web environment gives rise to criticisms of the objectivity, universality and neutrality of knowledge in the first place. New theory of knowledge emphasizes culture, contextuality, value and diversity of knowledge along with interaction between individuals and environment and interaction between individuals and the learning community. Moreover, in support of knowledge building of learners, knowledge engineering is moving towards ubiquitous knowledge acquisition, clear representation, orderly data organization, ontological content storage. Adapting to the direction mentioned above, the services for knowledge are hardly confined to simple knowledge management, which means that a series of changes should be made in certain elements ranging from searching, tagging and classification, communication, filtering, integration of knowledge to innovation, sharing, publishing of knowledge in order to form active, smart, personalized knowledge services. In the end, cloud computing and cloud services enrich the online learning environment where we can create personalized web learning environment easily and smoothly. In the mean time, cloud computing and cloud services play a crucial role in timeliness of knowledge building, integration of instructional resources and promotion of communication and collaboration. The knowledge building methods of human brains, the support for knowledge building by semantic web and the relationship between knowledge building of robots and human beings will be explored as to the future research goals concerning the web-based knowledge building.

6. References

Abernethy, N. F. et. Al. Sophia: A Flexible, Web-Based Knowledge Server. IEEE Intelligent Systems, 14, 4 (1999), 79-85.

Simard A. , Understanding knowledge services at naturalZ resources.[2007 - 03 - 18]. http://dsp-psd.pwgsc.gc.ca/collection_2007/nrcan-rncan/M4-45-2006E.pdf.

Sheth A & Ramakrishnan C. Semantic (Web) technology in action: Ontology driven information systems for search, integration and analysis. IEEE Data Engineering Bulletin, Special issue on Making the Semantic Web Rea1. 2003, 26 (4) : 40 - 48.

Shi ZhongYing, Pattern of knowledge growth and educational change [J]. Educational Research and Experiment, 2001, 4.

Sure Y. & Studer R. Semantic Web technologies for digital libraries.[2007 - 03 - 24]. http://www.aifb.unikarlsruhe.de/WBS/ysu/publications/2005_sw_for_all.pdf.

Thomas E. Hill, Modern theory of knowledge [M]. China Renmin University Press, 1989.

William E. Doll, Jr. A post-modern perspective on curriculum. New York : Teachers College Press, c1993

3

E-Learning and Desired Learning Outcomes

Ralph Palliam
American University of Kuwait, Division of Business and Economics, Kuwait

1. Introduction

A "net generation" of computer literate and computer sophisticated students are arriving at the gates of primary, secondary and tertiary institutions. The commensurate ability of faculty is now in question. The revolutionary socio-cultural transformations created by e-learning in the manner knowledge is generated, organized, retrieved, managed and purveyed across the different geographical, political, socio-economic and cultural boundaries must be thoroughly considered for any advancement in pedagogics. Proposals have been forthcoming to reform teaching and learning and make it compatible with the new competitive information and communication technologies environment. The architecture, diversity and apparent contradictions between these proposals render the public policy dialog scattered and confused. Within this context this chapter considers the identity, variety and destiny in productive e-learning with specific reference to desired learning outcomes and introduces the idea of a 'virtual space' delineated by two dimensions—'learning experience, namely, face to face intervention' and 'geographical space". These lay out the contours of the emerging intellectual landscape by placing past practices as well as present proposals on the same conceptual plane. The current approach to universal education continues to be bound by the self-imposed limitations of past regulations and that a heterogeneous universal educational policy is likely to be more suited to the new e-learning environment. Undoubtedly, effective learning through e-learning has become an issue of major discussions. As a result a set of vocabulary associated with lifelong learning is being developed to accommodate learning outcomes associated with e-learning. Having identified issues surrounding productive e-learning, desired learning outcomes are then presented. The two questions bearing on educational institutions are: how will these changes affect the institutions' academic mission and conduct? And secondly, how would institutions react to these changes? Finally, student motivation in terms of hierarchy of needs is considered in the light learning outcomes.

2. E-learning - Didactics

Conceptually, learning outcomes are associated with the learner being able to do a required task by the end of a defined period of time. The knowledge or skills will need to be demonstrated. Traditionally learning outcomes were easily stated and observed in behavioral terms. However, with the onslaught of e-learning the challenge is to equate learning outcomes with artificial intelligence. This brings one to the issue: how does one measure inquiry and analysis, critical and creative thinking, written and oral communication; quantitative literacy;

information literacy; teamwork and finally problem solving. Katz & Oblinger (2000) contend that the prevailing research on e-learning that focuses predominantly on instructional programming, and on the development of hardware and software, essentially neglects the more social, human and cultural perspectives on e-learning. The continued technological revolution, as a result of the introduction of the internet and upgraded and affordable computers, has changed the fabric of human society in fundamental ways. Every facet of business, commerce, governance, politics and education are being redefined. Moreover, Katz & Oblinger (2000) suggest that in a networked world, one can add an "e" to almost anything. There is no question that education is becoming an issue of major concern within e-learning. Understanding how one learns in an information age is critical to the advancement of a society. This would ensure that society will be able to maximize the learning outcomes by applying it strategically to improve the quality of life for all.

At the European Council in Lisbon in March 2000, Heads of State set an ambitious target for Europe to become within ten years "the most competitive and dynamic knowledge-based economy in the world, capable of sustainable economic growth with more and better jobs and greater social cohesion". They also placed education firmly at the top of the political agenda, calling for education and training systems to be adapted to meet this challenge. As governments focus on more private participation in higher education and e-learning in particular, the quality of education also remains a major area of concern. These concerns include: creating lifelong learning and learner mobility a reality, improving the quality and efficiency of provisions and outcomes, promoting equity and active citizenship and enhancing innovation and creativity at all levels of education and training. In an era where knowledge is the key to economic growth and development, education has never been so vitally important. The 'knowledge gap' between rich and poor countries is certainly widening, causing less developed countries to become further marginalized, socially, politically and economically. Establishing productive e-learning solutions to the challenges faced by poor countries in particular is paramount. E-learning becomes a major solution as other alternatives are becoming economically untenable.

The ICT (information and communication technologies) have provided the tools for easy access to quality education. The possibility for educational programs to be targeted to different group settings is enormous. These group settings could include *inter alia,* women and men who are faced with cultural and religious barriers, the socially, physically and mentally challenged, learning disabled and handicapped, the marginalized and those seeking continuing education. Education, once considered largely the prerogative of the rich becomes ubiquitous as a result of ICT. A comparison of the opportunities that are accorded by e-learning is reflected by the following Table 1.

While Table 1 is self explanatory, traditional schooling which was the manifestation of the industrial age required learners to achieve certain outcomes consistent with the demands of that time. The content was designed to meet certain minimum requirement. An analysis of textbooks would suggest that a mastery of the content provided a learner with the minimum knowledge required for the subject discipline. Educators who played a meaningful role were the custodians of what ought to be studied at the various different levels. During this age one could leave the education policy making to the policy makers, educational administrating to the administrators, parenting to parents, and teaching and learning to educators. Each had a specific role to play. In the information age everything becomes so

INFORMATION AND COMMUNICATION TECHNOLOGIES (Information Age)	TRADITIONAL SCHOOLING (Industrial Age)
World of learning	World of knowledge
Customized	Standardized for groups
Freedom with certain accountabilities	Predetermined control
Co-operative and social relations	Individual performance
Collective decision making	Unilateral decision making
Taking on initiatives	Compliance
Rich and diverse thinking	Conformity
Shared networks	One way communication with some feedback
Holistic	Systems
Concerned with process	Concerned with parts
Learning and learners are paramount	Teaching and teachers are paramount
Multiple media	Usually face to face with print media

Table 1. Comparison of the opportunities that are accorded by e-learning

blurred. However, despite the vast advancements made, teachers are still the principal agents of education but the methodology and roles are vastly different. Educators become an agent not only to represent learners but to match learners' needs with the overall aim and outcomes of education. Educators facilitate the learning process and become caring mentors. Learners become gainfully engaged in their pursuits. An underlying assumption associated with learning within the information age is that learners have the capacity for responsible actions, that they have a natural desire to learn and understand things, and that they have the desire to do their best. In this regard Self Determination Theory (SDT) addresses several basic issues associated with cognitive, affective and psycho-motor development. Regulation and perception of the self, one's psychological and emotional needs, life goals and aspirations, individual dynamism, culture and the impacts of social environments are key issues that determine the learners' ability to self actualize. Self actualization is the focus of the information age. Motivation within this assumes a different dimension. Technology facilitates record keeping for student learning in several different forms: standard inventory of learning, personal attainments inventory, and personal characteristics inventory. Accomplishments in learning can be immediately assessed and evaluated by the learner.

3. ICT and knowledge capital

ICT endows one with capital. In this regard the working population is offered a pragmatic way of upgrading their **human capital** which is traditionally considered as the knowledge, skills and competences and other attributes embodied in individuals that are relevant to economic activity. One's duration of schooling and one's level of qualification were the standard metrics used to measure human capital. Whilst, these metrics do not adequately capture the extent of human capital, **cultural capital**, on the other hand, is a more academic notion, referring to the credentials and cultural assets embodied in individuals and their families. Cultural capital is used to explain the reproduction of social hierarchy. Elite families usually endow their children with the cultural capital which enables them to succeed in maintaining their elite position. Countries that are well governed and show a high concern for human dignity also endow their citizens with cultural capital too. In these countries an investment in education allows one to move from non-elite positions into elite positions.

Finally, **social capital** could be defined in terms of faith, trust, norms and at levels of expressed trust in other people. Social capital allows agents and institutions to be more effective in achieving common objectives. The most common measures of social capital include one's participation in various forms of civic engagements, membership to voluntary associations, place of worship and political parties. Social capital has been deployed to explain a wide range of social phenomena, including general economic performance, levels of crime and disorder, immigrant employment and health trends. Despite some ambiguity, social capital is generally understood as a matter of relationships, as a property of groups rather than the property of individuals. Moreover, social capital itself can have socially undesirable effects, where trust and mutuality operate to enhance inequalities, exclusion or even criminality.

Undoubtedly, education plays a major role in the creation and development of each of these capitals. The key question is to what extent e-learning through ICT will be able to raise these capitals to higher levels than traditional schooling. In this regard the role of social media and networking in creating an awareness and a certain mode of conduct cannot be underestimated.

FORMS	DESCRIPTION	METRIC
HUMAN	Knowledge, skills and competences and other attributes embodied in individuals that are relevant to economic activity.	Traditional: Duration of schooling; level of educational and professional qualification. ICT Metric: would include constant engagement in ICT learning and knowledge environment
CULTURAL	Is a more academic notion, referring to the credentials and cultural assets embodied in individuals and their families. Used to explain the reproduction of social hierarchy - elite families and elite societies.	Traditional: Governance standards. Role of the governments in empowering societies and nation-building. ICT Metric: Use of ICT communication
SOCIAL	Capital that allows agents and institutions to be more effective in achieving common objectives. Usually deployed to explain a wide range of social phenomena, including general economic performance, levels of crime and disorder, immigrant employment and health trends. Generally understood as a property of groups rather than the property of individuals.	Traditional: Participation and engagement in civic roles, membership to voluntary associations, places of worship and political parties. ICT Metric: Developing social networks and moral lives.

Table 2. Human, social and cultural capital mission of universities

Upon examining the missions of universities as a formal educational institution, the following, amongst others, would emerge as key words: life-long learning; critical thinking and empowerment. "Learn, think and become" is a slogan that eloquently captures the pivotal role of the university in countries that have a satisfactory record of good and clean governance (democracy). These countries would immediately instill in their universities minimum standards of good and clean governance and values associated with the pursuit of truth. Within this universities would have to determine what is relevant in terms of epistemology (knowledge) and axiology (values). Moreover, Deer (2001) maintains that universities also play a vital role in ensuring that minimum standards of civil conduct exist. Public universities in democratic countries are usually in the public domain and tend to make this their pre-occupation and keep political institutions in check and balance and thereby establishing themselves as institutions for common good. In these counties, private or corporatized universities in particular tend to pursue different objectives. Countries where poor governance structures exist and where corruption is a manifestation, private universities tend to play another meaningful role. Institutions within this environment having indomitable courage become agents of change. Table 3 reflects the meaningful roles played by formal educational institutions in different types democracies. In essence Table 3 shows that poorly governed economies tend to endure lower standards of public education. This is a major cause for concern and therefore ICT constitutes a solution.

	Formal Public Educational Institutions	**Formal Private Educational Institutions - Accredited**
Poor to moderate governance structures	Usually to the right of the government. Institutions are in the public domain. Tend not to question the government - sole providers of the funds. Usually do not respond to the enormous pressures of the day. **ICT potential - poor.**	Usually to the left of the government. Institutions are not in the public domain. Tend to challenge governments discretely. Pro-democracy institutions. Establishing themselves as agents of change. **ICT potential - could be limited.**
Moderate to rich governance structures	These institutions reflect themselves as institutions for common good. Ensure that society receive the basic education at minimum acceptable levels. Funding is received from public coffers. **ICT potential - minimum.**	Tend to take education to higher levels. Have highly enriched curriculum and attract highly motivated students. Funding is external. **ICT potential - enormous.**

Table 3. Role of educational institutions - taking learning to another degree medieval education identified as T_{-2} - traditional learning

Prior to the introduction of formal schooling, education was imparted at home or to groups of children by village elders. The only children who went to school were those of the wealthy and the nobility who were taught classical languages and history. This would accord them a certain status and did not particularly make them creative members of society. Private home tuition actually began with the advent of primitive man. When the first cave dwellers taught their children how to hunt, they were being privately educated. Even today, private home education is a part of every child's upbringing. Everything a child knows that allows him to function in society is a result of knowledge imparted in the home by the parents. In the United States of America, the early colonists had little time to worry about formal education. What the children learned was what they needed to know to keep the household going. The few parents who were themselves literate would, at the most, pass on the ability to read and write. It was only when the country began to move from an agrarian economy to a manufacturing and trading one that education as a means of earning a living came into being. Since the U.S. was still primarily a rural society, once again it was the parents who set up the informal home schools - teaching their children what they knew, asking for help from the local elders and, when money was available, paying for a teacher to come for a few weeks or months to teach the children. Enlightened governments throughout the world out of a concern for education made schooling somewhat mandatory for all children. Schooling was on its way to becoming universal. However, a backlash began to develop towards the regimented and often mindless way formal schooling tried to impart education. The low standards of the schools were also a cause for concern.

4. Common good education during the industrial revolution T_{-1}

The Industrial Revolution had a profound effect on all levels of society in the late 18th and early 19th centuries. How people lived and worked changed significantly during this time. As a result education consistent with the revolution changed the productive capacity of England, Europe and United States. The revolution was something more than just new machines, smoke-belching factories, increased productivity and an increased standard of living. It was a revolution which transformed English, European, and American societies. Like the Reformation or the French Revolution, no one was left unaffected. Everyone was touched in one way or another, peasants and nobles, parents and children, artisans and captains of industry. The Industrial Revolution serves as a key to the origins of modern Western society. Perkin (2009) has observed, the Industrial Revolution was no mere sequence of changes in industrial techniques and production, but a social revolution with social causes as well as profound social effects.

5. Education for economic change identified as T_0

Vast differences exist between earlier and current forms of flexible learning. The earlier type was characterized by print media and then notably computer-based instruction which focused on the interaction between the student and technology namely the computer. The current prevailing paradigm is technology mediated communication where the primary form of interaction is between students and instructors, mediated by the computer. Computer-based instruction entailed individualized (self-learning) whilst computer mediated communication involves human facilitation. According to Williams (2002) the nature of learning and the possibilities of learning open to learners are numerous. E-learning becomes an answer to the challenge of lifelong education in the globalised market.

Traditionally the fundamental objective of good institutions generating and purveying knowledge is the ability to inculcate critical and noble thinking for common good. Within this framework, one should enquire as to what entails a reasonable return on investment in education. Undoubtedly, one should not expect a response associated with a student that can think critically and nobly and act with goodness despite the fact that these are missions of academic institutions. Traditionally, academic institutions in a particular society recruited students from diverse different communities and these institutions became more agents of socio-economic and political changes. Brick and mortar institutions facilitated socio-economic and political changes through diverse productive activities, one being face to face teaching and learning activities. The power of spoken words in this didactic approach creates an awareness and develops an *esprit de corps* among faculty and students in pursuing common objectives and at times these objectives are revolutionary in nature and institutions become more a geographic location where students and faculty vent their feelings and at times in violent ways.

Virtual institutions or flexible learning institutions are a major paradigm shift from the traditional brick and mortar institutions which for centuries have been the custodian of rich human thinking and pedagogy. One can consider e-Learning as another mode of learning in a continuum ranging from completely virtual to completely brick and mortar. The quest for universities to move the boundaries of the classroom is ever increasing. Utilizing technology has not only impacted on organizational and logistical procedures but also on learning outcomes and curriculum that is no longer linear. It therefore becomes imperative to match technological driven solutions to problems with desired learning outcomes. Garrison and Anderson (2002) contend that in order to make virtual e-Learning a viable future didactic approach one has to determine whether the use of modern technology enhances productive student learning consistent with the overall objective of education. Should the economic and social performance of a country be determined to a large extent by the citizens' relationship with technology, then the economy needs to exploit the potential of new technologies in its education. The incorporation of captivating media into a web-based teaching and learning experience is what the future holds for e-Learning. If this holds true then an educator will change how (s)he teaches, and this necessitates a change in what students need to learn. Consequently, the issue of quality is at the forefront of many debates on e-Learning. While this may be an issue, one needs to progress beyond and determine the identity of e-education, the variety of e-education and the destiny of e-education within the changed paradigm.

6. Education for social and cultural change identified as T_{+1}

Developing countries which invest in better education, healthcare, and job training produce surging economic growth and sharply reduced poverty. Failure to seize this opportunity to train citizens more effectively for the workplace, and to be active citizens, could lead to widespread disillusionment and social tensions. 'Culture' (in its simplest sense) is said to be 'the way of life' or 'the way in which one does things. Faculty need to adopt student-centred approaches and consider teaching in an outcomes-focused environment. This is quite a degree of cultural change. What many staff are faced with is a massive reassessment of their role – what they are expected to know, to do and to be – even those who thought they were (and were acknowledged as) good teachers in the first place. An outcomes approach to education requires a shift in emphasis from focusing on teaching to focusing on learning. A student-centred approach to education requires focusing on the learner rather than on the syllabus. For most academics, this is a major shift in their understanding of 'the way in which we do things' in a university.

7. The future of education T_{+2}

Advances in technology have produced numerous alternatives to the traditional brick and mortar institutions. Typical examples would include call centers. Classroom methods of delivery would need to change to accommodate changes in learning. Therefore the manner in which teaching and learning is accomplished needs to be considered in the light of technological advancement. Moreover, the use of computer networks unites educators and learners. This study firstly, identified the evolution of education from traditional and bureaucratic structures to highly technological laissez faire driven e-Learning. Since education is an industry, this necessitates flexible learning. A radical shift in brick and mortar institutions education began with distance learning that commenced with print technology. Major technological advances were made subsequently to distance education. This entailed the use of audio-video equipments. Traditional institutions are identified in the accompanying Figure 1 as those having high investment in brick and mortar and high

T_{-1}(Traditional institutions) Distance Education (Print Media satellite based) Private Education T_{-2} (Traditional learning) T_0 (Today)	Low Brick and Mortar High	T_{+1} (Tomorrow) Conversion of traditional schooling
HIGH LOW Learning experiences enabled by face to face		LOW HIGH Learning experiences enabled by technology
	H Virtual Environment L	T_0 (Today) (Technology driven distance education) *"I never try to teach my students anything, I only try to create an environment in which they can learn."* T_{+2} (Future) Conversion of traditional instructors to virtual support.

Fig. 1. The evolution of e-learning

investment in learning experiences through face-to-face contact. Virtual institutions are identified as institutions having high investment in learning experiences enabled by technology and a high investment in the virtual environment. The identity, variety and destiny in pedagogy are identified in terms of different time periods T_{-2}, T_{-1}, T_0, T_{+1}, and T_{+2}, where T_0 represents today.

Exploratory studies considering students learning taking place in two different positions in T_{-1}, and T_0 were conducted among corporate financial students who were able and willing to attend classes and students who were unable to attend the regular classes. They were subjected to a series of examination. In both periods T_{-1} and T_0, the findings suggest that students who did not attend classes but continued learning online performed worse than students who attended classes regularly and participated in class discussions. Students who did not attend classes tended to seek help from the proctors more often than students who attended the classes. Face to face learning experiences ensured a more holistic evaluation of the student than technology driven e-Learning.

8. Changes in the academia

E-Learning has rapidly become a major influence on how instructional materials are provided. As institutions are increasingly turning to e-Learning to deliver teaching and learning material, the underlying conceptualization of many e-learning courses is based on models found in traditional classroom instruction. New technology may not be found relevant in a model of classroom-based instruction that is suited for traditional brick and mortar institutions.

Educational professionals are required to change as a result of ICT. These changes do not only include the manner in which one teaches, and the manner in which they conduct and publish research. Student progress, catalogs, course guides, course schedules, and syllabuses will all be online and linked to each other. Changes will entail a development of key learning outcomes consistent with taxonomy of objectives in the cognitive domain: knowledge, comprehension, application, analysis, synthesis and evaluation. **Knowledge** entails remembering recalling terms, facts, and details without necessarily understanding the concept. **Comprehension** entails understanding and students could summarize and describe main ideas in own words without necessarily relating it to anything. **Application** entails transferring learning to own life or to a context different than one in which it was learned. **Analysis** entails relating and breaking material into parts, describing patterns and relationships among parts. **Synthesis** entails creating something new by combining parts to form a unique solution to a problem. **Evaluation** entails judging and expressing own opinion, judge or value based on expressed criteria, ideas and methods. Following the 1948 Convention of the American Psychological Association, Benjamin Bloom took a lead in formulating the classification of "the goals of the educational process". While the cognitive domain involves knowledge and the development of intellectual attitudes and skills, the other domains are the affective Domain and the psychomotor domain that needs to be addressed.

Applying Bloom's taxonomy to e-learning will result in a taxonomy of this nature:

	BLOOM'S TAXONOMY	RECOMMENDATION E-LEARNING
Knowledge	Remembering	Content awareness
Comprehension	Understanding	Online chatting
Application	Transferring	Meaningful online conversation
Analysis	Relating	Drawing on other's experiences
Synthesis	Creating	Developing own arguments based on analysis
Evaluation	Expressing	Learning in action

Table 4. Taxonomy of e-learning

In developing the cognitive objectives one need to establish at what level of motivation the students are. In E-Learning systems that utilize the computer networks, it is difficult to grasp the students' motivation to learn because there is little face-to-face communication between the instructors and the students. Despite this, faculty instructors are required to make very effective teaching strategies. In this regard the theories of Maslow who presents a hierarchy of five levels of basic needs may be best used. Maslow has set up a hierarchy of five levels of basic needs. In the levels of the five basic needs, the person does not feel the second need until the demands of the first have been satisfied, nor the third until the second has been satisfied, and so on. Maslow's basic needs are as follows: **Physiological Needs** These are biological needs. They consist of needs for oxygen, food, water, and a relatively constant body temperature. They are the strongest needs because if a person were deprived of all needs, the physiological ones would come first in the person's search for satisfaction. **Safety Needs** When all physiological needs are satisfied and are no longer controlling thoughts and behaviors, the needs for security can become active. Children often display the signs of insecurity and the need to be safe. **Needs of Love, Affection and Belongingness** When the needs for safety and for physiological well-being are satisfied, the next class of needs for love, affection and belongingness can emerge. Maslow states that people seek to overcome feelings of loneliness and alienation. This involves both giving and receiving love, affection and the sense of belonging. **Needs for Esteem** When the first three classes of needs are satisfied, the needs for esteem can become dominant. These involve needs for both self-esteem and for the esteem a person gets from others. Humans have a need for a stable, firmly based, high level of self-respect, and respect from others. When these needs are satisfied, the students feel self-confident and valuable. When these needs are frustrated, the students feels inferior, weak, helpless and worthless. **Needs for Self-Actualization** When all of the foregoing needs are satisfied, then and only then are the needs for self-actualization activated.

Maslow describes self-actualization as a person's need to be and do that which the person was "born to do." Educators at all levels need to understand student motivations. Students take online classes with every intention of completing them, but may fail for a variety of reasons. Studies have shown completion rates to be 40% lower for online learning. Success or failure of online instruction can be related to student motivation (Picar, 2004). Successful students manifest the following characteristics: highly motivated to accomplish learning goals; have some familiarity with subject; college level reading and writing comprehension; strong study and time management skills; achievement oriented; support network of friends or family; good physical and emotional health; and has access to other learning resources.

Intrinsic and extrinsic motivators affect students when participating in an online class. Intrinsic motivation is the completion of a task for the sense of mastery, competence and well being connected to the work done in class. The task motivates itself. Extrinsic motivation is the external reward after completion of the task. A few examples include grades, recognition from an instructor. According to Keller (1999), four elements of motivation must be addressed in on-line education. These include, attention; relevance; confidence and satisfaction. **Attention -** When a student feels isolated by working independently attention problem occur. Presentation of online content must be engaging to the student. Perception Stimulation is needed to surprise student by being shown the unexpected. An instructor can ask a thought provoking question online. The students can also generate their own questions to help guide their learning. This will help the instructor see what is important to the students and be able to reach their expectations. Different types of examples could be used to demonstrate a concept. **Relevance-** Students must find the content to be relevant to their goals and intentions. Instructors should determine student's knowledge and skills before presenting content. Students can fill out a quick online assessment so that the teacher can teach concepts that build on student's previous experience and knowledge. Course objectives should be related to the students' goals. Have the students relate their goals to the instructional objectives for the course and share this with the instructor and students online. Content should ideally be matched to student's preferences and knowledge. Teach what students want to learn. If there is a content area in class that students want to focus on, let that guide topics for the class. **Confidence** - Students only gain confidence when they achieve course goals. Student should be made aware of performance criteria for success. Performance criteria should include online participation in class as well as assignments. This should always be posted in online. Instructors can allow students to set the assessment criteria to evaluate their performance. Student can also choose areas of interest that are related to their learning goals and personal interests. This can be done through posting on chat lines where students collaborate and the teacher can review the postings. Providing immediate feedback for an online class is important so that the student does not feel isolated. Feedback can be immediate through an online test to confirm an answer. Informative feedback directs students to other resources. Analytical feedback guides a student to the correct answer. Immediate feedback keeps a student on track. **Satisfaction –** Student satisfaction is more likely if he can transfer the learning to his own experiences. Student can apply their knowledge to a real situation. The student can solve the problem by choosing the correct actions. Immediate feedback within the program provides reinforcement. This helps motivate students to be more engaged in their learning.

9. Teaching and learning in the information age

One of the fundamental tenets of education is preparation of students for life. Moreover, information is the major component of education. The availability of high speed computing infrastructure was the primary movement in the learning revolution. Combining a multitude of resources with the accessibility of personal computing devices give students access to vast amounts of information and have move the locus of power from the teacher to the learner. Traditionally, educational pursuits of societies and intellectual functioning of individual have their origins in social life. This position stresses the role which stakeholders play in learning and points to the importance of creating "classroom environments" which support the communication and exchange of ideas. Ideally students will become engaged in learning by participating in communities where learning is valued. These communities may be virtual and may be mediated by technical and cognitive tools. Cole & Engestrom (1993) contend that the master tool broadly conceived is language, the ability to communicate one's thought consistent with that of any face to face discussions. Educators need to consider the learner in relation to his technological and social resources whose interaction and their contexts are central to understanding the conditions for human learning. Learners are becoming active constructors of new knowledge and understanding based on what they already know and believe.

The modern day infrastructure places unimagined power in the hands of individual learners who have come work according to their own abilities and at varying speeds. The traditional classrooms typically having rows of students sitting side by side, gazing straight ahead at a teacher who is the purveyor of knowledge are slowly becoming a thing of the past. Realizing that computing technologies have impacted every aspect of human endeavor, educators need to transform learning activity into an innovative form of experience. The increasing interest in e-learning stems from several dynamic changes that include direct changes in social, political and economic conduct. Corporate conduct and market behavior have also played an important role in this regard. Corporations in particular see advantages in making their products and services ubiquitous through technology impacting upon society in numerous different ways. The internet has significantly changed the way lifestyle is delivered and facilitated in both educational and non-educational settings. The proponents of e-learning are largely positive and optimistic about its potential. Education is inherently a social endeavor. It therefore becomes essential to understand the various effects of space - geographic, temporal, and psychological between educators and learners. ICT offers tremendous potential that influences education. It therefore becomes paramount for educators to reflect upon many issues. Firstly, what is the desired outcome of a program of teaching and learning?; How would critical thinking be embodied in the program of teaching and learning?; What would sustain learners' quest for continued education?; What teaching styles would emulate critical thinking?; and finally how new knowledge would be generated and purveyed? Intertwined among these challenges is how to meet the expectations and needs of employers and employees in this new environment.

In this regard an inventory of teaching and learning documented in the form of a portfolio becomes essential. Such an inventory of teaching and learning should demonstrate the learners' knowledge in a particular discipline. Creativity of thought and reading beyond the subject is also enhanced and learners can contribute to an electronic discussion board. These discussion boards become a form of social networking where thoughts are challenged and knowledge is shared.

10. Conclusion

In conclusion, the question of whether universities will be necessary in the future has never been asked because it has never been a possible question before. The study commenced with two questions: What does one do when a "net generation" of computer literate and computer sophisticated students arrive at the gates of institutions? What is the commensurate ability of faculty? Until the rise of the World Wide Web there was no alternative to university education. As a result, educators are faced with a rich array of opportunities and at the same time hazards. The simple fact that it is now possible to ask the question mandates a discussion. It is difficult to predict the future. In the short run, e-Learning represents a threat to traditional institutions. The faculties of these institutions are obliged to take advantage of the technology toward two ends. First, they must use this most powerful intellectual tool to free them from classroom drudgeries and shifting from one traditional technology to other non traditional and time saving devices where studies is less and less boring encouraging creative, enriching, and exciting thoughts. Corporations are run with more intelligence (and information) than ever before and they need intelligent, creative employees more than ever before. Universities can and should respond to this need. A need still exists for intelligent citizens who lead examined lives, who make informed choices and conduct themselves intelligently at all times. Educators need to be aware of student motivation when teaching an online class. Student motivation is even more difficult to assess online, especially with the lack of face to face contact. Strategies were identified in the study to engage the students and keep them interested. Most importantly, be aware that more technology does not lead to better learning and finally facilities are important but facilitators become paramount in e-learning.

11. References

[1] Argyle, M. (1991) Cooperation: *The basis of sociability.* London: Routledge.

[2] Cheng, Hui-Chuan, Lerman, J. & Armstrong, P. (1991) Comparison of performance and attitude in traditional and computer conferencing classes, *The American Journal of Distance Education,* 5:51-64.

[3] Cole, M & Engestrom, Y. (1993) A Cultural-historical approach to distributed cognition, Salomon, G. (ed) *Distributed Cognition,* CUP, Cambridge

[4] Commission of the European Communities (2003) Commission Staff working paper elearning: Designing tomorrow's education:A mid-term report as requested by the council resolution of 13 July 2001.

[5] Garrison, D.R. & Anderson, T (2002) *E-learning in the 21st century: a framework for research and practice,* London: Routledge.

[6] Katz, R. N. & Oblinger, D. G. (Eds.). (2000) *The "E" Is for Everything: E-Commerce, E-Business, and E-Learning in Higher Education.* San Francisco: Jossey-Bass.

[7] Keegan, D. (1996) Foundations of Distance Education. 3rd Ed. London: Routledge.

[8] Keller, J.M. (1999) Using ARCS motivational process in computer-based instruction and distance education. New Directions For Teaching and Learning, 78, 39-47.

[9] Perkins H (1969) *The Origins of Modern English Society, 1780-1880*

[10] Picar D., (2004) http://itec.sfsu.edu/wp/860wp/F04_860_picar_elearning_motivation.pdf

[11] Simons, J A, Erwin D B & Drinnien B. A.(1987) *The Search for Understanding,* West Publishing Company, New York.

[12] Seufert, S, Lechner, U & Stanoevska, K. (2002) 'A reference model for online learning', *International Journal on e-Learning* (January to March): 43-55.

[13] Steeples, C. & Jones, C (2002) *Networked learning: Perspectives and issues*. Computer Supported Cooperative Work-series.

[14] Williams, C. (2002) 'Learning on-line: a review of recent literature in a rapidly developing field', *Journal of Further and Higher Education* 26 (3) 263-272.

Part 2

Design

4

Innovative E-Learning Solutions and Environments for Small and Medium Sized Companies (SMEs)

Ileana Hamburg
Institute for Work and Technology – FH-Gelsenkirchen, Germany

1. Introduction

Europe experienced one of the most difficult periods in the economic history. The economic recession seems to end in December 2009 but many European countries recover slowly and European companies particularly small and medium sized ones (SMEs) have difficulties in facing todays challenges. The requirements in working life increase: more knowledge is necessary as well as flexibility referring to a fast familiarization with new working environments.

In order to cope with such requirements and changes of the labor market, beside a good organized labor market policy, flexibility and fast improving measures in the education programs are necessary. The future of many companies depends on the ability of their staff to learn how to use knowledge for acquiring the competences to adapt to constantly changing environments (Hall, 2006).

"The only thing that gives competitive advantages to an organization is what it knows, how it uses that knowledge and how fast it can learn something new" (Rosenberg, 2000). That means organizations should develop a strategy of Life Long Learning (LLL) integrated in their work and business environments and giving support "just in time". The use of e-Learning within this strategy can be an answer to these needs of nowadays organizations with geographically distributed workforce, for acquiring knowledge which changes fast, for increasing performance without more costs and for "just in time" learning (Wild et al., 2002). The SMEs need such strategies based on e-Learning, and new IT media embedded into work processes, responding not only to requirements of work/career situations but also to employees interests and supporting collaboration, knowledge sharing and performance support. E-Learning through its flexibility and adaptability can bring advantages to the SMEs. It is an important tool that can support knowledge development empowering people with the skills and knowledge needed to turn change to an advantage. Learning by using e-Learning 2.0 (Hamburg, 2010), which is based on Web 2.0 (O'Reilly, 2005) focusing on community and social interactions, has the potential to support sharing, development and transfer of individual and organizational knowledge through interactive methods of online delivery of information, collaborative procedures, targeted training and through blending of e-Learning with other education methods (Engert et al., 2008).

Social media based on Web 2.0, i.e. media for social interaction offer the premises for a fast knowledge acquisition and support transforming learning in a continuous „lifelong process". Andreas Kaplan and Michael Haenlein (2009) define social media as "a group of Internet-based applications that build on the ideological and technological foundations of Web 2.0, which allows the creation and exchange of user-generated content."

Communities where individuals share a domain of interest and knowledge about which they communicate and learn to increase their knowledge via formal or informal methods in order to solve problems are proper environments for learning (Wenger, 1998, 2002: Hamburg, 2008, 2010).

But results of projects show that the use of e-Learning and of cooperation in European SMEs is very low. Some of them and also big organizations tried to implement e-Learning but many of these attempts failed in the last years (Atwell, 2003; Beer et al., 2008; European Comission, 2003; Robinson, 2008).

In this paper, results of projects, of expert interviews and case studies referring to readiness of SMEs for e-Learning and attempts to transfer existing best practice of e-Learning solutions and learning strategies to other SMEs are presented. Communities oriented to learning and examples of projects aimed also at building communities and learning strategies for SMEs by using social media and some conclusions are given.

2. Readiness of SMEs for e-learning: Results of projects, expert interviews, case studies

Results of studies and European projects (e.g. ARIEL www.ariel-eu.net, SIMPEL www.simpel-net.eu, ReadiSME www.readisme.com) show that one of the most critical but important aspect to be considered is an evaluation of e-Learning readiness. Many companies which have to make the decision whether to integrate e-Learning into their vocational strategy do not know if the company, the staff and infrastructure are "ready" for this or not.

A "possible" exact description of the situation at the time of introducing e-Learning in order to develop/adapt a training model can be realized through a methodical evaluation of e-Learning readiness.

The Economist Intelligence Unit cited by Psycharis (2005) published some models of e-Learning readiness.

Rosenberg (2000) identified the following four factors – the "Four C's for Success": Culture, Champions, Communications, and Change. He considers corporate-policy factors very important for the success of an e-Learning project: an open learning culture, the manager support of the project, the successful communication of the project and its advantages for the staff and a change process which integrates these factors of success into the further development of the organization and of the staff. These elements have to be clarified previously to a project in order to assure its success.

He developed 20 key-questions which were classified in the categories: entrepreneurial readiness, changing nature of learning and e-Learning, value of teaching and information design, management of change, re-invention of educational organization, industry of e-Learning and personal commitment.

Chapnick (2000) considers that the main readiness factors for the implementation of e-Learning are the pychological readiness, the sociological readiness, and the environmental readiness, the readiness of the human resources and the economic readiness.

Broadbent (2002) affirms that the successful implementation of e-Learning in an organization requires right people, right place and right resources.

The following factors are considered by Worknowledge (2004) important when implementing e-Learning: the readiness of the staff, the readiness of administration, the economic readiness, the environmental readiness, the technological readiness and the readiness of the culture.

Borotis and Poulymenakou (2004) suggest seven factors that should be checked before an e-Learning solution is adopted including entrepreneurial readiness, readiness of content, technological readiness, readiness of culture, of human resources and economic readiness.

We would like to add a further two models of e-Learning readiness. Habermann and Kraemer (2001) identify (similar to Rosenberg, but rather forming a methodical point of view) five typical problem fields previously to a project, which can influence the strategically and operative planning: problems of complexity, information, resources, decision and of coordination ones.

Stacey (2001) preferred professional-content aspects. His "Big 8 questions to Answer in Planning and Implementing e-Learning" contain questions of organizational and didactical processing as well as some to measuring success.

Psycharis tried to connect the factors of e-Learning readiness mentioned in the literature and to classify them into 3 major categories (Figure 1):

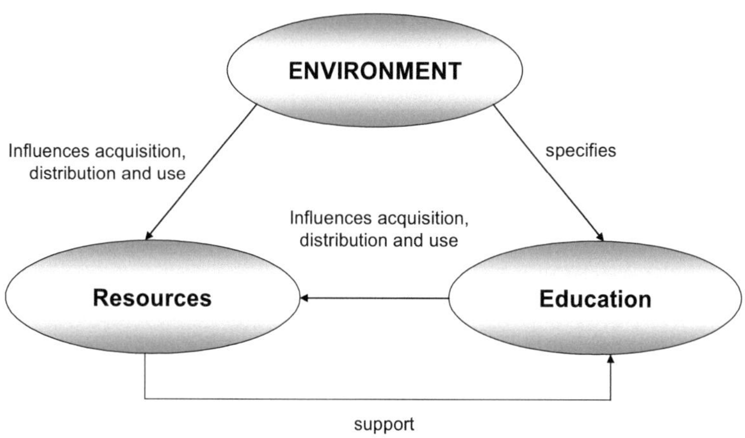

Fig. 1. Criteria of readiness and correlation between them (Source: Psycharis, 2005).

All these models try to group the content that belongs to specific areas, e.g., technological readiness, human resource readiness, etc. but the content of the categories of the different models are appreciatively the same. The authors regard e-Learning projects less on the basis of technical implementation processes but more of needed organization development and organizational integration.

The models add value in sorting the factors that need to be investigated before an e-Learning project starts. Some observations within these models particularly when applying them to SMEs are the following:

- before e-Learning readiness can be measured, a decision should be made if this is the best choice of training delivery or not,
- special pedagogical requirements and face to face contact are not to be neglected,
- organizational readiness is a difficult problem for SMEs particularly for small business,
- the models should be adapted to be applied not only before e-Learning started but also during and after the e-Learning event,
- not only managers should answer the questions of these models, but also trainers and specialists,
- some models are oversimplified and do not include all the fields that needs to be ready before starting e-Learning.

In the followings, factors considered in our model will be presented which influence the successful adoption of e-Learning and which can be used to build a readiness model that will assist the SMEs, consultants and providers in determining what should be done in order to prepare the staff, the trainer and the organization for the learning event. In our model, a list of questions for the evaluation of e-Learning readiness has been provided in a reference catalogue taking into consideration the main criteria Organization/Management, Technology/Services, Staff/Human Resources.

The following questions are to be used in form of a catalogue:

Organization/Management

Strategic and economic readiness

- Which are the strategically objectives and reasons for implementing/using of e-Learning?
- Economic readiness (financial resources available) for e-Learning

Entrepreneurial readiness

- Are the requirements necessary for a successful implementation of e-Learning fulfilled?

Readiness of culture

- Is the learning culture of the organization an innovation supporting one?

Management readiness

- Does the company management support the implementation of e-Learning?

Technology, Services

IT readiness

- How are the IT equipment and connection of the workplaces with the Internet?
- Are IT and Web used for learning and communication by staff?

Readiness of learning environments

- Which are the existing learning platforms in the organization?
- Do virtual learning communities exist in the organization?

Readiness of content

- Is the content to be learned suitable for e-Learning?

Staff/HR

Trainees' readiness

- How are the IT skills of the target groups for e-Learning?
- Are they motivated and ready to learn?

Trainers', tutors' readiness

- Are trainers, tutors educated for e-Learning?
- Which are the most used vocational training forms in the company (formal, informal, etc.)?

Readiness of vocational training plans and strategy

- Which are the plans and tools for the staff development in the company?
- Do long term training strategies based on e-Learning exist in the company?

We tried to keep the catalogue for e-Learning readiness as short as possible The staff does not respond if the questionnaires are too complex.

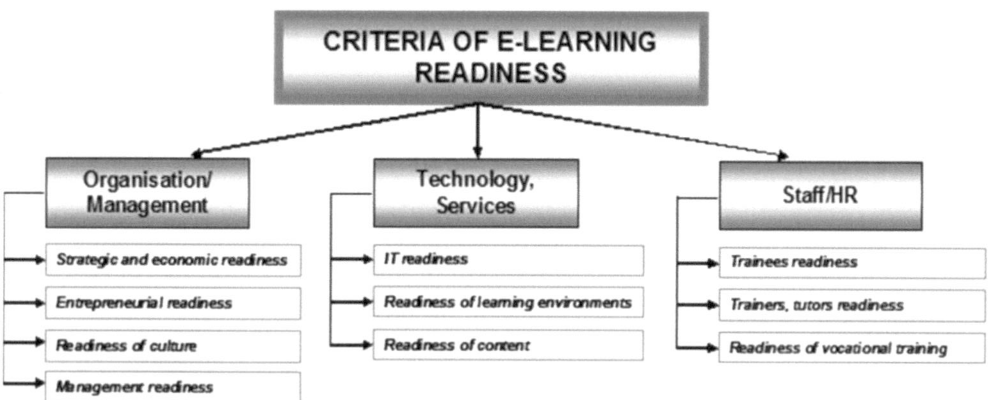

Fig. 2. Factors for e-Learning readiness - Project SIMPEL www.simpel-net.eu

In this context and with partners from universities and SMEs in Ireland (coordinators), Portugal, Romania and Hungary, the author works within the EU Leonardo project LLL Readiness in SMEs (ReadiSME -http://www.readisme.com/).

The project is mainly an innovation transfer project of best practice and results of successful e-Learning strategies and projects from recent years. It is focused on methods to establish degrees of LLL readiness based on e-Learning in SMEs and on impacting knowledge management. The project adopts a step-by-step approach to implement LLL according to different levels of readiness whilst simultaneously working towards higher levels of readiness.

The project uses the results of the SIMPEL project involving researchers, higher educators and other training providers, SMEs, e-Learning experts and providers (Beer, 2008).

Comparative analysis of the results of projects undertaken by the SIMPEL partners and results of national seminars within this project show aspects which have to be considered when implementing e-Learning as a part of the LLL strategy of the company if it is to be sustainable:

- identification of needed skills/competences which could be achieved by e-Learning,
- readiness for e-Learning,
- adequate tutor and technical support for education and integration with more traditional forms of learning, learning infrastructures,
- organizational perspective,
- transfer of knowledge,
- economical aspects,
- quality and (self) evaluation criteria.

Within ReadiSME, 20 German SMEs have been interviewed and 2 case studies have been carried out in order to evaluate e-Learning readiness of German SMEs taking into consideration the categories presented above. The results of interviews not only from Germany but also from project partner countries are summarized below.

The majority of companies responded that they are LLL ready but e-Learning is not sufficiently applied and they are still not up taking it as a competitive tool. The reasons for this are sometimes unknown. In previous studies, done in projects like Ariel and SIMPLE, regarding barriers to training issues in SMEs, some similar issues, like in the ReadiSME, have been found. However, there is a little more detail:

- A reactive approach to learning
- A lack of electronic content which can be found easily
- Lack of time to explore relevant training options to achieve the competitive strategy
- Lack of relevant ICT applications
- Lack of staff motivation
- Lack of understanding all the advantages of e-Learning particularly by managers and person responsible with further education in companies.

Because it appears that most SMEs seem to be LLL ready and there is still a low uptake, the ReadiSME partnership highlights that there may be more to these reasons than a lack of time and a lack of content. One must go into the psychology theories of change and encouraging individual change in one's lifestyle. These have be looked in further work within ReadiSME in the context of the levels of SME readiness for LLL. It can be said that there are different levels of company readiness with regard to the evaluation of the questionnaires used within ReadiSME. Several levels of readiness can be derived from the results of the questionnaires:

- Those with a high level of ICT, high level of organizational readiness and a high level of staff readiness.
- Those with a low level of ICT, high level of organizational readiness and a high level of staff readiness.
- Those with a high level of ICT, low level of organizational readiness and a high level of staff readiness.
- Those with a low level of ICT, high level of organizational readiness and a low level of staff readiness.

- Those with a high level of ICT, low level of organizational readiness and a low level of staff readiness.

At an individual level there are also different levels of readiness:

- Those with a high perceived ability to undertake LLL.
- Those with a low perceived ability to undertake LLL.

It is recommended that a questionnaire needs to be developed in order to assess the level of individual readiness bearing in mind motivational and psychological theories and that different techniques should be used to manage the process of increasing readiness and incorporating change.

3. Transfer of existing innovative e-learning solutions to other SMEs

The main content of this part is to present some innovative solutions for SMEs within the on-going innovation transfer Leonardo project Net Knowing 2.0: Web 2.0 Technologies and Net Collaborating Practices to support learning in European SMEs *(*www.netknowing.com*)*.

The aim of the project Net Knowing 2.0 is to help European SMEs to turn their daily work into a source of corporate learning for all their employees. Like this, the integration of the e-Learning in the daily work life will be facilitated, as well as the opportunity for companies to build their own formative resources. The project focuses on the development, testing and dissemination of a didactical package to enable managers and directive staff of SMEs to benefit from e-Learning particularly based on Web 2.0 technologies, Networking and e-Collaborating practices as an instrument for their own personal learning and for the support of corporate informal learning systems in their enterprises. Some special objectives are:

- To enable managers and directive staff of SMEs to improve their learning opportunities by the use of Web 2.0 technologies and networking practices.
- To enable and encourage them to participate in social professional and entrepreneurial networks and communities of practice in order to obtain the maximum benefits of sharing knowledge activities.
- To improve the knowledge sharing culture in SMEs supporting them to make better use of their organizational knowledge as a corporate learning resource.

One of the project tasks was to collect and structure results of the SIMPEL project and other ones which could be transferred within Net Knowing 2.0 for other SMEs. A catalogue of recommendations has been developed for the transfer process which used also results of discussions with representatives of German SMEs which have been interviewed in this context by the author. In the following, we describe the issues for transfer and some of the transferred products.

Some issues for transfer schemas were title of the product/result to be transferred, general description/aims for which it has been developed in the past or description of the context, how can be it re-used in Net Knowing 2.0, aims which could be addressed with the transfer of this product, needs of successful transfer, methods to be transferred, resources needed to attend a successful transfer.

Two products to be transferred from SIMPEL are:

1. A draft for a sustainable training strategy for SMEs based on e-Learning.

The strategy has been developed in cooperation between SIMPEL partners and consultants for SMEs, discussed and improved so that it could be adapted to specific national requirements. Interesting discussions during seminars with SMEs contributed to the development of some e-Learning models within this strategy.

Within Net Knowing 2.0, the strategy and the models have to be discussed with SMEs in all partner countries in order to be improved taking into consideration the actual economic and financial situation, new profiles of working places, etc.

Some models (best practices) for training strategies for SMEs based on e-Learning could also be transferred from SIMPEL by being customized together with SME representatives from companies which would like to apply them.

Methods used for the strategy transfer and for strategy models are discussed in each partner country with SMEs. Discussions were also hold with e-Learning and Web 2.0 experts, presentation of them at special fairs, workshops and conferences, within networks where partners are members have been done.

Some objectives of this transfer process are:

- Improvement of difficulties of SMEs to survive/be competitive due to qualification.
- Helping SME to implement sustainable training strategies and innovative work places.
- Using e-Learning and Web 2.0 tools for improving their learning models.
- Learning from best practices SMEs from Germany already use.

2. The SIMPEL Community of practice (CoP)

Within SIMPEL a Community of practice (CoP) with e-Learning experts and practitioners has been established in order to cooperate in improving the use of e-Learning in SMEs. More about CoPs is presented in part 4. The CoP is supported by the standard virtual learning environment (VLE) Moodle. The activities of the SIMPEL CoP to improve LLL in SMEs and other organizations by using e-Learning were successful.

The layout of the CoP has to be changed according to the objectives of Net Knowing 2.0.

The functionality of the SIMPEL CoP has been improved and used for building a CoP in Net Knowing by using TikiWiki CMS. Tiki is a powerful web-based application created by a large team of contributors. In the part 4 of this chapter the CoP developed within Net Knowing 2.0 will be described.

By using the CoP within SIMPEL, the SMEs staff and consultants, Web developers can cooperate also with experts from other countries to quickly find practical solutions to SME problems. The training modules developed within the project Net Knowing will be also available on the CoP platform and training sessions of these modules will be moderated by project partners during the project period.

4. Framework for improving e-learning readiness and building LLL strategies

The Framework uses the readiness results and suggests measures to improve LLL readiness and steps to develop LLL strategies. It uses a combination of the trans-theoretical model which is a model for behavior change and recommendations from the ARIEL and SIMPEL projects. The Framework is based on a top-down and bottom-up approach targeting both the individual and the organization. It aims first to raise awareness of the potential benefit of LLL to the individual and the organization and to change the attitude and behavior of individuals and companies towards LLL. Last but not least, the frame should help companies to implement sustainable LLL strategies based on e-Learning.

Results of the projects SIMPEL and ARIEL show that first some organizational measures are required which will be presented within the following steps. These measures correspond to the planning, action and maintenance stages in the building of a LLL strategy by using the trans-theoretical model for organizational behavior change. At each stage we have added electronic tools, which may contribute to master the stage effectively.

Analysis of company situation and needs of qualification including:

- Analysis of business goals and the company's situation and of difficulties the company has to achieve these goals
- The determination of the qualifications needed by the staff to solve the difficulties
- Methods to achieve such qualifications (LLL strategy, e-Learning, short term qualification, etc.)
- Electronic Tool: for gathering documents in various versions and making them available throughout the company (or according to differentiated access rights): Wiki (either stand-alone or as part of a Learning Management system like Moodle), this may be accompanied by a forum for discussion, again either as stand-alone or as part of an LMS)

Concept

- Finding of suitable offers and services for the qualification needs required by the work tasks. Determination of learning contents, forms and media used for the LLL strategy.
- Determination of relevant knowledge and data flows.
- For internal communication and gathering information by wiki and/or forum may be continued to be used. Feedback sheets and/or databases such as provided in learning management systems (LMS) such as Moodle help gather the information even more precisely.
- To find suitable offers, researching the web and particularly social networks such as Xing, meanwhile also Facebook can be useful.

Planning

- LLL measures as well as the time, the actors, the technological and organizational infrastructure and the tools needed for an efficient realization of these measures.
- The preparation of a financial (business) part of the LLL model providing a framework for the economical dimension of the LLL strategy in the company, linking the planning with the process level of the implementation.
- An excellent planning instrument for SMEs is Mindmanager, linking mind maps with basic project management features. For the financial planning it is necessary to draw on the data of business or enterprise management software (depending on the size of the company this may range from simple spread sheets up to very specific enterprise planning resource planning packages, which vary greatly according to size, branch and needs of the companies concerned

(http://en.wikipedia.org/wiki/List_of_ERP_software_packages).

Implementation

- LLL solutions which correspond to the learning culture of the company will be produced (or purchased and adapted) and introduced.
- This may cover the whole range from buying standard learning software packages to subscribing to podcasts and other web-based offerings to running a CoP and using/running an LMS with self-developed learning contents. For SMEs it may be useful to band together or to make use of offerings by branch associations etc. in order to minimize costs.
- A further step may involve tests and certification. In all likelihood, SMEs will not go further than running online quizzes for testing knowledge. Certification will most likely be taken out of offerings by craft chambers and other officially recognized certification agencies (including universities).

Evaluation and improvement

- How effective and financial efficient the training was.
- A complete evaluation concerns human and financial resources, developed measures, participation, changed knowledge, behavior, competences and expectations of the participants to the LLL program, practical changes in the company.
- This raises the issues of quality control of e-Learning and return on investments (ROI). It is not possible here to point to one or two tools which do it all. Many different parameters may play into this. See for example: http://www.prescientdigital.com/articles/learning/measuring-the-success-of-e-Learning-initiatives/. It is important not to follow a narrow, purely economic frame in this evaluation.

Results of some tasks carried up within ReadiSME show that many SMEs have the technical infrastructure, organizational capability and personnel procedures in place to facilitate learning. However, these companies are still slow to undertake learning and an improving of your awareness is useful.

The trans-theoretical model is a method of changing behavior in individuals using interventions. It has been widely used to increase physical activity, raising health literacy and encouraging the cessation of smoking.

It aims to allow individuals to make conscious decisions in order to change their behavior about a specific topic. It deals with people at different levels of readiness on the behavior change spectrum. The spectrum ranges from people who have no intention to change, to those who have made a change and do not wish to regress. In the trans-theoretical model there are five stages of change:

1. Pre-contemplation - the individual is not intending to take any steps to make the change in behavior. They are usually unaware or uninformed about the benefits the change in behavior can bring.
2. Contemplation - people are intending to change in the next six months. However, if they do not recognize that the pros outweigh the cons they may remain in this stage for a very long time. For example, if a person decides that in September they are going to do a training course in Java programming.

3. Preparation - a person is taking steps to make the change in order to take action in the immediate future. For example, if a person starts looking for different java courses and buying java books in order to prepare or attends an open night in the local university.
4. Action - the person actually makes the behavior change. For example, enrolls in a course, starts attending a course.
5. Maintenance - Working to prevent relapse.

The Framework has been discussed with consultants and representatives of European SMEs particularly German ones and to improve it. Scenarios will also be used for explaining the Framework to managers and SME staff.

Scenarios create a sense of common understanding and indicate certain strengths and weaknesses of education and training systems in companies.

Scenarios are different from forecasts in that they provide a tool that helps SMEs to explore the many complex business environments in which they work and learn and the factors that drive changes and developments in those environments. Furthermore, scenarios include "narrative descriptions of assumptions, risks and environmental factors and how they may affect operations. Scenarios attempt to explore the effect of changing several variables at once with objective analysis and subjective interpretations" (Wikipedia, 2005).

Within a company, scenarios provide a common vocabulary and an effective basis for communicating conditions and options.

Scenarios can help SMEs to be innovative by:

- Identifying white spaces between old and new economies (e.g. e-commerce changing companies' business).
- Engaging and inspiring the SME`s stakeholders to make the changes for transformation and to articulate the future of a city, region, etc.
- Sparking innovation and new forms of value creation (new products and services replacing traditional ones).
- Creating alignment and energy around an organization's vision and purpose (what is the 21st century business idea).

There are a number of organizations who are working with scenario planning on a consulting basis as well as a method for internal strategic planning. One example is the GBN (Global Business Network - http://www.gbn.com) which has worked together with a large number of big and small companies to explore the future of their industries. GBN uses scenario thinking in a variety of contexts and in conjunction with other processes and tools that they have developed over the years particularly focused on illumination of the short- and long-term risks and on opportunities associated with specific decisions and investments.

Shell has been producing Global Scenarios for more than 30 years (http://www.shell.com/). At Shell, in order to create analytical clarity, the scenarios no longer tell particular "stories", they rather consider the interplay between essential forces and contrasted ways in which different groups can pursue their objectives. While providing more complex and sometimes technical analyses of business environments, Shell Scenarios are based on a map which provides a simple, unified context which is very powerful to better understand the various conditions under the company has to operate in different circumstances.

We give an example of a scenario- It can be developed after the analysis of the company situation.

A medium-sized retailer - active in Germany with about 20 locations - introduced the question of how it can position itself strategically new. In recent years, it became increasingly difficult to compete successfully in the highly competitive market. New distribution channels (discounters and internet) gained importance and fought for the same customers. Clients became more prices sensitive and the margins continuously lower. The question came up how the company could secure its long-term success. The decision about a strategy for the next year (or next years) should be in the light of a thorough assessment and a clean sounding of realistic options for the company. Using the technique of scenario thinking in options is encouraged. The aim is not to establish a precise position. Instead, future versions will be developed in the form of scenarios. The final decision is presented in the scenario below.

In the first phase, an analysis of the company's external and intern situation, of the business strategy, of the staff qualification needs has been done during a one day workshop. The conclusion was that the company has on the one hand, a strong business unit with a diverse range of products. On the other hand, the company's focus cannot be identified. The company offers products in many areas, but it is not really excellent or clearly perceptible in one of these areas. New media are not used for advertising the products. No customer focus can be seen. There exists no more knowledge about concurrent products. Most of the staff did not attend qualification courses in the last 4 years. The extern trainer-driven training is mostly used. Informal learning was not a recognized method in the company.

After the analysis it was decided not to concept a new active strategy with an review of the organization, business, etc. but to use the strategy of minimal changes: e.g. improvements of the business strategy and introduction of new media and LLL learning concepts like informal learning (not only for today needs and requirements) should involve only minimal changes in the existing structures and processes of the company.

In the planning phase taking part during another workshop, the changes have been discussed. It was decided to use entirely own strengths of the company. If the company goes into completely new areas of business and a complete new strategy in which they have little knowledge and little experience, the risk for the company is quite large. In addition, this would be associated with large investments. A repositioning of the current business model and introducing informal learning, e-Learning and new media like Web 2.0 for learning, cooperation and product advertising seems promising instead of a completely new business, organization and learning model that the company cannot control and where competitors are one step ahead.

5. Social media for the development of innovative communities for SMEs

Social media based on Web 2.0 services i.e. media for social interaction offer the premises for a fast knowledge acquisition and support transforming learning in a continuous „life long process" also within the communities.

Social media can take many different forms, including Internet forums, weblogs, social blogs, micro blogging, wikis, podcasts, photographs or pictures, video, rating and social bookmarking. By applying a set of theories in the field of media research (social presence, media richness) and social processes (self-presentation, self-disclosure) Kaplan and Haenlein created a classification scheme for different social media types in their Business Horizons article published in 2010. According to Kaplan and Haenlein there are six different types of social media: collaborative projects, blogs and micro blogs, content communities, social networking sites, virtual game worlds, and virtual communities. Technologies include: blogs, picture-sharing, vlogs, wall-postings, email, instant messaging, music-sharing, crowd sourcing, and voice over IP, to name a few. Many of these social media services can be integrated via social network aggregation platforms.

The technical skills needed to use social media are rather low. Blog software, for example, can replace sophisticated and costly content management systems. It enables content providers from reporters, writers, educators to concentrate on their content without bothering too much about the underlying technicalities. It is even faster and less demanding to communicate and thus through social networks, such as Facebook, Twitter and others.

Another important characteristic of such applications and "spaces" is the decreasing differences such as the one between teachers and taught, between formal and informal learning processes, between education and knowledge acquisition/management. This gives rise to new integrated and world-wide forms of learning such as in "Communities of Practice" where a community based on shared interests learns in a community of equals by exchanging expertise and experience without building a hierarchy, because any of the participants is considered teacher and taught at the same time. This may be well combined with more formal learning processes, for example, the acquisition of language skills. A low-cost and easy access virtual room to accommodate formal and informal learning practices, group collaboration and the gathering and exchanging of learning materials might be realized in an e-Learning environment based on the Social media tool TikiWiki CMS Groupware.

TikiWiki CMS Groupware, originally and more commonly known as TikiWiki or simply Tiki, is a free and open source wiki-based, content management system written primarily in PHP and distributed under the GNU Lesser General Public License (LGPL) license. In addition to enabling websites and portals on the internet and on intranets and extranets, Tiki contains a number of collaboration features allowing it to operate as a Geospatial Content Management System (GeoCMS) or Groupware web application (2010). It has been actively developed since 2002, making it a very mature open source Wiki-CMS-Groupware solution. More than 200 people have contributed source code to the Tiki project; this makes Tiki one of the largest open source teams in the world.

Tiki includes all the basic features common to most CMSs such as the ability to register and maintain individual user accounts within a flexible and rich permission/privilege system, create and manage menus, RSS-feeds, customize page layout, perform logging, and administer the system. All administration tasks are accomplished through a browser-based user interface.

Tiki has four major categories of components: content creation and management tools, content organization tools and navigation aids, communication tools, and configuration and ad-ministration tools. These components enable administrators and users to create and manage content, as well as letting them communicate to others and configure sites (TikiWiki, 2010).

For example, some of the main features are:

- Wikis (like in Wikipedia)
- Forums (like in phpBB)
- Blogs (like in WordPress)
- Articles (like in Yahoo News)
- Image Gallery (like in Flickr)
- Map Server (like in Google Maps)
- Link Directory (like in DMOZ)
- Multilingual (like in Babel Fish)
- Bug Tracker (like in Bugzilla)
- RSS Feeds (like in Digg)
- Free Open Source software (LGPL)

In addition, Tiki allows each user to choose from various visual themes. These themes are implemented using CSS and the open source Smarty template engine. Additional themes can be created by a Tiki administrator for branding or customization as well.

Tiki is an international project, supporting many languages. The default interface language in Tiki is English.

Communities, where individuals share a domain of interest and knowledge about which they communicate and learn via formal or informal methods in order to solve problems are proper environments for learning.

One approach which we discuss and used are CoPs. CoPs are made up of voluntary members who share knowledge, ideas and interests and who act as mentors to each other. They offer new opportunities for knowledge management and learning processes by using new forms of interaction between team work and loose contact between the actors (Hamburg, 2006).

At present, most European SMEs act alone in facing their training problems. A successful and suitable solution would be for SMEs to build/join communities of practice in different forms in order to share knowledge, apply best practice in workplace design and to develop business-oriented models of training. In CoPs knowledge is created when people participate in common problem-solving and exchange the knowledge needed. Sharing knowledge makes more sense in the context of a CoP because its members have common learning interests. Therefore, experience exchange within their specific activity areas reciprocates trust. Trust is a key facilitator necessary for knowledge sharing and is also important for the creation of a common pool of knowledge which can be used for a new/innovative product or service. Therefore, CoPs play a critical role in the promotion of learning in an organization and can become a powerful tool in generating sustainable competitive advantages for SMEs. They are an alternative to building teams particularly in the context of an innovation. The tacit knowledge accumulated over years from the experiences of CoP members can be processed for new products or services which will add value to SMEs.

Internet technologies (Palloff, 1999) extend the interactions within communities of practice beyond geographical limitations and make possible the building of virtual CoPs (VCoP). These communities free their members from the constraints of time and space. In comparison to technical solutions for knowledge management, VCoPs can mark a change from "managing knowledge" to "enabling knowledge." Web 2.0 has a vast potential to improve environments for emerging CoPs and is able to efficiently support activities within a community. It supports the collaboration of SME staff through interactive Web-based procedures. It also supports Siemens's (2005) concept of connectivism whereby information is said to be constantly changing, that learning which takes place in distributed networks of people is based on diversity of opinion and where content and services are adaptable and responsive to the specific needs and goals of SMEs.

The use of social media with Web 2.0 services and e-Learning 2.0 in learning communities improves the ability of members to socially interact with the technology used (communication with technology). Social media tools like Internet forums, weblogs, social blogs, micro blogging, wikis, podcasts, photographs or pictures, video, rating and social bookmarking are easy to use can help to create a more dynamic community and provide an on-going conversation benefiting the members.

By using social media tools in learning environments supporting the community the potential exists for the combination of synchronous and asynchronous communication, access to - and from geographically isolated communities (Hlapanis & Dimitracopoulou, 2007) and international information sharing.

Supporting learners' communication includes assisting students in coping with the technology, providing multiple means of access, helping students to achieve text based communication skills, setting personal goals and priorities and dealing with conflict and tension.

The use of e-Learning specifically based on Web 2.0 (e-Learning 2.0) in CoPs also impacts on formal learning settings where it is particularly useful for pedagogical approaches such as collaborative learning and problem and enquiry based learning.

Despite its great potential, there are barriers and limitations particularly of current technologies in relation to virtual communities of practice. The lack of face-to-face contact within a CoP can often be an advantage because it helps to suppress traditional group norm behavior. On the other hand, it remains open whether community of practice where face-to-face contact is entirely excluded, can be sustained over a long period. Face-to-face interaction and socialization processes consolidate relations between members and group membership. Trust is important for a VCoP and is developed primarily through face-to-face interactions.

Another aspect in relation to VCoPs is that because virtual community infrastructures can be set up across cultures via the Web, cultural and language differences can change interactions and hinder CoP activity flows. The use of technology to bridge geographical gaps can lead to a misinterpretation of messages whereby cues and feedback are often missing. Crossing virtual boundaries between institutions can involve legal issues wherein knowledge transfer such as data protection, becomes intellectual property.

A further important barrier to VCoPs refers to selectivity in the choice of ICT to support the CoPs. VCoPs need to use Internet standard technologies such as bulletin boards and Web boards and if possible, platforms already known to participants. Many authors (Hong, 2003) have stressed the difficulties of members' ICT access and ICT skills referring for example, to the use of on-line forums and e-Learning training. In order to assure optimal interaction between users and the ICT platforms which support KM in VCoPs with SME participation, methodologies and processes should be used for the interfaces which acknowledge not only a CoP's functionality but also the ICT competences and learning abilities of staff members. Interfaces should have a basic real level of usability (Johnson, 2001).

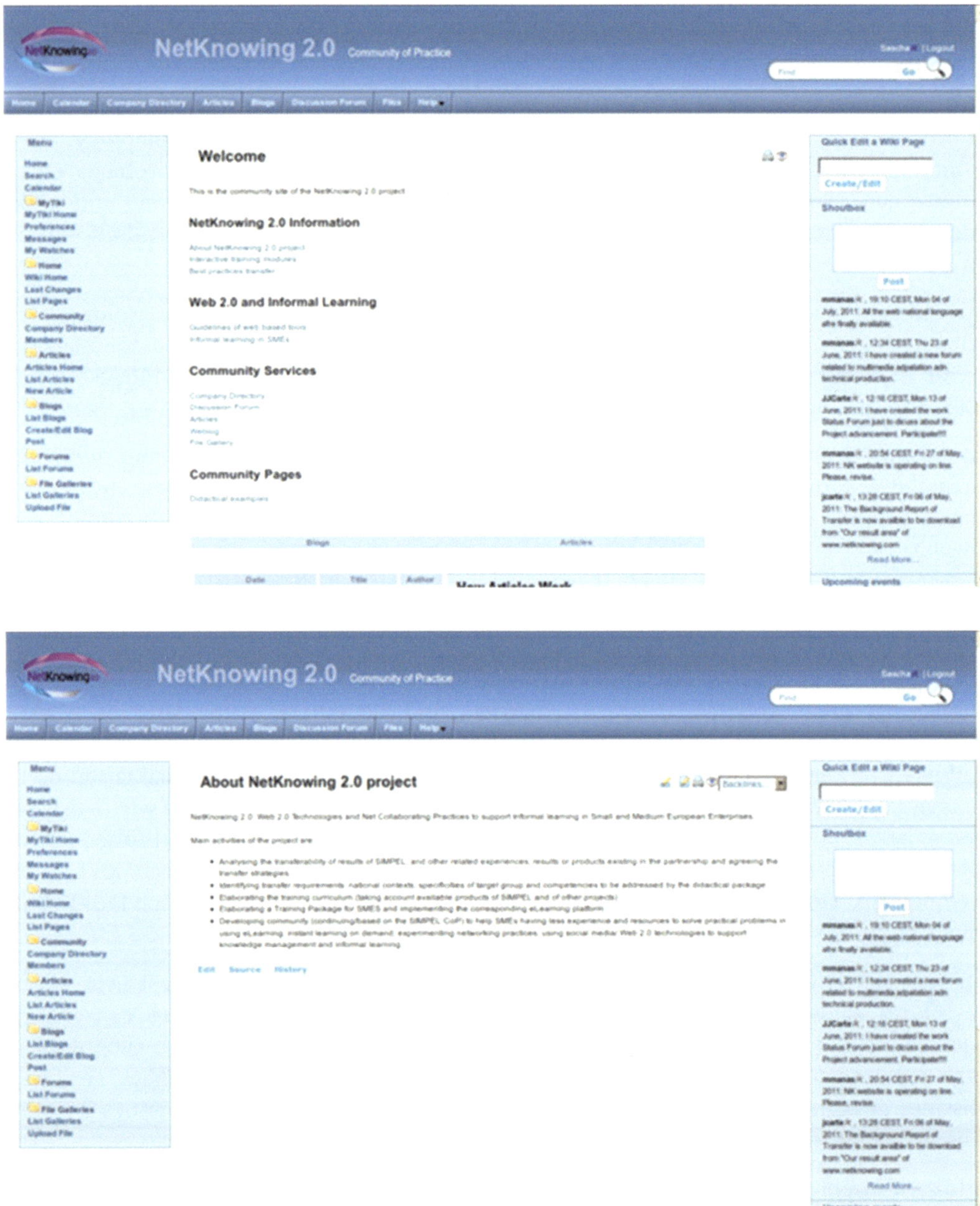

Source IAT: http://cop.netknowing.eu

Fig. 3. CoP of the project NetKnowing 2.0.

But in designing learning projects or CoPs to manage change, there is a continuous need for the many specific constraints of SMEs to be taken into account. Learning, communication and many other activities are significantly more short-term oriented in SMEs than in big companies because of the small numbers of employees.

Some screenshoots of the CoP developed within the project Net Knowing 2.0, by using social media tool TikiWiki are given.

6. Conclusions

In this paper, it was argued that readiness for LLL by using e-Learning and CoPs signal two important approaches to improve the competitiveness of SMEs and the continuing professional development of individuals within them.

However, there are some remaining research questions to be answered, in particular, the identification of creative strategies in LLL which could contribute to the removal of barriers such as inertia to change and knowledge struggles and political issues and refinement of innovative methods, guidelines and good practices for companies and organizations for supporting not only competitiveness but also social integration, innovation, etc.

Determining the factors that affect LLL readiness and initiating knowledge sharing and transfer processes and the development of CoPs is a complex process. There are currently many tools and technologies for e-Learning 2.0, web 2.0 and social media which could be exploited or used in an innovative way to address the diversity occurring in virtually every organization worldwide. These need to be explored further in terms of their ability to address the strategic needs of SMEs.

It is important to help SMEs and individuals to have an open and adaptable attitude to such tools and methods by initiating corresponding cooperative projects.

7. Acknowledgement

This paper describes work within the SIMPEL project which was supported by the EU within the e-Learning initiative and work within the ongoing ReadiSME and Net Knowing 2.0 projects supported by the LLL Leonardo da Vinci sub-program.

8. References

Attwell, G., D. Dirckinck-Holmfeld, P. Fabian, A. Kárpáti & P. Littig (2003). E-Learning in Attwell, G., Dirckinck-Holmfeld, D., Fabian, P., Kárpáti, A. & Littig, P. (2003) "ELearning in Europe - Results and Recommendations". Thematic Monitoring under the LEONARDO DA VINCI Programme. Bonn, Germany. Report., Impuls 010.

Beer, D., Busse, T., Hamburg, I. & Oehler, C. (eds.) (2008). "Improving ELearning practices in SMEs. Proceedings of the SIMPEL final conference". Brussels, 14.04.2008. Universitas-Györ.

Beer, D., Busse, T., Hamburg, I., Mill, U. & Paul, H. (eds.) (2006). "eLearning in European SMEs: observations, analyses & forecasting". Münster, Waxmann.

Broadbent, B. (2002). Tips to held decide if your organization is ready for e-Learning. Available at http://www.serprofessoruniversitario.pro.br/ler.php?modulo=11&texto=700.

Borotis, S. & Poulymenakou, A. (2004). "E-Learning Components: Key issues to Consider Before Adopting e-Learning Interventions". Proceedings of eLearn, Washington, DC. Available at http://www.ois.dmst.aueb.gr/analysi/pages/eLReadiness_ELEARN2004.pdf.

Brook, C. & Oliver, R. (2003). Online learning communities: Investigating a design framework Australian Journal of Educational Technology 2003, 19(2), pp. 139-160.

Chapnick, S. (2000). Are you ready for E-Learning? Learning Circuits Update (Online serial). Available at http://www.learningcircuits.org/2000/nov2000/Chapnick.htm.

Cross, J. (2006) "Informal learning: rediscovering the natural pathways that inspire innovation and performance". John Wiley and Sons.

Davis, J., Kay, J., Kummerfeld, B., Poon, J., Quigley, A., Saunders, G. & Yacef, K. (2003). Dougiamas, M. (2004) "Moodle: Using Learning Communities to Create an Open Source Course Management System". Perth, Australia.

Dougiamas, M. (2004). "Moodle: Using Learning Communities to Create an Open Source Course Management System", Perth, Australia.

Duguid, P. (2005). "The Art of Knowing: Social and Tacit Dimensions of Knowledge and the Limits of the Community of Practice". The Information Society (Taylor & Francis Inc.): pp. 109-118.

Economist, The (2003). e-Learning readiness rankings, Economist Intelligence Unit. Available at: http://www-304.ibm.com/jct03001c/services/learning/solutions/pdfs/eiu_e-Learning_readiness_rankings.pdf.

Engert, St., Hamburg, I., Marin, M, & Petschenka, A. (2008). Improving e-Learning 2.0-based training strategies on SMEs through communities of practice. In: The International Association of Science and Technology for Development: The Seventh IASTED International Conference on Web-Based Education, March 17-19, 2008, Innsbruck, Austria. Innsbruck, pp. 200-205.

European Commission (2003). "Observatory of European SMEs".

Habermann, F. & Kraemer, W. (2001). „Envision E-Learning: Von der Strategie zum detaillierten Projektplan". In: W. Kraemer & M. Müller (eds.), Corporate University und E-Learning. Wiesbaden: Verlag, pp. 233-258.

Hall, R. (2006) "Knowledge Management in Australian Oragnisations: Development or Deeping Inequalities?" In: M. Carton & J.-B. Meyer (eds) The Knowledge Society. Paris: L'Harmattan pp. 127-142.

Hamburg, I. & Lindecke, Ch. (2005) "Lifelong learning, eLearning and business development in small and medium enterprises". In: Szücs, A. (ed.) & Bo, I. (ed.): Lifelong eLearning: bringing eLearning close to lifelong learning and working life; a new period of uptake: proceedings of THE EDEN 2005 Annual Conference, 20-23 June, 2005. Budapest: Univ. of Technology and Economics, pp. 79-84.

Hamburg, I. (2007). Shifting eLearning in SMEs to a Work-based and Business Oriented Topic. In: European Distance and ELearning Network: New learning 2.0? Emerging digital territories - developing continuities - new divides, THE EDEN, Annual Conference, Budapest, June 13-16, 4. Naples: CD-ROM.

Hamburg, I. (2010). eLearning 2.0 and social, practice-oriented communities to improve knowledge in companies. In: Ortiz Bellot, G., Sasaki, H., Ehmann, M. & Dini, C. (eds.) ICIW, 2010. The Fifth International Conference on Internet and Web Applications and Services; 9-15 May 2010, Barcelona, Spain. Barcelona: CPS, pp. 411-416.

Hamburg, I., Engert, St., Marin, M. & Petschenka, A. (2008). "Improving eLearning 2.0-based training strategies on SMEs through communities of practice". In: The Internat. Association of Science and Technology for Development: The Seventh IASTED International Conference on Web-Based Education, 17.-19.03.2008, Innsbruck, Austria. Innsbruck, pp. 200-205.

Hlapanis, G. & Dimitracopoulou, A. (2007). The school-teacher's learning community: matters of communication analysis. Technology Pedagogy and Education 16 (2) pp. 133-152.

Hong, K.-S., Lai, K.-W. & Holton, D. (2003). "Students' satisfaction and perceived learning within a web-based course". Educational Technology and Society 6(1), pp. 116-124.

Johnson, C. (2001). "A survey of current research on online communities of practice". Internet and Higher Education, 4, pp. 45-60.

Kaplan, A.M. & M. Haenlein (2009). "Users of the world, unite! The challenges and opportunities of Social Media". Business Horizons 53 (1): pp. 59–68.

Kaplan, A.M. & Haenlein, M. (2010). "Users of the world, unite! The challenges and opportunities of Social Media". Business Horizons 53 (1): pp. 59–68.

McMillan, D.W., & Chavis, D.M. (1986). Sense of community: A definition and theory. Journal of Community Psychology, 14, pp. 6-23.

O'Reilly, T. (2005). "What is Web 2.0. Design patterns and Business models for the next generation of Software". http://www.oreillynet.com/lp/a/6228.

Palloff, R. & Pratt, K. (1999). Building Learning Communities in Cyberspace. San Francisco: Josey-Bass Publishers.

Psycharis, S. (2005): Presumptions and action affecting an e-Learning adoption by the educational system. Implementation using virtual private networks, European Journal of Open and Distance Learning 2/2005. Available at http://www.eurodl.org/materials/contrib/2005/Sarantos_Psycharis.htm.

Robinson, D. (2008). "Keeping pace with change in SMEs: creating and maintaining congruence and consistency in SMEs in Transition economies" http://works.bepress.com/david_robinson/2.

Rosenberg, M.J. (2000). The e-Learning readiness survey: 20 key strategic questions you and your organization must answer about the sustainability of your e-Learning efforts. Available at
http://books.mcgrawhill.com/training/elearning/elearning_survey.pdf

Schwen, T. & Hara, N. (2003). "Community of practice: A metaphor for online design?" The Information Society 19, pp. 257-270.

Siemens, G. (2005). "Connectivism: A learning theory for the digital age". In: International Journal of Instructional Technology and Distance Learning.

Stacey, P. (2001). "E-Learning - The Big 8-Questions to Answer in Planning & Implementing E-Learning", 27.07.2001. Available at http://www.bctechnologycom/statics/pstacey-jul2701.html.

TikiWiki CMS Groupware. http://info.tiki.org. Retrieved 2010-01-03.

Watson, I., Buchanan, J., Campbell, I. & Briggs, C. (2003). "Fragmented Futures: New Challenges in Working Life". Sydney: Federation Press.

Wenger, E. (1998). "Communities of Practice: Learning, Meaning and Identity". Cambridge MA: Cambridge University Press.

Wenger, E., McDermott, R. & Snyder, W.M. (2002). "Cultivating Communities of Practice". Harvard Business Press; 1.edition.

Wikipedia. http://en.wikipedia.org/wiki/Tikiwiki. Retrieved 2010-01-03.

Wild, R.H., Griggs, K.A. & Downing, T. (2002). "A framework for e-Learning as a tool for knowledge management". Industrial Management Data Systems, 107(7), pp. 371-380.

Woelk, D. & Agarwal, S. (2002). Integration of e-Learning and knowledge management. In: World Conference on E-Learning in corporate, Government, Health Institutions, and Higher Education. Volume 1. pp. 1035-1042.

Worknowledge (2004). "E-Learning Assessment Readiness".

5

Reciprocal Leading: Improving Instructional Designs in E-Learning

Kathleen Scalise and Leanne R. Ketterlin-Geller
University of Oregon, Southern Methodist University
USA

1. Introduction

This chapter discusses new approaches for e-learning instructional designs in distance learning and virtual settings. Called reciprocal leadership, students under the direction of an instructor take turns in leadership roles at distributed locations in person or virtually via synchronous social media sites, through facilitating groups and developing leadership skills. Three approaches of reciprocal leadership for e-learning are discussed and examples presented: structured, unstructured and semi-structured reciprocal leading. The approaches are useful in addressing the difficult challenge for both distance and hybrid e-learning courses of how to facilitate interesting and effective group interaction.

One of the most difficult challenges for both distance and hybrid e-learning courses is how to effectively facilitate group interaction. Student centered designs that focus on learners constructing understanding often employ small groups for reflection, dialogue and interaction (Bransford, Brown, & Cocking, 2000). Effectively facilitating multiple groups in e-learning, whether synchronously or asynchronously, requires different approaches than in the traditional classroom (O'Neil, 2003; Thompson, 1999). The three reciprocal leadership approaches discussed here are explored in several contexts, and implications are discussed.

Assigning students to leadership roles as part of class activities is nothing new (Olson & Torrance, 1996). But in e-learning this group facilitation can take on both new urgency and a new look (Clark & Hooley, 2003; Taylor, 2002). The new urgency comes about because distributed groups often stumble in carrying out small group activities when the instructor is not physically present. Special preparation and strategies are necessary to make it work well.

One of these strategies, reciprocal leading, rotates students in the role of leader. Students take on facilitation roles as well as sometimes teaching, organizational and other responsibilities at distributed sites or in virtual activities. Reciprocal leadership can increase successful group interaction, be very engaging for students and reinforce emerging leadership proficiencies for students. Here we discuss three approaches for reciprocal leading in e-learning, and compare some strengths and weaknesses. The three approaches differ in part in the degree of structure applied to the leadership role, with a structured, semi-structured, and unstructured example discussed here.

2. What we mean by reciprocal leading

The term reciprocal leading is used here as a parallel term to reciprocal teaching. Reciprocal teaching (Palincsar & Brown, 1985) is an approach to instruction originally created to help with reading comprehension. Classrooms were organized into small reading groups, with one member of the group assigned to act as the teacher for each reading. He or she was responsible for holding a discussion about what the article, story or other writing meant. Although every member of the group was expected to complete all readings, the reciprocal teaching role rotated to a new person for each reading, until all members of the group had a chance to "teach" a reading.

Reciprocal leading broadens this role to include not only teaching but taking turns monitoring and moderating group activities, facilitating, organizing and leading groups. Leaders rotate and often a new leader is selected for each class session or reciprocal activity. For e-learning, goals can include that all members of the group experience the leadership role as well as that more facilitation and leadership capacity is available across distributed and virtual sites. Group activities that can be led with reciprocal leading strategies including many collaborative learning and small group designs, online or offline.

Reciprocal leading, like reciprocal teaching, can serve numerous purposes and functions in different learning environments. Though not yet a common topic in the education literature, mentions of reciprocal leading are beginning to be discussed (Michigan State University Extension, 2007; Sawicki, 2003). In general, the concept of leadership in general at least in the U.S. where we are situated is moving toward increasingly a distributed organizational responsibility with shared accountability for affecting system change and improvement (Kaufman, 2007). Reciprocal leading acknowledges the leadership roles that students can take in a distributed community of learners.

In the original design of reciprocal teaching, the reciprocal teacher begins by asking the group a question about the article and ends with summarizing the article. The basic elements of reciprocal teaching often are categorized as involving questioning, clarifying, predicting and summarizing activities.

The basic elements of reciprocal leading center around facilitating and mentoring group behaviors. The basic goal of facilitation is to help a group accomplish its goals. Understanding group dynamics, the roles that individuals play in groups, and guidelines for facilitation are all principles that can be taught. Basic facilitation skills include preparation and planning for group work, establishing ground rules, staying on task with work goals, methods of intervention when groups need to move in new directions, data or other product management within the group, and presentation of deliverables. As reciprocal leaders become more skilled, they can grow in their ability to lead by considering such topics as how rigid or flexible should the structuring of group activities be, what should the pace of activities be, and to whom should the group look for checking and validation of their work, such as whether adjudication should be internally or externally focused.

2.1 Some strengths and weaknesses of reciprocal leading

The idea behind reciprocal teaching is that during peer-to-peer discussion, problems of understanding often come to light. One student attributes meaning to a part of a reading, and others bring their thoughts and reflection to clarify or refocus the meaning. Thinking is externalized in the discussion.

Similarly in reciprocal leading, a type of meta-thinking is externalized. The facilitator moves between groups and can compare and contrast approaches between and among groups. Since the facilitator is a classmate, peers are often more generous in their inclination to cooperate with the group task, and to discuss approaches or seek alternate solutions. The search for common ground helps ensure that students are finding best approaches in a very situated fashion.

Like in reciprocal teaching, in reciprocal leading more skilled and less skilled members of the group can participate together. In a reading setting, group members with a range of skills can participate together as initial reading is done outside the group, at everyone's individual pace. But then the group forms to share opinions about what the reading means. Peer-to-peer instruction helps to clarify parts of the reading that may not be understood. Additionally, participants can point out passages that are meaningful to them and situate the learning in the local context by sharing personal experiences, ideas and thoughts. In the end, the reading task is ultimately simplified not through decomposition into basic skills but rather by providing a variety of expertise from the group to negotiate meaning.

When doing reciprocal leading, once again the temporary group leader has access to all the skills of the group to clarify activities, suggest guidance and provide a rich variety of expertise. Like reciprocal teaching, reciprocal leading serves multiple purposes. First, it is a distributed learning design that allows complex activities to be carried on by inclusive groups, without requiring the continuous presence of the teacher or course instructor. This makes it a good choice when there is only one teacher present for many students. Small groups can differentiate instruction naturally, since the leader-teacher-student ratio is reduced to a level where everyone's understanding can be addressed.

Reciprocal leading also gives students more opportunities for leadership experiences, even at early ages such as middle school. In reciprocal teaching, a consistent theme throughout the variations of the approach is that the teaching role is assumed by the students, and that this teaching role rotates to all members of the group. It is distinguished from some other forms of peer tutoring by who gets to assume the teaching role. Other forms of peer tutoring often involve specifying one or more peers as more capable — the tutor — while others are the learners, or tutees. Reciprocal leading offers some of the same egalitarian advantages to training who leads, and to showing that the leading and following roles can rotate to everyone within a group.

Encouraging students to engage in leadership experiences can reinforce key habits of mind as well as group interaction skills. Rotating the leadership role helps to break students out of group roles they may have become identified with in the regular school social context. It can also provide sheltered environments for language learners and international students, for instance when a native speaker or domestic-born reciprocal leader is assigned to facilitate groups that may need assistance in understanding some specific terms in English, if that is the language of instruction, or to offer a local perspective on policy, structure, organization and so forth if that is pertinent to the learning goals. The opportunity to exchange information across cultural or national contexts through the reciprocal leading role is powerful for global education, we have found, helping both the temporary leader and those in the supported environment. When roles shift, in this case the language learners and international students can then take a lead position in an area of their own expertise. For instance we found this last year in University of Oregon classes with a German student to the U.S. holding a graduate degree in an important areas of cognitive psychology for our class, and a Korean student who was able to lead us in podcast creation activities for shared learning using her enlightening social media skills, while the international students each enjoyed a supported language and cultural environment at other times in the course, through swapping reciprocal leading roles. This draws on the strength of the class, especially for adult learners but also possible for younger students.

By specifically teaching students skills in how to facilitate group interactions and offering them leadership experiences in doing so, students gain valuable skills they can use in moderating interactions across groups. Group facilitation skills such as these are important in conflict management and in allowing many students to become "ambassadors" of leadership in and out of school settings. Rotating leadership reinforces an expectation that all students can lead. Instruction and practice in developing leadership skills builds confidence. Like reciprocal teaching, reciprocal leading can have a lot to offer students and classes.

There are also substantial weaknesses in the reciprocal leading approach. Some of these are the flip side of the strengths. While students may gain leadership capabilities as they take on leadership roles, this also presumes that students may not have these proficiencies to start. Calling on students to lead activities that they are just mastering themselves can be a challenge. It places demands on the confidence of the reciprocal leader, who can feel they are not sufficiently expert to lead such activities, and also can impede the success of the group if the reciprocal leader indeed does need more knowledge or skills to lead the activity. Establishing trust, encouraging participation, organizing the work of teams and redirecting group focus that goes astray are all complex skills to ask of students. Implicitly acknowledged group roles that are already present *de facto* in some classes may also derail the efforts of students to lead. Of course, the age and maturity of students may enter into the picture. But the challenges and expectations of group tasks also tend to grow over time so the challenge to leadership abilities also tends to keep pace with growing maturity, meaning that leadership can remain relevant early and then grow even as stages of development and skills advance.

Some students may also simply not be comfortable in the leadership role. Self-confidence, shyness and a variety of other attributes can influence student anxiety. Reciprocal teaching often handles this by encouraging students to participate, while creating both a supportive environment and an expectation that all students will be able to participate, which would also be appropriate for reciprocal leading. Differentiation strategies can also be used, if necessary, to meet the needs of students, such as offering enough of an array of tasks for choices that may suit individual needs and preferences, while also offering leadership experiences.

With reciprocal leading, the variety of leadership expertise within the class can be tapped to make an intriguing array of student-centered designs possible. Here we take up a few examples in distance learning in higher education.

3. Three examples of reciprocal leading instructional models in e-learning settings

The three examples in this paper draw on different degrees of upfront structuring of the student leadership roles. They also show different synchronous and asynchronous uses of reciprocal leading.

3.1 Example 1: Traditional reciprocal teaching as reciprocal leading in e-learning

In the following example, a form of reciprocal teaching was reframed into reciprocal leading for use in a hybrid distance education course on research methodology. This course is part of a larger graduate-level program in Educational Leadership in which a portion of the students attend classes on-campus with the instructor and another group of students attend off-campus via video streaming. In this context, students at each site often form collegial relationships with other students at their site but frequently do not interact with students across sites, thereby limiting the collaborative nature of whole-class interactions. To facilitate and encourage cross-site communication and discussions, online reciprocal leading groups with members from both sites were formed to discuss the weekly readings.

The purpose of the reciprocal activity was two-fold. First, the discussion groups were designed to stimulate students' thinking about course topics by engaging in critical discourse about the readings. Second, the discussion groups were intended to encourage students from both sites to meaningfully interact with each other and develop professional relationships. To accomplish these goals, the instructors formed the reciprocal leading groups at the beginning of the course to reflect a balanced composition. Each group of five students represented approximately equal numbers of on- and off- campus students, new and returning students, and males and females. Students remained in the same group for the length of the term.

The online reciprocal activity described here was conducted in much the same way as traditional reciprocal teaching experiences, with a leadership element added. Each student assumed the role of the leader for one reading assignment while the other students participated as group members. To initiate the discussion, the reciprocal leader wrote and posted to a virtual discussion board a summary of the readings, a synthesis integrating the readings with other course topics or readings, and discussion questions that were designed to extend the readings to other contexts or situations and encourage thoughtful analysis. Group members were responsible for reading the assigned material and responding to one unique discussion question. All group members had access to and could comment on the postings. After the group members responded to the discussion questions, the leader rejoined the discussion with specific feedback to individual group members that offered another perspective, integrated responses from different group members, or provided clarification about the readings or application of the material. As such, the reciprocal leader moderated over the course readings, providing students with opportunities to seek clarification, apply the readings to address novel situations, and interact with each other.

We found that though many of the students in the course were familiar with hybrid e-learning from previous classes, they first expressed considerable anxiety with the hybrid reciprocal leading format. Concerns included whether it would be complicated and time-consuming to participate in the leadership activities, and also whether they would be able to sustain the activity without direct intervention by the course instructors. However, as students engaged they became much more comfortable.

Group discussions did occur independently of the course instructors in the reciprocal leading format. The instructors monitored the content of the discussions for appropriateness and alignment with the assignment expectations; however, the course instructors did not join the discussion or provide feedback to group members on their engagement in the discussions. The reciprocal leader received individual feedback on his or her summary, synthesis, and discussion questions. The leader received full credit for the summary if he/she described the main theoretical issues presented in the readings, included the major and relevant findings or conclusions, and included details from the text. The synthesis was evaluated based on the analysis of the main issues as well as the integration of multiple sources into a unique perspective. Lastly, the leader received feedback on the ability of the discussion questions to elicit higher order thinking, extend the discussion beyond the perspectives described in the article, and prompt students to relate the information to other contexts and/or situations. Because the discussions occurred outside of class and required group members to react, timeliness of the initial posting and responses was also evaluated.

Overall, the student leaders successfully completed the reciprocal activities within the appropriate timeframe and actively engaged with their group members in discussion and clarification. Most earned satisfactory scores for their summary, synthesis, and discussion questions. The online discussion sessions facilitated by the reciprocal leaders were interactive and dynamic. The leaders generated thoughtful questions that were responded to with equal care. Many of the interactions exceeded the course instructors' expectations in length and depth, indicating that the discussions were engaging both the leaders and students.

Following the reciprocal leading episode, the course instructors facilitated a whole-class discussion about the readings to further clarify the topics and situate the discussion in the course content and goals, promote discourse across groups by inviting the reciprocal leaders to discuss unique perspectives or thoughtful applications generated by their group, and generalize the material across contexts. These discussions enable class members to learn from other groups and develop a broader understanding of the material. Furthermore, these activities help develop verbal and written communication skills necessary for discussing complex issues. As such, the reciprocal activities as well as the whole-class discussions contributed to the community of learners in which everyone worked together to develop expertise and problem solving skills.

Through the use of a virtual discussion board, the reciprocal leading activity described above provided an avenue for accomplishing the course objectives within a distributed distance education environment. The reciprocal leader was the instrument through which students engaged with the course readings and gained a deeper understanding of the course content. Additionally, the reciprocal leader encouraged collaboration and communication within his/her group by helping group members make connections to each other's thinking and bring clarity to their own thinking. Because the reciprocal leader changed with each reading assignment, all members in the class experienced the role of leader, thereby gaining additional leadership and facilitation skills.

While student leadership was quite successful in this course, another course using a similar but different reciprocal leading activity found a weak link when including a stage in which the reciprocal leaders responded to the student postings. In other words, the reciprocal leaders were successful in creating and posting the synthesis and discussion questions, and these materials elicited good group response on target for the reflection and discussion expected for learning goals. However, in this second course, having the reciprocal leader then respond to and facilitate this discussion rather than returning to the course instructors as in the first example did not work as seamlessly. This pointed up weaknesses in the ability of the students to "stretch" their skills and synthesize the material in areas where they themselves were also learners. One possible explanation for these differences is the varied student demographics between the two courses. The first example described above was offered in an Educational Leadership program, while the second course was with pre-service teachers with may have had fewer leadership experiences in the past. Differences in career goals across these two student groups could have accounted for some of the different outcomes, and this suggests more coaching and practice may be needed for some students in reciprocal leading settings; however, these students also may be most likely to benefit from enriching their leadership skills and knowledge, through such supported practice opportunities.

3.2 Example 2: Paper discussion threads as a semi-structured reciprocal leadership role

Another e-learning strategy for increasing communication and collaboration across students in a distributed distance education model is to use student work to lead ongoing discussion threads to highlight specific topics. In this example, the online discussion thread was used as a venue for sharing students' writing samples.

In a separate assignment, students were required to read a research article of their choice and provide a critique on the quality of the theoretical framework, methodology, results, and discussion using the course framework as a guide. After students received feedback from the instructors, they were encouraged to share their written perspectives with their classmates on a discussion thread. Once a student posted his/her article and critique, classmates were invited to provide a thoughtful and constructive response to the author that reflected on the author's use of vocabulary and concepts discussed in class. In addition, students were encouraged to consider differences in writing style, research traditions, and topical themes. In providing these responses, it was the intent of the instructors that the students would develop and refine their vocabulary of research-related terms, seek clarification of concepts where necessary, and have exposure to multiple styles of communication.

This reciprocal leading approach was somewhat less structured than in the first example, where specific discussion questions were required to be generated and used to frame the group responses. Here, the threads provided a looser guide to the leadership format, and allowed a more fluid exchange of ideas.

In the end, the discussion threads uncovered a variety of patterns in the responses. Many students engaged in discussion about the topic of the original article, either seeking clarification about the purpose of the article or the methodology that was used. Several students suggested ways in which the original article could be improved or replicated. Others commented more specifically on the student's critique of the article, suggesting ways in which he/she could improve the presentation of the material, recommending other readings, or asking for more details about why certain recommendations were made and how they would address the shortcomings. Below are excerpts from three discussion threads that highlight these instances.

3.2.1 Critique A

Classmate response to author of critique: I really liked your critique. As a practitioner, I would read you. Your presentation is very user friendly and your logic is easy to follow. I thought that you provided an excellent summary of the strengths and limitations of the study and you acknowledged what was also included in the original article.

You mentioned limited literature in the review. How would you have expanded the search, or what would you have included? Sounds to me like they are attempting to put a new slant on an old idea and by so doing, add to the literature and what they did sounds reasonable. I just ask the question as it is often a challenge for me. I often select subjects for which there is relatively little literature.

Our district is one that is examining the idea of smaller schools, specifically the K-8 route. I agree with you that I'd like to see more research before taking these ideas into implementation. Where would you like to see this research go next? I'm a bit surprised that there aren't more cost/benefit analyses on this issue with education dollars being scrutinized so.

Author's response to classmate: In response to your questions: You make a good point that there should be more cost-benefit studies on the issue of school size. I think there are more. What makes this [article] unique is the focus on cost per graduate rather than cost per pupil. Also, the authors say that most previous studies do not have access to school level budget data (only district-level data). So other studies haven't been able to use the school as the unit of analysis.

Classmate's response to author: It's a great and novel perspective. I enjoyed reading your critique from that angle (graduate). Are you entertaining a dissertation topic in that area, or still mining?

3.2.2 Critique B

Classmate response to author of critique: I chose your critique because I, too, am very interested in how to turn reluctant readers into avid ones. A few reactions: 1) I would have expected the author to employ reading aloud to the Caribbean youth as a way to pique their interest; 2) I don't see much of a difference between reading magazines, the internet, comic books, the sports page, and novels - who cares, as long as a student is learning by accessing the text, my intuition tells me that there should be solid literacy gain through reading; 3) It looks like a fun study to try and replicate . . . particularly the Caribbean component.

Well done! I didn't know we could do the final draft in an outline format. That was interesting to see.

Author's response to classmate: Thanks for the feedback. Yeah, I remember [the instructor] saying we could use the outline format. I even have it in my notes. It kept it clean and tidy for me.

My biggest beef was that [the intervention] was 45 minutes once a week - with REALLY reluctant readers (they told me [the author] so, which told me that they [the students] had something to prove to me [the author]). Scarcely enough time to put a dent in their reading. But yes, I remain convinced that high-interest reading in any form can have an impact.

3.2.3 Critique B

Classmate response to author of critique: I don't have a lot of feedback, but here's what I have! First, just knowing a little about your background and interests, this article seemed to be a really good match.

My only other question is was this really action research? I may be mistaken in my definition, but I thought action research was done by a practitioner at his/her own school site. It doesn't sound like that was the case here because I thought you mentioned something about how the school was chosen. I probably just need more clarification on the definition and perhaps reading the article makes it more obvious! It sounds like all the other methods were aligned with that type of research.

Author's response to classmate: That's a great question. Action Research can be done in cooperation with a researcher, but the practitioner will be on the front lines. But you are correct in that it's conducted in response to a need or problem. Information is gathered, a plan constructed, implemented, results reviewed, plans adapted and the spiral continues. It's not often the type of research one would see in a peer-reviewed journal, and from what I understand definitely not the type of research one would do her dissertation around. But, from a teacher-researcher perspective, where change happens organically, it makes sense.

3.3 Example 3: Cascading as an unstructured reciprocal leadership role

The final example of reciprocal leading we will share here, which we call "cascading," was the least structured. In the first two examples, specific reciprocal leaders were identified by the course instructors and tasks assigned to the leaders. In the first example, groups were carefully formed by the course instructors and tasks including direct discussion questions were specified as required of the reciprocal leader. In the second example, the threaded reciprocal leading role was somewhat looser. Dialogue and conversation tended to move in the direction of the group interest, with less specification both by the course instructor and the reciprocal leaders. In this third example, the reciprocal leader may not be designated at all, nor their tasks clearly defined. Rather, students coalesce into groups more naturally of their own accord, as described below, to achieve a small objective that has a clearly defined goal: solve a statistics problem, learn how to use some aspect of a software product, complete a portion of a laboratory activity. Generally, some groups at each site may identify the solution more quickly and achieve the objective before others. This can result in sites where some students are impatiently waiting to go on while others are still struggling with basic procedures or problem setup.

In cascading, this differential pace is turned from a problem into an advantage. While participating in cascading designs, those students who have completed a task, project or subgoal successfully then move briefly into the role of reciprocal leader and join other teams to facilitate their work. Productive dialogic inquiry often results, with those who join groups querying the group about what they have tried and what problems they are encountering.

Having just been successful on the task themselves, the reciprocal leaders become a valuable body of expertise for the striving group. The term *cascading* is used because the expertise then cascades throughout the distributed site, either offline or online, with problem solution propagating multiplicatively as one successful group can readily divide and disseminate their knowledge, to assist two, three, four or more other groups or individuals.

The term "cascading" is drawn here from the biological sciences, where the process of cascading is found in many living systems to speed them up and to amplify the impact of the result, on a molecular level such as in chemical pathways of the body. This concept of cascading, or propagating change multiplicatively by dispersing groups of change agents, allows some of the fastest biological processes in living systems to occur. Here in this application of reciprocal leading, we apply the mechanism to social systems, for the purpose of increasing learning opportunities for all students, in a way that can help support distance and virtual education.

Cascading is a form of differentiated instruction for students. Differentiated instruction is an approach to teaching that acknowledges people have multiple paths for learning and for making sense of ideas (Hall, 2002; Reis et al., 1988; Sizer, 2001; Tomlinson, 2001; Tomlinson & Allan, 2000; Tomlinson & McTighe, 2006; Willis & Mann, 2000). As instructors when we differentiate instruction in the classroom, we are saying that we know students come to us with different backgrounds, preferences and needs. We believe how we respond will make a difference. With the use of electronic technologies, differentiated instruction is beginning to play out in some new forms (Scalise, 2005; Taylor, 2002; Trivantis, 2005; Turker, Görgün, & Conlan, 2006). These include new media inclusion for differentiation, levels of interactivity, response actions, and enhanced ability to collect data on the fly and to deliver custom content (Bennett, Morley, & Quardt, 2000; C. G. Parshall, Spray, Kalohn, & Davey, 2002; C. G. Parshall, Stewart, R., Ritter, J., 1996). Here in cascading we see an example of differentiation of e-learning through peer-to-peer reciprocal leading.

One interesting aspect of differentiated e-learning in general — or e-diff — is how quietly personalization or individualization, one form of differentiation, is slipping into electronic learning products (Hopkins, 2004; Trivantis, 2005). Differentiated instruction through technology is contributing to such diverse purposes as adaptive delivery of content, individualizing learning materials, dynamic feedback, cognitive diagnosis, score reporting and course placement (Gifford, 2001). In cascading, it is applied to a spontaneous format of peer tutoring, through which students adopt rotating roles of leadership and sharing expertise in activities.

Taken all together, the potential of differentiation to affect student learning can be great (Tomlinson & McTighe, 2006). In the e-learning context, it also becomes faster and easier to do for some types of differentiation, so it is important that differentiation is well done, just as is true in the classroom-based context.

3.3.1 Distinctions important for instructional designers to understand

When instruction is differentiated in the classroom, it is often clear that multiple approaches are spiraled into the curriculum. For instance, experiences repeat in different forms or students are grouped and regrouped for course placement and learning activities.

When the differentiation is done entirely within electronic technologies, it can be much less apparent that differentiation is taking place in virtual settings. If one learner is given something different on the computer from some other learner, either locally or at a remote site, it can be hard to tell since the two learners aren't looking at the same screens. Typically there is no basis for comparison. The learner may not even realize that had he or she interacted differently with the computer, it would have interacted differently with them. Also, unless disclosed, we don't necessarily know what e-interfaces are gleaning about a learner or the purposes to which the inferences are being put (Nielsen, 1998).

Furthermore, differentiation in e-learning products can have a different intent from classroom-based approaches. In traditional classroom-based approaches, some researchers argue that the result of differentiated instruction should not be different learning outcomes but rather different ways to access the same learning outcomes (Tomlinson & McTighe, 2006). The argument often is that the strongest classroom-based differentiation ensures all students work with the essential understandings for a segment of learning, thus stabilizing the most substantial learning goals. E-learning products are often designed to stretch the individual student's opportunity to learn. The intent can be to tap areas were interest and engagement are strong, or to give the learner choice among objectives. Cascading can help support all of these goals in some circumstances, where the instructional design may show good fit to student abilities and needs.

3.3.2 What is meant by differentiation in e-learning or virtual settings?

Many teaching approaches that focus on meeting the readiness, interest or learning profile needs of individual students tend to involve one of five types of differentiation, which we briefly review here before continuing with cascading. (Hall, 2002; Reis, et al., 1988; Sizer, 2001; Tomlinson, 2001; Tomlinson & Allan, 2000; Tomlinson & McTighe, 2006; Willis & Mann, 2000).

- Differentiation of content – when students start at different places in the curriculum and/or proceed at different paces.
- Differentiation of process – emphasizing many modalities of learning profiles, including individual learning skills profiles (Boyatzis & Kolb, 1991), learning inventories (Dunn, Dunn, & Price, 1984; Lovelace, 2005), cognitive dimensions (Sternberg, 1997), and multiples intelligences (Gardner, 1999).
- Differentiation of product – different students have different assignments and turn in different products. This is a somewhat controversial type of differentiation, since it may appear to establish different standards for students.
- Differentiation of affect – the feelings and attitudes of the learner may be a differentiation premise in e-learning. This can include choice for preference or confidence building exercises such as dynamic assessment, where hints are provided to the learner until he or she grasps the learning objective.
- Differentiation of learning environment – in the e-learning context this can include individual, small or large group learning; incorporating hybrid instruction that combines elements of technology with offline or classroom-based instruction; distributed learning location; or synchronous and asynchronous learning.

Cascading is a form of reciprocal teaching that can bring about differentiation in all these areas, if desired. It is less commonly used for differentiation of product, where a more a structured form of reciprocal teaching typically takes place when the role or product is differentiated, such as in the prior examples.

However cascading is one of the tools of e-learning that can most directly contribute to differentiated instruction in the classroom through reciprocal leading. It is one way to answer the question about when we differentiate, how do we decide who gets what? In cascading, rapid short cycles of peer evaluation help to create an active, small-scale differentiation going on as a continuous improvement process in the classroom. It is mentored and monitored through the active more-able-peer role taken on by students, if they have established strong skills in reciprocal leading and can rotate their skills into play to help their learning communities, whether virtual or classroom-based.

3.3.3 A framework of five approaches to differentiation in virtual settings

Before we specifically discuss cascading further, it may be helpful to consider a framework for the most common e-diff strategies in use today (Scalise, 2007a, 2007b). The framework is organized into five general categories, based on what type of decision-making process and evidence is used to establish the adjustment choices. Approaches can also be combined, or blended, in e-learning products. The five general strategies are:

1. "Diffuse" approaches to differentiation, in which students receive the same content but have multiple opportunities for learning and are provided with different approaches for making sense of ideas planfully "diffused" throughout the content.
2. Self-directed approaches, in which students receive different content by a mechanism of self-selection built into the instructional design. This introduces differentiation through student choice.
3. Naive differentiation, in which the computer alone is determining the course of differentiation, not the user, but no specific plan or overall strategy is in place in the e-learning content for why differentiation is happening, or what it is intended to mean in the learning context.
4. Boolean differentiation, in which the software itself does the differentiation as above but uses types of Boolean logic, such as rule-based frameworks or decision trees, to determine how to adjust content for different students.
5. Model-based differentiation, in which expert opinion is combined with a variety of data mining techniques to generate ideas for how content might be appropriately differentiated, with again the differentiation is delivery via some type of computer adaptive process.

Differences in the five strategies are numerous, and here each type is taken up briefly and described.

In *diffuse differentiation*, there is no direct intention to assess or match the needs of individual users, or to customize content or feedback, as all students receive the same content. But enough variety and different sources of stimulation are provided to interest and engage diverse audiences. This is a very common approach to differentiated instruction in a traditional classroom teaching setting. The hope is that with enough variety provided, everyone's needs can be addressed.

The second strategy, *self differentiation*, allows students to select their personal choices as they work their way through online content. This can consist of simply selecting the order of completion among a fixed menu of learning activities or modules, or can allow much more range of choice. The courseware design determines where choice points are. Self differentiation is also very common in online content.

Naïve differentiation comes about almost inadvertently in many e-learning products. It involves changing portions of content in a more random way, not based on the specific needs of individual students, but simply rotating content and graphics so that screens have different images, representations and so forth each time viewed. This might involve a randomizing factor or a shuffle function. Though diffuse and self-directed strategies can be quite consistent with improved learning objectives of differentiated instruction, it can be harder to make the case for naïve differentiation. Gains in motivation and engagement as learning displays change, for instance, are hard to argue for if the same student only sees one of the displays.

The next strategy, *Boolean differentiation,* uses assessment evidence to change the flow of content for different students. Boolean here simply describes logic that computers use to determine if a statement is true of false. Main Boolean operators include "and," "not" and "or." Operators get used with a series of rules to describe what happens with the content as students make their responses. There are many distinctions among different rule-based methods, including various planning agents, bug bases and chaining algorithms. But the idea is that a set of rules have been devised, often by very carefully studying many students.

These rule-based Boolean methods make up some of the oldest forms of e-diff. The simplest types look like a checklist of learning objectives. Students go down the list and complete the objectives. If they successfully complete 1 AND 2, they go onto 3, for instance. But 1 and NOT 2 and maybe the student is redirected to 2A, or given some additional feedback or other learning intervention that passing students don't get. Rule-based methods can take much more elaborate forms, and have been in very fine-grained ways to describe the multitude of conceptions and misconceptions students hold in certain subject matter areas, and what to do about them. Challenges come in mapping the knowledge space and coming up with effective rules that work, especially for more open-ended and less codified learning objectives, where the permutations of student reasoning quickly grow NP hard to model.

The final form of e-diff to be mentioned here, *model-based,* is actually a large family of approaches that will be grouped together here for the sake of discussion. Some of the approaches are among the newer e-diff forms and others have been around for some time. Most use some form of expert opinion, including from teachers and other subject matter experts, combined with data mining to generate ideas about how content might be differentiated. Common data mining techniques include a variety of regression and Gaussian statistical models, Bayesian networks, neural networks, item response models, and mixed method approaches that combine quantitative and qualitative data to make interpretive or generative predictions.

On the plus side, data mining approaches can be faster and easier than deriving complex rule-based forms. Also they can allow predictions to be compared to actual student learning data to fine tune models. However, the question often is which model to use, and why. Also crucial in the case of e-learning is whether the model really is doing an appropriate job of telling you something about students.

3.3.4 Relationship of cascading to the framework of five approaches to differentiation in virtual settings

Cascading as a form of differentiated instruction draws on the reciprocal leading resource available in the learning environment to help meet the needs of many students. Differentiated instruction though a powerful approach to student learning gains in many settings can suffer from resource issues, and how to get enough expertise applied to the differentiation need. Cascading draws on a continuously refreshing cycle of more-able peer resource in the classroom, with the flow of trading the reciprocal role, just as in reciprocal teaching, allowing everyone to participate both in providing assistance, which can extend student understanding through teaching practices, and receiving assistance, which extends opportunities not only for learning but also for elaboration, extension and reflection.

Working with students to develop their cascading skills for reciprocal roles is important. Developing good reciprocal leading skills here includes understanding the role of the leader, and how to help teams frame their work by asking elucidation questions and encouraging scaffolded reflection. Note too that learners need to see coached examples of how to *receive* reciprocal leading assistance in differentiation. Under the right circumstances, cascading may be able to infuse critical expertise throughout a distributed or virtual site quickly. It is especially useful in situations that would be difficult to take place at all at distributed sites without one or more instructors present, for instance in technology workshops and science laboratories.

Cascading must be used carefully, and students must in advance be shown how to be effective reciprocal leaders in this approach, just as in the more structured approaches described above. It can sometimes result in some students feeling rushed by others who complete tasks and take on reciprocal leading roles, although in our experience this does not happen if specific attention and acceptance of how to provide the rotating assistance and *how to accept the rotating assistance* is introduced when reciprocal leading is taught. It also may be less appropriate in more open-ended problem solving efforts where extensive individual reflection is desired in advance of collaboration, although even here it does allow for cognitive engagement through elaboration and reflection as mentioned. In the right situations and with proper training of the role that reciprocal leaders should play — not doing the work for the other groups but facilitating their problem solving processes — it can be a very effective approach. Virtually, it has been used in both adult learning, where it is very helpful for online and distance settings, and also synchronously face-to-face with even young children, when they are working with e-learning products. It likely is possible to effectively use cascading beyond e-learning settings, but the focus of this article is specifically on instructional designs for e-learning, so we will not take that up here.

4. Conclusion

Distance and hybrid e-learning approaches often call for new ways to facilitate group interaction. Rather than moving away from student centered and group designs, students themselves can be encouraged to take on meaningful reciprocal leadership roles that can expand what can be done at distributed sites, synchronously or asynchronously. By placing students in the role of rotating leaders, they can help facilitate effective small groups for reflection, dialogue and interaction. Such facilitation of multiple groups at a distance in e-learning is different from the classroom. Structured, semi-structured or unstructured leadership formats can be employed but all call on developing student leadership ability to take on such roles. Critically, students must be able to organize a group to get to a goal. How to divide work, frame discussion and encourage participation are some of the leadership skills that need to be explicitly taught. Good resources for short lessons in this area include *Tools for Teaching* (Davis, 1993) and *Classroom Strategies for Interactive Learning* (Buehl, 2001).

When students lead, they must know how to rephrase and reframe when they meet challenges in advancing the progress of their group. Experienced instructional leaders know what to do when their efforts are met with blank looks: for instance, come at it again from another direction.

Reciprocal leaders who are unfamiliar with taking charge can readily lapse from the leadership role. They may even be startled when the group stalls and they are reminded to stay on task. As the course instructor, it might be tempting to step in and take charge for the leader. However, a more effective strategy would be to remind the leader of the role and let him/her make attempts to move forward. Encourage the leader to consult the group for help if they don't know what to do.

School culture and school climate can help in the degree to which students can lead successfully. Supportive environments where students feel free to take on more risk in their group roles are important. When efforts to stretch are themselves valued as a form of success, this is especially helpful. A culture of inquiry and exploration is empowering and helps to propagate leadership through a bootstrapping process of sharing new knowledge.

How the course instructor facilitates success is also very important. Communication efforts are key. Students need to know the leadership roles they are expected to take and have information on how they can be accomplished. Even if the role is to be unstructured like cascading, this needs to be made clear so students know when they are in the position of becoming reciprocal leaders. Communication of expectations reduces anxiety about assuming leadership in learning settings, where by definition students are not yet fully proficient.

Students who are reciprocal leaders will likely have fragmented knowledge in the topic area. Even in the context of reciprocal leadership, course instructors need to make the transitions from topic to topic clear and to organize the relationships sufficiently for students to make the conceptual connections among big ideas clear. Something as simple as a class agenda for each session helps students know and anticipate what is going on, and can help students make the conceptual ties between class activities and the learning objectives. Instructors must also be prepared to step into the reciprocal leading process at the appropriate places, so that students are well guided as they negotiate new territory.

Finally, instructors should be aware of their assumptions. While scaffolding of the reciprocal leadership role always needs to be addressed, this may be especially important when students are coming to reciprocal leadership with a different epistemology or set of ontological relationships than is common for the methodology, discourse language and other tool sets for the subject or grade-level area. Instructors can help students to connect the thinking of the new field with their prior knowledge as they engage in leadership activities.

Leadership thus becomes a joining of the old with the emerging knowledge of the new, to benefit the whole.

5. Acknowledgement

We appreciate the assistance of the University of Oregon in helping to develop innovative instructional designs for new approaches to distance and virtual teaching and learning.

6. References

Bennett, R. E., Morley, M., & Quardt, D. (2000, April). Three Response Types for Broadening the Conception of Mathematical Problem Solving in Computerized-Adaptive Tests. Paper presented at the National Council of Measurement Education (NCME), San Diego, CA.

Boyatzis, R. E., & Kolb, D. A. (1991). Assessing Individuality in learning: The learning skills profile. Educational Psychology, 11(3,4), 279-295.

Bransford, J. D., Brown, A. L., & Cocking, R. R. (2000). How People Learn: Brain, Mind, Experience, and School. Washington, D.C.: National Academy Press.

Buehl, D. (2001). Classroom Strategies for Interactive Learning. Newark, Delaware: International Reading Association, Inc.

Clark, D., & Hooley, A. (2003). Epic Survey 2003: The future of e-learning. Brighton: Epic Group PLC.

Davis, B. G. (1993). Leading a Discussion Tools for Teaching (pp. 63-74). San Francisco, CA: Jossey-Bass.

Dunn, R., Dunn, K., & Price, G. E. (1984). Learning style inventory. Lawrence, KS, USA: Price Systems.

Gardner, H. (1999). Intelligence Reframed: Multiple Intelligences for the 21st Century. New York: Basic Books.

Gifford, B. R. (2001). Transformational Instructional Materials, Settings and Economics The Case for the Distributed Learning Workshop. Minneapolis, MN: The Distributed Learning Workshop.

Hall, T. (2002). Differentiated instruction, National Center on Accessing the General Curriculum, Wakefield, MA: Retrieved November, 2006, from http://www.cast.org/publications/ncac/ncac_diffinstruc.html.

Hopkins, D. (2004). Assessment for personalised learning: The quiet revolution. Paper presented at the Perspectives on Pupil Assessment, New Relationships: Teaching, Learning and Accountability, General Teaching Council Conference, London, England.

Kaufman, M. (2007). Learning Organizations, EDLD 644. University of Oregon.

Lovelace, M. K. (2005). Meta-Analysis of Experimental Research Based on the Dunn and Dunn Model. Journal of Educational Research, 98, 176-183.

Michigan State University Extension. (2007). Welcome to 4-H Citizenship, Leadership & Service, Michigan 4-H Youth Development: Leadership & Citizenship, 2007, from http://web1.msue.msu.edu/cyf/youth/leadership.html.

Nielsen, J. (1998). Jakob Nielsen's Alertbox for October 4, 1998: Personalization if Over-Rated Retrieved Nov. 8, 2006, from http://www.useit.com/alertbox/981004.html.

O'Neil, H. (2003). What Works in Distance Learning. Los Angeles: University of Southern California/CRESST, Report to the Office of Naval Research.

Olson, D. R., & Torrance, N. (Eds.). (1996). Handbook of Education and Human Development: New Models of Learning, Teaching and Schooling. Oxford: Blackwell.

Palincsar, A. S., & Brown, A. L. (1985). Reciprocal teaching Teaching reading as thinking. Oak Brook, IL: North Central Regional Educational Laboratory.

Parshall, C. G., Spray, J., Kalohn, J., & Davey, T. (2002). Issues in Innovative Item Types Practical Considerations in Computer-Based Testing (pp. 70-91). New York: Springer.

Parshall, C. G., Stewart, R., Ritter, J. (1996, April). Innovations: Sound, Graphics, and Alternative Response Modes. Paper presented at the National Council on Measurement in Education (NCME), New York.

Reis, S. M., Kaplan, S. N., Tomlinson, C. A., Westbert, K. L., Callahan, C. M., & Cooper, C. R. (1988). How the brain learns, A response: Equal does not mean identical. Educational Leadership, 56(3).

Sawicki, M. (2003). Thinking Like a Fugitive Slave: Categorical Imperatives at the Mall. Paper presented at the Annual International Conference on Philosophy and Geography, Towson, Maryland.

Scalise, K. (2005). Data Driven Content in e-Learning: Integrating Instruction and Assessment. Paper presented at the American Association for Higher Education (AAHE) Virtual Assessment Conference, Strand 1: Promoting and Institutional Culture of Integrated Assessment, http://www.aahe.org.

Scalise, K. (2007a). Differentiated e-Learning: Five Approaches through Instructional Technology. International Journal of Learning Technology, 3(2), 169-182.

Scalise, K. (2007b). Differentiated e-Learning: What it is and five approaches. i-manager's Journal of Educational Technology, 4(1), 24-28.

Sizer, T. R. (2001). No two are quite alike: Personalized learning. Educational Leadership, 57(1).

Sternberg, R. J. (1997). Thinking Styles. New York: Cambridge University Press.

Taylor, C. R. (2002). E-Learning: The Second Wave, Learning Circuits. Retrieved July 10, 2006, from http://www.learningcircuits.org/2002/oct2002/taylor.html

Thompson, M. (1999). Distance Learners in Higher Education. What are the learners' circumstances? World Bank Global Distance EducatioNET: Teaching & Learning. Retrieved from http://www1.worldbank.org/disted/Teaching/Design/kn-02.html

Tomlinson, C. A. (2001). How to differentiate instruction in mixed-ability classrooms (2nd ed.). Alexandria, VA: ASCD.

Tomlinson, C. A., & Allan, S. D. (2000). Leadership for differentiating schools and classrooms. Alexandria, VA: ASCD.

Tomlinson, C. A., & McTighe, J. (2006). Integrating Differentiated Instruction + Understanding by Design: Connecting Content and Kids. Alexandria, VA: Association for Supervision and Curriculum Development.

Trivantis. (2005). Present Day Custom eLearning. Retrieved July 12, 2006, from http://www.trivantis.com/custom-elearning/custom-elearning.htm

Turker, A., Görgün, I., & Conlan, O. (2006). The Challenge of Content Creation to Facilitate Personalized E-Learning Experiences. International Journal on E-Learning, 5(1), 11-17.

Willis, S., & Mann, L. (2000). Differentiating Instruction. Curriculum Update, Education Topics, ASCD Retrieved Nov. 2006, from http://www.ascd.org/ed_topics/cu2000win_willis.html.

6

adAstra: A Rubrics' Set for Quality eLearning Design

Patrizia Ghislandi
University of Trento, Cognitive and Education Sciences Department, Italy

We can only see a short distance ahead,
but we can see plenty there that needs to be done
A. M. Turing,
Computer Machinery and Intelligence, Mind, New Series,
Vol. 59, No. 236. (Oct., 1950), pp. 433-460.

1. Introduction

The question that, from the very beginning, inspired our inquiry was "*When you can say that an eLearning academic course is a "good" course?*".

The question sound simple, but the answer it is not.

While we are moving forward with our studies the environment to be explored is more and more widening, but we think that the time had came to share our state-of-the-art knowledge with other scholars.

We will analyze, in this paper, why this topic is a complex one and we will present the lessons we learned during our research, the path we followed up to now and our goals, that are:

1. to define the characteristics of a good academic online/blended course;
2. to find the most suitable methods to monitor these characteristics;
3. to create the tool (a rubrics' set) to evaluate —ex ante, in itinere or ex post— an academic online/blended course.

As a "laboratory" to improve the tool we were designing we used the six editions of the eLeaning course TIA (Tecnologie dell'Istruzione e dell'Apprendimento, i.e. Instructional and Learning Technologies), Cognitive Faculty, University of Trento, Italy.

We gather the lessons learned in a rubrics' set that we call *adAstra*, borrowing the name from the famous saying "per aspera ad astra" (i.e. through hardships to the stars), from Lucius Annaeus Seneca, philosopher and politician that lived in the ancient Rome around the beginning of the Christian era. *adAstra* would like to be a guide in designing, developing, delivering and evaluating the academic online courses.

In this chapter we will present:

1. the scientific foundation of *adAstra* idea;
2. the "laboratory" environment we used to test our solutions;
3. the research methodologies;
4. the *adAstra* rubrics and the lessons learned in these years;
5. the future developments.

2. The theoretical framework

From the very beginning we decided it was very important to found the characteristics of a quality academic eLearning module on a theoretical framework. In the scientific literature we appreciated the Sloan-C model and the Community of Inquiry model.

2.1 Sloan-Consortium Five Pillars

Sloan-C is a not for profit consortium based in Newburyport, near Boston, Massachusetts, that intend to promote quality in the academic courses. In the paper *The Sloan Consortium Report to the Nation: Five Pillars of Quality Online Education* (Lorenzo & Moore, 2002) the two authors define the "5 pillars" that are the quality eLearning mainstay:

1. **Learning effectiveness**: eLearning quality have to be at least equal to the traditional education quality. The key to obtain this result is the interaction among the students, with the teacher and with the content.
2. **Students satisfaction**: reached when the students learn successfully and are satisfied by the online experience, thanks to timely and personalized services and to their "feeling" to be involved in a quality learning environment.
3. **Faculty satisfaction**: when teachers teach online successfully, they are morally and administratively supported by the institution, and they can count on mutual respect and esteem when working with traditional teachers.
4. **Cost effectiveness**: when the institution control the budget through the use of technologies to improve the teaching effectiveness, to reduce the drop out, to optimize the spaces.
5. **Access**: when all the students (with or without disabilities) can attend the online lessons successfully. Digital divide, far from to be only a memory, is also a concern.

We concentrated our study on the first one of the parameters, i.e. *learning effectiveness*, because we consider that the academic course quality principal criterion is the attainment of a deep and meaningful learning.

Deep and surface are two approaches to learning, derived from original empirical research by Marton & Säljö (1976) and since then elaborated by Ramsden (1992), Biggs (1987) and Entwistle (1981), among others. Jonassen defined the meaningful learning, a concept near to deep learning, like an active, constructive, intentional and focused, collaborative, authentic learning (Jonassen et al., 2008).

We are fully aware of the importance, to design quality eLearning, of the other four aspects of the Sloan-C model: students satisfaction, teacher satisfaction, cost effectiveness, accessibility. But we postpone to future researches the detailed analysis of these parameters, only partially consider in this paper.

2.2 Community of Inquiry

During our studies we asked ourselves which strategies the teacher have to use to promote deep and meaningful online learning. About this topic we found particularly interesting the idea of Community of Inquiry by Garrison, Anderson & Archer (Garrison et al., 2000), that later on benefited from many other authors contributions.[1] These authors started from the study of the impact of written interaction in the eLearning forum, building up a model of a "deep and meaningful learning" environment, the Community of Inquiry Model, that includes: Teaching, Social and Cognitive Presence.

1. The **Teaching Presence** is the teacher attention to the eLearning design and development, to obtain deep and significant learning. Including what the teacher do before, during and after the module's delivery to determine the outcomes and facilitate the *Cognitive* and the *Social Presence* (Anderson et al., 2001);
2. The **Social Presence** is the student possibility to project him/herself socially and affectively in the computer mediated communication, so that he/she is perceived like real person (Rourke et al., 2001);
3. The **Cognitive Presence** is the possibility for the student to build and consolidate his/her knowledge through the reflection, the meaningful discussion, the critical thoughts and the "practical inquiry" (Garrison et al., 2001).

The goal is to help the teacher to improve its online courses, understanding which characteristics can facilitate the meaningful debate and the critical thinking development.

3. adAstra: A tool for the design phase

Garrison and his colleagues, beside giving a description of each one of the "presences", provides an indicators' set that allow to evaluate the three presences during the forum analysis. The tools' set, as far as I understand, is created to be applied on the forum transcription and it is useful during and after the end of an online course.

This approach is also found in most papers of the scientific literature in which the eLearning quality is analyzed ex-post, when the course is over. Indeed the monitoring phase is often seen as the final collection and analysis of the students and teachers impressions about the course. The benefits of this kind of evaluation are for the future editions of the course, but is limited for the course under construction.

In our *adAstra* approach we choose to scaffold the teachers and the professionals in the design phase. We are strongly convinced that the evaluation is an activity that have to be conducted before, during *and* after the delivery of an online course.

Therefore we decided to investigate what the designer, the teacher and the eTutor have to do to create an online course that bring to a meaningful learning:

- *before the course:* during the design of the learning environment, the textual and multimedia materials, the assignments, the assessment methods and the feedback.

but also:

- *during the course*, monitoring the students' and teacher's social and cognitive activities;

---

[1] See communitiesofinquiry.com for a papers' collection about the Community of Inquiry theory

- *after the course*, for an efficient monitoring of the process, of the project and of the course's effectiveness .

The main goals of our *adAstra* tools are:

1. to help designing a quality course avoiding rough mistakes for the inexperienced, and slips for professionals;
2. to maintain high the interest for quality during all the course stages;
3. to keep track of the problems encountered by the designers and to store the more effective solutions found, constantly improving *adAstra* by the inclusion of the experiences gained from different students, teachers, technologies, media and methods. This drill & practice philosophy toward mastering a quality design reminded us the saying "per aspera ad astra", or briefly "*adAstra*", that we adopted in our research team, initially joking, and to which we afterward became affectionate.

The rubrics that we have up to now validated are about:

1. analysis
2. design and development
3. teachers/eTutors/instructional designers feedback
4. students feedback

The idea is to build up a guide that lists the "good" online course characteristics, founded on the experience accumulated by our group in years and years of eLearning design for our Faculty and successively validated during our research work.

4. TIA- instruction and learning technologies

The "laboratory" that allowed us to design and test the *adAstra* solutions is the course TIA- Tecnologie dell'Istruzione e dell'Apprendimento (i.e. Instruction and Learning Technologies), that here following we would like to present. Tecnologie dell'Istruzione e dell'Apprendimento (thereafter TIA) is an optional course of the Cognitive Faculty, Trento University, Italy, delivered in the academic years from 2003/2004 to 2008/2009 and today replaced by a mandatory course, with the same educational strategies, but with larger contents and more students. The optional course's number of students was from 15 to 25, and formed 3/5 goups of people, followed by one teacher and 3 part-time eTutors

The TIA goal was to allow the students to experiment, in eleven weeks, the distributed learning community dynamics, the collaborative learning, the online communication and the eTutoring principles. The educational strategies used to reach this goals are: collaborative design and creation of a multimedia ipertext; role play; online collaboration; asyncronous forum discussions; self-evaluation and peer assessment. The course was based on socio-constructivistic learning paradigm (Brown et al, 1989, Lave & Wenger 1991, Rogoff 1990, Wenger, 1998).

In the first three year the course was based on a proprietary LMS-Learning Management System (screen shot in Fig. 1).

From the 2006/2007 edition Moodle (release 1.7) replaced the previous LMS. The Fig. 2 show the Moodle home page.

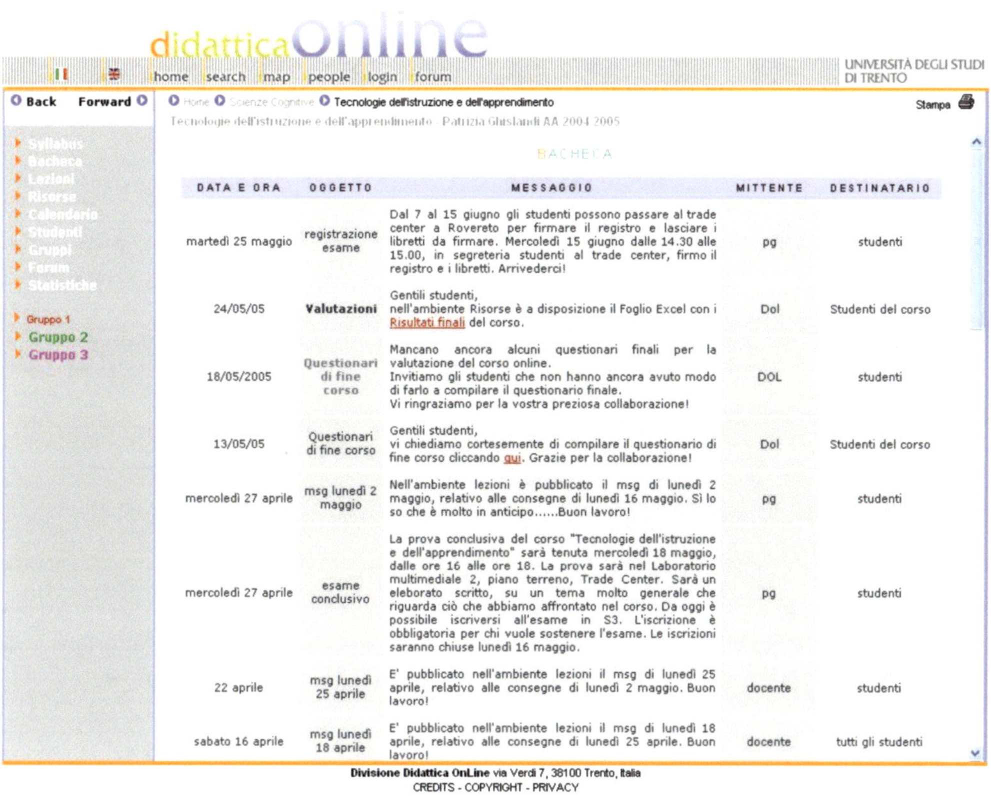

Fig. 1. TIA 2005/2006: the home page on the proprietary Learning Management System

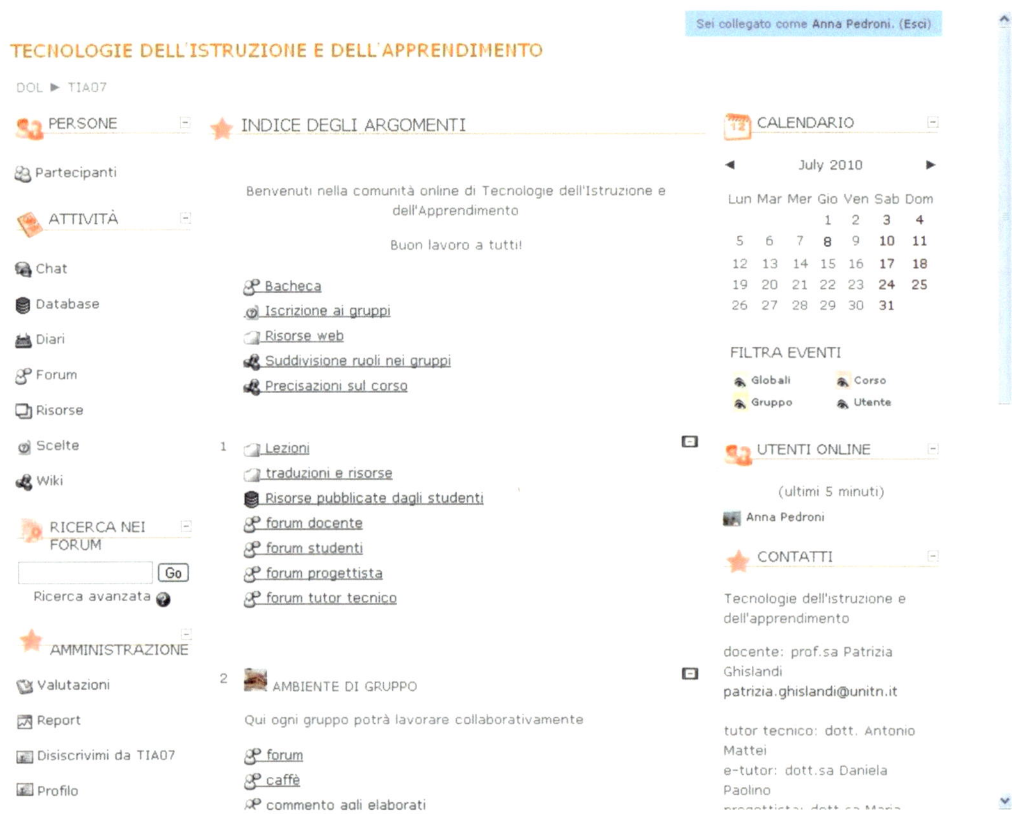

Fig. 2. TIA 2006/2007: home page on the Moodle environment

The home page presents:

1. the **information environment**, with all the general information about the course, the bulletin board for the most urgent announcement, the environment for the group registration;
2. the **communication environment** for the syncronous and asyncronous communication among the teacher/ eTutors/designer and the students during the whole course;
3. the **content environment** for multimedia and text contents publishing by the teacher and the eTutors;
4. the **group environment** that supply the students with all the tools and the resources for the collaboration:
    i. the *forum* for the discussion among the students about the contents and about the group organization; the *"caffè"* for the informal socialization among the students; the *teacher and eTutors comments forum,* about the weekly students assignments;
    ii. the *wiki*, where the group publishes the assignments;
    iii. the *chat* for the synchronous group discussions;
5. the **student environment**, a metacognitive tool to draw up a weekly personal self-evaluation by the student, that receive a timely feedback by the teacher/eTutors;.
6. the **agenda** to share with the students and groups the deadlines.

5. TIA teaching strategies

During the various TIA editions many methodological and design choices remained unchanged.

Based on the collaborative and constructivistic strategies we promoted the **responsible engagement and the continuous partecipation** asking the students to autonomously form small groups (from 4 to 6 people) to work together on the teacher assignments. This approach is important to support the motivation and to facilitate the participants involvement.

The *scripted collaboration*, a role play collaborative strategy, invite the students to hold by rotation one from the six roles established by the teacher and let them, every week of the course, to have personalized tasks.

The weekly roles are:

1. **chairman**: sets the agenda, defines, at the beginning of the course, the roles for all the weeks, sends at the module beginning the message to the group, manages the face-to-face meeting and possible conflicts;
2. **editor**: publishes the final version of the group paper/multimedia no later than the 12 p.m. of Sunday;
3. **moderator:** moderates and enlivens the forum communication, organizes and creates the new threads for a better forum organization;
4. **researcher**: every week researches and publishes, making them available to the group, two meaningful url (site or papers) about the topic under study;

5. **editor**: publishes, no later than the 12 p.m. of Sunday, the weekly diary, i.e. five row about the group week;
6. **spy**: lurks in the other groups and takes back in its own all the strategic information about the other students work in progress.

The responsibility towards the group, but also towards himself and the teacher, guarantees the continuous participation, clearing the drop out risk. In six edition of the course, with circa 110 students, we didn't have any drop-out.[2]

Initially many students complains of the pressing pace. Nevertheless to be part of a group that have to work hard, but also warrants, in case of difficulties, a psychological support, a concrete help and an often warm social environment, lets the majority of the students say that they are satisfied of the experience. And many of them express their regrets when the course close down.

Another way to guarantee the participation is to ask the students to send, no later than the Sunday at 12 p.m. a **personal diary**, a message of 3-5 row about how well went off the week. To this message the teacher or the eTutor gives always a timely feedback, that gives to the student the feeling that there are a recurrent moment of communication with the teacher, and that she/he can asks if needed. Moreover gives to the student the impression that his/her presence in the course and the contributions he/she gives are appreciated. In the traditional course the teacher interact with the student only when he have to judge him/her, and only in the case of oral examination, that are more and more infrequent, due to the students increasing number. In the eLearning course the teacher assure a continuous help in the knowledge construction.

Another strategy that we use is to facilitate the student in the initial choice to participate to the online course.

The critical moment is at the course beginning, when the student have to enter in the learning environment, understand how it work, what he has to do, how he has to interact with the others. Everything is new. Indeed online courses based on the collaboration, on the interaction with the teacher, on the metacognitive self-evaluation are not so common today, at least in Italy. And moreover the students don't understand if eLearning is "advantageous", compared to the traditional course, from the point of view of the time and energy that have to be dedicated. We can imagine they ask themselves: "If I can pass the exam like non attendee student, why I have to complicate my life attending a demanding online course?

To overcame this situation and avoid the initial drop-out the first fourteen hours of TIA lessons are face-to-face and we present:

1. goals, contents, prerequisites, technologies, activities organization, assessment criteria, educational agreement, teachers, eTutor, designer, reference, agenda, etc.
2. the course environment: how to enter, how it is organized, which tools are available, how to reach the teacher and to communicate with the other students.

---

[2] We calculate the drop-out rate considering only the students that participated to the group for at least one week. We do not consider in the students' number the "lurkers" that explored the course in the very initial days, but that were not involved in any way in the collaboration.

Moreover a socialization activity is promoted. We ask the students to register to a group when they enter the first time in the course site. Every group coin a name and create a self-presentation video. We experienced that this activity, during which the students have to call upon both in the personal plane and in the competences to be shared, is an excellent way to learn to interact, to know each other, to present him/herself and its own potentials and limits to the team mates.

6. *adASTRA*: The rubrics' set as "lessons learned" history

TIA educational and organizational strategies have been improved during the academic years, thanks to the constant attention to our pedagogy best practices, the colleagues advices, the design suggestions and tools found in the scientific literature and in the web and, above all, thanks to our research activities. We registered everything we learned in a set of criteria, that we selected and organized in the rubrics' set (Fig. 3).

The rubrics' set in the present release is a tool for monitoring ex-ante, in itinere ed ex-post, the design, development and delivery of academic eLearning courses based on socio-constructivistic paradigm.

We use the "rubric" term because our tool is not only a check list of criteria to be verified. It includes the basic elements that have to be present in the course design and also gives suggestions to create a good constructivistic course.

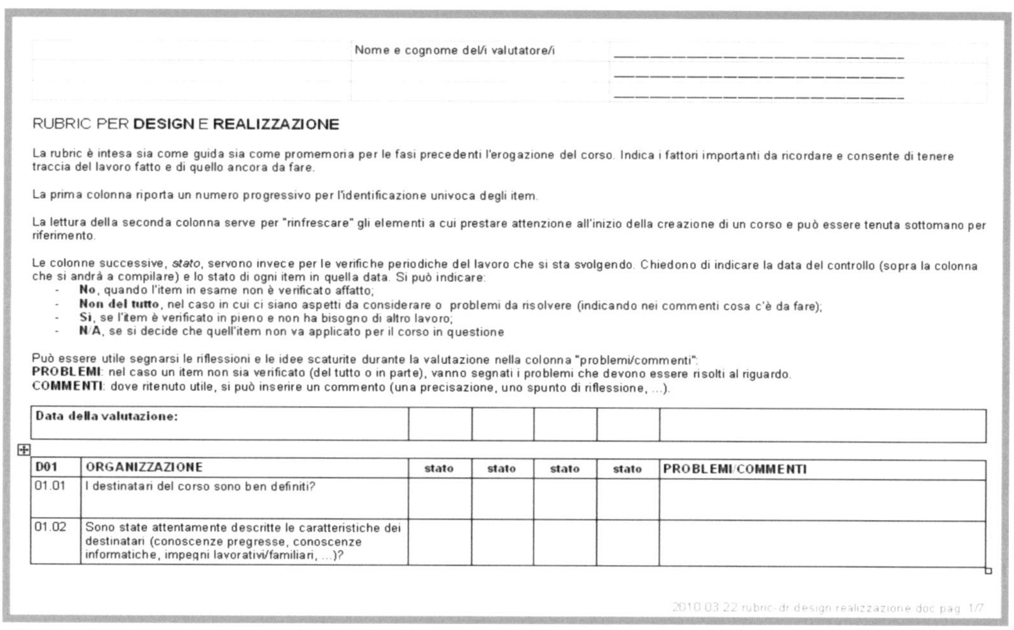

Nome e cognome del/i valutatore/i ____________________

____

____

RUBRIC PER **DESIGN** E **REALIZZAZIONE**

La rubric è intesa sia come guida sia come promemoria per le fasi precedenti l'erogazione del corso. Indica i fattori importanti da ricordare e consente di tenere traccia del lavoro fatto e di quello ancora da fare.

La prima colonna riporta un numero progressivo per l'identificazione univoca degli item.

La lettura della seconda colonna serve per "rinfrescare" gli elementi a cui prestare attenzione all'inizio della creazione di un corso e può essere tenuta sottomano per riferimento.

Le colonne successive, *stato*, servono invece per le verifiche periodiche del lavoro che si sta svolgendo. Chiedono di indicare la data del controllo (sopra la colonna che si andrà a compilare) e lo stato di ogni item in quella data. Si può indicare:
- **No**, quando l'item in esame non è verificato affatto;
- **Non del tutto**, nel caso in cui ci siano aspetti da considerare o problemi da risolvere (indicando nei commenti cosa c'è da fare);
- **Sì**, se l'item è verificato in pieno e non ha bisogno di altro lavoro;
- **N/A**, se si decide che quell'item non va applicato per il corso in questione

Può essere utile segnarsi le riflessioni e le idee scaturite durante la valutazione nella colonna "problemi/commenti":
PROBLEMI: nel caso un item non sia verificato (del tutto o in parte), vanno segnati i problemi che devono essere risolti al riguardo.
COMMENTI: dove ritenuto utile, si può inserire un commento (una precisazione, uno spunto di riflessione, ...).

Data della valutazione:					

D01	**ORGANIZZAZIONE**	**stato**	**stato**	**stato**	**stato**	**PROBLEMI/COMMENTI**
01.01	I destinatari del corso sono ben definiti?					
01.02	Sono state attentamente descritte le caratteristiche dei destinatari (conoscenze pregresse, conoscenze informatiche, impegni lavorativi/familiari, ...)?					

2010 03 22 rubric-dr design realizzazione doc pag 1/7

Fig. 3. Design and development rubric.

7. The rubrics' set validation and the research methodologies

We wanted to be sure that both the contents and the form of our tool were valid (complete, correct, consistent, easy-to-use, effective, efficient) and for that we submitted the rubrics' set to a multiple check:

1. we asked an audit to the designers of the Trento University eLearning Division;
2. we offered the rubrics' set to the students of an eLearning design course we organized in 2010, and asked them to validate it;
3. we offered the rubrics' set to the eTutors of the Firb (i.e. Investement Fund for Basic Research) project whose title is "Net@ccessible: teaching/learning together and for all in a lifelong project". Net@ccessible is a project funded by the Italian Ministry of Public Education, University and Scientific Research to design and create an accessible online learning environment.

We had mainly a qualitative research approach.

We conducted semi-structured interviews with 20 eLearning designers and 5 eTutors. Some of them were new to the eLearning design and some very experienced people.

We collected eLearning designers needs and requirements and positive or negative remarks about the rubrics' set and we used them to improve our tool.

We discovered that *adAstra* is very useful for the eLearning design apprentices but it is also considered quite good, at least like pro memory, by the experts.

8. TIA and the "*adASTRA*" rubrics

In the following paragraphs we will look through the TIA course using the rubrics like a guide.

8.1 Needs and resources analysis rubric

I would like to start this paragraph with a simple example of how the rubric use would have allowed us to bypass a design mistake. Last year during IATI (Artificial Intelligence and Informatics Technologies, the course that replaced TIA from the academic year 2009/2010) in spite of all the experience made in the six previous years, we had to ask to two visually handicapped person to attend the course externally. Indeed nor the course site nor the educational materials were designed to be suitable for the software/hardware equipment (like text reader or enlangers) that allow visually handicapped person to use the PC and internet. A better initial analysis, and the use of an accessibility rubric (that we immediately created after this experience), would have allowed us to design an accessible course.

In the analysis rubric we consider three kind of elements:

- **the needs** that the course would like to respond to;
- **the resources** that are available;
- some **design choices** (es: educational technologies) that could be anticipated already in this phase and that is good to know to plan the necessary resources.

We can refer to TIA like an example. The course have been created to let the students know the dynamics of a learning community, the online communication and the eTutoring principles. Essentially these are the needs we settled with TIA, because we think this topics are more and more important for learning. Due to the course content and to the fact that we designed a constructivistic learning environment, we had to plan the presence of an extended teachers staff (designer, eTutor, technical help desk, teacher: who?, how many?) and to decide which Learning Management System to use.

It was also necessary to create a user profile. We collected the data about the students age, the previous education, motivational factors, working situation (part-time worker, non worker, etc.), ICT- Information and Communication Technologies familiarity, english knowledge, collaboration and working in group ability, possible disabilities.

The designer had to collect many of this data also about the teacher and the eTutors.

If they are novice in the use of eLearning it will be necessary to foresee an individual support so that they can interact effectively with the students and among them. We had to plan in a different way the interaction between the teacher and the eTutor if the latter had competencies about the eLearning facilitation but not about the course content.

At the analysis' end we will have available these type of information:

- goals, needs and objectives, educational contents;
- course length, credits number, budget, technologies;
- available educational materials (textual and multimedia), copyright, prerequisites;
- users, teacher, eTutors, staff characteristics;
- methods of quality monitoring;
- some general idea about teaching strategies and assessment methods.

All these information will ease the following phases and, at the same time, will produce the design of a course feasible with the available resources and suitable for the specific users.

8.2 Design and development rubrics

The course design and development are intimately connected and developed together.

For making the design and development rubrics more useful we divided the elements to be planned and verified in seven criteria:

1. organization,
2. educational materials,
3. pedagogy,
4. assessment,
5. communication,
6. technologies,
7. accessibility.

For all this areas we prepared a series of questions that help the teacher to remember the course more important elements and the possible choices. It happen that a parameter is not suitable for the course we are developing and in this case we do not consider it.

For every parameter we analyze the characteristics that, following the rubrics, we considered for the TIA course.

1. **Organization**: users characteristic; prerequisites (basic knowledge about computer, internet and english), frequency of student access to the site to follow all the online course activities; frequency of teacher and eTutors access to the forum; maximum answer time delay to the students questions, so that he/she doesn 't feel neglected; face-to-face and online meeting agenda, qualitative monitoring by questionnaires and interviews.
2. **Educational materials:** they included a bibliography, a webliography, the teacher slides. The rubrics' set helps to monitor the coherence with the objectives but also the completeness, the contents updating and its adequacy to the users characteristics and to the credits number, accessibility, copyright.
3. **Pedagogy**: we choose a collaborative constructivistic teaching strategy, following the Jonassen thoughts (Jonassen, 2007), and also the Wenger community of practice (1998). The students formed a small group of 4-6 persons, so that the communication was more effective. The teacher proposed a scripted collaboration, i.e. the interpretation of some roles to facilitate the involvement of all the people. We foresee a weekly self-evaluation by the participants, commented by the teacher feedback. To make this design architecture effective was very important to explain to the students the teacher's pedagogical approach, what he will expect from them, and in which time frame.
4. **Assessment**: we decided to assess the students according to their participation (access, forum messages, etc.); to the group's assignments quality; to the result of a final written examination. Whichever assessment method is used is really important that it is coherent with the adopted teaching strategies and that it is explicitly declared since the course beginning.
5. **Communication**: our course was based above all on the forums (news, student/teacher; student/eTutor, helpdesk, caffè, group's forum). We used the email for solving possible access problems to the course site. Recently we began to use skype. And, if necessary, we used also the telephone.
6. **Technologies**: we integrated Moodle with some web 2.0 tools. We employed Delicious for social bookmarking; Skype for audioconferences; MediaWiki for collaborative writing/multimedia publishing. Another software that was extremely useful was CMap, to build collaboratively conceptual maps. Everything that could be helpful for the course was used. Paying attention not to confuse the students asking them to use too many different software environments. We gave all the necessary information about the software in classroom, and published them on the course site.
7. **Accessibility**: the course has to be as ergonomic as possible, allowing teachers, students and eTutors to navigate without any problems, using meaningful labels, essential links, clear information, etc... Environments and educational materials have to consider all the accessibility rules. Publishing the educational materials, the textual and multimedia assignments, and using the communication environment have to be very easy and "natural". After we discovered our course was not accessible for visually handicapped students we decide to create an accessibility rubric, that explain how to design and implement a site for student with disabilities, following the World Wide Web Consortium and the WCAG-Web Content Accessibility Guidelines (World Wide Web Consortium [W3C], 2008).

8.3 Teacher's and students' feedback rubrics

The rubrics about the teacher's and students' feedback bring to mind the classical idea of monitoring through the participants (teachers, eTutors and students) impressions, opinions, and comments.

The students feedback have to give information about their satisfaction regarding some elements:

- educational and organizational aspects: if there is something not clear is better if it surfaces as soon as possible, otherwise the participation will decline;
- technological and communication aspects: no problems have to be found for what is concerned the access, the use, the participation;
- the course in general: the positive and productive atmosphere and the adequacy of the workload are two fundamental elements. The problems concerning other aspects influence the former: if for example a student write a message many time without receiving a timely answer his feeling concerning the course will get worse (and that could cause dissatisfaction also in the group mates). Every problem detected or directly stated by the students have to be confronted and solved as soon as possible. If it is impossible to find an acceptable solution, it will be necessary to give a satisfactory explanation. In every case, it is mandatory not to let the answer in abeyance.

The problems' and suggestions' collection during the course allow for immediate in itinere adjustments.

The students' feedback is collected in many ways and in different moments.

- in the middle of the course —or more often—at the end of the course, through the two purposely rubrics;
- all through the course, by means of the teacher's, eTutors' and technical helpdesk's forum

The teacher's and eTutors' self-evaluation satisfy two requirements:

- allow the designer to verify that there are no obstacles concerning the organization, the technologies, the communication. Indeed whether the teacher has a problem in publishing the educational material or the eTutor is not able to monitor the forum, the course will have for sure some problems. In fact delays and shortcomings from the teaching staff, if not explained at the right time and exhaustively, may give to the students the impression to be neglected.
- allow the teacher and the eTutors to verify if they are doing what was established in the design phase regarding their tasks and the time to perform them (communication environments monitoring, assignments comments, textual and multimedia material publishing, etc.) maintaining the often pressing pace of an online course.

9. Conclusion

Many interviews and focus group with teachers, experts or novices in designing eLearning module, testify that our *adAstra* rubrics' set is a valid help for creating effective socio-constructivistic eLearning courses.

Nevertheless we know that we are still far from creating a complete and validated tool useful to scaffold the teachers and the instructional designers in creating whichever eLearning course, with different teaching strategies, different multimedia environments, different students characteristics. And that this goal will be completed in many years, through the work of many researchers, teachers and Ph.D. students.

There are many topics we would like to consider in our studies, to be tested preliminary on the field and to be included in a comprehensive rubrics' set. We list the two more urgent here following:

1. we would like to consider how the affectivity influence the eLearning participation and the eLearning effectiveness, considering the theories recently presented in scientific literature by many authors (Campbell, 2006; Clore, & Palmer, 2009, Damasio, 1994; Salovey & Mayer 1990, Kort et al., 2001).
2. we would like to widen our rubrics to include different teaching models. *adAstra* is now a good scaffold for designing socio-constructivistic courses. Although it can offer useful hints also for self-learning environments or transmissive courses, we need more researches to have a complete set of theoretically founded tools to scaffold the design of eLearning courses based on various pedagogical frameworks and to monitor their quality.

Next year, in the 2012, will be celebrated the Alan Mathison Turing year. Turing is an English mathematician, logician —that lived in England from 1912 to 1954 and was treated in an "appalling" way for being homosexual— widely considered to be the father of computer science and artificial intelligence. I would like, to honor him, closing with the words he used to conclude his most famous paper: *Computing machinery and intelligence,* published in October 1950 by the *Mind* review (Turing, 1950)

We can only see a short distance ahead,
but we can see plenty there that needs to be done

10. Acknowledgement

This paper was developed within the FIRB project 2007 RBNE07WBKL_004, entitled *Net@ccessible: teaching - learning for one and all in a lifelong plan,* funded by Miur (Italian Ministry of Public Education, University and Scientific Research) and by the Universities involved.

The Trento research team includes Patrizia Ghislandi (coordinator), Marco Dallari, Massimiliano Tarozzi, Antonio Mattei, Daniela Paolino, Chiara Eberle, Federica Cumer. The following institutions also participate in the research: Roma University Foro Italico; Napoli University Federico II; Roma Tre University; Bologna University; Bologna Don Gnocchi Foundation.

11. References

Anderson, T., Rourke, L., Garrison, D. R., & Archer, W. (2001). Assessing teaching presence in a computer conferencing environment, *Journal of Asynchronous Learning Networks,* Vol. 5, N°2.

Biggs, J. (1987) *Student Approaches to Learning and Studying,* Hawthorn, Vic: Australian Council for Educational Research

Brown, J. S., Collins, A. & Duguid, P. (1989), Situated Cognition and the Culture of Learning, *Educational Researcher,* Vol. 18, N°01, Washington, DC: American Educational Research Association

Campbell, P., (2006), *Affect as a Presence in the Community of Inquiry Model* (master thesis), Athabasca University, Alberta. 06 August 2010 available from http://library.athabascau.ca/drr/download.php?filename=MDE/priscacampbellThesis.pdf

Clore, G. L. & Palmer, J. (2009) Affective guidance of intelligent agents: How emotion controls cognition, *Cognitive Systems Research*, Vol. 10, N° 1, March 2009, Pages 21-30

Damasio, A. R., (1994), *Descartes' Error: Emotion, Reason, and the Human Brain*, London: Putnam Publishing

Entwistle, N (1981) *Styles of Learning and Teaching; an integrated outline of educational psychology for students, teachers and lecturers*, Chichester: John Wiley, ISBN 0 471 10013 7

Garrison, D. R., Anderson, T. & Archer, W. (2000). Critical inquiry in a text-based environment: Computer conferencing in higher education, *The Internet and Higher Education*, Vol. 2, N°2-3, pp. 87-105.

Garrison, D. R., Anderson, T. & Archer, W. (2001). Critical thinking, cognitive presence, and computer conferencing in distance education, *American Journal of Distance Education*, Vol. 15, N°1

Jonassen D. H. (2007), Promuovere e sostenere il problem solving nell'eLearning , Engaging and supporting problem solving online, in Ghislandi P. (ed.), *Verso la eUniversity. Contributi per una nuova didattica universitaria, Towards eUniversity. Contributions for innovative teaching/learning in higher education*, Trento: Editrice Università degli Studi di Trento.

Jonassen, D.H., Howland, J., Marra, R.M. & Crismond, D. (2008). *Meaningful learning with technology*, 3rd Ed. Columbus, OH: Merrill/Prentice Hall

Kort, B., Reilly, R. & Picard, R. W., (2001), An Affective Model of Interplay between Emotions and Learning: Reengineering Educational Pedagogy, in Okamoto T., Hartley R., Kinshuk & Klus J. (Eds.) (2001). Advanced Learning Technology: Issues, Achievements and Challenges, Los Alamitos, CA: IEEE Computer Society (ISBN 0-7695-1013-2)

Lave, J. & Wenger, E. (1991), *Situated learning: Legitimate peripheral participation*, Cambridge, UK: Cambridge University Press

Lorenzo, G., & Moore, J. C., (2002), *The Sloan Consortium Report to the Nation: Five Pillars of Quality Online Education*. 05 August 2010 available from http://www.sloanconsortium.org/publications/books/pillarreport1.pdf

Marton F. and Saljo F. (1976), On Qualitative Differences in Learning — 2: Outcome as a function of the learner's conception of the task, *British Journal of Educational. Psychology*, Vol. 46, N° 115-2

Ramsden, P. (1992) *Learning to Teach in Higher Education*, London: Routledge, ISBN0-415-06415-5

Rogoff, B. (1990), *Apprenticeship in thinking: cognitive development in social context*, New York, NY: Oxford University Press

Rourke, L., Anderson, T. Garrison, D. R. & Archer, W. (2001). Assessing social presence in asynchronous, text-based computer conferencing, *Journal of Distance Education*, Vol.14, N°3, pp. 51-70

Salovey, P. & Mayer, J. D. (1990), Emotional intelligence, *Imagination, Cognition, and Personality*, Vol. 9, pp. 185-211

Turing, A. (1950), Computing Machinery and Intelligence, Mind, New Series, Vol. 59, No. 236. (Oct., 1950), pp. 433-460, ISSN, 0026-4423, 18 August 2008 available from http://loebner.net/Prizef/TuringArticle.html

Wenger E. (1998), *Communities of practices. Learning, meaning, and identity*, Cambridge: Cambridge University Press,

World Wide Web Consortium [W3C], (2008), Web Content Accessibility Guidelines (WCAG) 2.0. 21 February 2011 available from http://www.w3.org/TR/WCAG20/

Part 3

Software

7

Learning Objects and Their Applications

Selahattin Gonen and Bulent Basaran
Dicle University
Turkey

1. Introduction

Education and technology are two important factors that have an important role in human life. Education helps reveal the cognitive, affective and psychomotor potential that human owns from birth. Thanks to education, people have survived against nature and become more powerful, more constructive and more creative beings. This change and development caused by education both made people's lives easier and helped technology emerge. Technology can be defined as activities to develop tools that will facilitate people's lives with the help of their knowledge and skills. While developments in the field of education caused more advanced technologies to emerge, technological developments caused new information and scientific fields to emerge. Educational technology is a community of academic systems that help design learning and teaching environments effectively and solve problems experienced in the learning and teaching process as well as increase the permanence and quality of learning.

The development of the Internet and multimedia technologies and their use in distance education programs resulted in the educational model defined as "web-based learning" or "e-learning". This educational model occurred as a result of the synthesis of the Internet, distance education and computer-supported education. The most important feature of the e-learning model is that it provides individuals with the opportunity for education in any place at any time with the help of Internet support. In addition, web-based distance education allows establishing synchronous and asynchronous communication among students and teachers with the help of interactive web pages, e-mail and file transfer. Students who visit various web pages with different contents, who are members of various clubs, who participate in e-mail groups, who enter web sites from different parts of the world to obtain information (such as virtual libraries, news services and so on) and who are in constant communication/interaction with the trainer in the Internet environment can reach a great amount of information requiring the use of various tools. Since students face new information in this process, incidental learning occurs as well (Atack & Rankin, 2002; Hawatson, 2004; All & Madran, 2005). In order to carry out an effective learning activity, an e-learning material should have such components as texts, audios, simple graphical presentations, video presentations, animations, simulations, games, testing systems and interactions supported with feedback (Friesen, Fisher & Roberts, 2001). Among the tools that allow effective presentation of learning contents developed in these environments are learning objects. Learning objects are small software applications which are similar to such real-world physical objects as books, notebooks and pencils and which have their own unique features. In order to use learning objects for various purposes and in different environments, these learning objects should be defined and should include explanatory information. This process is carried out with "metadata" meaning "defining information". According to Wiley (2000), a learning object is any digital source that can be used to support learning. This part first introduces learning objects and their features and then presents applications of these objects in physics education.

2. Learning objects

Learning objects can be defined as "information pieces which are structured independent of one another, which can be updated and used again for different purposes and needs, which can be combined to create a whole content, which are labeled with defining information and which can be accessed via a network and used for educational purposes." Learning objects have great importance in distant education applications.

In recent years, learning objects have been widely mentioned as a new concept in the areas of e-learning, design and development. There are studies to define this new concept to develop related standards, and there are great efforts to transfer these standards into practice.

According to Learning Technology Standards Committee, or LTSC, an organization that aims at developing and spreading standards regarding instructional technologies (Kelly, 2002; Learnet, 2003):

"It is defined as a digital or non-digital thing that can be used, reused re referred to during technology-supported instruction." Multimedia contents that can be used as a source during technology-supported instruction are objects that include instructional content, learning goals, instructional software and software tools, people, organizations or events."

This is quite a general or comprehensive definition and even covers non-digital environments. Therefore, learning objects can be said to include various things ranging from a simple piece of music or a text to a whole lesson and even to more complex structures such as a pool of lessons given in an institution. However, mostly, there are digital objects in practice. Thus, David Wiley (2000) suggests a more simplified definition: "A learning object is any digital source used to support learning." This can be considered as a definition good enough to use and comprehensive enough to cover terabytes of data on the web. A learning object is any object that has the potential to be used in educational activities, and in order to explain this subject, it should have at least a special educational purpose or an educational meaning (Slater, 2002). Learning objects are pieces which can be included within the scope of a lesson, which are used as an educational material, which are labeled with defining information, which can be used again and which can be accessed via the Web for educational purposes (Sharples,2002). Learning objects are information units that can be used in a number of applications to teach a special concept or a technique.

2.1 Features of learning objects

Learning objects provide a learning and/or educational vision that is automatized, directed and computer-guided. In other words, learning objects provide such opportunities as "taking just what is enough", "reaching quickly in time" and "giving education specific to the person". If one wants to learn only the piece of a lesson not the lesson as a whole, the necessary learning objects can be used to meet this demand. Since they have defining information, learning objects can easily be found. In this way, there will be an opportunity to access the instructional content on time. As learning objects are separate and independent objects, they provide opportunities for specialized learning by helping create lessons appropriate to each individual's own learning method or style.

The advantages and benefits provided by learning objects are primarily as follows (Karaman, 2005):

- **Reusability** - Learning objects are objects that can be reused for different purposes in a number of environments. Once created, they can be used for various purposes in different settings. Reusability provides the advantage and potential to decrease the cost, efforts and the time spent for their development.
- **Producibility** - Learning objects can be automatically combined in a way to perfectly meet the learning needs of a certain student. At the same time, this means that the student can take the control and determine his or her own way of learning.

Competency-based learning is an approach that focuses on the intersection of skills, knowledge and attitudes within core competency models rather than the lesson model. Regarding the application of this approach favored by educators and workers, the problem experienced up to now has been the lack of content modular enough and appropriate to the purpose. Labeling learning objects provides an appropriate competency-based approach by matching the object-defining information with individual competency differences.

- **Adaptability:** Learning objects can be adapted to different environments and different student needs.
    - **Customization:** For institutions or individuals in need of the customization of the content, the learning object approach facilitates customization. Modular learning objects maximize the software potential via recombination and material supply together with separation into units as desired.
    - **Interoperability:** The object approach maintains interoperability between institutions and other learning systems as well as other learning platforms. Also, the approach helps design, develop and present learning objects specific to institutional needs.
- **Salability**: Developing small pieces with less cost and fewer mistakes is easier than developing bigger pieces. When an object created is used again and again, the gains will be doubled each time. For an institution, the value of a content increases when used. This helps make saving from the cost of the redesign and development process and provides the opportunity to sell content objects and to transfer a certain subject to sharers in pieces.
- **Flexibility:** If the material is designed in a way to be used for multi purposes, the material can be reused more easily without being rewritten for each of the new subjects or purposes. Excluding an object from the scope of the lesson is more difficult than dealing with it as a piece of the design and development.
- **Convenience of content management, search and update:** Meta-data labels facilitate content management via choosing and filtering the related content for a specific purpose and rapid update and search.

2.2 Examples for learning objects

- A digital video showing a surgery,
- A web page describing the symptoms of diabetes,
- A "flash" animation explaining the derivative of function in mathematics,
- A "realmedia" audio recorded in a face-to-face lesson,
- A web-page including "html, flash and realmedia audio records" and explaining normal distribution in the course statistics.

The examples given above are appropriate to all educational grades and include instructional materials that can be used in a number of disciplines ranging from medicine to physics and engineering education. One of the most important standards of these instructional materials includes the SCORM objects.

3. Sharable Content Object Reference Model (SCORM)

SCORM is a reference model created based on adaptation via the standards developed to make e-learning software durable, reusable, accessible and interoperable with other software. This model was established by the American Ministry of Defense in 1997. The ADL(Advanced Distributed Learning) organization was asked to develop standards regarding technology-based education to be used for the purpose of leading the federal and private institutions and to support the educational needs. Besides a number of international organizations especially in England and Canada, universities provide academic support as well. In line with the studies by ADL, many standards and specifications in the field of e-learning have been gathered under a single reference model. The first version of this model, called SCORM 1.0, was made available for use in January in 2000, and its following versions 1.1 and 1.2 were available in January and October in 2001. The latest version was made available by ADL in January in 2004 with a new name as SCORM 2004.

The SCORM lessons can be restructured as reusable learning objects that make the lessons highly effective and beneficial. This new content is also compatible with the criteria called R.A.I.D.

- **Reusable**: It can easily be adjusted and used when compared to other development tools.
- **Accessible**: Educational objects in a distant place can be presented in an easily accessible way.
- **Interoperable**: It can work well with a wide range of hardware, operating systems and web browsers.
- **Durable**: It does not require important changes with new versions.

Learning Management Systems (LMS) have an important role in SCORM.

4. Learning Management Systems (LMS)

As can be understood from its name, Learning Management Systems (LMS) is a management tool as integrated system that provides opportunities to manage the educational contents, monitor the learners and the teachers and individualize the learning-teaching processes (http://www.knowledgebank.irri.org/elearningfordev). The purpose of

LMS is to facilitate and carry out e-learning activities in a more systematic and planned way. It allows presenting the learning material, sharing and discussing the learning material presented, managing the lessons, taking homework, taking exams, providing feedback regarding these exams and homework, organizing the learning material, keeping records of the students, teachers and the system and taking reports (Morten, 2002) .

According to Weller (2007), these learning areas, known as Virtual Learning Environment (VLE), were called software systems designed to support learning and teaching. A VLE typically provides a tool via the Internet for wikis, blogs, chats and forums, for the management of student groups, for responding to and transforming students' works, for uploading the content and for communication, monitoring, questionnaires and evaluation.

A VLE is a computer program that facilitates electronic learning. Such e-learning systems are called LMS, Course Management System (CMS), Learning Content Management System ((LCMS), Managed Learning Environment (MLE), Learning Support System (LSS) or Learning Platform (LP). Instruction in this way is considered as computer-supported or online education. In USA, Web-Based Learning (WBL), Learning Management System (LMS) and Course Management system (CMS) are widely-used terms. In England and in a number of European countries, Virtual Learning Environment (VLE) and Managed Learning Environment (MLE) are commonly used. In addition, since VLE is considered to be a sub-system of ML, these two systems are interrelated.

There are various LMSs. Among these, the most well-known LMSs are as follows: 1-ATutor (www.atutor.ca), 2- DrupalEd (www.funnymonkey.com/come-and-get-it), 3-Interact (www.interactlms.org), 4-SiteAtSchool (siteatschool.sourceforge.net), 5-SyndeoCMS (www.syndeocms.org), 6-Sakai (http://sakaiproject.org/portal), 7-eFront (http://www.efrontlearning.net/), 8-Claroline (www.claroline.net), 9-Decobe Suite (http://www.docebo.org), 10-ANGEL_Learning (http://angellearning.com/), 11-Blackboard (http://www.blackboard.com/), 12-Desire2Learn (http://www.desire2learn.com/), 13-ILIAS(http://www.ilias.de/docu/),eCollege (http://www.ecollege.com/index.learn), 14-Webct (purchased by Blackboard), and 15-Dokeos (www.dokeos.com).

While some of these softwares are commercial, some are open-source software (OSS). All these programs have a number of common features. Among these applications, the most striking one is Moodle.

5. MOODLE

Moodle is a course management system. The Moodle was developed by commercial and non-commercial users from all over the world and has globally spread out via the Internet. Although Moodle was originally designed by Martin Dougiamas (http://dougiamas.com), today, it is directed by the Moodle Company in Pert in Western Australia. The most important feature of this design adopted by Moodle is its ease and elegance in the development of course materials (Berggren et. al., 2005).

5.1 General features of Moodle

The most important feature of Moodle is that everybody (teachers, students and so on) can use it quite easily.

- Moodle is totally free.
- The software can run under both operating systems: Windows and Linux.
- The system includes 50,000 students and thousands of courses.
- It competes with commercial packages alone and has a big share in the educational industry.
- It has quite a big thematic community and a large population of end-user trainers (100,000 registered users in its website alone).
- It has a language support in 150 countries in 70 different languages. In this system, you can choose any language you want. If you want, you can choose all the languages at the same time (Moodle); you can choose three languages at the same time (Distant Education); and you can choose one language (for questions).
- It has a large population of developers.
- Thanks to its large population of developers, the product life cycle is fast. That is, in quite a short time, its new versions are developed.
- Since it is free, it has a large population of testers.
- Most end-users use Moodle without having any experience in programming and databases. When a problem occurs, the problem is solved faster than it is in commercial systems.
- Since it is an open-source system, its security deficits is covered faster than it is in commercial systems.
- A number of new features are constantly added and distributed freely (block or module)

5.2 Some features in Moodle concerning the system administrator

There are some basic features in Moodle LMS concerning the system administrator. These features are as follows:

- Moodle can run on Unix, Linux, Windows, Mac OS X, Netware and on any other system with PHP support (it covers almost all companies that give hosting service).
- Moodle is designed in a modular way and has a number of functions at different levels.
- Moodle can easily be updated from one version to another. Moodle can update itself thanks to its own mechanism of recognition of new versions. In addition, it allows fixing itself and its related database files by recognizing the compatible databases.
- Moodle needs only one database (and if necessary, it can share this database with other applications).
- Moodle support a number of database management systems thanks to its developed database abstraction ability (For example, Moodle can run under Oracle).
- Moodle is a system focused on strong security in all its versions. All the forms are controlled; data validity is provided; and cookies are managed by encoding them.
- Moodle adopts social constructionist pedagogy and supports such instructional methods as activity-based education, critical reflection and target-based education.
- Moodle is appropriate to 100% online classrooms and can be used to support face-to-face education (synchronous education).
- Moodle needs a simple, effective and compatible Internet browser that requires low level of technology. Internet Explorer, Firefox or any other browser can help.

- Course lists can serve all the courses on the server via guest or another developed access methods on the Internet. You can index your courses via the Google research engine as a guest.
- A Moodle site can manage thousands of courses.
- Most text areas (sources, forum messages, written entries and so on) can be arranged with the WYSIWYG HTML editor found in Moodle.
- Multimedia sources (for example YouTube videos, Flash documents and so on) can easily be managed within the system.

Use of Moodle in physics lessons has an important place among educational applications.

5.3 Use of Moodle in physics education

Teachers can develop the Moodle platform by applying web-based peer assessment. These studies also allow developing students' perceptional schemes and structuring their knowledge as well as help them improve their abilities to make discussions and establish connections between similar things.

Computer use in physics education started in 1970s. Since then, a number of studies have been carried out investigating the effectiveness of technologies on physics education. In addition, there are comprehensive discussions regarding the use of WBLs in physics education (Kenny et. al., 2006). Giving physics education as a paradigm of solving a scientific problem is claimed to be more effective and efficient than using traditional approaches (Landau, 2006).

5.3.1 Quizzes

Quizzes are useful tools for measuring the levels of students' knowledge. Moodle provide comprehensive quiz samples. In Moodle, while answering the quiz questions prepared, students have more than one opportunity to test themselves.

5.3.2 Problems and exercises

One of the vital aspects of physics education is that students develop their ability to solve problems that represent different physical situations. Generally, students experience difficulty in applying the rules and equations they have learnt in lessons. Therefore, while doing this, it is important to provide them with exercises that will be beneficial for them.

5.3.3 Java applets

Presentation of standard formats (texts, Java applets, films, flash animations) is a perfect tool in terms of understanding simultaneous dynamic physical rules. Undoubtedly, applets are among the most successful sources used in physics education. Since applets are simultaneous computer experiments, they allow students to recognize the current relationships by giving values to the subject-related variables in a way different from animations.

Although Java applets are not specific to Moodle (these applets can run with any Java-supported web-browser), they can be used in related activities. Watching an animation is not a passive activity. With animation, students can learn real and dynamic information about the physical systems that they experience difficulty understanding.

Moodle is an important way for teachers to organize their course materials. When considered from the point of instructional view, use of multimedia tools to organize more attractive activities makes the instructional process more interesting. Consequently, these activities increase students' interest in the course of physics. Here, due to lack of time in the classroom, teachers can provide their students with a comprehensive source of information. In addition, Moodle facilitate the interactions between teachers and students in the virtual environment, and this provides the opportunity to take their views and suggestions as a learning committee. Moodle allows students to share their knowledge and difficulties. In this way, students can help each other via forums and chats. Thus, teachers can understand in which courses their students experience difficulty.

6. Whiteboard Movies (WBM)

Whiteboard Movies (WBM) are screen images which can be distributed via CDs and the Internet and which include texts and/or audios that can be transformed into various formats such as flash movies explaining mathematical concepts and solutions to problems. WBMs could be a one-minute long record without any sound and could be complex like a fully interactive educational video, which allows learners to understand the answers of questions or the solutions to their own similar problems. It is the latest form of asynchronous learning that opportunities for simple and inexpensive interactive education.

In 1997, WBMs were pioneered by Tim Fahlberg (Fahlberg, 2004; Fahlberg and Nonis, 2005). After this method was proved and favored, it started to be used in education from elementary schools to higher education institutions. The current state of Whiteboard Movies initiated as a big project has resulted from long-term studies.

6.1 WBM applications

WBMs actually have a simple logic of use. Within the frame of this logic,

- Seeing and listening to the subject being taught,
- Listening to and rehearsing the subject anytime you want,
- Seeing and listening to each step,
- Carrying out activities for understanding the method used.

6.2 Short story of WBMs

WBMs were originally considered as a supportive and effective way of out-of-class instruction method different from the educational support of private teachers, the family or other sources. Initially, Tim Fahlberg applied this method by creating a mathematical multimedia website that provided visual and aural instructions. Later, between 2000 and 2003, using TechSmith's Camtasia Studio, Tim Fahlberg created a number of high-quality WBMs with Corel Grafio with the help of a graphics tablet or a tablet PC and distributed them via the Web or CDs.

The WBM is a technique for learning in numerical instruction. Generally, there are two questions directed regarding WBMs:

1. How easy is it to create WBMs?

2. What is the cost of WBMs?

It is quite important that instructors should be knowledgeable about how to integrate WBMs into the educational process in order to obtain the desired learning gains in visual and aural dimensions. In physics education, because mathematics and geometry have a very important place in both experimental and theoretical basis, WBMs used in mathematics education can also be used in physics education. Figure 1 presents how WBMs are integrated into the education process.

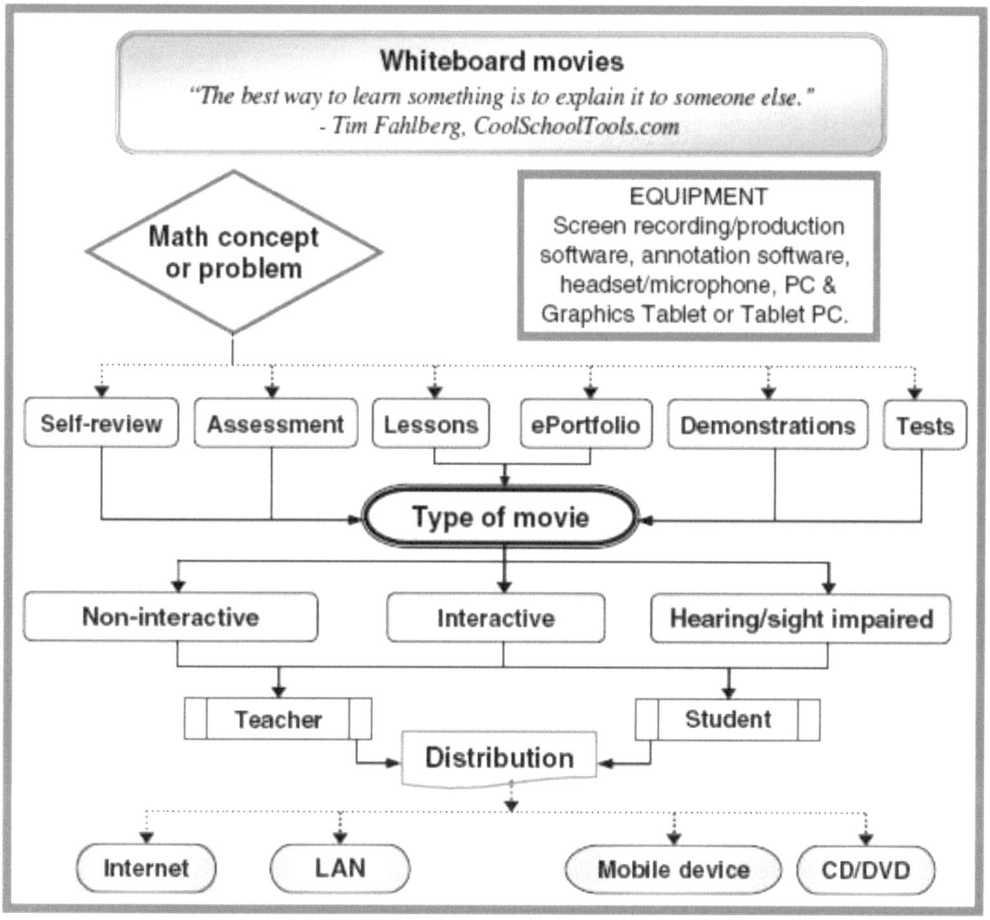

Fig. 1. Use of Whiteboard Movies in Mathematics Education (MacNeil,2006)

6.3 Current WBM techniques

Today, rapid developments in computer technology have led to the use of several facilities in education such as various effective and preferable software (e.g. TechSmith Camtasia Studio), cheap cable and wireless tablets and annotation software (SmartTech's SmartNotebook or Blade's NotateIt or Microsoft OneNote). In the integration process of WBMs in education, there are numerous alternatives provided by technology in creating equations and texts by using graphical calculators and animations. Today, among these alternatives, people can choose and use the most appropriate one. Of all these, a simple personal computer (Desktop, laptop or tablet PC), headphones with a microphone, screen capture and annotation software and a digital pen can be used as effective educational alternatives with fairly little cost.

Although WBMs are considered by people who have a traditional education understanding as quite unprofessional, the images in CDs or on the Internet is just like the blackboard in the classroom.

6.4 Equipment necessary to create WBMs

In creating WBMs, basic standard tools include headphones with a microphone, pen graphics tablet, screen capture and annotation software

- **Pen Graphics Tablet**: Depending on personal preferences, a small 6x4 inc. tablet or a big 8x6 inc. tablet can be used. Cable tablets are cheaper and more reliable.
- **Screen Capture Software**: These programs allow recording the whole screen, a certain part of the screen, the selected part of the screen, the selected object or all the actions we carry out on the screen. Generally, the standard area of 640x480 pixel or 480x320 pixel is used for solving little problems. Screen-capturing programs allow combining a number of small records and creating files in the format of avi and swf.
- **Annotation programs**: These programs help use pen, shapes and lines to make WBMs more interesting and comprehensible.

6.5 Phases of creating WBMs (Fahlberg & Stojanovska, 2005)

To make them more comprehensible, it would be better to mention the WBM step by step. The most difficult thing to do here is typing on the graphics tablet. Typing on the Tablet practically takes 15 to 20 minutes. If disorders occur regarding the software during the records, these disorders should not be considered as a problem. The reason is that screen-capturing programs allow doing additions and corrections quickly and easily on the record and cutting the bad writings and mistakes easily in the last phase. The mistakes that occur during audio-recording can be corrected during re-recording. During production, the audio level can be increased or decreased, and the frame rates can be changed.

The basic steps are as follows:

Step 1. Open the annotation software.
Step 2. Turn on your tablet PC with your pen.
Step 3. Prepare your necessary material (figures, texts and so on regarding the problem that you will solve). For solving the problems that will take longer time, we can prepare more than one page by using the properties of the annotation software.
Step 4. Run the screen-capturing program and make sure the record window is easily visible. Do not type outside the screen by mistake.
Step 5. Check your microphone and make sure the screen-capturing program records the audio.
Step 6. Run the screen-capturing program.
Step 7. Solve the problem. If you make a mistake in your speech during the problem solving process, stop talking, take a deep breath and start your statement again. If

you are typing, turn back to the annotation program and start typing and speaking again. While following these, you do not need to close the screen-capturing program because this program allows you to exclude the unwanted parts from the WBM.

Step 8. Import the WBMs to the screen-capturing program. Here, you can make additions, extractions and arrangements in your video.

Step 9. Thanks to screen-capturing programs, you can transform WBMs into the format of swf.

In applications, in order to obtain information about which students watched the WBMs for how long and how many times, it is better to transform them into the SCORM standards.

6.6 Who can create and benefit from WBMs

- Teachers can create WBMs to support their students' learning outside the classroom.
- Teachers can create WBMs for each other in terms of the teaching techniques.
- Students can create WBMs to express their own thoughts and to show their teachers how well they have understood the materials.

A study carried out in LosAngles (Unified School District) in 2004 demonstrated that there was a clear increase in students' performances in algebra and geometry (http://www.unitedstreaming.com/homePages/evaluation2004.cfm).

WBMs are expected to increase students' learning more. Although studies conducted on the benefits and use of WBMs generally were related to mathematics education, applied studies can be carried out on physics education as well depending on the belief that WBMs can also be used in other fields.

Since use of WBMs clearly increases students' learning and facilitates teachers' cooperation with their students, they also increase teachers' professional satisfaction. WBMs are now considered to be an educational technique which is creative in visual and affective respects and which teachers can use for their students at any educational level during their education lives without spending much money. WBM technology is also important for numerical instruction. The thing that authorities give importance to is the fact that the result obtained is worth the time and money spent. In addition, it is important note that the traditional instruction method should not be totally avoided. Therefore, it is better to remember the traditional instruction method briefly. Traditional teaching is concerned with the teacher being the controller of the learning environment. Power and responsibility are held by the teacher and they play the role of instructor (in the form of lectures) and decision maker (in regards to curriculum content and specific outcomes). They regard students as having 'knowledge holes' that need to be filled with information. In short, the traditional teacher views that it is the teacher that causes learning to occur (Novak, 1998).

7. Learning materials commonly used in education

In order to facilitate students' learning, different teaching techniques can be used. Students can be provided with alternatives which will help them entertain while learning. If they want, they can learn the subjects via audible slides, video-recorded lessons or WBMs.

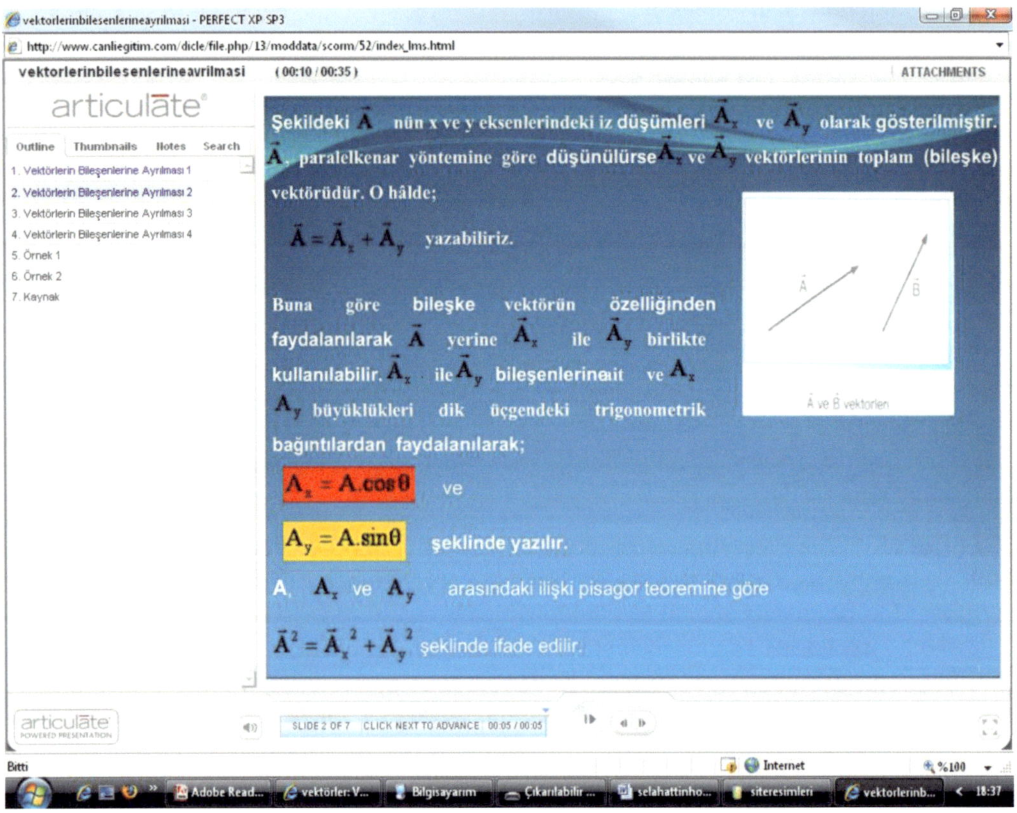

Fig. 2. Teaching via slides

Moreover, students can learn the subjects via audible slides. They can not only see the slides but also reach the slide they want by clicking the subject-headings found on the left side of the screen.

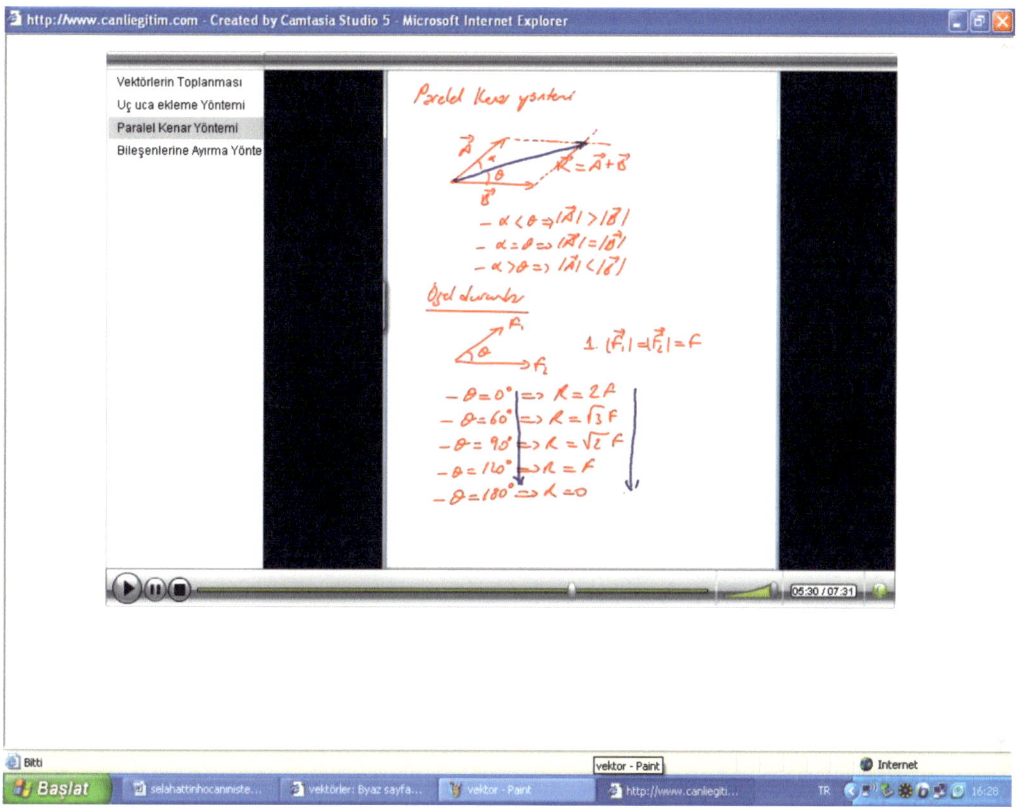

Fig. 3. Teaching via WBMs

One of the most important features of the WBM material is that it allows students to learn the subject in an audible and visual way.

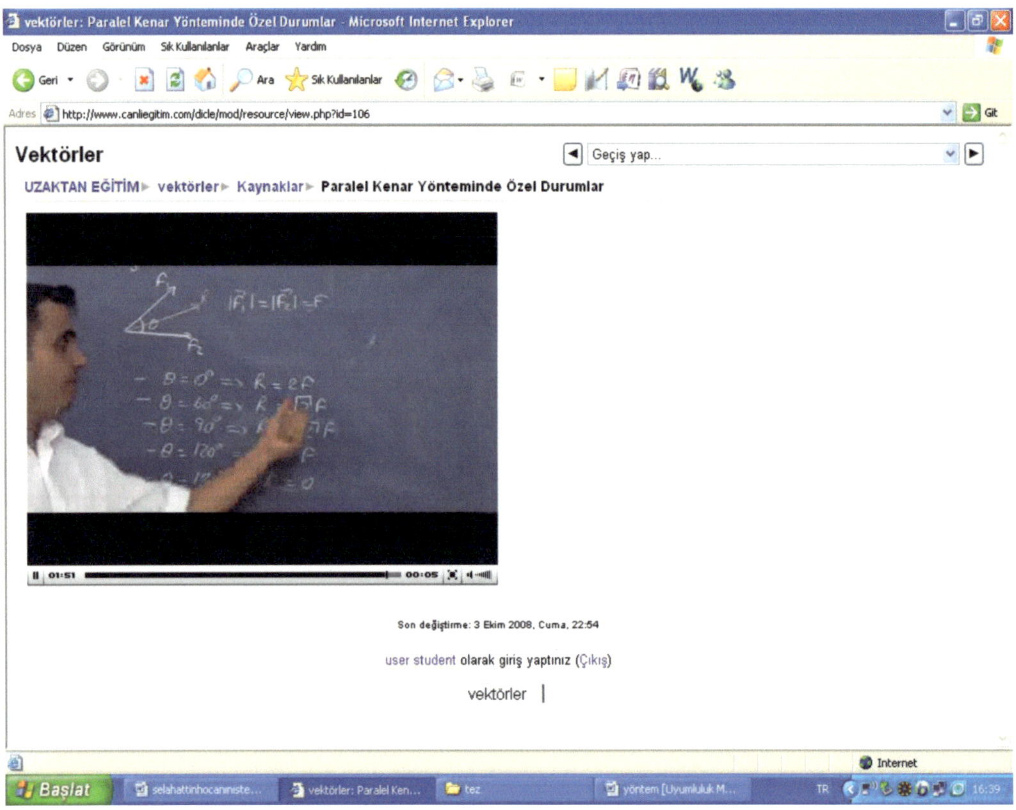

Fig. 4. Teaching via video-records

The purpose of video-records which includes teaching of the subject is to provide students with visual instruction. The video-records should focus on basic concepts and gains. In order to avoid uploading long-file videos in the web environment and to enable these videos to open fast, the picture quality should be low and the picture size should be small. In addition, video-records allow watching the videos again and again and analyzing the processes in detail (Yıldırım & Şimşek, 2005).

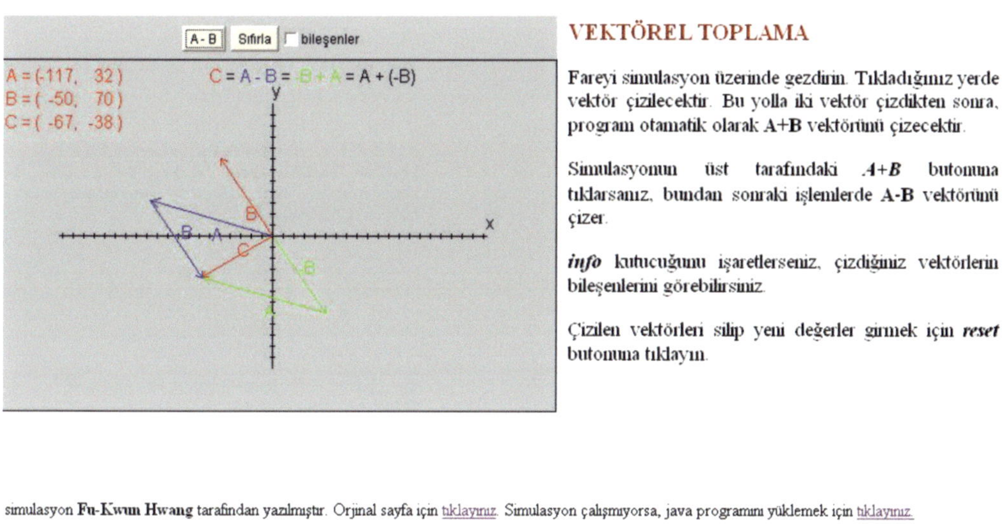

Fig. 5. Sample Java Applet Simulation -1

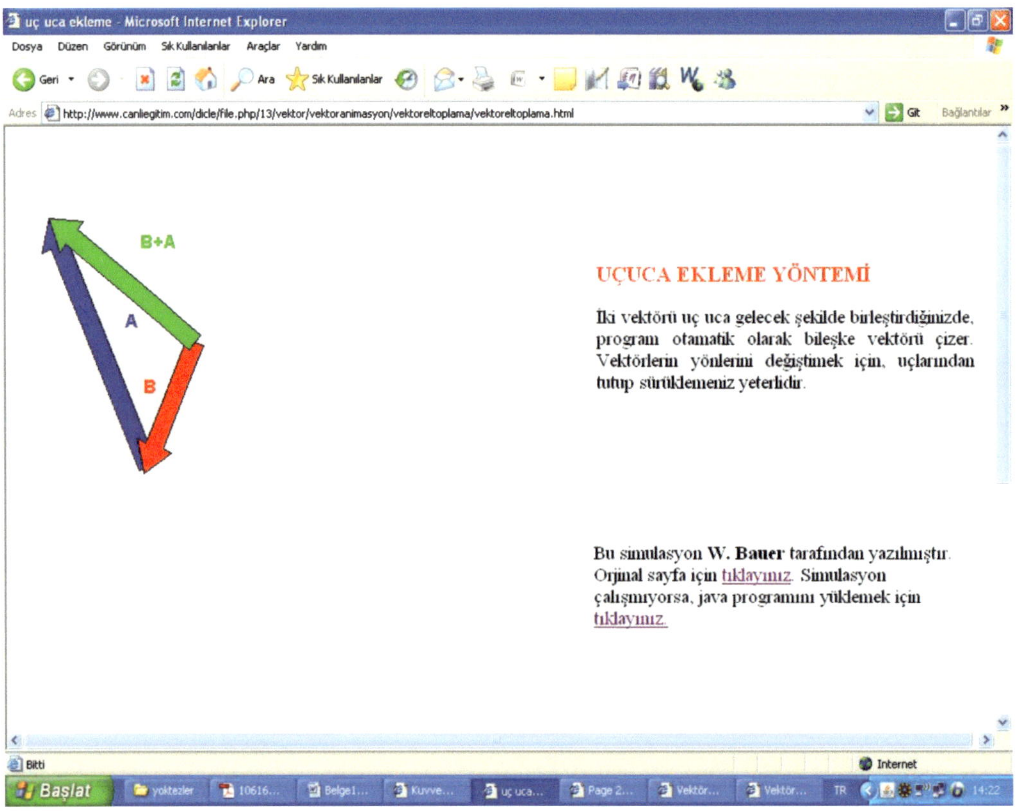

Fig. 6. Sample Java Applet Simulation -2

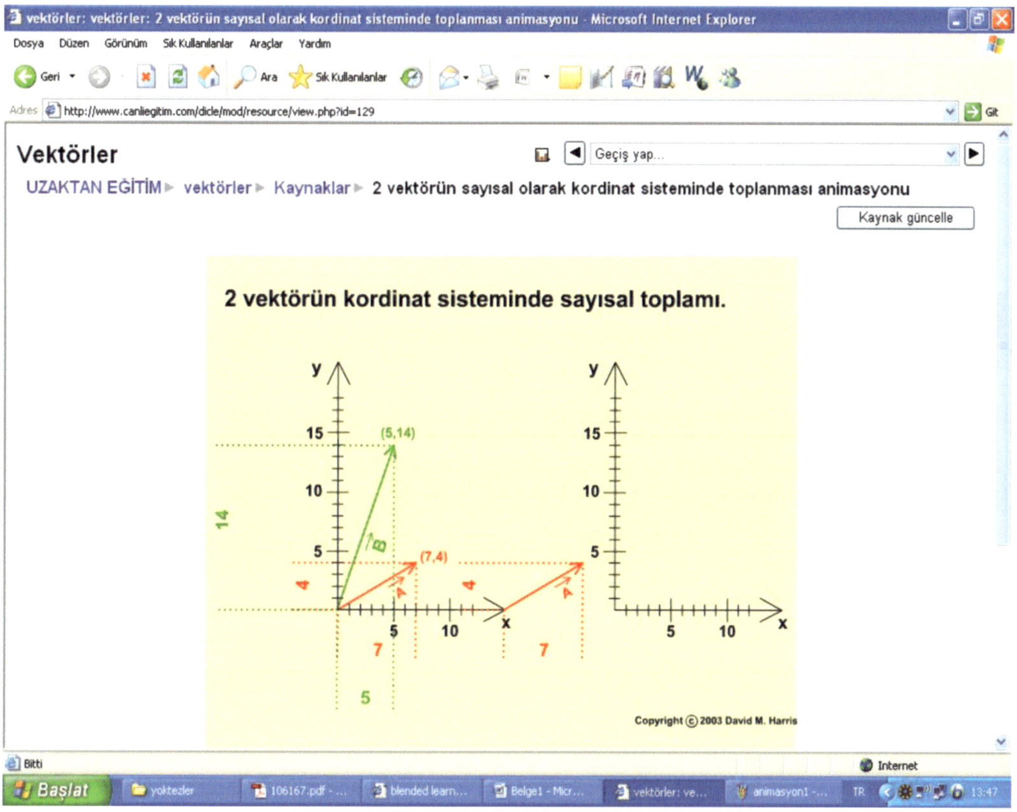

Fig. 7. Flash Animation Screen

In order to explain the subject better in course contents, various simulations and animations can be used. It is known that simulations and animations used allow concretizing the abstract information, increasing students' motivation, enforcing learning and storing the information permanently in the mind by addressing more than one sense organ. In addition, simulations and animations can present a large amount of information to users at a time and allow watching the videos again and again (Çalışkan, 2002). Figure 5, Figure 6 and Figure 7 present a sample screen of a page of simulations and animations included in Moodle as a lesson activity.

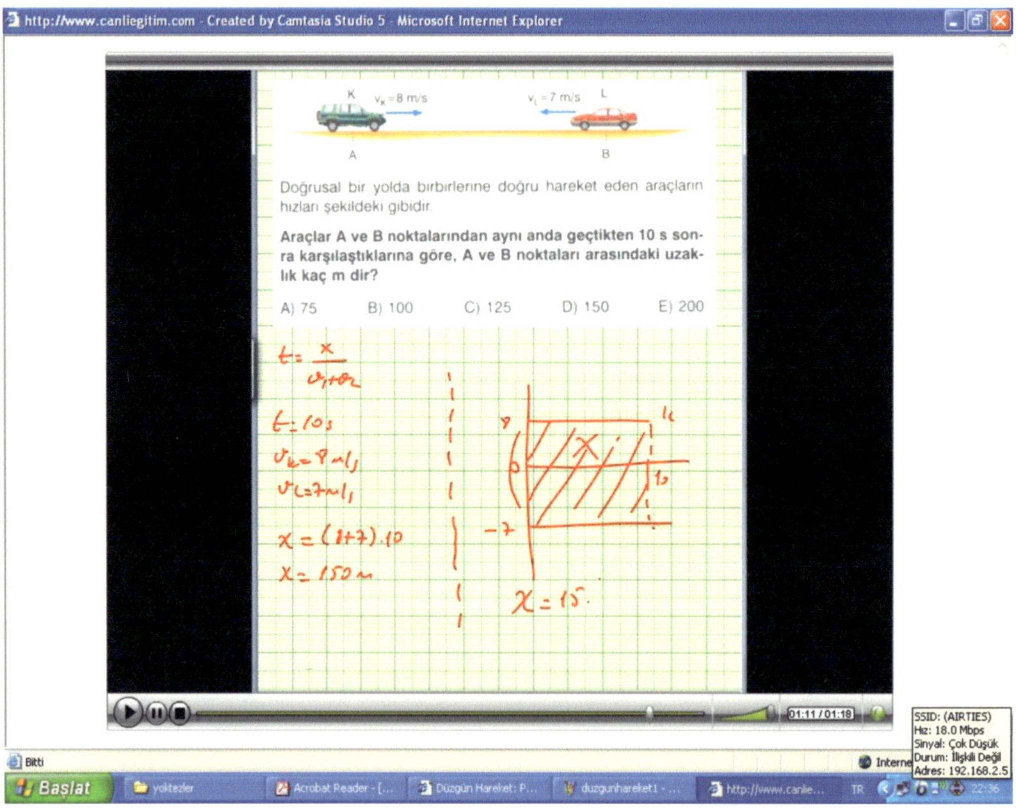

Fig. 8. WBM Screen

At the end of each subject, WBMs can be prepared to improve students' problem-solving abilities and to allow enforcing their learning and understanding the subject better. Thanks to WBMs that help enforce understanding the subject, students can not only follow the process in an audible and visual way but also watch the solutions to the problems. In order to obtain data regarding how many times and how long students have watched the solutions to the problems, all WBMs can be arranged in the SCORM format.

8. Conclusion

This part presents learning objects and related applications in physics education in e-learning environments.

The need for information and the rapidly-developing technology brought renovations not only to the society and the work life but also to educational applications. Among these technologies is the e-learning environment used in different fields. E-learning environments are now in our daily lives and have become a subject for scientific research and studies.

Since the use of learning objects in e-learning environments is new in practice, the benefits of these objects for the learning environments and the facilities they provided for distance education should be introduced both to the students and to the teachers. In the applications that we carried out with high school students, it was seen that learning objects were quite beneficial for the students and teachers and even for the parents in many respects when the learning objects were prepared effective. These applications also revealed that the students established communication not only with each other but also with their teachers. Moreover, it was possible for the parents to know about the academic development of their children. In short, learning objects allow information sharing, numerous revisions and feedback. Thanks to these features of learning objects, they allow permanent learning, student-centered learning and learning by doing. In addition, thanks to reusability of learning objects, an object once produced can be used a number of times, which helps avoid high cost and waste of time.

Learning objects can be used in various in-class or out-of-class activities such as activating students' background knowledge, supporting conceptual change, allowing multiple demonstrations, transferring learning and developing the skills.

For the spread of such applications, it is necessary to develop a number of different types of object stores. In addition, teachers should be trained on how to create, choose and apply learning objects.

9. References

Berggren, A., Burgos, D., Fontana, J. M., Hinkelman, D., Hung, V. & Hursh, A., (2005). Practical and Pedagogical Issues for Teacher Adoption of LMS Learning Design Standards in Moodle LMS. *Journal of Interactive Media in Education (02).*

Çalışkan, S., (2002). Uzaktan Eğitim Web Sitelerinde Animasyon Kullanımı, *Açık ve Uzaktan Eğitim Sempozyumu, Anadolu Üniversitesi*, Eskişehir.

Fahlberg, T. (2004). *Creating Whiteboard Movies That Teach and Foster Collaboration (Whiteboard Movie Presentation).* New Orleans, USA: NECC.

Fahlberg, T. & Nonis, J. (2005). *Creating Whiteboard Movies to Teach, Add to ePortfolios, and Collaborate*, 2005, Philadelphia, USA: NECC.

Fahlberg-Stojanovska, L. (2005). Technology in Education, Presentation for SimLab 2004 and SimLab 2005, *sponsored by DAAD, Bitola, FYR Macedonia.*

Karaman, S.(2005). Öğrenme Nesnelerine Dayalı Bir İçerik Geliştirme Sisteminin Hazırlanması ve Öğretmen Adaylarının Nesne Yaklaşımlı İçerik Geliştirme Profilerinin Belirlenmesi. (http://tez2.yok.gov.tr).

Kelly, J., (2002). Introducing Learning Objects Tutorial. *(In partial fulfillment of MSc. in Information Technology in Education for Trinity College Dublin, Ireland, http://www.cs.tcd.ie/Jim.J.Kelly/103_eLearning_investigations_files/103_intro_lo_tutorial/103_intro_lo_tutorial_introduction.htm*

Kenny, R., Bullen, M., & Loftus, J. (2006). A Pilot Study of Problem Formulation and Resolution in An Online Problem-based Learning Course. *The International Review of Research in Open and Distance Learning, 7(3).*

Landau, R. (2006). Computational Physics: A Better Model for Physics *Education? Computing in Science & Engineering*, 8(5), 22–30.

Learnet, (2003). *What Are Learning Objects*? http://learnet.hku.hk/objects.htm

MacNeil, G. (2006). "New Ways of Implementing the Syllabus", "What can Students do?", "Whiteboard Movies and Investigations in Mathematics", "Thinking, Reasoning and Working Mathematically out loud with MathCasts". *Presentations for the "Implementation of the 1–10 Mathematics Syllabus"*, Toowoomba, Dalby, AU.

Morten,P,F,.(2002).Online Education Systems: Discussion and Definition of Terms, (URL:http://www.nettskolen.com/forskning/DefinitionTerms.pdf)

Novak, J. (1998). Learning, Creating and Using Knowledge: Concept Maps as Facilitative Tools in Schools and Corporations; *Lawrence Erlbaum Associates, Inc; New Jersey*, pp 24-25 .

Sharples, M., (2002). E-learning for Doctors and Dentists, Centre for Educational Technology and Distance Learning, *University of Birmingham.* http://www.edu.bham.ac.uk/research/crmde/conference/ppt/sharples http://www.lru.bcit.ca/portfolio/oursamples/learningobjects/index.shtml

Slater J., (2002). *Learning Object.* CETIS Reference. http://www.cetis.ac.uk/encyclopedia/entries/20011120111052/view

Weller, M. (2007). *Virtual Learning Environments: Using, Choosing and Developing Your VLE.* London: Routledge.

Wiley D. (ed.), (2000). *Instructional Use of Learning Objects, Online Book,* http://reusability.org/read/

Yıldırım, A., & Şimşek, H., (2005). *Sosyal Bilimlerde Nitel Araştırma Yöntemleri*, Geliştirilmiş 5. Baskı, Seçkin Yayıncılık, Ankara

8

Evolutive Platform – A Genetic E-Learning Environment

Jorge Manuel Pires and Manuel Pérez Cota
Universidade de Vigo
Spain

1. Introduction

It is now a widely accepted fact that IT can radically change educational practices and learning processes. The technological revolution requires better cognitive skills, either through the innovation or creativity, cognitive attributes par excellence. These attributes are not stratified by class or social status. A low cognitive functioning, with implications in poor school performance, are not indicators of lower classes or marginalized ethnic groups, i.e., their intelligence is not limited to the models of society. There will be one cognitive dysfunction ("Input," preparation, "Output") that in most cases, those responsible for education are not formed to overcome it, or do not make use of strategic resources to avoid waste of the cognitive potential of individuals (Fonseca, 1999).

Therefore the objective to be achieved is to build a self-regulating system that enables the improvement of different cognitive factors, allowing the student to fill certain gaps in their learning process by using genetic algorithms combined with statistical functions and evaluation learning models properly defined.

1.1 The cognitive approach

Cognition, as an act of assimilation, integration and ability to express and develop information, prepares us as a species to understand our past and build our future. Surroundings of an evolutionary process as a species stems from the informational and communication between plurineuronal sensory systems (Input) and motors (output) and is unavoidably in the genesis of adaptability and learning (Fonseca, 1999). A motivated individual be automatically a better skills receiver; a genius is 1% talent and 99% work (Edison 1902).

Cognition has grown as a doctrine based on the various time-empirical observations, and hard data of field research evidence proof, that are mental structures underlying not only thought, but also emotion, as well as the very perception and interpretation of both, inner/internal and outer/external source information (Lazarus, 1999, as cited in Kerkiri et al., 2010). (Gardner, 1993, as cited in Kerkiri et al., 2010), whose multiple intelligence theory is based on cognitivism, asserts that mind consists of numerous fairly specific and independent computational mechanisms, and it is in this context that research on learning styles has also been promoted. Based on cognitive learning theory, the structure of content of the cognitive matter should be organized hierarchically. Relevant research (Deshler, 1986, as cited in Kerkiri et al., 2010) has surely led to the conclusion that students learn mainly from the progressive and relation-linked construction of knowledge. This approach may well find applications in a Learning Management System (LMS) with a psycho-pedagogically driven learning path creation module (Kerkiri et al., 2010).

1.2 The co-constructivism approach

From constructivist point of view, the knowledge "built" by an individual and not broadcasted, is itself both a reflective and active process. The interpretation that the individual performs of the new experience is influenced by their prior knowledge introducing in social interaction, multiple perspectives of learning. Learning requires understanding of the whole and the parts, and should be understood in a global context. In this perspective, Reuven Feuerstein introduces one new dynamic, co-constructivism (Feuerstein, 1990).

The theory of Structural Cognitive Modifiability - (SCM), far transcends the purely cognitivist approach, and advocates that every individual is modifiable, a process that is inherent to the human species (Feuerstein, 1990).

1.3 Conditioning the learning process

Considering that in terms of learning, we retain 20% of what we see and 90% of what we practice and that the two stages of learning are supported on know how to make and know evolve, and that three of the most important processes of learning are learning studying, learning reflecting and learning by doing, we must reflect on the dangers of abandonment or the demotivation on the incentive on the learning process, that result on an extinction of the knowledge acquired. Extinction occurs, when one previously conditioned response becomes less frequent and finally disappears (Feldman, 2001).

The conditioning in the learning process can be obtained through an educational incentive structure built extremely well, so that the individual is identified with the learning process. The positive and negative reinforcements in weighted measures are also two instruments for consolidating the learning model, helping to maintain the incentive, because the behavior can be modeled by the administration of positive and negative reinforcements, which also implies a causal relationship of reinforcement (cause) and behavior (effect). As mentioned, these stimuli must be used carefully, since the short / medium term may create a dependency on the user, if eventually ceased to exist. This is because human beings however much they want or wish, to shape their humility, are always waiting for a feedback regarding their performance.

In this study, these reinforcements may result from the machine itself through the use of happy smiles or pleasing sounds - for positive reinforcement, or sad smiles and unpleasant sounds - for negative reinforcement. In both cases, we can use more advanced techniques as the use of subliminal messages.

For these reasons, we conclude that individuals follow standards and models imposed by society; however, the reality is quite different, since the profiles of learning and speed of acquisition of knowledge in each of us are different. This is the purpose of this investigation; prove that we can improve our multiple intelligences/ cognitive profiles.

2. Targets

2.1 The outlook

When moving from traditional learning to educational e-systems, students get increasingly involved in their learning process. Technological systems are the new vectors used to disseminate knowledge between and provide feedback amongst the learning process (actors, pedagogues, the tutors and the learners). The use of IT in education covers a wide range of very different activities; e.g. learning environments, course management, and much more. Because the *one-size-fits-all* paradigm cannot be applied to individual learning, adaptability is a must. Hence, courseware is meant to be tailored according to the learner's needs. Two main families of computerized applications aspire to offer this adaptability: Intelligent Tutoring Systems (ITS) (Brusilovsky, 1992, as cited in Madhour & Forte, 2010) and Adaptive Hypermedia Systems (AHS) (Brusilovsky, 1996, as cited in Madhour & Forte, 2010).

Intelligent Tutoring Systems (Brusilovsky, 1992, as cited in Madhour & Forte, 2010) rely on curriculum sequencing mechanisms to provide the student with a path through the learning material. An adaptability algorithm computes this so-called personalized path, corresponding to the course construction and curriculum sequencing (Shang et al., 2001, as cited in Madhour & Forte, 2010). The process is twofold:

- Find the relevant topics and select the most satisfactory one;
- Construct dynamically page contents based on the tutor decision for what the learner should study next

ITS usually provide an evaluation of the learner's level of mastery of the domain concepts through an answer analysis and error feedback process that eventually allows the system to update the user's model. This process is called intelligent solution analysis (Serengul & Smith-Atakan, 1998, as cited in Madhour & Forte, 2010).

Adaptive Hypermedia (AH) (Brusilovsky, 1992, as cited in Madhour & Forte, 2010) was born as a trial to combine ITS and AH. As in ITS, adaptive education hypermedia focus on the learner, while at the same time it has been greatly influenced by adaptive navigation support in educational hypermedia (Brusilovsky, 1996, as cited in Madhour & Forte, 2010). In fact, adaptability implies the integration of a student model in the system in the framework of a curriculum, which sequence depends on pedagogical objectives, user's needs and motivation.

Hence, the use of adaptive and/or interactive hypermedia systems was proposed as a promising solution (Brusilovsky, 1996; Prentzas & Hatziligeroudis, 2001, as cited in Kazanidis & Satratzemi, 2009). Adaptivity in e-learning is a new research trend that personalizes the educational process through the use of Adaptive Educational Hypermedia Systems (AEHS). These systems attempt to create an individualized course according to the user's personal characteristics, such as language, learning style, preferences, educational goals and progress. In this way, instructors expect to solve some of the main problems of web courses and hope to succeed in achieving a better learning outcome (Kazanidis & Stratzemi, 2009)

However, there is still a problem in the presented families; information comes from different sources embedded with diverse formats into the form of metadata making it troublesome for the computerized programming to create professional materials (Shih et al., 2007, as cited in Liu & Shih, 2010). The major identified problems are (Liu & Shih, 2010):

- Difficulty of learning resource sharing;
- Even if all e-Learning systems follow the common standard, users still have to visit individual platforms to gain appropriate course materials contents. It is comparatively inconvenient;
- High redundancy of learning material;
- Due to difficulty of resource-sharing, it is hard for teachers to figure out the redundancy of course materials and therefore results in the waste of resources, physically and virtually;
- Even worse, the consistency of course content is endangered which might eventually slow down the innovation momentum of course materials;
- Deficiency of the course brief;
- It is hard to abstract course summary or brief automatically in efficient way. So, most courseware systems only list the course names or the unit titles. Information is insufficient for learners to judge quality of course content before they enroll certain courses;

2.2 The new environment paradigm

Web courses and hypermedia systems deliver knowledge to a wide number of users with different characteristics, preferences and knowledge of the domain, irrespective of where they live, their age or their study credentials. However, these systems do appear to have some quite major problems which have been identified and documented through research studies and have differentiated into three distinct categories (Kazanidis & Stratzemi, 2009). The first deals with problems related to disorientation, cognitive overload, discontinuous flow (Murray et al., 2000, as cited in Kazanidis & Stratzemi, 2009), content readiness and distraction. The main solution that research proposes is the use of adaptive and or interactive systems. The second category of problems is those that arise from the absence of a common development framework for course construction. Course content, thus, lacks reusability, durability and interoperability. A suggested solution is the adoption of common educational standards for course construction and delivery. The third category involves instructors who come up against difficulties during course construction as most of the time course development requires not only specific programming capabilities but also deep knowledge of adaptive strategies and educational standard specifications (Kazanidis & Stratzemi, 2009).

This research is based on work of a PhD thesis. The idea has emerged because the authors - that are teachers in various education institutions in Spain and Portugal, feel that the students /learners needed a new way of acquiring knowledge. The need for a new paradigm with regard to learning processes and educational practices, led authors to begin the process of research on the state of the art and later, the investigation of a unique process that would use a single tool / environment that would allow the concentration of the student / learners exclusively in the acquisition of knowledge. Personalization consists in adapting the behavior of the system according to some specific information related to an individual user (Madhour & Forte, 2010).

Creating this new paradigm implies that both a new industry, that will emerge, as the creators content, for example, teachers or trainers are the responsible for creating content and the implied level of difficulty. The difficulty inherent to each block of knowledge, is set in a consciously way by the creators, and the "market", will be the quality evaluator of each. Teachers and Trainers can also adapt old methods, such as the traditional manuals, or Power Point presentations, to the new paradigm, since this follows the Sharable Content Object Reference Model (SCORM) standard, and can be accepted in virtually any kind of (LMS), although initially be developed using the Moodle. The use of universal normative and free software - such as Extensible Markup Language (XML), JAVA, Hot Potatoes or Reload Editor, among others, will be an additional advantage of this paradigm.

Thus, this structure addresses in a single way, the problems identified by (Shih et al., 2007) and (Liu & Shih, 2010) have exposed. Regarding what (Murray et al., 2009, as cited in Kazanidis & Stratzemi, 2009) and (Kazanidis & Stratzemi, 2009), claimed, adaptability, interactivity, lack of reusability, the durability, the interoperability and the difficulties in the construction of materials, are guaranteed by the use of the Knowledge Block (KB) and by the inherent structure.

Sharable Content Object Reference Model

On the other hand, students have greater flexibility in learning, since there will be an exclusively - if it is so desired - man-machine interaction, with no third party involved, thus reducing certain constraints to progress, that might occur with traditional methods.

Another advantage is that the solution delivers in a single structure - the KB, several sources of information (Fig. 4), thus solving the problem of diversity in content origin.

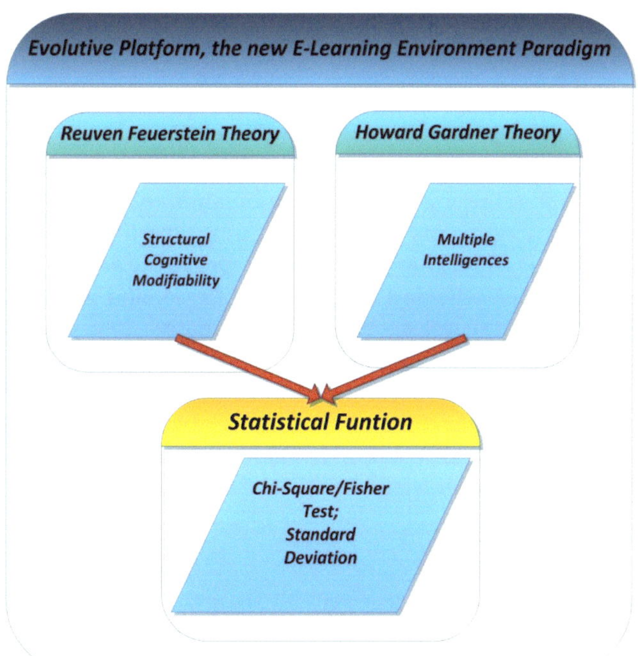

Fig. 1. Global Block Diagram

3. Method

A host of research has been devoted to the way individuals acquire and perceive educational material in relation to their personality (Wallace et al., 2007, as cited in Kerkiri et al., 2010). Early efforts that approached provision of personalized learning paths were either based on the performance of the learner (Carchiolo et al., 2007, as cited in Kerkiri et al., 2010), or on indicators of her/his preferences (Graf et al., 2008, as cited in Kerkiri et al., 2010).

Individuals present distinct ways of learning, different background, and diverse preferences. By composing these characteristics, aspects of the student learning process and knowledge, construction process can be inferred by computational systems and registered in a profile (Stiubiener et al., 2010).

Each individual has her/his unique way of learning. Thus, learning style greatly affects both the learning process and the outcome (Carver and Howard, 1999, as cited in Kazanidis & Satratzemi, 2009). In order to achieve better learning outcomes, several research streams are attempting to provide adaptivity of the learning process. One of these streams exploits educational theories about student learning styles in order to gain a better learning outcome. Some of the most well known learning styles are (Kazanidis & Satratzemi, 2009):

- Kolb's learning style theory (Kolb, 1984).
- Honey and Mumford (1992)
- Felder & Silverman (1988) Learning Style Model (FSLSM)..
- Witkin's Field Dependent- Field Independent Model (Witkin et al., 1977).
- Dunn & Dunn (1978) Model.
- Grasha-Riechmann Student Leaming Styles Scale (GRSLSS) (Riechmann & Crasha 1974).
- Gardner's theory of multiple intelligences (Gardner, 1993).

Various studies have been done that have applied several techniques in e-Learning:

- Becker and Vanzin (2003) tried to detect meaningful patterns of learning activities in e-Learning using the association rule.
- Minaei-Bidgoli, Kashy, Kortemeyer, and Punch (2003) proposed a method of predicting a learner's final test score by using a combination of multiple classifiers (CMC) constructed from learning-history data in e-Learning, and they reported that a modified method using a Genetic Algorithm (GA) could improve the accuracy of prediction.
- Talavera and Gaudioso (2004) and Hamalainen, Laine, and Sutien (2006) proposed a method to prediction final test scores using the native Bayes model obtained from learning-history data in e-Learning.
- Ueno (2010) does not simply propose a system of predicting a learner's final status using a data-mining technique, but an agent that acquires domain knowledge related to the content from a learning-history-log database that automatically generates adaptive instructional messages to guide the learners.

3.1 The adaptive system structure

Adaptive systems (Kobsa, 1996 & Kobsa, 2001, as cited in Stiubiener et al., 2010) include a user model that represents student's knowledge, objectives, interests, and other characteristics that enable a system to differentiate among its users. The system gathers information, models users, and uses that information to provide adaptation. This enables the system to interact with several users, in the same context, but in different ways. The sources of information on which the adaptation is based might range from user's interaction to a direct request for information (Stiubiener et al., 2010).

The proposed system adapts itself and guides the user through the available KB, individualizing student outcomes through identifiers in the database. This information is used to determine what lessons should be selected to achieve the objectives.

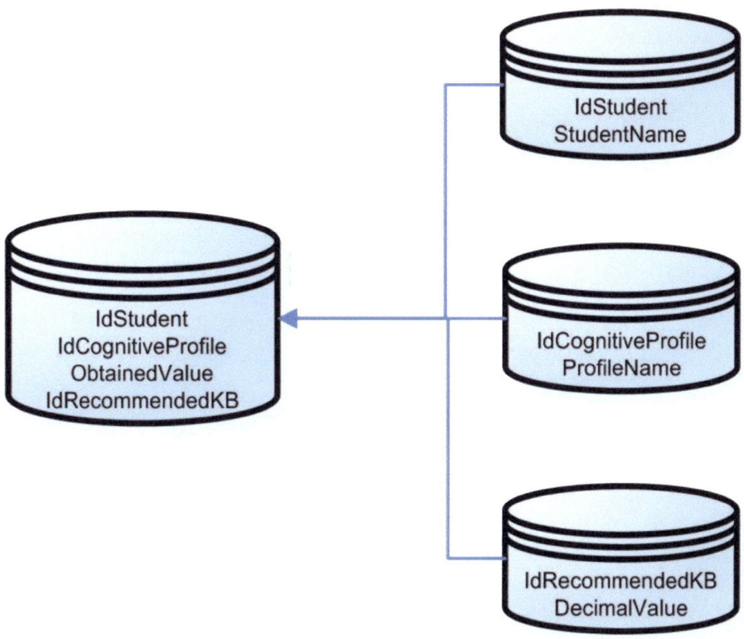

Fig. 2. Database Structure

The user's knowledge level is a crucial parameter for adaptive systems (Kazanidis & Satratzemi, 2009). The proposal agent uses learner's history data, which is stored in a database to individualize learners.

A computational agent that learns using machine learning or data-mining technologies from data is called a "learning agent". This article proposes a learning agent for e-Learning (Ueno, 2010).

In the social context, artificial intelligence can take advantage of biological observations of certain species to imitate their experiences. This trend, called evolutionary computation, uses genetic algorithms (GAs) on one hand and swarm intelligent techniques on the other hand (Madhour & Forte, 2010). This learning agent, in particular, uses a GA that enables extraction of the necessary values to choose the most appropriate KB, based on two statistic functions.

The learning model (LM) (fig. 4), defines the learning activities in which the individuals learn. The content is structured information, consisting of multimedia resources, texts, lectures and other materials. The content is a set of circumstances that are relevant to the student to build knowledge through its connection with it.

In this model the teacher, has a bipartite role in the presentation of content and creation the learning context. The context can be a classroom or a virtual learning activity, in which the role of teacher is more focused on content in the case of a classroom, and the context in the case of a virtual learning activity. In this study the LM is transformed in the KB with the following structure (Fig. 5).

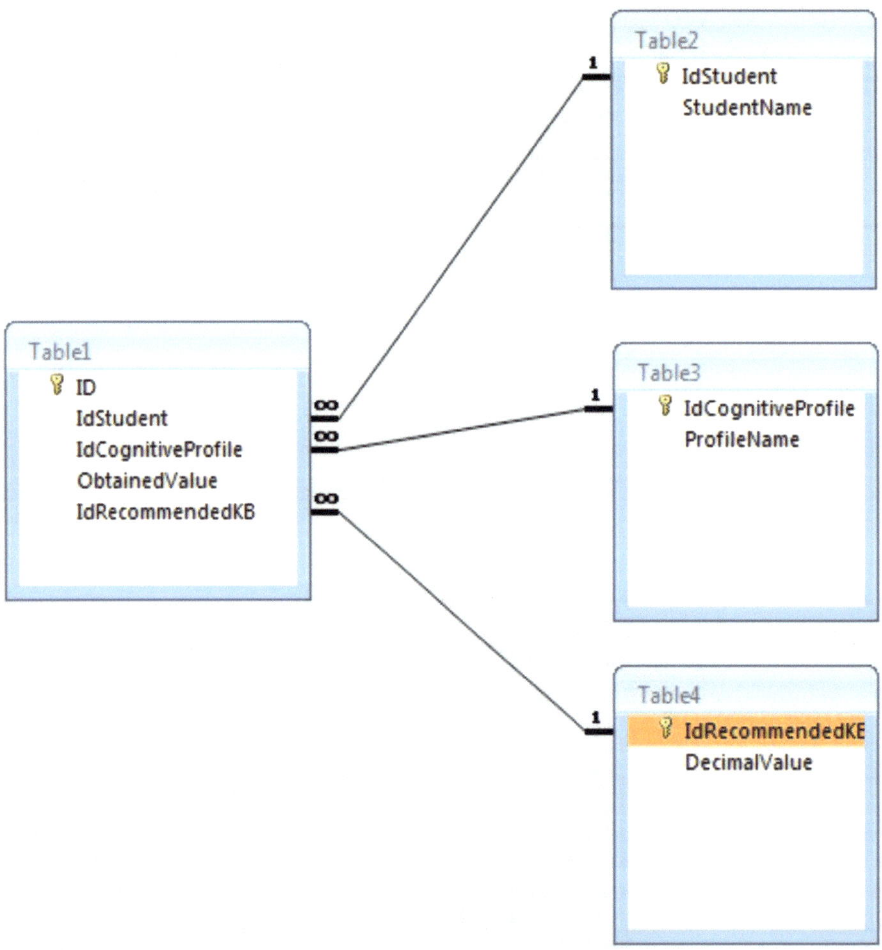

Fig. 3. Database Relations

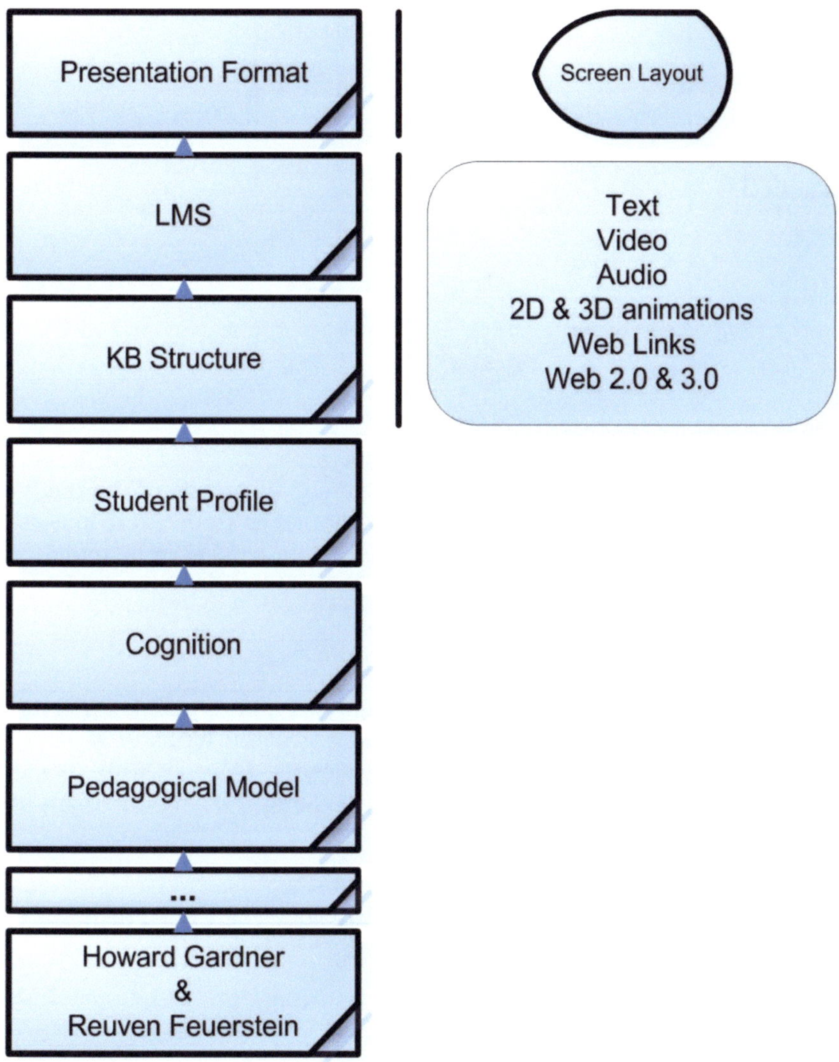

Fig. 4. Learning Model Orientation Layer Structure

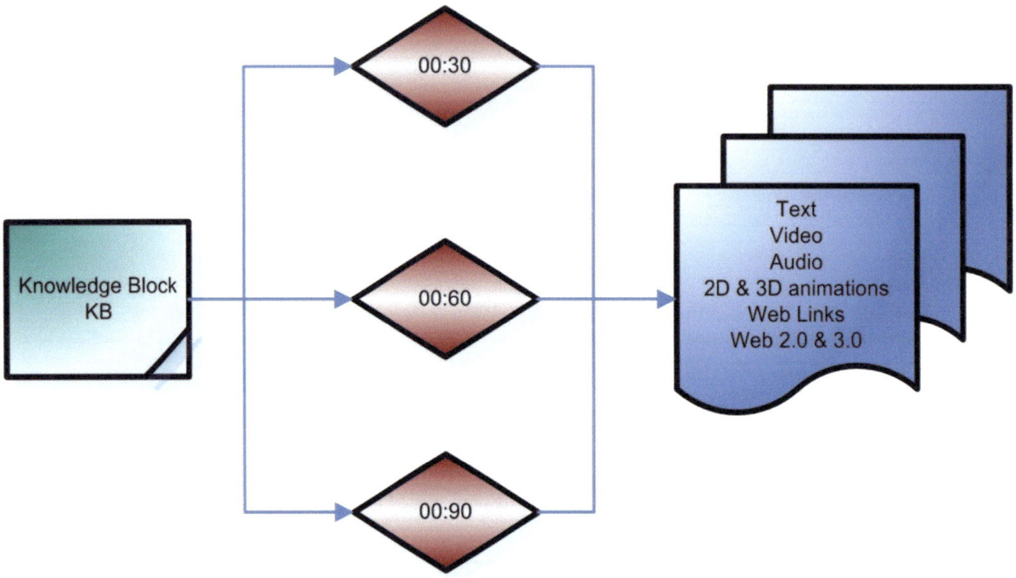

Fig. 5. Knowledge Block Structure

The KB represent 30, 60 or 90 minutes lessons, covering all aspects of Gardner's multiple intelligences (Gardner, 1993) using a variety of content that go from text to images, sounds, video and web links. This structure can be prepared by the teacher or by multidisciplinary teams or companies that want to develop contents.

4. The core

Student centered learning is an educational paradigm that gives students greater autonomy and approach is very similar to the Bologna Process goals in terms of student centered model based on learning outcomes and competences (Alves, 2010). Some of the characteristics of effective learners in the student centered learning paradigm are (de la Harpe et al., 1999, as cited in Alves, 2010):

- Have clear learning goals;
- Have a wide repertoire of learning strategies and know when to use them;
- Use available resources effectively;
- Know about their strengths and weaknesses;
- Understand the learning process;
- Deal appropriately with their feelings;
- Take responsibility for their own learning;
- Plan, monitor, evaluate and adapt their learning process;

The majority of virtual learning environments (VLE) are used as mere repositories of content, based on the classroom paradigm and don't support the individualization of the learning process (Alves, 2010). According to Dias (Dias, 2004), building spaces for online learning is a challenge that goes beyond the simple transfer of content to the Web. This approach tends to transform the environments in online repositories of information rather than in the desired spaces of interaction and experimentation (Alves, 2010).

The integration of the intelligent systems in the learning process support, allows an adaptation of content and contexts to the learning style of each student, providing adaptive tools to support collaboration (Lesgold et al., 1992; Goodman et al., 2003, as cited in Alves, 2010).

To allow a greater adaptation of the learning environment based on the student's profile the adoption of theories of artificial intelligence in education is proposed, based on the learning experience, adapting contents and contexts to the student needs (Alves, 2010).

In the last three decades, artificial intelligence has been adopted in various forms of education. One of the most important issues in the adaptation of an intelligent tutoring system is the modulation of student behavior in order to adapt the pedagogical model to the student model. For this adaptation to be more effective the student profile must be identified. In this context, the development of adaptive learning environments based on the student profile is one of the most important challenges in the adoption of artificial intelligence systems in education, in order to improve the educational process. This approach is based on new pedagogical methodologies to provide learning environments adaptable to the needs of each student (Alves, 2010).

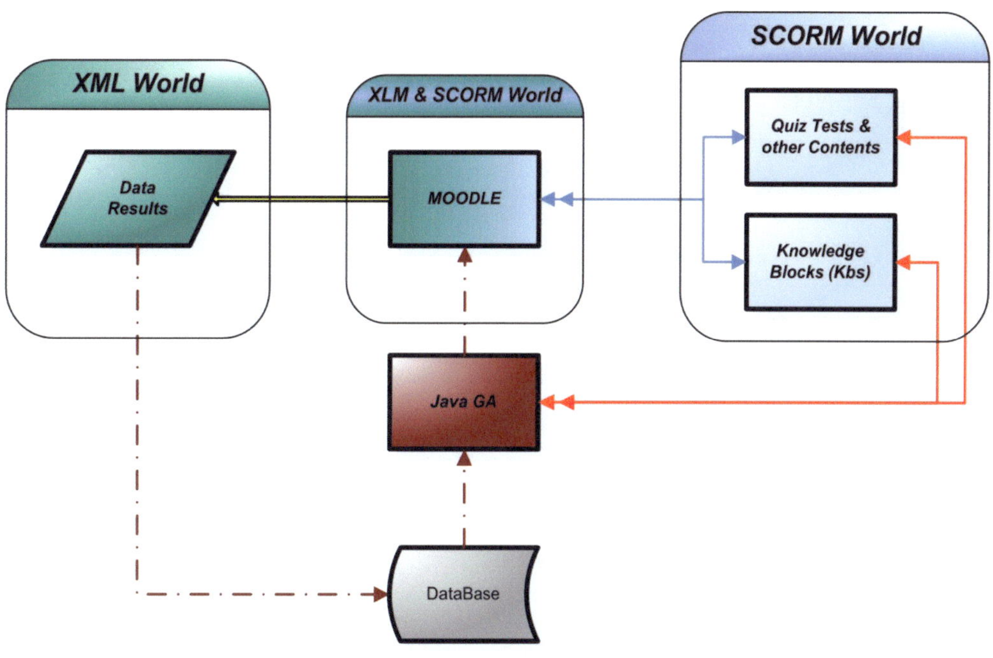

Fig. 6. Evolutive Platform Structure

1. Quiz Test & other Contents are created with SCORM compliant software[1] and imported to the (LMS), after be chosen by the Java GA, consulted the database that contains the student statistics data;
2. KB are created with SCORM compliant software[2] and imported to the (LMS) after be chosen by the Java Genetic Algorithm (JGA), consulted the database that contains the student statistic data;

[1] e.g. Hot Potatoes, Reload Editor or others;

Fig. 7. Algorithm Structure - first samples – training phase

[2] e.g. Hot Potatoes, Reload Editor or others;

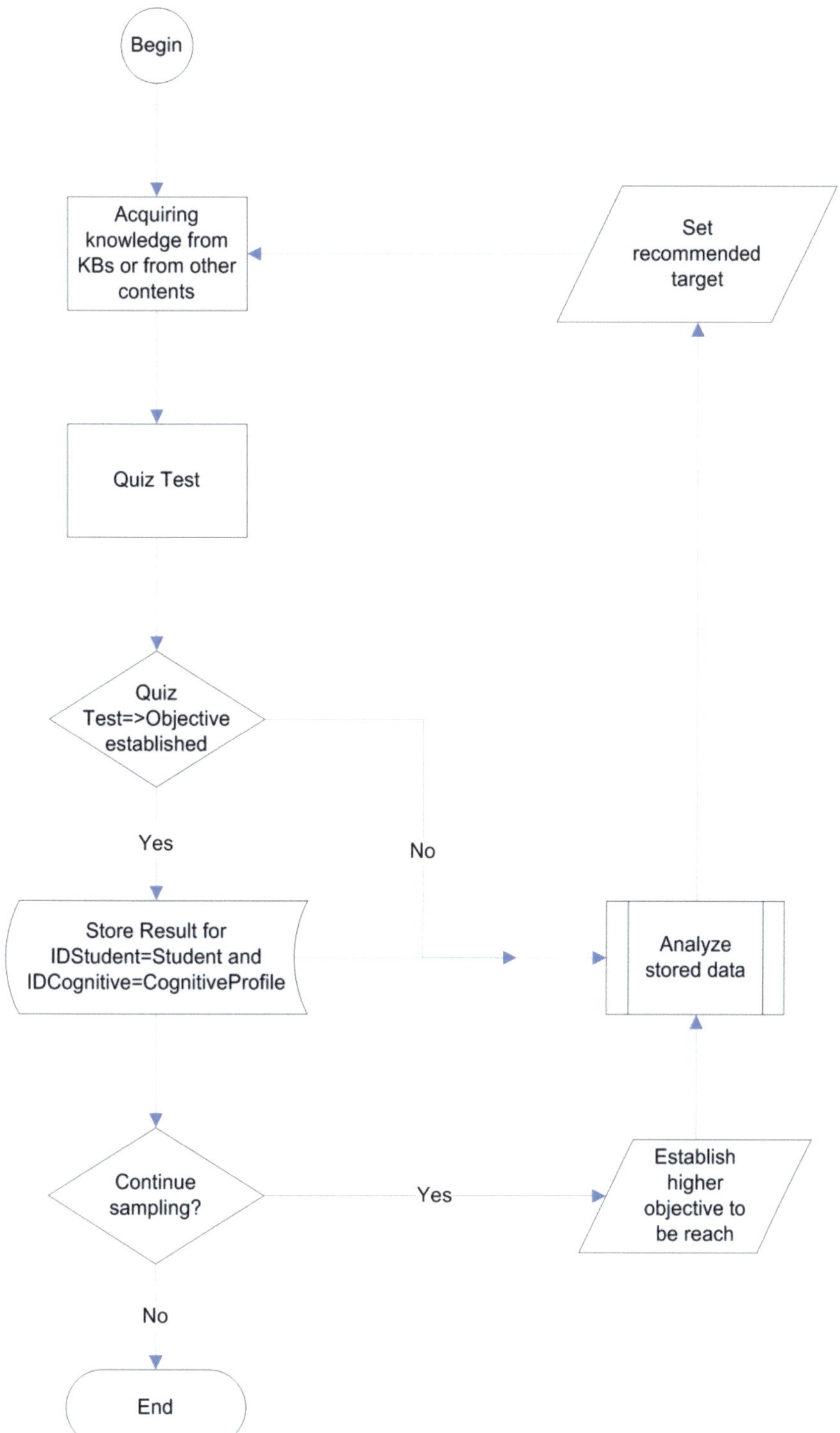

Fig. 8. Algorithm Structure - cruising speed

3. The Moodle (LMS) produces results in XML format, which are stored in a database system for subsequent consultation by the JGA;

The flowcharts from (Fig. 7 and 8), represent the sequence of actions to meet to get the best KB. They differ only in one point. From the moment the algorithm has sufficient sampling, no longer need an intervention, passing to auto regulatory mode, using the information contained in databases on a particular student and their profile.

4.1 The genetic algorithm

The GA has an important role in implementing this solution, since its performance will greatly affect the final results. It should be as dynamic as possible in order to achieve various goals, according to the predetermined guidelines. This should be achieved by giving weights to the cognitive profile or profiles, which are meant to be improved. The basic idea is to get the "fitness function" to be improved as much as possible in order to get a better approach to the most correct KB, according to the previously achieved results.

The student results after activity sequence builds a set of binary values. The idea is to maximize the minimum obtained by the individual, i.e., find what difficulties are visible and redirect all the intellectual effort to overcome the problems, never forgetting the positive objectives already achieved.

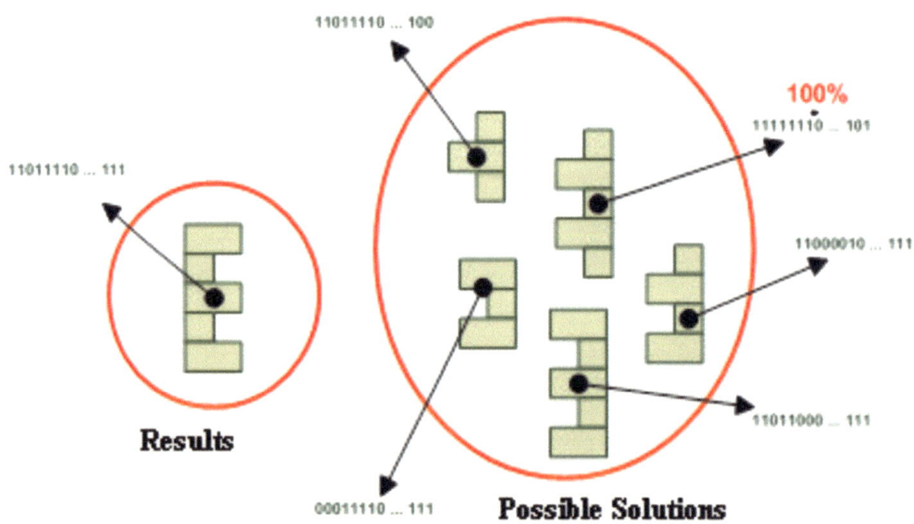

Fig. 9. Binary correspondence of the population and possible solutions

The GA will select the KB that matches the student's difficulties. If the match is not 100% exact, 80% will be considered a fair value in the acquisition of the new block.

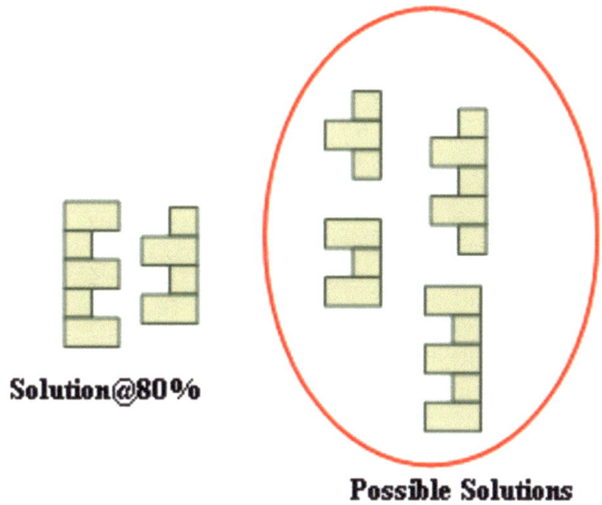

Fig. 10. Solution @ 80%

The 100% match will be an ideal situation that the GA mechanisms will try to achieve.

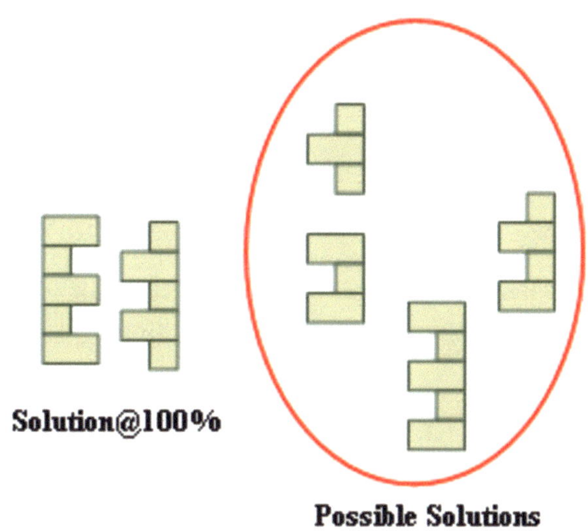

Fig. 11. Solution @ 100%

This ideal situation will be only achieved after several cycles of study of the behavior of the individual. This ideal situation is also dependent on the availability of the block that has the desired binary value.

4.2 The fitness function

The fitness function allows assigning probabilities to the units likely to be visited by the learner. The highest probability is that relating to the most suitable unit. In this case we use two statistical functions to get the necessary values to choose the most appropriate KB.

4.2.1 Chi-square

The chi-square is defined as a discrepancy measure between the observed frequencies and the expected ones (Spiegel, 1994).

$$Q = \sum_{i=1}^{k} X_i^2$$

Equation. 1. Chi-Square distribution

The GA uses this discrepancy measure, as its evaluation function. The obtained value will be used as a weight, to select the best candidate block.

$$x^2 = \frac{(o_1 - e_1)^2}{ej} + \frac{(o_2 - e_2)^2}{ej} + \cdots + \frac{(o_k - e_k)^2}{ej} = \sum_{j=2}^{k} \frac{(o_j - e_1)^2}{ej}$$

Equation. 2. Chi-Square distribution in extended form

The two observation tables (Fig. 12), represent a possible situation of what is sought as a final value - the expected, and obtained through "simulated reality" - obtained. The difference between what is expected and what we get is the deviation that must be compensated to achieve the objective - the expected value. In the simulation (Fig. 12), there are two blocks to simulate a process of classifying a given KB. As it is observed in the (Fig. 12) illustration, χ2 suffered a decrease from the 1st to 2nd KB, which can be understood as an improvement in the GA orientation, as the 2nd block better approach the individual's cognitive reality. It is still observed - and in spite of the illustration represents a random simulation of what is desired that the orientation of GA is forced immediately when the discrepancies between expected values and obtained values are significant (between points 5 and 7 in the χ axis in the graph to the right, and between 5 and 8 in the graph to the left).

4.2.2 Standard deviation population

When all available values are used, it is called a population; when only a subset of available values is used, it is called a sample.

$$s = \sqrt{\frac{1}{N-1} \sum_{i=1}^{N} (x_i - \overline{x})^2},$$

Equation. 3. Standard Deviation Population

Where $\{x_1, x_2,\ldots x_N\}$ are the observed values of the sample items and $\overline{x}$ is the mean value of these observations. This correction (the use of $N - 1$ instead of N) is known as Bessel's correction. The reason for this correction is that s^2 is an unbiased estimator for the variance σ^2 of the underlying population, if that variance exists and the sample values are drawn independently with replacement. However, s is *not* an unbiased estimator for the standard deviation σ; it tends to overestimate the population standard deviation. The term *standard deviation of the sample* is used for the uncorrected estimator (using N) while the term *sample standard deviation* is used for the corrected estimator (using $N - 1$). The denominator $N - 1$ is the number of degrees of freedom in the vector of residuals, $(x_1-\overline{x},\ldots,x_n-\overline{x})$ (Wikipedia - Standard Deviation, 2011). In order to get the increase by which the GA will guide the choice of the degree to be achieved, we turn to the second statistical function - Standard Deviation Population, which collects the values of the individual result from several samples from the calculation of Chi-square. This value will allow us to pick a particular KB, guiding the student in obtaining their optimum value.

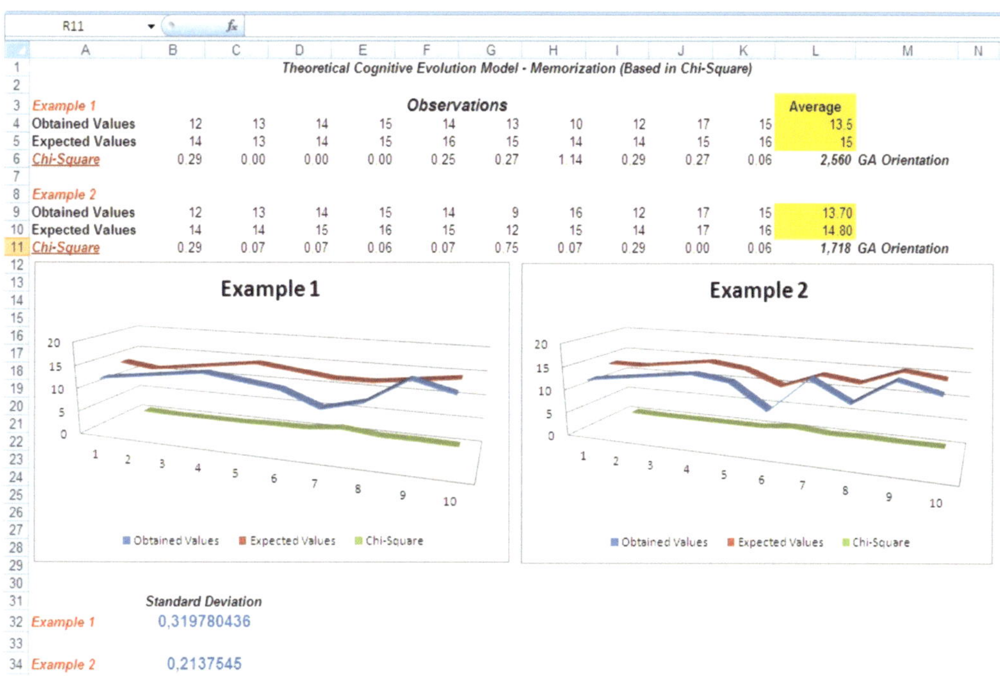

Theoretical Cognitive Evolution Model - Memorization (Based in Chi-Square)

	Observations										Average	
Example 1												
Obtained Values	12	13	14	15	14	13	10	12	17	15	13.5	
Expected Values	14	13	14	15	16	15	14	14	15	16	15	
Chi-Square	0.29	0.00	0.00	0.00	0.25	0.27	1.14	0.29	0.27	0.06	2,560	GA Orientation
Example 2												
Obtained Values	12	13	14	15	14	9	16	12	17	15	13.70	
Expected Values	14	14	15	16	15	12	15	14	17	16	14.80	
Chi-Square	0.29	0.07	0.07	0.06	0.07	0.75	0.07	0.29	0.00	0.06	1,718	GA Orientation

	Standard Deviation
Example 1	0,319780436
Example 2	0,2137545

Fig. 12. Theoretical Cognitive Evolution Model - Memorization

4.2.3 Genetic algorithm pseudo-code

The theory is based mainly on the following two assumptions:

- H_0 is ignored until the learning curve of the individual is understood;
- H_0 is considered for future evolutionary terms after 1st premise has been achieved;

The use of the two hypotheses is due to the fact that the 1st objective is to understand the cognitive reality of the individual, and then improve it.

Algorithm for Individual Cognitive Sequence (10 samples example):

1. Establish objective to be reached (0-100% or 0-20);
2. Start ranking process (w/ sample = target);
3. Get cognitive binary of the individual;
4. Perform statistical operation on results;
5. Repeat (1) at least 9x (or as desired);
6. Get Final Sum;
7. Apply acquired weight (next module=objective to be achieved + obtained weight);
8. Repeat (1) N times until obtain binary or objective;

The algorithm begins by setting up a target, regardless of prior knowledge of the cognitive profile of the individual. The sequence (1 to 4) will be repeated at least 10 times and the value statistically treated to obtain a weight. The result will be used in obtaining the next module by the GA, with the aim to get closer to the maximum desired.

4.3 Knowledge blocks

Notwithstanding their indisputable assets, the reusability and inoperability of learning objects has been presented as a major problem in adaptive learning, inasmuch solutions of their technical linking are not directly presupposed. Standards have been thus adopted by the e-learning community to facilitate and foster interoperability and reuse of learning artifacts among different e-learning platforms. The pertinent use of predefined sets of metadata promotes the exchange of Learning Resources (LR) among different e-learning systems and content providers, while offering higher potentials for finding existing learning content as well. Such standards for the learning resources are Learning Object Metadata (LOM) and Sharable Content Reference Model SCORM[3] (Kerkiri et al., 2010).

Adopting educational standards, like SCORM, comes as a solution to the above problems for content reusability, accessibility interoperability and durability. It's expected that the adoption of such standard will help authors to construct more effective courses faster with less effort and at a lower cost (Kazanidis & Stratzemi, 2009).

Authors would save much time and effort if they could easily find and reuse qualitative educational content from other courses and or platforms. Moreover, they would save time if there where no need to update their courses when the host platform was updated to a new version. Thus, the need to have reusable, accessible, interoperable and durable (RAID) content has led to the creation of learning technology specifications. For the time

[3] specifications of SCORM can be found in Advanced Distributed Learning (ADL, 2004)

being the most popular educational standard is SCORM (ADL, 2009) which was implemented by the ADL (Advanced Distributed Learning) Initiative (Kazanidis & Stratzemi, 2009).

SCORM is a collection of specifications and standards for the development, packaging and delivery of educational content. More specifically, it describes the components used in learning and how to package them for exchange between compliant systems; how they should be described using metadata in order to enable search and discovery; and how to define sequencing rules for the content objects (ADL, 2009). SCORM consolidates the work of other standards and organizations, such as ARIADNE, AICC, IMS, and IEEE's LTSC into one unified reference model. The application of SCORM ensures the reusability, accessibility and durability of the educational material, as well as interoperability between (LMS) (Kazanidis & Stratzemi, 2009).

4.3.1 The knowledge block structure

The KB is a simple structure that has SCORM compatibility and a binary codification, allowing the GA to be the most suitable choice to which specific case.

Reserved for Future Use	Educational Level	Cognitive Profile ID	KB difficulty level
00000000	00000	000	0000000000000000

Table 1. Knowledge Block Coding

Regardless of the used operator - crossover, mutation or both, 16 bits are up front considered enough for a KB selection to be uploaded in the (LMS), without the risk of a premature convergence into a specific solution by the GA.

Binary Value	Decimal Value
0000000000000000	0
...	...
111010111000110	9,20 ≈
...	...
1100110000000110	15,94 ≈
...	...
1111111111111111	20

Table 2. Knowledge Block Difficulty Level

$$20_{10} - <65535_{10}><1111111111111111_{2}>$$

$$9{,}20_{10} - <X_{10}><Y_{2}>$$

$$X = <30150_{10}><111010111000110_{2}>$$

After being provided the results in decimal base, by the GA, those will be converted by an internal mechanism - a 3 simple rule in order to achieve the corresponding binary value of KB closer to the desired.

Cognitive Profile	Binary Representation
Logical-Mathematical	000
Linguistic	001
Musical	010
Spatial	011
Naturalist	100

Table 3. Knowledge Block Cognitive Profile ID

Considering that of the 10 (ten) cognitive profiles universally recognized (Gardner, 1993), only 5 (five) will be subject to analysis, since the remaining four - Corporal, Intrapersonal, Interpersonal and Existential can not be considered in the context of this work, because they are virtually impossible to quantify due to their strong abstract nature, we therefore will need only a 3 bit code to represent them.

Educational Level	Binary Representation
1st Grade	00000
...	...
Bachelor's	01000
...	...

Table 4. Knowledge Block Educational Level

In a similar way, the remaining 5 bits will identify the educational level best befitting the KB. The choice of such a wide identifier is related to the possibility of reaching 32 possible levels of identification, in a specific educational system. In Portugal, these values can easily go up to 23 levels. The exchange of the information between KB and the GA will be made through XML files. The (LMS), in turn, will provide the user with the KB appointed by the GA, in a dynamic way, changing the links according to the information received.

4.4 XML

XML and Java technology are recognized as ideal building blocks for developing services and applications that access services. Java Architecture for XML Binding (JAXB) is an XML binding model that defines the way of automatic mapping XML documents into objects in a programming language.

Two major processes, marshalling and unmarshalling, take care of the mapping between Java objects and XML documents, which makes JAXB surpass traditional Simple API for XML (SAX) and Document Object Model (DOM) approaches. Its advantages are (Liu & Shih, 2010):

- Simplicity: It is Java procedure to derive the classification (Schema-Derived Classes & Interfaces) through the outline that Binding Compiler compiles out, so does not need to deal with XML file by oneself, and does not deposit and withdraw the content tree without according to the order;
- Extensibility: The programmer can revise the schemas and derive the classification independently, and let the procedure accord with systematic requirements even more. Additionally, when XML Schema is changed to some extents, it just needs to recompile

Schema, and increase some more procedures newly, instead of needing to revise the original procedures.

- Efficiency: Because all content tree data is produced by JAXB according with the definition of XML Schema, no invalid methods on objects exist. Even it could use the Unmarshaller class to verify whether XML file is effective.

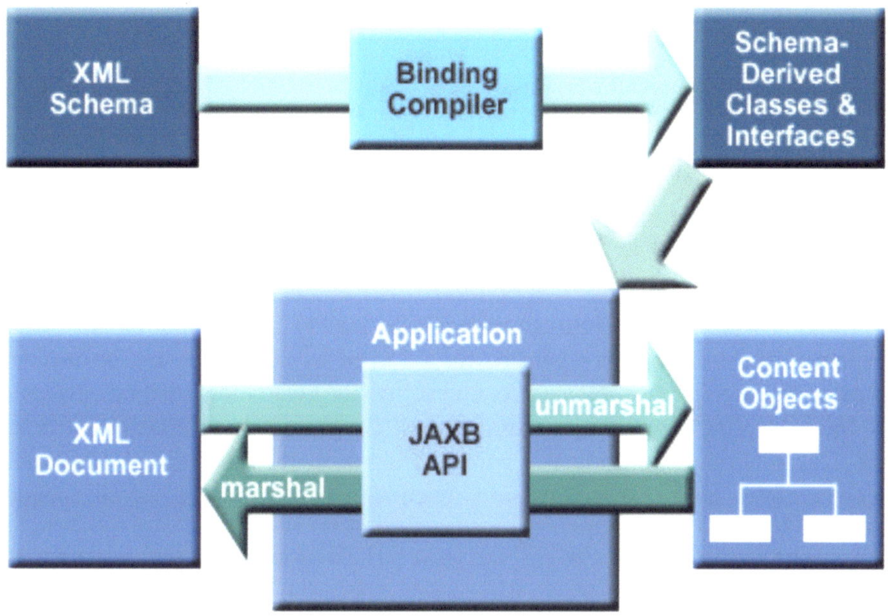

Fig. 13. Java Architecture for XML Binding (JAXB)

```
<language>
      <typename>
            <tysource sourcetype="imsdefault"/>
      <tyvalue>German</tyvalue>
      </typename>
      <contentype>
            <referential>

                  <indexid>language_01</indexid>
            </referential>
      </contentype>
      <proficiency profmode="OralSpeak">Excellent</proficiency>
      <proficiency profmode="OralComp">Excellent</proficiency>
      <proficiency profmode="Read">Good</proficiency>
      <proficiency profmode="Write">Poor</proficiency>
</language>
```

Fig. 14. XML example of a record containing information of classifications

The exchange of all the information between KB and GA will be made through XML files (Fig.14). The (LMS), in turn, will provide the user with the KB appointed by the GA, in a dynamic way, changing the links, according to the information received.

5. Conclusions and future work

The theoretic part of the work is ready. The authors have already designed all the interactions and mechanisms that will allow proceeding to the development phase. Field-testing will occur during this development. There is already a partner - a local kindergarten which has volunteered to test the results.

In order to evaluate the proposed system, a class of students (21 children involved) has been divided randomly into two groups. One group uses the described system, while the other follows the normal route. The tests will be performed during the current school year, after which we will get the results. During this period, the algorithm will be modified simultaneously in order to improve performance.

In the future, it will be taken into account the possibility of this solution to include the capacity to make several choices regarding the KB to be selected, allowing the improvement of two or more cognitive profiles. We intend to use evaluation methods by computer through the algorithm Cota-Groppo (Groppo, 2010), using a new interface to communicate with the GA, in order to introduce a better accuracy in the results. The introduction of psychological states, such as emotional and affective responses should also be considered in future work (Lin and et. al., 2010).

6. References

ADL (2009) Advanced Distributed Learning, SCORM, Available at: <http://www.adlnet.gov/scorm/>, [Last Visit 14/02/2009].

Alves, Paulo (2010). Advances in Artificial Intelligence to Model Student-Centered VLEs, Advances in Learning Processes, ISBN 978-953-7619-56-5.

Becker, K. & Vanzin, M. (2003). Discovering increasing usage patterns in web based learning environments, *Proc. Int. Conf. on Utility, Usability, and Complexity of e-information systems*, pp. 57–72

Dias, P. (2004). Comunidades de aprendizagem e formação online, Nov@Formação, Revista sobre a Formação à Distência & E-Learning, Inofor, pp. 14-17.

Dunn, R., Dunn, K. (1978). Teaching students throught their individual learning styles: A pratical approach. Reston Publishing, Reston, VA.

Edison, Thomas Alva, In: The Phrase Finder, 10.09.2011, Available from http://www.phrases.org.uk/meanings/genius-is-one-percent-perspiration-ninety-nine-percent-perspiration.html

Felder, R.M. & Silverman, L.K., (1998). Learning and teaching styles in engineering education. Engineering Education, Vol.78 No.7, pp. 674-681.

Feldman, Robert S. (2001). Compreender a psicologia, Editora McGraw-Hil de Portugal, 5ª Edição, Lisboa, Portugal.

Feuerstein, R. (1990). The theory of structural modifiability. In B. Presseisen (Ed.), Learning and thinking styles: Classroom interaction. Washington, DC: National Education Associations.

Fonseca, Victor (1999). Aprender a Aprender: A Educabilidade Cognitiva, Noticias Editorial, 2ª Edição, Lisboa, Portugal.

Gardner, H. (1993). Multiple intelligences: The theory in practice, Basic Books, New York, USA.

Groppo, Mario Alberto (2010). Métodos de Evaluación por Computadoras, para Reforzar la Interacción Docente-Alumno, Tesis Doctoral, Vigo, Spain.

Honey, P. & Mumford, A. (1992) The manual of Learning Styles, Peter Honey, Maidenhead, BerkShire.

Lin, Hongfei et al. (2010). Affective Computing in E-Learning, E-learning, ISBN 978-953-7619-95-4.

Liu, Feng-Jung and Shih, Bai-Jiun (2010). Application of Data-Mining Technology on E-Learning Material Recommendation, E-learning Experiences and Future, ISBN 978-953-307-092-6.

Madhour, Hend; and Forte, Maia Wentland (2010). Personalized Learning Path Delivery, Advances in Learning Processes, ISBN 978-953-7619-56-5.

Minaei-Bidgoli, B., Kashy, D.A., Kortemeyer, G., and Punch, W. F. (2003). Predicting student performance: an application of data mining methods with an educational webbased system, *Proc. IEEE conf. on Frontier in Education*, Vol. 1, pp. 13–18

Kazanidis , Ioannis and Satratzemi, Maya (2009). Towards the Integration of Adaptive Educational Systems with SCORM Standard and Authoring Toolkits, Advanced Learning, ISBN 978-953-307-010-0.

Kerkiri et al. (2010). A Learning Style - Driven Architecture Build on Open Source LMS's Infrastructure for Creation of Psycho-Pedagogically - 'Savvy' Personalized Learning Paths, E-learning Experiences and Future, ISBN 978-953-307-092-6.

Kolb D. (1984). Experimental Learning: experience as the source of learning and development, Prentice-Hall, New Jersey.

Riechmann, S.W., and Grasha, A.F. (1974). A Rational Approach to Developing and Assessing the Construct Validity of a Student Learning Style Scales Instrument. Journal of Psychology, Vol. 87, pp. 213-223.

Spiegel, Murray R. (1994). Estatística, MAKRON Books do Brasil Editora Lda, 3ª Edição, São Paulo, Brasil.

Standard deviation, In: Standard deviation, 24.09.2011, Available from http://en.wikipedia.org/wiki/Standard_deviation

Stiubiener, Itana ; Ruggiero , Wilson Vicente and Rosatelli, Marta (2010). An Approach in Personalistion and Privacy in E-Learning Systems, E-learning, ISBN 978-953-7619-95-4.

Talavera, L. & Gaudioso, E. (2004) Mining student data to characterize similar behavior groups in unstructured collaboration spaces, *Proc. of the Workshop on Artificial Intelligence in CSCL, 16th European Conference on Artificial Intelligence, ECAI2004*, pp. 17–23

Ueno, Maomi (2010). Bayesian Agent in e-Learning, E-learning Experiences and Future, ISBN 978-953-307-092-6.

Witkin, H.A., MMoore, C.A., Goodenough, D.R., Cox, P.W. (1977). Field dependent and field-independent cognitive styles and their implications. Review of Educational Research Vol.47, pp. 1-64.

9

A Multimedia Integrated Framework for Learning Management Systems

Nishantha Giguruwa, Danh Hoang Anh and Davar Pishva
Ritsumeikan Asia Pacific University
Japan

1. Introduction

In recent years, increasingly developing information and communication technology has altered the landscapes of social life and industrial activities for mankind. Every day, new Internet applications and more efficient ways of doing existing tasks are being discovered. Proliferation of the Internet, decreasing cost of hardware, enhancements in wireless communication, emergence of smart phones, and development of high resolution display technologies etc. are all leveraging technologies of the state of IT development that we witness today.

Development of information technology has been changing the way of teaching as well as learning; in that, e-learning opens new dimensions for education ranging from simple *file sharing* systems that facilitate dissemination of didactic material to sophisticated *smart classrooms* (Pishva, 2007) that transfer technology and know-how cultivated through years of rigorous academic/research endeavor from one location to many other locations. Forms of e-learning in today's context dominantly use computer software for delivering, tracking, and managing lectures; televised broadcasts and video conferencing characterize the earlier generations of distance education. Starting from educational policy concerns that e-learning initiatives are justified on the basis of cost efficiency, or the need to provide access to learners in educational settings, where face-to-face instruction is not feasible; today, we face a challenge of enhancing the quality and accessibility of educational resources via means that adapts to the lifestyles of learners. This challenge has opened interesting research streams to investigate technologies that leverage the best blend of *face-to-face* and *distant* education, referred to as *blended education*.

Today, *Learning Management Systems (LMS)* (Bersin, 2007) have become a readily available resource that provides an array of functionalities for content dissemination, student evaluation, and administration, to ensure effective delivery of education. Notwithstanding these functionalities, LMS in its current shape appears to be a system that has not captured the lifestyles of students (and teachers) in the modern society. A current day student (Veen, 2009) is a dynamic character immersed in a networked society, where education has to compete with many other vices in the *virtual marketplace*. This competing marketplace has not only detracts learners from academic efforts via many interesting vices such as online games, social networking systems, virtual avatars, on-demand video etc., but also bombards academic repositories with loads of information due to ever accumulating unsorted knowledge on the Internet. Additionally, decreasing study efforts due to "study while working" habits has placed a special demand for creating user-centered LMSs that adapt to the lifestyles of students and teachers.

In Ritsumeikan Asia Pacific University in Japan (APU), the authors have developed a prototype version of multimedia enhanced learning management system. APU, whose mission is to create world leaders in science, management and economics through a bilingual curriculum, has shown an increasing interest in adopting computer supported methodologies in its education system. Recent statistics show that the use of web-based instruction, as a supplement means to face-to-face instruction, has increased rapidly in APU (Nisantha, 2009), where Blackboard is used as an integral part of its education system since its establishment to serve nearly 6000 concurrent students and more than 200 teachers. Hence, the authors believe that their findings of the research endeavors in this very conducive environment, APU, will not only provide the reader with knowledge on practical and cost effective solutions on the authors' experience in custom tailoring an LMS with home grown technologies, but also conceptual framework solution for upgrading IT enabled education to accommodate modern students.

1.1 Leaning Management Systems (LMS)

Computer modalities and software systems, which are used to achieve blended learning objectives coupled with support to administrative and monitoring of educational courses, are generally termed Learning Management Systems[1] (LMS) (Bersin, 2007). The ever growing competition for education, which is mainly attributable to the vast amount of free form of information available over the Internet, has enforced the typical LMS systems to evolve from the conventional forms of mere record keeping and simple file distribution systems to complex systems with broader functionalities. This section explains the functional modules of a generic LMS, and presents a rationale to build up the thought process for future LMSs.

1.1.1 Learning Management Systems functions

The basic description of LMS is an application (usually a web based application) that automates the administration, tracking and reporting of learning/training events. The concept of LMS in today's context — range from simple systems for managing lecture notes to complex systems that provide an array of functionalities such as content authoring, course building, online examination, student evaluation, grade book, and collaborative learning — illustrated in Figure 1.

Some system modules, which are generally considered as complementary such as video conferencing, distance collaboration, and smart classrooms, are also included in the latest versions of LMS. However, not every LMS has all of above listed features — depending on

[1] Conventionally, LMS is referred to as the domain that takes control over the user interaction and user management of the learning process whereas *Learning Content Management System* (LCMS) is referred to as the domain that is responsible for managing the content. When the functionality of the learning platform concentrates more on handling courses it is called a course management system (CMS). In this paper we have been referring to the term LMS as a common term for LMS, CMS, and LCMS.

scale and needs, organizations can choose a suitable LMS for their operation. According to a survey conducted by Learning Circuits, the most valuable features of an LMS are shown in Figure 2.

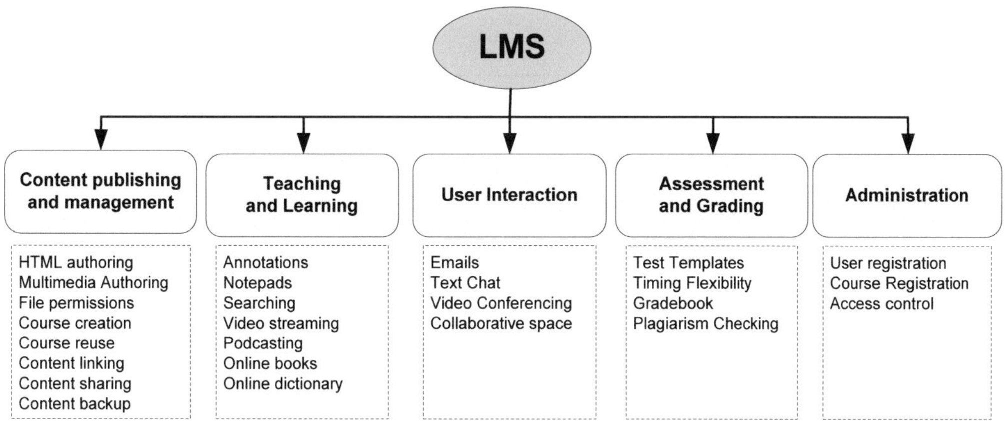

Fig. 1. General LMS functions categorized according to usage purpose

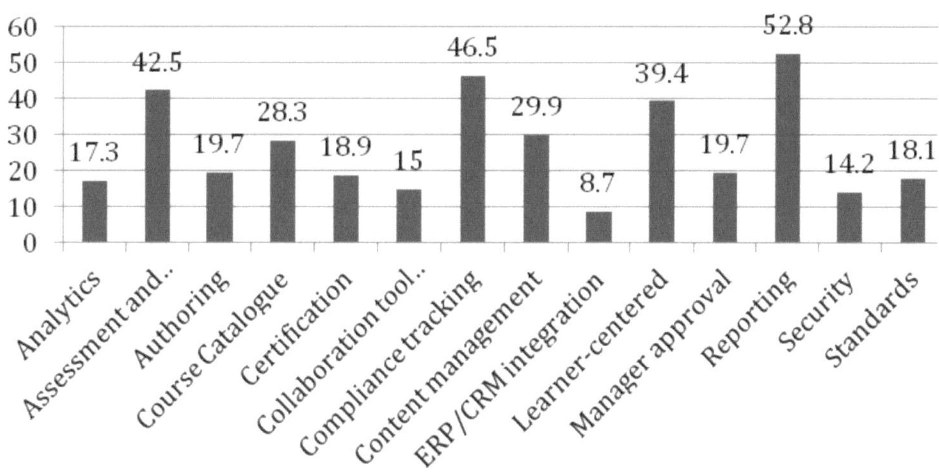

Fig. 2. Most valuable features of an LMS (%)

1.1.2 LMS Market

LMS solutions are currently available in both open source and commercial forms; popular representative solutions include Blackboard and Moodle. According to LMS evolution information, as illustrated in Figure 3, emergence of LMS has been very active in the late 1990s followed by its rapid evolution through many LMS generation in the next decade. Blackboard, which has claimed biggest share among the market players, acquired Prometheus in 2001, WebCT in February 2006, and Angel Learning in May 2009. It now clearly dominates the LMS market, with around 80% shares among US universities and over 50% among all universities around the world. Moodle - the most popular open source LMS solution also has achieved a great growth in recent years. Number of registered educational sites has increased from 25 thousand in 2008 to around 50 thousand as on March of 2010 giving evidence for the great trends and potentials of open source LMS.

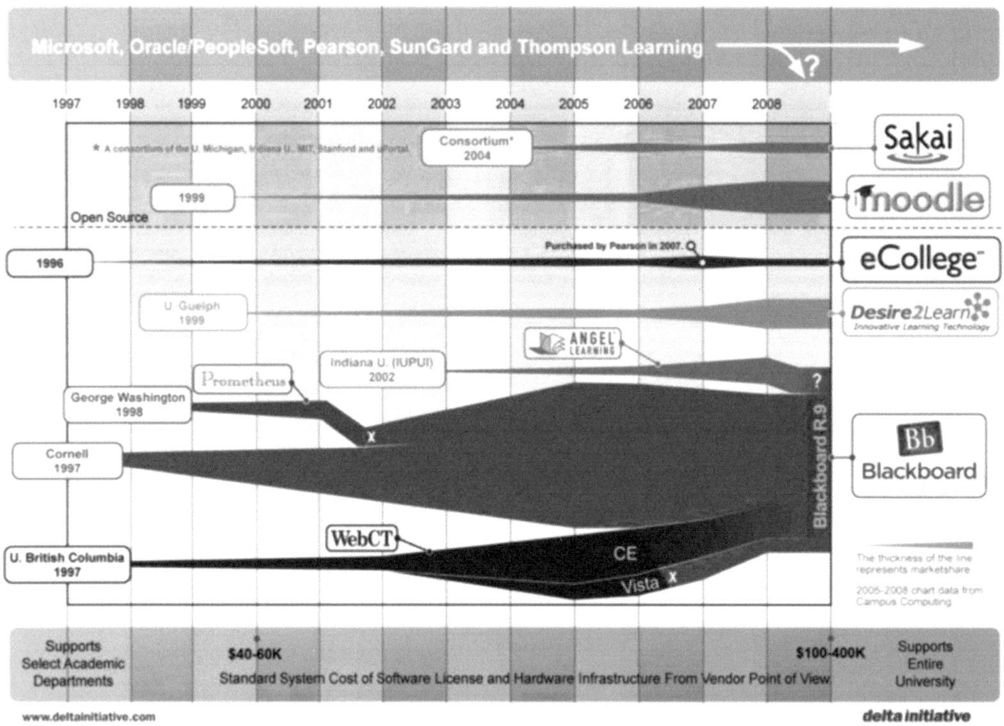

Fig. 3. LMS market share time line (Copyright http://www.deltainitiative.com)

1.1.3 LMS potential

The launch of new generation LMS such as Blackboard 9.0, D2L 2GO has resulted in a significant improvement in interaction among various parties: learners, teachers, instructors, and administrators. The potential of mobile technologies have also enhanced the functions available in LMSs with increasing numbers of mobile devices that can access Internet resources conveniently. Emergence of smart phones and smart devices such as iPod, iPhone, iPad, and Android are now being supported by major LMS like Blackboard Learn 9.0. Other LMS providers are also aware of the importance of LMS services via mobile devices. For instance, Desire2Learn Inc. ("D2L"), a global provider of enterprise e-Learning solutions, has also developed a mobile learning application called "Desire2Learn 2GO" which allows users to access course information from a BlackBerry mobile device. Moodle has also stated supporting mobile devices, including all Japanese mobiles, iPhone, and iPod touch since 2009.

According to The Instructional Technology Council, the top 5 growing areas of LMS segments are, namely: (a) online student organization and web services, (b) online counseling and advising, (c) online plagiarism evaluation, (d) online Audio\Video streaming, and (e) online textbook sales.

2. Multimedia in e-learning

As the name suggests, multimedia is a combination of different forms of media that contains information stored at varying granularities of time and space resolution. For example, a still image represents certain time of space with varying special resolution whereas an audio/video segment represents both time and special information in continuous form at varying resolutions. Text on the other hand is human interpreted state of certain event or series of events in time and space.

People understood the efficiency of using multimedia since long time ago: surgery model has become standard equipment in the biology class, the molecular model is a standard equipment of chemistry, and there is no geographic lecture if there are no maps. Modern multimedia encompasses assimilation of more media forms to deliver its contents to the consumers in a highly usable manner, in that, people can make use of their multiple senses at the same time to grasp information quickly and accurately. Virtual reality and augmented reality technologies have enabled perceiving things even beyond the perception of human senses.

2.1 Impact of multimedia in e-learning

Use of multimedia has been identified as an important element (Evans, 2007) in educational systems. High efficiency of using multimedia in education is caused by its characteristics, which includes:

- Mirrors the way in which the human mind thinks, learns, and remembers.
- The combination of media elements in a multimedia lesson enables trainees to learn more spontaneously and naturally, using whatever sensory modes they prefer, extending their experience to discover on their own, enable them with varying levels of literacy and mathematical skills to learn by using sight, hearing, and touch.
- Multimedia programs (expert systems) are designed to allow learners to pause, branch, or stop for further remediation, exploration, or enhancement opportunities; encouraging non-linear thinking.
- With the rapid development of mobile technology, the transfer speed of wireless mobile networks has dramatically increased with mobile access to multimedia contents, such as high quality on-demand video, video call, on-demand TV, etc. Multimedia is the only viable and effective content format that could be used effectively for education due to the mobile nature of users as well as due to small screens of devices.

Figure 4 illustrates positive effects of multimedia usage in education for two example cases. According to United States Department of Defense data (Oblinger, 1991), some useful conclusions are made on the effect of multimedia in education: short-term retention of approximately 20% of what is heard, 40% retention of what is seen and heard, and 75% what is seen, heard and done. Trainees can complete courses with multimedia in one-third of the time and reach competency levels up to 50% higher, compared to the performance of traditional instruction modes. Furthermore, in most of the cases, the overall cost of instruction is lower.

According to a separate study in CERT® (CERT, 2007) virtual training environment (VTE), as illustrated in Figure 5, it is a known fact that the best way to ensure mastery and retention of a specific instructional subject is to present the subject to the user in multiple increasingly-engaging formats. In an experiment where students read about a topic, hear about it, see it, and then put it into practice; the subject mastery level continues to increase as one utilizes more of his/her sensory powers.

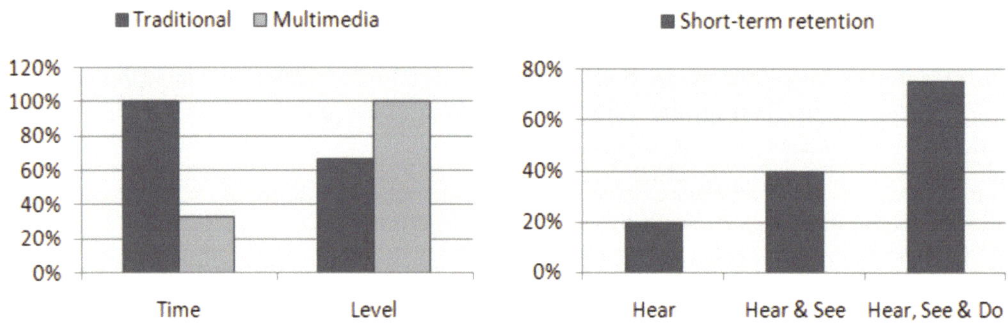

Fig. 4. Positive affection of multimedia on education

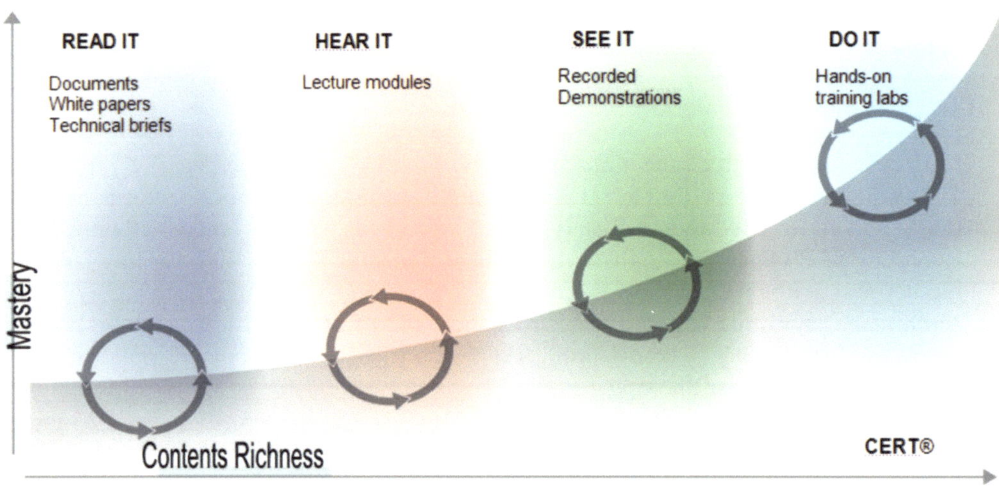

Fig. 5. Multi-modal learning reinforcement in VTE

2.2 Multimedia usage in current LMS

Despite the mighty of multimedia content in didactic material, its usage in learning management systems is still not straightforward due to many reasons. First, multimedia handling involves large amount of computing power and storage volume requiring improvements to current equipment; second, multimedia dissemination requires high-band width links which needs costly investment for network improvements; third, student-side gadgets are not readily available for all students to capture and render multimedia; and fourth, teaching pedagogies have not yet captured the important semantics of multimedia based learning.

Due to the reasons explained above, multimedia content usage in LMS is not fully explored yet. The way multimodal contents is used in education, today, is by making use of classic file transfer and media handling technologies to disseminate multimedia in parallel to LMS operation. In Ritsumeikan Asia Pacific University, a content authoring dissemination system that uses a combination of FTP server, multimedia server, and Blackboard has been used for this purpose, as illustrated in Figure 6.

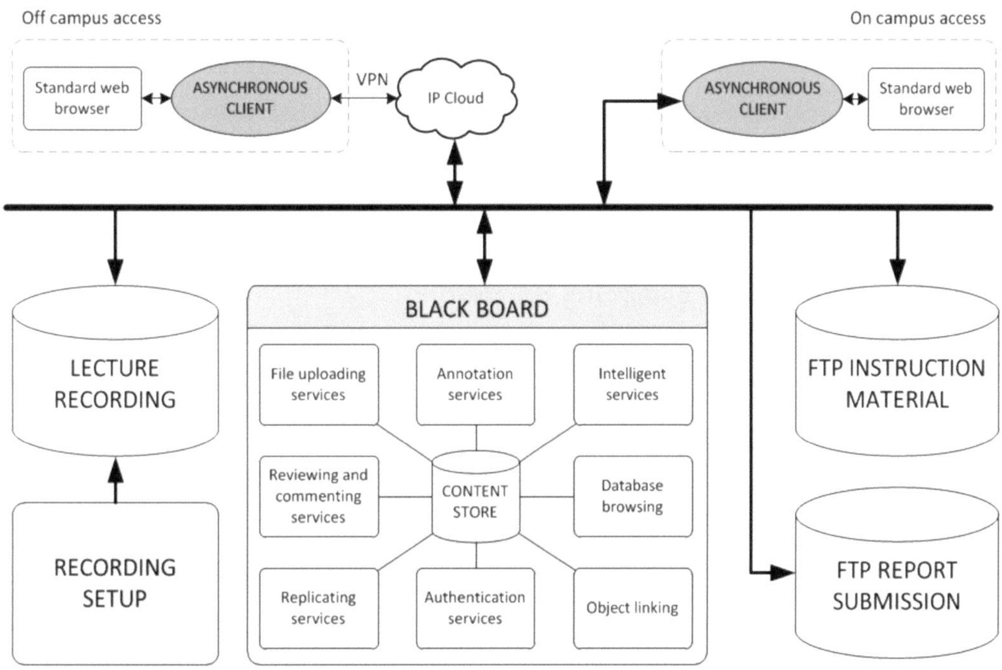

Fig. 6. Components of the ICT based educational platform in APU

- **FTP file server**: File Transfer Protocol file server holds two sub-folders, Instructional Material and Submit Report for all lectures. Instructional Materials contain course contents while the Submit Report folder is used for students to submit their assignments.
- **WebCT/Blackboard system**: From the year 2000 to 2007 APU used WebCT, a web-based course management system and in 2008, APU upgraded the LMS system to Blackboard because it was found to be more user-friendly and supports more functions. Presently APU is still using Blackboard and the Blackboard site is accessible off campus requiring virtual private networks (VPN) for some specific pages.
- **Lecture recording and Multimedia streaming server**: Class discussion and lectures can be recorded using a special mobile recording equipment set (fixed installation is limited to a few lecture rooms) and the recorded clips are uploaded to the multimedia streaming server that uses synchronous multimedia integration language (SMIL).
- **Custom-made LMS**: Some lectures in APU are using their own LMS. In the ICT institute in APU the creators use a custom-made LMS, basically a modified version of Claroline, to best accommodate their teaching pedagogy.

It can be also observed that trials of close integration of multimedia in LMS are emerging. WebCT/Blackboard system (BlackBoard inc., 2009), heavily used commercial LMS today, has integrated virtual classroom/collaboration functionality in its latest (Windows Vista compatible) version. Moodle, a heavily used open source LMS, has also integrated a multimedia plug-in, named DimDim, to facilitate primitive video conferencing capability. Many academic institutions reportedly have added an array of custom multimedia functionalities either as an integrated tool to the LMS or as and independent tool to quickly cater the demanding needs for multimedia functionalities. While the technology is moving toward a multimedia rich learning management system, its practical deployments is still far away, due to many unsolved technical and pedagogical problems. Therefore, in Asia Pacific University in Japan, we have started developing a Ubiquitous Multimedia Enhanced Learning Management System (umeLMS) to enhance its education quality while reducing the user burden. The term ume (ゆめ：pronounced as Yume) in Japanese Language means dream: hence we envision an ideal LMS (dream LMS) to enhance the quality of education.

3. Multimedia integrated e-learning framework

In devising the integrated framework for LMS implementation, requirement of all stake holder groups are to be addressed: a user-centric, customized, content rich, and ubiquitous learning environment is aimed. The target LMS must ensure a leaning environment that characterises a consolidated system with many tangible features, such as (a) reduced cost and time consumption, (b) reduced workload, (c) enhanced educational quality, (d) enhanced system accessibility, and (e) enhanced usability. This section elaborates the integral components of multimedia integrated framework, namely: input integration, content generation, and access integration scenarios used to accomplish this task.

3.1 LMS content model

Figure 7 illustrates the life cycle of a generic course indicating its didactic contents, associated access scenarios, and interaction of its stakeholders (i.e. administrators, teachers & lectures). Involvement of multimedia in this model covers major portion of content volume and plays a significant role in supporting the learner and teacher in understanding the course content, evaluating students' progress, report back to the lecturer, and participate in group discussions. Although continuous multimedia is recorded with relevant time-space information in full, its usefulness is a relative measure; without user having access to smooth reception of multimedia, and without user having required access modalities to traverse a multimedia clip over its full length of duration, usability of multimedia content is very low. Multimedia should always reach users with high availability both in time and space with adequate metadata embedded, supporting application metaphors to implement semantic navigation modalities (through book marking, cross linking, filtering, and data mining etc).

3.2 Integrated framework architecture

The LMS framework proposed in this work essentially addresses several important design aspects through a modular design approach. Figure 8 illustrates this modular architecture with corresponding implementation technologies shown on the right side of the diagram. *Content Store* (CS) facilitates storing of content in the hard disk with required backup and synchronizing support. *Content management and integration module* (CMIM) is responsible for content management functions such as authoring and versioning. Two separate modules

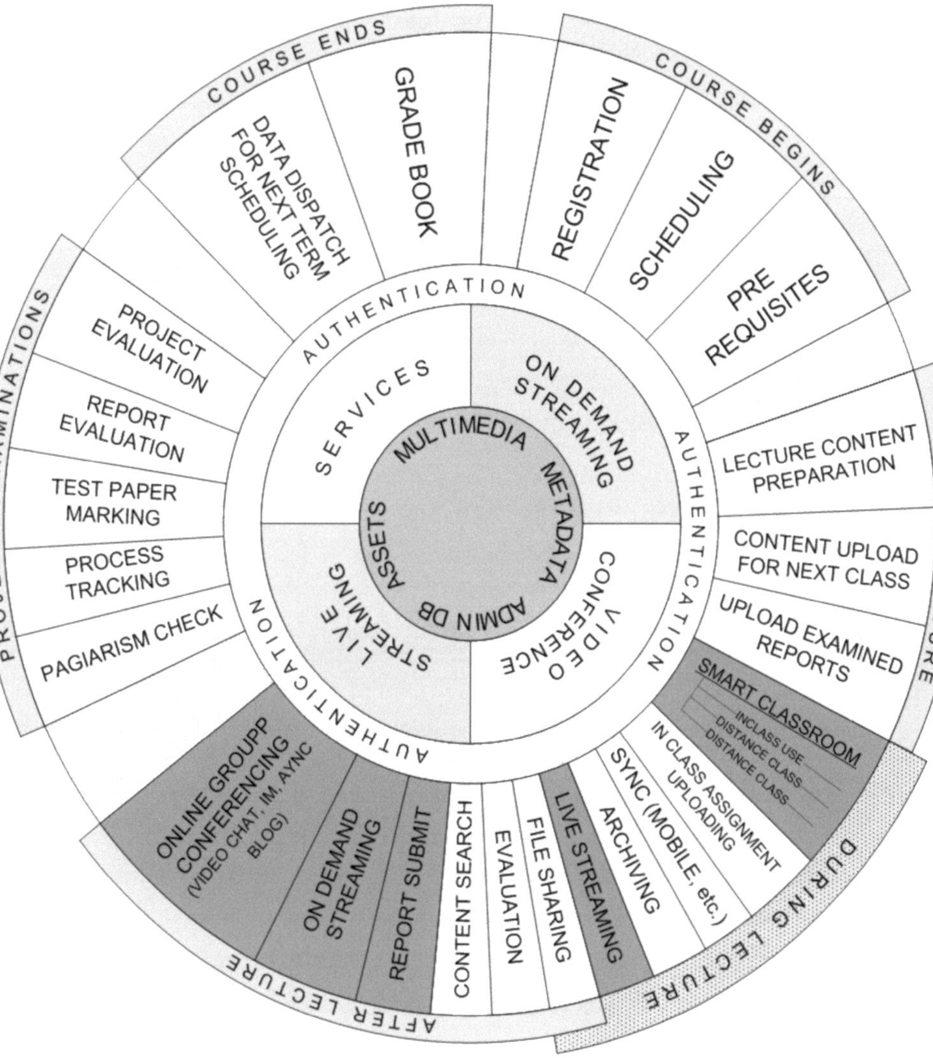

Fig. 7. Content model and access scenarios for a course life cycle in integrated LMS

that operates on top of CMIM are dedicated for input and output functionalities namely; *learning management module* (LMM) to support various learning/teaching scenarios and *multimedia management module* (MMM) to house functionality to handle multimedia content authoring and dissemination metaphors associated with LMM functions. *User management module* (UMM) module is indispensible to manage the front-office of the system such as registration, authentication, and notifications. UMM manages users as well as user groups and implements access authorization to the system resources through the functional modules LMM and MMM. UMM also passes very important parameters to its underlying service interfaces on the access behavior of users, which makes sophisticated user-centric implementation possible. This modular design also enables interfacing with complementary modules that the authors have proposed as separate work such as project management and evaluation system (Long, 2008) industrial student internship program (SIIP) (Tanaka, 2009) and smart classrooms (Pishva, 2008). These modules essentially support a framework that characterizes three modes of system integration, namely: (a) input integration, (b) content integration, and (c) access integration.

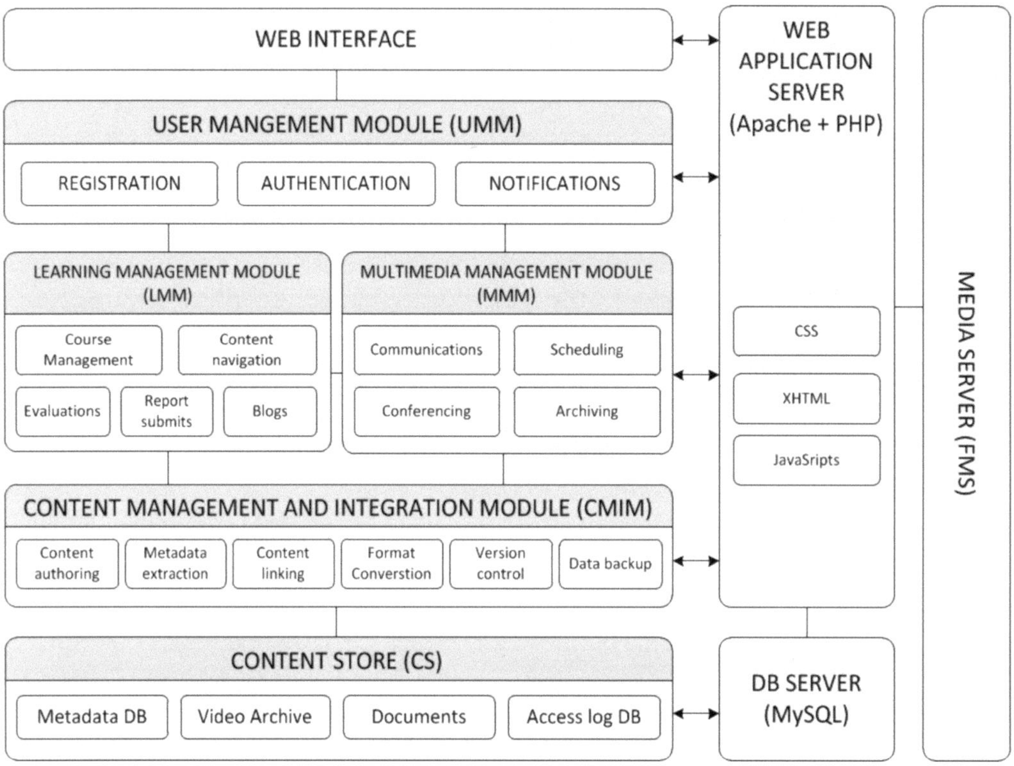

Fig. 8. Modular architecture of umeLMS

Figure 9 illustrates multimodal sources of content originated by both teachers and learners, devices involved, and various access scenarios of the proposed *user centric learning* (u-learning) framework.

3.3 Input Integration

Input integration refers to capturing various multimedia inputs to enhance the richness of lecture content. Following multimedia input methods are of major concern for maximizing multimedia richness in teaching as well as learning:

3.3.1 Lecture recording

Lecture recording has become more and more popular in all types of academic institutions, nowadays. However, in most cases it is used as a single stream audio video recording and often not integrated to the LMS, but facilitated as an adjunct multimedia dissemination system supported by loosely coupled cross links with the LMS. In most systems (e.g. the recording system currently used in Asia Pacific University), human interaction is required for recording, uploading, and creating a hyperlinks. The recording mechanism proposed in

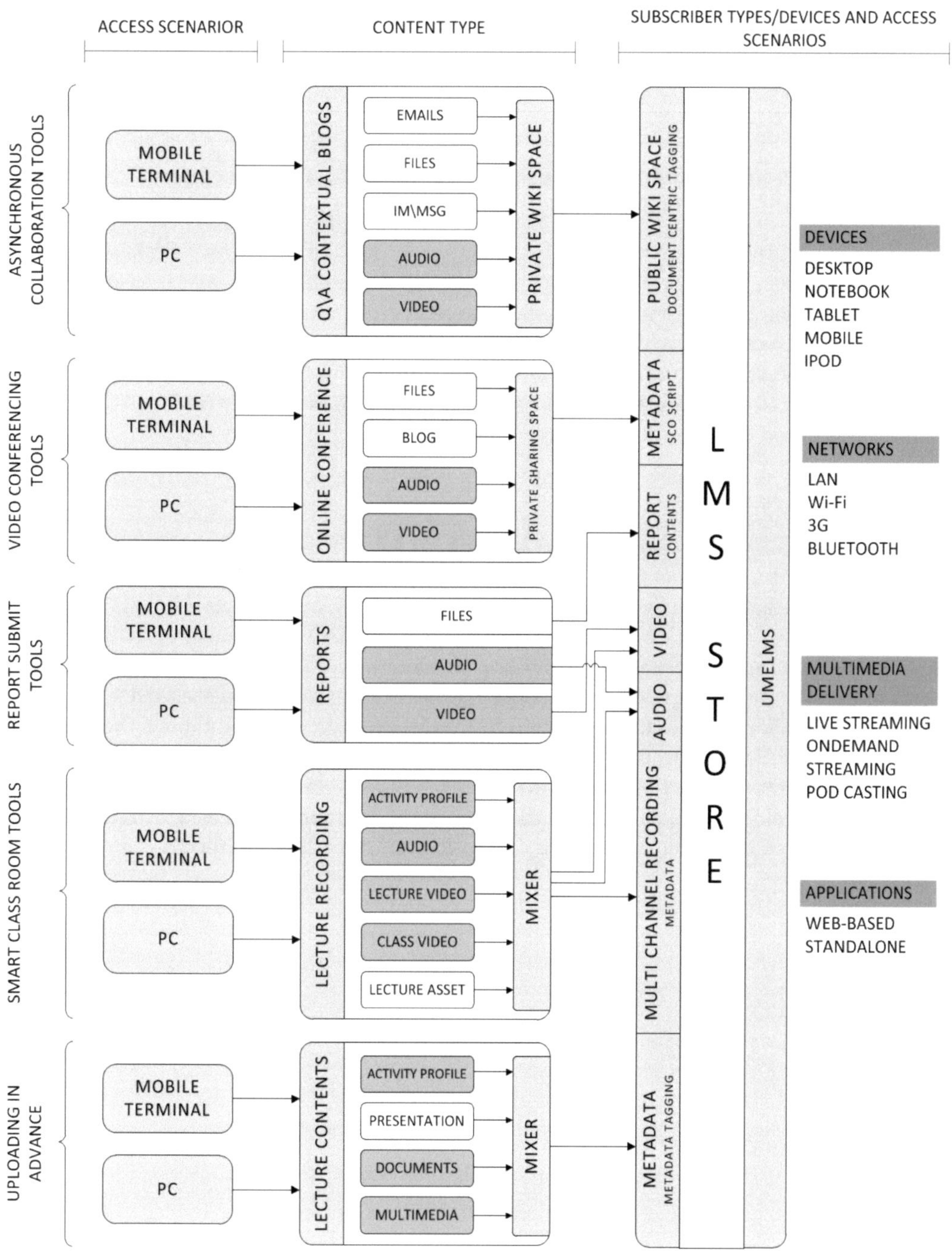

Fig. 9. Content, devices and access scenarios in multimedia enhanced u-Learning framework

these papers essentially involves automated capturing of multiple video channels, multiple audio channels, and projector/PC screen on which the teacher is presenting. The recording captures the important activity of the classroom by automatically analyzing the behavior of signals in various input streams and then forming a combined streaming for recording. This form of recording is proposed by other research as well such as *smart classroom* implementations (e.g. Pishva, 2008), but they often require sophisticated and costly equipment.

In this work we propose a cost effective methodology that uses a single dedicated PC per classroom to process multiple audio-visual inputs and form a composite stream for recording as illustrated in Figure 10.

Video inputs are captured from three IP cameras pointing to the lecturer's desk, whiteboard and the students. Voice of the teacher is captured from the main audio system in the classroom and the audio from the students is captured from the microphones in IP cameras. The lecturer's screen is used as the default video input. Depending on the classroom activity inferred by the system on various inputs, the recording PC forms a composite video stream and transmits it to the video server for archiving. Flash Media Server (FMS) (Adobe, 2010) technology is used to implement the streaming functionality at the server.

3.3.2 User side recording

Existing LMSs allow the user (teacher/student) to submit their reports, suggestions, and comments as document attachments. The user centric learning framework proposed in this work suggests that the users should be facilitated with application metaphors submit multimedia reports through devices they use in daily life. This enables enhanced interaction among students and teachers by providing an interface to query and answer without wasting time, without the need to purchase special devices and software, and without the need to be familiar with multimedia processing knowledge. By combining the user-side recording function with content integration feature, users are given privilege to manipulate their own multimedia rich resource database, which is attributable for establishing a sustainable learning process. A client side recording solution involves a similar, but less complicated, system implementation as in the lecture recording architecture illustrated in Figure 10.

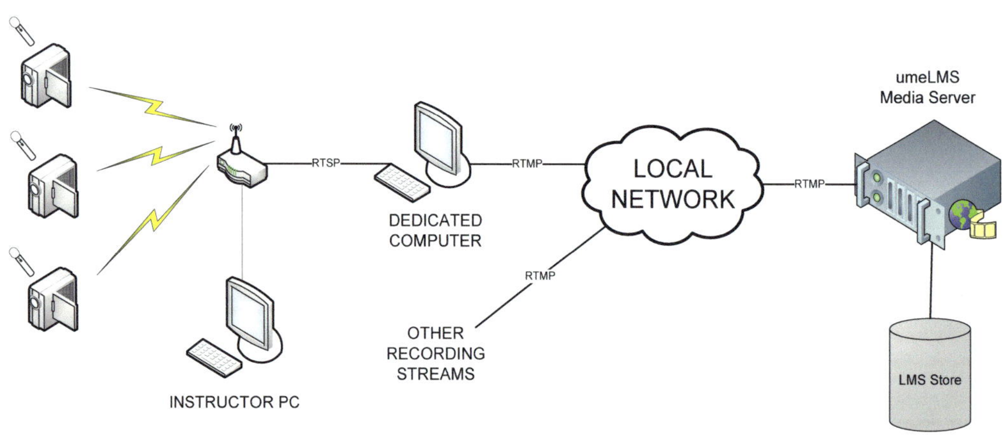

Fig. 10. Lecture recording architecture

3.3.3 Live conferencing

Live conferencing features are used in many fields including education, office management, business interactions, clinical activities, and e-commerce services. In education, live conferencing is strongly supported by commercial LMS; open source LMS have less built-in-features for live conferencing. Existing live conferencing modules, anyway, are not fully integrated in to LMS – some complementary tools like Skype, and conferenceXP, are used in collaboration with LMS, in most cases. The proposed framework deploys flash media server (FMS) that can provide high quality and flexible synchronous media streaming ,which can closely integrate live conferencing with the core LMS. Media contents are streamed via links between client and FMS through RTMP protocol (HTTP tunneling supported). LMS media server implements many support functions such as, stream forwarding, multi-stream recording, and multi-party session controlling to enable close integration of live conferencing with LMS. In live conferencing, each client will receive the downstream multimedia streams from the media server and transmits the upstream components into the media server, synchronously. The media server receives all video streams and forward multimedia to respective members, as governed by its session controlling mechanism.

3.3.4 Multimedia blogs

The proposed e-learning framework support blog based asynchronous group scenarios to use more multimedia contents. This means using of multimedia objects (image, video, audio, and vector graphics) to replace the conventional modes of text based interaction in blogs.

3.4 Content integration

Having built up the content store with a mixture of related hypermedia elements (i.e. lecture contents, lecture recording, report submissions and client side multimedia), it is required to relate different elements for enhanced accessibility. We adopt a metadata model to implement a semantic linking mechanism as presented in (Hiromitsu, 2005) to relate different elements in the LMS store. The content model we adopt allows context aware navigation rather than conventional hierarchical browsing, which enables flexible content views such as lecturer centric, student centric, course centric and activity centric as illustrated in Figure 11.

The students/lectures are given an interface to store the contents in an inter-related way using semantic cross-links such that the content navigation becomes easier and faster. The need for creating manual links is avoided as far as possible. Different elements inherit relations are based on the context that it creates. The access rights are also defined on contextual grounds at the time the object is created. The lecturer/course admin are given privileges to override these access rights.

3.4.1 SCO content model

We propose a Sharable Content Model (SCO) that enables content sharing and in the LMS. We adopt this model, similar to SCORM, to facilitate a well defined content structure while keeping the content development burden as low as possible to the teachers. However, in order to keep this SCO methodology less complex, we keep away from the standard SCO models, but use a simple and structures custom SCO model for content management. Here,

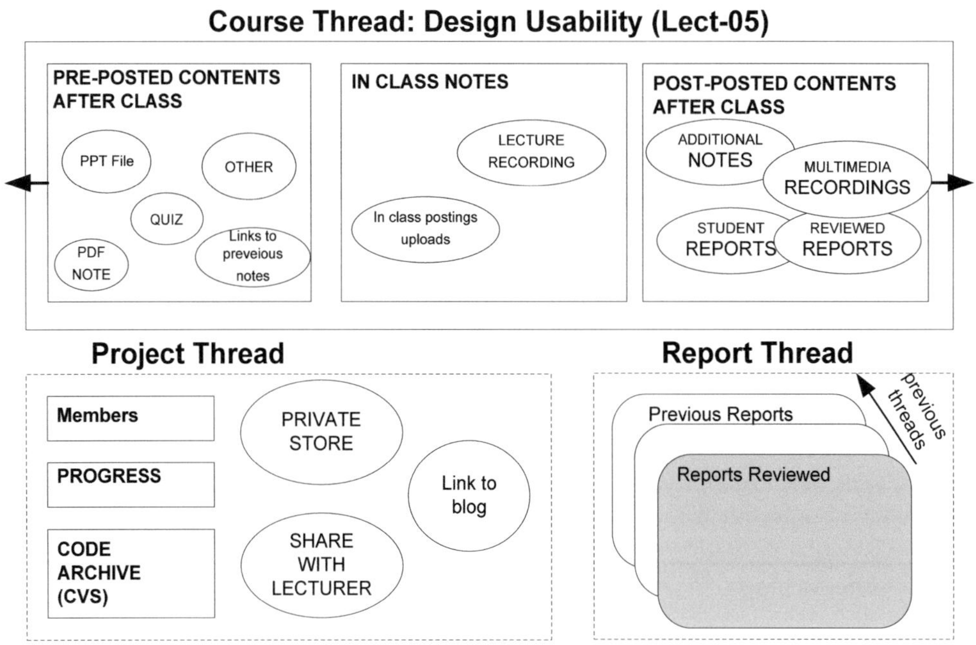

Fig. 11. Schematic of the integrated content model. (Relate this to SCO)

content associated with a course are stored physically in a flat file store, but conceptually placed within an abstract folder as dictated by metadata-content relationships. All metadata is stored in a single file named manifest.xml (here we use the same methodology adopted in SCORM), and content files (i.e. documents, multimedia files) are stored in the file store without any alterations.

3.4.2 Content authoring

Figure 12 (left side) shows the formation of SCO script in manifest.xml. The SCO publisher assimilates different types of hypermedia inputs as shown in (II.b) and generates manifest.xml file (III.b). Hypermedia input in (II.b) is saved in the proper service location (ie. Data Server, Web Server or Media Server). Metadata for generating the SCO object is captured from user behaviour, user input, and scanning the input content by the system. Input files that do not generate any metadata description, will all be stored as linked *assets* of the course contents. In this approach, content corresponding to one course are packaged in to one abstract container with a *manifest* file.

3.4.3 Content rendering

With reference to Figure 12, when a client request to access an object from Web Server (1) , the web Server will check the data server and get the metadata information of that object (SCO compliant) (2,3). After receiving the requested information from the data server (objects permission, file info, etc.) (4), web server will render the HTML output, with embedded objects or hyperlinks to contents. In case of media streaming, the web server will pass the required information for the client to communicate directly with the media server (6,9) and instructs the media server to service the client (7,8).

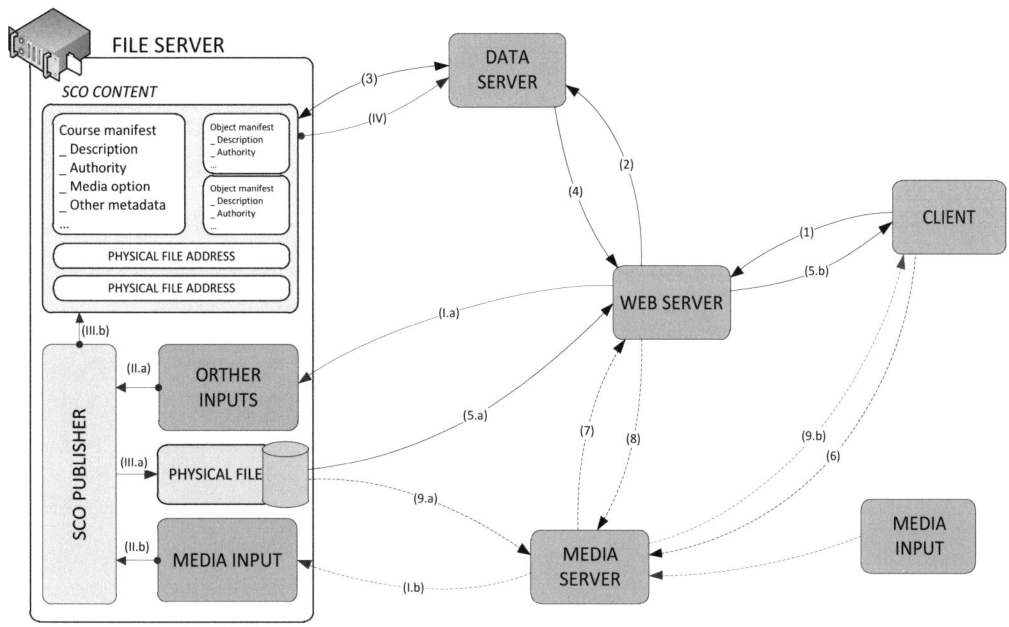

Fig. 12. SCO content integration

3.5 Access integration

Ubiquitous access is one of major goals of the development of proposed e-learning framework by which the LMS system is open to ubiquitous access through desktop as well as mobile devices. This is made possible by using *flash streaming technology* which currently a dominating element of *rich Internet application* (RIA) market. Flash technology is supported by almost all internet browsers and installed virtually in all computers irrespective of the operating system. The media streaming system in this framework adopts Flash Media Server (FSM), which provides the ability to stream live videos or video on demand contents, flexibly. Using FMS, multimedia can be accessed by almost all desktop platforms as well as mobile devices without the need for tedious software installations.

Mobile clients can access the content store using most of the smart phones. Moreover, the mobile network having been dramatically developed over the last 5 years and 3G/4G streaming is capable of smooth streaming of high data rate videos such as live TV, even in fast moving environments (e.g. while traveling by busses, trains etc.) There is not much differences in developing desktop applications and mobile application, due to the advent of Flash 8, which brings the gap between mobile and desktop content closer by supporting FLV video, H.264 video, as well as On2 VP6, and Sorenson video codecs. This framework majorly adopts streaming in FLV video format, which can be realized by FSM in a highly scalable manner.

4. Implementation of UMELMS

UMELMS, *Ubiquitous Multimedia Enhanced Learning Management System*, has been prototyped and tested in Ritsumeikan Asia Pacific University (APU) in 2010 for six months, as a supplementary system, to support the delivery of some selected course. Especially, the lecture recording system of UMELMS was used to record some of the lectures (ICT courses) in the university followed by an attempt to cross link all other didactic materials to lecture recording through meta data tagging. Using this LMS, the course creators can manage and create new multimedia content including lecture records by a central control panel. The experiments conducted in APU network environment resulted good performance proving the system efficiency in many aspects, such as system robustness, device compatibility, and scalability.

4.1 Working environment

APU is a pretty young and international university, where nearly 6000 foreign and domestic students are served with a bilingual curriculum. Currently, around 2500 PCs are used in APU to realize IT enabled education; PCs are connected through a 100Mbps local area network with an external connection operating at 400Mbps. A fast Wi-Fi network that covers a large area over APU campus and facilitate concurrent access to a large number of mobile phones and other smart devices. In conclusion, APU's network environment is highly conducive to reap the best potential of multimedia rich content delivery for education, making it an ideal place to benchmark the UMELMS system. APU's IT enabled resources setup is illustrated in Figure 13.

Fig. 13. Classrooms and device setup in APU

4.2 UMELMS system setup

UMELMS system is developed using the framework explained in Section 2. A Web Server is built upon the resources, L(W)AMP stack (which stands for Linux or Windows), Apache, MySQL and PHP. UMELMS Media Server, powered by Flash Media Interactive Server, was hosted in another dedicated Windows server. All the servers of UMELMS are connected with the APU network through 100Mbps Ethernet connection. The testing server is equipped with Intel Xeon X3353 2.66GHz, 4GB of RAM, Broadcom NetXtreme Gigabit Ethernet Card, and Barracuda ES.2 SATA 3.0Gb/s 500GB HDD x 2 with average speed of 80MB/s. UMELMS does not require any complicated installation in order to perform a new recording, editing, and playback. For example, the only requirement to perform a new class record session is a camera connected to a certain computer that can access the APU network. The recording process is mangled through a web interface on the PC with camera connections. In the practical system, a dedicated computer with Adobe platform applications can be used as a part of recording system to manipulate videos before streaming them up to the server; the process can be done either automatically or manually.

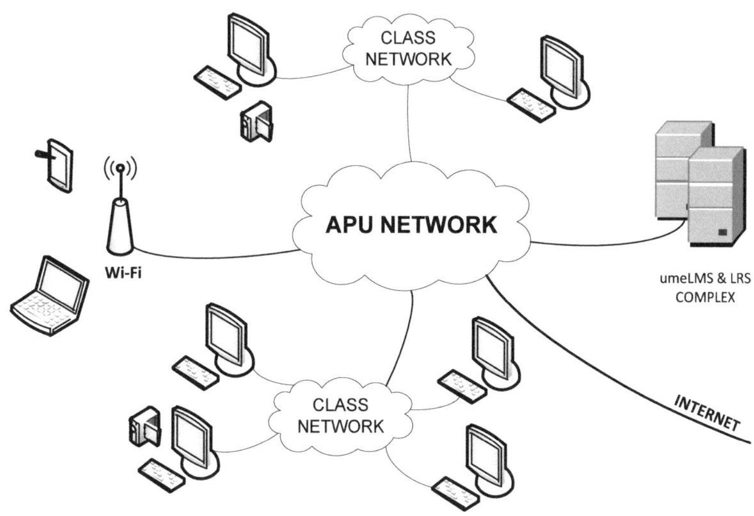

Fig. 14. Network environment in APU

4.3 Implementation and deployment

UMELMS Web Server and *UMELMS* Media server communicate with each other through a low-level API system (i.e. interface of multimedia management module (MMM) and learning management module (LMM). When Media Server wants to communicate with the web server, it will uses the web service (written in PHP) and make an XML-RPC (Remote Procedure Call) to request the user authenticating data. On the other hand, when Web Server wants to initiates media services (e.g. make a Live Conference through Media Server), it will request Media Server through a similar method. The client (desktops or handheld device) only need a Flash supported browser to access Web Server, everything will be taken care in server-side.

Figure 15 illustrates a snap shot of UMELMS showing video playback and student's personal notes. By this way, each student can maintain his/her own study profile.

Fig. 15. A snapshot of umeLMS showing video playback and student's personal notes

4.4 Evaluation

Experiments show that the system requires 1Mbps bandwidth to handle one streaming session at high quality (720px*405px 24fps). According to the estimation from evaluation result, the archiving server is able to handle approximately 360 concurrent recordings while keeping the system workload under 70%. The number of current recording sessions is limited to this value mainly because of the memory usage.

As UMELMS multimedia controls are Flash based, users can access its content using a wide range of devices that supports flash. The Lecture Recording System is fully automatic and eliminates unnecessary delays caused by manual uploading, making the lecture record able to be used as live streaming during the lecture, and as on demand streaming after the lecture.

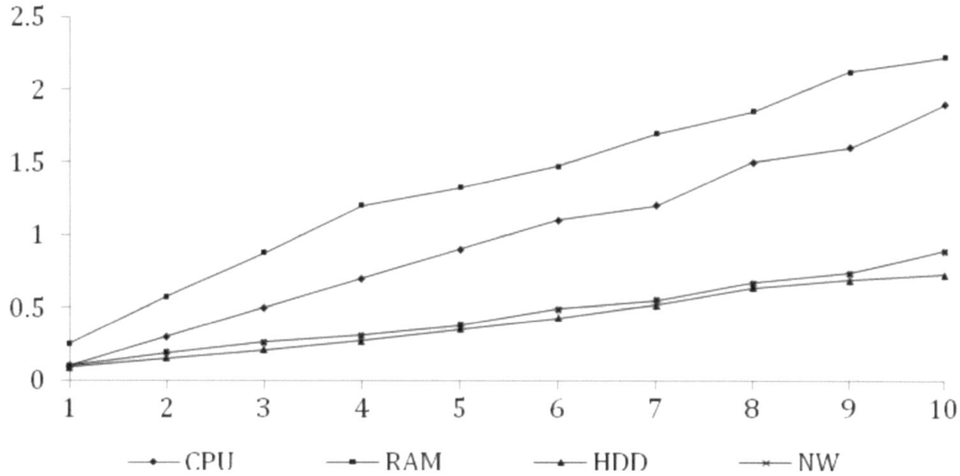

Fig. 16. Server resource usage (%)

5. Conclusion

In this work we presented a framework for implementing a content integrated learning management system with specific focus on multimedia enrichment in learning content. To implement this we propose SCO based content model and a flash based multimedia framework, with which content captured from various sources is integrated. This concept is demonstrated by implementing ubiquitous multimedia enhance learning management system (umeLMS) in Ritsumeikan Asia Pacific University.

6. References

Adobe - Flash Media Server documentation . (2010). Retrieved from Adobe Coorporation: http://www.adobe.com/support/documentation/en/flashmediaserver/

Bersin, J., Howard, C., & Leonard, K. O. (2007). *Learning Management Systems 2008: Facts, Practical Analysis, Trends and Vendor Profiles.* Bersin & Associates Learning Leaders® press.

Bersin, J., Howard, C., & Leonard, K. O. (2007). *Learning Management Systems 2008: Facts, Practical Analysis, Trends and Vendor Profiles.* Bersin & Associates Learning Leaders® press.

Blackboard home page. (2009). Retrieved from http://www.blackboard.com/

Chen, H.-Y., & Liu, K.-Y. (2008). Web-based synchronized multimedia lecture system design for teaching/learning Chinese as second language. *Computer Education , 50* (3), 693-702.

D, O. (2007). Introduction to multimedia in instruction. *Maximizing multimedia: A how-to-session for faculty.* Dallas County Community College District at Dallas.

Evans, C., & Gibbons, N. J. (2007). The interactivity effect in multimedia learning. *49* (4), 1147-1160.

Hiromitsu Hita, Nishantha, G. G., & Hayashida, Y. (2005). A File System with Semantic Links for Supporting Asynchronous Collaboration (in Japanese). *IEICE Regional Conference.* Fukuoka, Japan: IEICE Kyushu Branch.

Long, T., Nishantha, G. G., & Hayashida, Y. (2008). Integrating Project Management Feature in Learning Management Systems. *IEICE conference in Kyushu.* Oita, Japan: IEICE Kyushu Branch.

Nishantha, G. G., Anh, D. H., Pishva, D., & Claster, W. B. (2009). Multimedia Enhanced Learning Management Framework. *CSEDU 2009,* (pp. 267-272). Lisboa, Portugal.

Pishva, D., & Nishantha, G. (2008). Smart Classrooms for Distance Education and their Adoption to Multiple Classroom Architecture. *Journal of Networks (JNW) , 3* (5), 54-63.

Veen, W. Homo Zappiens, Learning in a Digital Age, key note address. *CSEDU 2009, International Conference on Computer Supported Education* (pp. 23-26). Lisbao, Portugal: 2009.

Woods, R., Baker, J., & Hopper, D. (2004). Hybrid structure: Faculty use and perception of Web-based courseware as a supplement to face-toface instruction. *Internet & Higher Education , 7* (4), 281-297.

10

Ontology Alignment OWL-Lite

Aammou Souhaib, Khaldi Mohamed and El Kadiri Kamal Eddine
LIROSA, Faculté des Sciences, Université Abdelmalek Essaadi, Tétouan, Maroc

1. Introduction

The term ontology was originally used in philosophy from the 19i-th century. In this area, it refers to the study of what exists, ie, the body of knowledge about the world (Welty et al., 2001). In the field of knowledge representation, ontologies are considered as relating to different fields of knowledge. They respond to problems of representation and manipulation of knowledge. Ontology is "is an explicit specification of a conceptualization" (Gruber, 1993). Ontologies are widely used in knowledge representation on the Web (Charlet et al., 2004). Nowadays, ontology embodies expert knowledge of a domain. Based on the fact that knowledge can take many different representations, there are nowadays several domain ontologies for the same scope. The alignment techniques represent a general framework in which several ontologies can be exploited.

The alignment also allows the exchange of a semantic point of view, the view of many people (Bach et al., 2004). Although some work on ontologies show the necessity of using domain knowledge (Aleksovski et al., 2006) in certain situations, several methods for ontology alignment that do not have domain knowledge been developed. The main methods are cited: ANCHORPROMPT (Noy et al., 2001), IF-MAP (Kalfoglou et al., 2003), ASCO (Bach et al., 2004), GLUE (Doan et al., 2004), QOM (Ehrig et al., 2004a) and OLA (Euzenat et al., 2004b). These main methods1 exploit ontologies in format markup languages (XML, RDF (S) and OWL-Lite2). In addition, most of these methods exploit similarity measures that cover more or less the whole structure of ontologies to align. These methods generally exploit a threshold of stability provided by the user, to ensure the cessation of the alignment process.

However, this level of stabilization does not spread wide for the calculation of similarity. The OLA is the only method to have the advantage of support for OWL ontologies format-Lie. The OLA method uses a threshold of stabilization to calculate the alignment. Alignment method proposed in this research can implement a new algorithm for automatic alignment of ontologies OWL-Lite. In each pair of entities belonging to the same category, the alignment algorithm calculates the similarity measures. It defines two models for calculating the similarity (local and global), while addressing the problem of circularity and user intervention in the alignment process. The experimental results show an improvement of evaluation metrics from OLA.

The paper is organized as follows. The second section provides a comparative study of the main methods of ontology alignment chosen. In the third section, our method of aligning ontologies OWL-Lite is described. The fourth section shows an experimental evaluation. The conclusion and future work are the subject of the last section.

2. Comparative study of methods of alignment

Ontologies created can be described in several languages, eg, XML (Marsh, 2001), RDF (S) (Klyne et al., 2004), DAML + OIL (Connolly et al., 2001) and OWL (Smith et al., 2004). The purpose of these languages is to represent the ontologies in a common language. OWL also enables the sharing, import and export ontologies. It is considered the standard ontology for the domain of Semantic Web (Berners-Lee et al., 2001). For these reasons any ontology that is not described in OWL drawbacks. The alignment of two ontologies is to find a match between their entities that are semantically similar (Ehrig et al., 2004b). In a formal way, alignment is defined by the map function as follows:

$$Map : O \rightarrow O' \text{ such that } map(e_1) = e_1' \qquad \text{if } sim(e_1, e_1') > t,$$

Where O and O′ are the two ontologies to align, means a minimum threshold of similarity belonging to the interval [0,1], $e_1 \in O$ and $e_1 \in O'$. This threshold indicates the minimum level for two entities are similar. Each entity e_i is more aligned to a single entity e_j'. Several criteria were used for the comparison of alignment methods, eg, the input format, output format, the measures of similarity and the quality of alignment (Do et al., 2002).

In the remainder of this section we detail the formats for input and output measures of similarity and the quality of alignment.

2.1 Formats in entry and exit

The type of data used must be specified for each method of alignment. Ontologies to be aligned can be represented with languages with beacons or the format of the conceptual graphs. The languages with beacons are XML, RDF(S), DAML+OIL and OWL. The dictionaries of synonymies or lexicons are extra information sometimes being able to be added and which necessary for the improvement of are returned process of alignment.

The format and the structure of the result of alignment are specified for each method. It should be specified if alignment is carried out between the whole structures or couples of entities of two ontologies. The result for the majority of the existing methods is a fi to shit of alignment (generally in format XML), indicating which are the ontological couples entities which correspond. All the methods of alignment determine correspondences between the ontological entities by using measurements of similarity.

2.2 Measurements of similarity

Following taxonomy are proposed for the classification of various measurements of similarity (Rahm and Al, 2001):

i. Terminological method (T): compare the labels of the entities. It is broken up into purely syntactic approaches (TS) and those using a lexicon (TL). The syntactic approach carries out the correspondence through measurements of dissimilarity of the chains (e.g., EditDistance). While, the lexical approach carries out the correspondence through the lexical relations (e.g., synonymy, hyponymy, etc.);

ii. Method of comparison of the internal structures (I): compare the internal structures of the entities (e.g., interval of value, cardinality of attributes, etc.);
iii. Method of comparison of the external structures (S): compare the relations between entities and others. It is broken up of methods of comparison of the entities within their taxonomies (ST) and methods of comparison of the external structures by holding account of cycles (SC);
iv. Method of comparison of the authorities (E): compare the extensions of the entities, i.e., it compares the whole of the other entities which are attached to him (authorities of the classes);
v. Semantic method (M): compare interpretations (or more exactly the models) of the entities.

2.3 Quality of alignment

Measurements of **Precision**, **Recall** and **Fallout** (Do and al, 2002) were the metric ones largely exploited to estimate the quality of alignments obtained. The EON "Evaluation of Ontology-based Tools" (EON, 2004, EON, 2006, Euzenat and al, 2006) retains these measurements for the evaluation of the quality of alignment. The main aim of these measurements is the automation of the process of comparison of the methods of alignment as well as the evaluation of quality of produced alignments. The first phase in the process of evaluation of the quality of alignment consists in solving the problem manually. The result obtained manually is regarded as the alignment of reference. The comparison of the result of the alignment of reference with that of the pairing obtained by the method of alignment produces three units: N_{found}, $N_{expected}$ and $N_{correct}$. The unit N_{found} represents the pairs aligned with the method of alignment. The $N_{expected}$ unit indicates the whole of the couples paired in the alignment of reference. The $N_{correct}$ unit is the intersection of the two units N_{found} and $N_{expected}$. It represents the whole of the pairs belonging at the same time to alignment obtained and the alignment of reference. The precision is the report/ratio of the number of found relevant pairs, i.e., "$N_{correct}$", reported to the full number of pairs, i.e., "N_{found}". It returns thus, the part of the true correspondences among those found. Thus, the function precision is defined by: precision = $|N_{correct}| / |N_{found}|$. The recall is the report/ratio of the number of found relevant pairs, "$N_{correct}$", reported to the full number of relevant pairs, "$N_{expected}$". It specifies thus, the share of the true found correspondences. The function recall is die fi denies by: recall= $|N_{correct}| / |N_{expected}|$. Fallout measurement makes it possible to estimate the percentage of errors obtained during the process of alignment. It is defined by the report/ratio of the erroneous pairs, "$(N_{found} - N_{correct})$", brought back to the full number of the found pairs, "N_{found}", i.e., Fallout = $1-(|N_{correct}| / |N_{found}|)$

Table 1 presents summary and transverse review principal know-discussed methods of alignment. The first entry of table 1 presents the formats of ontologies dealt with by each method of alignment. These formats are as a majority of the languages of beacons except for KIF and OCML. The second entry of table 1 indicates the nature of the fi to shit result which is a fi to shit XML or a fi to shit RDF(S). The third entry of table 1 gathers the various measurements of similarity exploited on the level of each method. The last entry of table 1 puts forward the terminals of measurements of precision for each method within the framework of the tests carried out by EON (EON, 2004). Thus, method OLA compared has a light advantage to method QOM. The "qualitative" performances of these methods are almost similar, since they take into account all the characteristics of ontology to knowing, the terminological similarity, and structural of entities of ontologies. Moreover, the quality of alignment produces by OLA is better. Indeed, the value of the minimal precision and the value of the maximum precision are higher than those provided by QOM. To note that, OLA proposes a method of calculating of similarity who solves the problem of circularity between the concepts during the process of alignment (Euzenat and Al, 2004b). The result of alignment is appeared as a file RDF/XML.

	GLUE	OLA	IF-MAP	ASCO
Input	XML	OWL-Lite	KIF, OCML, RDF(S)	RDF(S)
Output	XML	RDF	RDF	RDF
Similarity	E	T, TS, I, S, ST, SC, E	ST, E	T, TS, TL, ST
Precision	[0,3-0,6]	[0,6-0,8]	-	-

Table 1. Comparative table of the principal methods of alignment.

In the majority of the principal methods of alignment of ontologies, the stabilization of the measurement of similarity is exploited. This measurement of stability is provided by the user through a threshold. This threshold allows the propagation of the similarity to reach optimal alignment. This propagation is likely not to suitably exploit the vicinity of the various ontological entities. In this way, the method of alignment can stop without exploring of advantage the vicinity. This stop is due to the fact that the treatment of two successive neighbors does not bring a profit lower than the specified threshold. In the same way, the stop limits the treatment of the interesting entities and risk to harm the result of alignment obtained. These disadvantages encouraged us to propose a new method of alignment. The main advantage lies in the fact that it eliminates the intervention from the user by exploiting a wider vicinity of the entities to be paired. The following section introduces the new method of alignment of OWL-Lite ontologies developed which we then compare with method OLA.

3. Our approach to ontology alignment

The method of ontology alignment that we propose takes as input ontologies described in OWL-Lite. OWL-Lite ontologies are transformed to match the form of an OWL-GRAPH that we introduce. The OWL-GRAPH can represent all the information contained in the ontology OWL-Lite (Smith et al., 2004). Classes, properties and instances are nodes in the graph proposed. Nodes in the OWL-GRAPH represent the six types of entities that exist in an ontology OWL-Lite: concepts, instances of concepts, data types, values, data types and properties of classes (such purpose and nature of data type). Relations between entities in the ontology OWL-Lite are the arcs between nodes of the graph. Arcs that exist in the OWL-GRAPH reflect the semantic relationships between entities of an ontology. The OWL-GRAPH is used to represent four categories of specialized links, attribution, instantiation and equivalence. Figure 1 shows an example of two ontologies represented through two separate graphs OWL-Graph. The first ontology indicates that a teacher supervising a student who achieves his memory. The second ontology indicates that a memory is made by a student who is supervised by a teacher. OWL Graphs-Graph obtained by the construction module operated by the alignment module ontologies OWL-Lite. Indeed, the alignment module performs the course of two ontologies represented in the form of two graphs OWL-Graph. This course compares the nodes and arcs of graphs to determine the correspondences between different ontological entities operating in the diameter of the nodes. The diameter of a node is the number of nodes separating the end of the graph (instances).

The new method of alignment proposed is an approach basing itself on a model of calculation of the similarities local and total. This model follows the structure of the OWL-Graph graph to calculate measurements of similarity between the nodes of two ontologies. The module of alignment associates for each category of nodes a function of aggregation. The function of aggregation takes into account all measurements of similarities between the couples of nodes close to the couple to node to be paired. Thus, this function exploits all the descriptive information of this couple. Table 2 presents the notations used in the developed algorithms. The algorithm which implements the method of alignment proposed takes in entry two ontologies to be aligned in the form of two files OWL-Lite and produces a result in the form of a fi shitting XML.

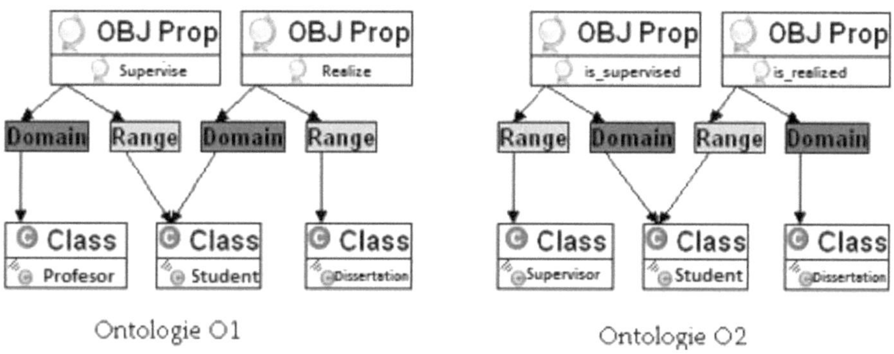

Fig. 1. Example of two OWL-Graph graphs of two ontologies.

- O1, O2: two ontologies to be aligned
- VS_T: terminological vector of similarity
- VS: semantic vector of similarity
- VD: vector of the respective diameters minimum to each couple of nodes

Each node of ontology presents among its characteristics the following fields:

- type: the type of the node
- diameter: the diameter of the node

Each element of the vectors V ST and V S is characterized by the following fields:

- the node of ontology O1
- the node of ontology O2
- the value of similarity

Table 2. Notations used in algorithms PHASE1_SIMTERM and PHASE2_SIMSEM.

It should be noted that our method operates in two successive stages. The first stage, implemented by the means of function PHASE 1_SIMTERM, makes it possible to calculate the local similarity (terminological). The second phase, c.f. function PHASE2_SIMSEM, makes it possible to calculate the similarity total, known as semantic.

3.1 Calculation of local similarity

The calculation of the local similarity is carried out only once for each couple of nodes. The measurement of local similarity of the couples of entities is calculated via algorithm 1 (c.f., function PHASE1_SIMTERM). The calculation of the similarity local (or terminological) is carried out between the descriptors of entities like the names, the comments, etc. the terminological similarity is made up of the syntactic similarity and the lexical similarity. Thus, the syntactic similarity is calculated via the functions of LEVEINSTEIN or EditDistance (Euzenat and Al, 2004a). While the API of WORDNET (Miller, 1995) is exploited for calculation of lexical similarity. Function PHASE1_SIMTERM makes it possible to calculate the terminological similarities of the couples of nodes of two ontologies. It takes in entry two ontologies O1 and O2 to be aligned, represented in the shape of two OWL-Graph graphs, as well as the function of terminological similarity to use and gives in return a vector of terminological similarity of each couple of nodes.

The function CalculSimTerm (Algorithm 1, line 8) takes in entry two nodes N1 and N2, and turns over a value of similarity. This function is provided by one of the methods of calculating of following similarity: the measurement of LEVENSHTEIN, the distance from the under-chains or the API of WORDNET. The local similarity for the various couples of entities is exploited thereafter for the calculation of the total similarity. The following section describes in detail the computing process of the total similarity.

1 **Function: PHASE1_SIMTERM**
    Data1: Two ontologies O1 and O2
    Data2: terminological Function of similarity
    Results: Vector of local similarity VS_T
2 **Begin**
3   /* course of the nodes of O1 ontology */
4   **For each** (N1 ∈ O1) **make**
5   /* course of the nodes of ontology O2 */
6   **For each** (N2 ∈ O2) **make**
7   **If** N1.type=N2.type **then**
8   Sim_T=calculSimTerm(N1,N2)
9   /* add: 2 nodes and the value of the terminological
10   similarity*/
11   add ((N1, N2, Sim_T), VS_T)
    return (VS_T)
End

Fig. 2. Algorithme1.PHASE1_SIMTERM.

3.2 Calculation of total similarity

The calculation of the similarity total, known as semantic, is done between the whole of close nodes by categories. Function PHASE2_SIMSEM organizes, by categories, the adjacent nodes with the couple of entities to be paired. Then, it calculates the measurement of similarity between each of the same pair category. To carry out this calculation, the measurement of similarity "Match-Based similarity" is used:

$$\boldsymbol{MSim(E,E')} = \frac{\sum_{(i,i')\in pair(E,E')} \boldsymbol{Sim(i,i')}}{\boldsymbol{Max(|E|,|E'|)}} \quad (1)$$

where E and E′ represent two whole of the same nodes category. This function, requires that the local similarities of the couples (i,i') are already calculated, gives like result the couples of the unit P = E×E′. The couples (i, i'), intervening in calculation, must present best measurements of similarity. To choose them, there exist two approaches: the algorithm glouton and dynamic programming (Boddy, 1991). The algorithm glouton carries out local choices. Indeed, when he is confronted with a choice, he takes what seems to him the best to advance, and hopes then that the succession of local choices contributes to an optimal solution. While the dynamic programming try to lead to an approach of global optimization. In our algorithm of alignment the algorithm glouton is implemented. Indeed, the algorithm glouton chooses a couple of entities having the greatest similarity and which is higher or equal to the fixed threshold. Then, it removes the two entities of the couple of the table of the similarities. The algorithm continues the checking for each couple until there does not exist anymore couples having a measurement of similarity higher than the threshold.

```
Function: PHASE2_SIMTERM
        Data1: Two ontologies O1 and O2
        Data2: terminological vector of similarity VS_T
        Data3: Weight of terminological similarity Π_L
        Results: Vector of global similarity VS
Begin
        /* calculation of the minimal diameter for each couple of nodes */
        For each (e ∈ VS_T) make
                VD_i =min (e1_O1.diametre, e2_O2.diametre)
                /*iterate until reaching the maximum of the diameters belonging
                to VD*/
                For (it=1; it ≤ Max_{j∈[1, V D.size]} VD_j; it++) make
                        /*to traverse the vector of the similarities of the
                        preceding iteration, the vector of similarity of the first
                        iteration is VS_T*/
                        For (j=0; J < VS.size; j++) make
                        /* verify number iteration and minimum diameter of
                        nodes to be aligned*/
                        If it < VD_j then
                                Simvois = CalculSimVois (VS_j.N_O1, VS_j.N_O2)
                                Sim = Π_L × VS_T (j) + Simvois
                                V Sj = (NO1, NO2, Sim)
                Return (VS)
End
```

Fig. 3. Algorithme2.PHASE2_SIMTERM.

In order to solve the problem of the dependences of similarity, the method of the system of equations at fixed point (Euzenat and al, 2004b) is exploited. It uses a quasi-linear function which formally allots to each category of nodes a weight Π., being given a category of nodes X and the whole of the relations implied N(X), the measurement of total similarity SimX: X → [0, 1] is defined by:

$$Sim_X(x, x') = \sum_{F \in N(x)} \Pi_F^X Sim_Y\big(F(x), F(x')\big). \tag{2}$$

The function is standardized since $\sum \Pi_F^X = 1$. In our approach of alignment, which we propose, the weights are fixed by defect for each category of nodes. This does not prevent that the user can assign the weights which it wishes. By using the equation (2), to calculate the total similarity of the various categories, a system of linear equations is obtained. The variables of this system are the similarities of the couples of nodes deduced from the equation (1). The resolution of the system of the equation (2) is done by iterations. Iteration 0 of algorithm 2 (c.f. line 10) exploits the terminological similarities, already calculated by intermediary of the algorithme1. Then, iteration 1 of algorithm 2 uses the equation (2) to calculate the total similarities between couples of the same entities categories. Measurements of similarities of the categories intervening in calculation of the similarity of a couple result from the preceding iteration. Thus, the iteration J functions in the same way as the preceding iteration. The calculation of the total similarity of each couple is based to the measures of similarities calculated with the iteration (j-1). In each iteration, the number of candidates to be aligned falls according to the minimum diameter of the couple of node to pair. The exploration of the diameter of each node allows the propagation of the similarity through the vicinity. The principle of this propagation is explained in what follows.

3.3 Propagation of the similarity through the vicinity

Our method carries out a propagation of similarity definitely better than that of OLA. Indeed, in its process of alignment, all the vicinity of the couple of entity to be aligned is integrated in the calculation of similarity. For example, let us consider the figure 1 which presents two ontologies O1 and O2. Being given the couple of entities (Student (O1), Student (O2)), the calculation of the similarity includes the close entities which enter in plays. The calculation of similarity of the couple in question evokes in this example the objectProperty type and varies for two algorithms our algorithm and OLA. Thus, table 3 presents the entities close to the couple (Student(O1), Student(O2)) for, respectively, our algorithm and OLA. Thus, our method integrates measurements of similarity of the couples of entities (supervise (O1), is_supervised(O2)) and (realize(O1), is_realized(O2)) in the calculation of similarity of the couple (Student(O1), Student(O2)), while OLA, is limited to calculate the measurement of similarity between (realizes(O1), is_supervised(O2)). Consequently, the measurement of similarity for this couple is encircled better with our algorithm than with OLA.

Moreover, our method, contrary to OLA, is not based on the stability of the measurement of similarity, by using a threshold die fi nor by the user. Indeed, algorithm OLA carries out successive iterations and in each iteration, measurements of similarities of the entities to be aligned are compared with those of the preceding iteration. If the variation is lower than the threshold, the entities in question are not treated more in the iterations which follow.

neighboring entities	**Student (O_1)**	**Student (O_2)**
For "our method"	Supervise, realize	Is_supervised, is_realized
For OLA	Realize	Is_supervised

Table 3. Table of the entities close to the couple (Student(O1), Student(O2)).

However, this method is likely to make lose couples of entities, whose measurements of similarity can increase the value of the similarity in the iterations later. To cure this problem, our method uses the notion of the diameter, i.e., the depth of the entity in the OWL-Graph graph. Thus, our method does not stop reiterating on a couple of entities only after having exploited all its neighboring structure.

The measurement of similarity of each couple of nodes varies from an iteration to another until it converges. The iteration count in our method is equal at least maxima of the diameters of the candidates to pair. In each iteration, algorithm 2, (c.f., line 12), check candidates to be aligned. The couples of nodes, whose minimum diameter is lower than the number of the current iteration, will not be treated. However, the diameter of each node in the graph must be given. To determine the diameter of a node, two aspects should be considered. The first consists in checking if the graph is directed or not. The second consists in taking account of the circular relations. The algorithm of the calculation of the diameter uses the representation of the OWL-Graph graph of ontology, and makes it possible to determine the diameters of the existing nodes. Moreover, the OWL-Graph graph considered is a graph not directed. However, there exist categories of nodes for which a diameter equal to zero is given. Indeed, these nodes must be only treated in the iteration of algorithm 2 (c.f., line 10), i.e., in the iteration of calculation of the terminological similarity.

These nodes are of nature standard of data (string, non-negative integer, etc.), or value of data (a numerical value, a character string, etc.). The measurement of similarity of each couple of nodes varies from an iteration to another to deal with the information incorporated in the vicinity. The iteration count in our method is equal to the maximum of the minima of the diameters of the candidates to pair.

In the following section, an experimental evaluation of our method is presented.

4. Experimental evaluation of ontology alignment method

Experimental evaluation of the proposed alignment method was conducted on two complementary aspects. The aspect of "intra-method" will focus on evaluating performance, ie, execution time, method vs. the change in the size of the ontologies to align, and the similarity measure used. The second aspect, called "inter-method" to compare the qualitative results obtained by the proposed method vs. the other methods, eg, OLA. As part of experiments conducted some tests provided in the benchmark base available to the community through competition EON (EON, 2004) are used. These tests are described by table 4 (EON, 2004). The ontology base consists of a set of references. It represents a simplified version number of ontological entities compared with real ontologies. Each test case benchmark base highlights a feature of the second ontology to align with the test database. The purpose of the test base is to take care of all aspects that exist in an ontology OWL-Lite and that could have a significant impact on the evaluation metrics of the result of alignment.

4.1 The aspect “intra-method”

In what follows, we will try to measure the evolution of the performances of our method compared to the increase of the composition structural of ontology. Table 5, presents the statistics raised as for three series of tests which were carried out. Indeed, same ontology was used, i.e., the ontology 101 described in table 4. Each test brings an incremental aspect of the composition structural of ontology. The tests carried out are three types of tests. In the

Test	Characteristics of ontology
101	Same basic ontology
103	The not recognized axioms are replaced by their generalization
205	The names of the entities are replaced by their synonyms
222	The hierarchy of the classes is strictly reduced
225	The restrictions of classes expressed by properties were removed
301	Ontology to be compared is real and similar to basic ontology
304	Ontology is also real and similar to basic ontology

Table 4. Ontologies of tests.

TEST1, the ontology of reference is only made up of classes. Thus, it is made up of 33 entities to align. In the TEST2, the 24 properties of nature object are added to the classes.

The number of entities thus becomes 57. In the TEST3, complete ontology is used, i.e., ontology is made up of 97 entities distributed as follows: 33 classes, 24 properties of nature object and 40 properties of standard nature of data. According to the results presented in table 5, the performances of the process of alignment depend on the two following aspects: size of ontologies to be aligned and the choice of the function of terminological similarity. Indeed, the time of execution increases considerably when the number of entities to be aligned increases and conversely. This increase is more considerable on the level of the module of alignment than on the level of the module of construction of the OWL-Graph graph. The choice of the terminological function of similarity also influences over the execution time of the module of alignment. Indeed, the use of a simple function, like that of LEVENSHTEIN, for the calculation of the terminological similarity reduced the time execution. On the other hand, the use of a function more complex as the WORDNET increases considerably the execution time of the process of alignment. This variation is due to the time spent by the algorithm of alignment for obtaining the value of syntactic or lexical similarity. This time this is much more important with the use of WORDNET than with another function of syntactic calculation of similarity like that of LEVENSHTEIN. Indeed, the use of the API WORDNET requires accesses expensive disc to seek synonymies.

	TEST1	TEST2	TEST3
TE: Construction OWL Graph	3,450	4,700	6,780
TE: Our method (LEVENSHTEIN)	110,465	225,677	357,561
TE: Our method (WORDNET)	148,542	301,978	455,843

Table 5. Execution time of OWL-Graph construction and our method in seconds.

4.2 The aspect "inter-methods"

While being based on the quality of alignment (measurement of precision), method OLA had better results (c.f., table 1). In the same way, method OLA exploits ontologies with the OWL-Lite format. For these reasons, method OLA would be used as method of reference in the facet intra-method. Within this framework, it is important to recall that our method carries out a propagation of similarity on all the vicinity of the entities. It exploits the concept of diameter of the ontological entities has fixed to explore the totality of the structure of ontology. The alignment, produced by our algorithm with each test, is compared with the alignment of reference. Thus, the results of measurements of qualities are calculated. Table 6 recapitulates the results obtained by the two methods of alignment" our method" and OLA (EON, 2004). The best results of the values of precise details of "our method" are obtained when the structures of ontologies are similar or identical, i.e., tests 101, 103, 222 and 225. Thus, "our method" obtains values of precision for these tests which are higher than 0,910. This is explained by the fact why our approach is more effectively exploits the structures of the entities to be aligned. From where, the entities which have almost the same structure are correctly aligned. The results of the tests where the value of precision is less good explains by two aspects. Firstly, our algorithm calculates measurements of similarities of the same entities category. This induces that certain couples of entities are not taken into account by the process of alignment, from where the whole of the pairs belonging at the same time to alignment obtained and the alignment of reference, $N_{Correct}$, is weak. Consequently, the value of precision is weakened. Moreover, the couples which were excluded from the process of alignment can help with the increase measurements of similarities of the couples of close entities and consequently, to increase the number of correctly aligned couples. Secondly, our algorithm does not use in its process of alignment a comparison between the wording or the comments of the entities.

		Precision		Recall		Fallout	
Test	**Similarity**	**"our method"**	**OLA**	**"our method"**	**OLA**	**"our method"**	**OLA**
101	**LEVENSHTEIN**	1,000	0,587	1,000	0,970	0,000	0,400
103	**LEVENSHTEIN**	0,985	0,540	0,985	0,901	0,011	0,430
205	**WORDNET**	0,500	0,470	0,500	0,802	0,493	0,500
222	**WORDNET**	0,917	0,530	0,957	0,901	0,063	0,430
225	**WORDNET**	0,953	0,570	0,953	0,967	0,027	0,400
301	**WORDNET**	0,610	0,483	0,740	0,607	0,347	0,493
304	**WORDNET**	0,592	0,428	0,680	0,618	0,353	0,541

Table 6. Comparison between "our method" and OLA.

In order to evaluate the results of the approach of alignment proposed, table 6 compares the results of two algorithms "our algorithm" and OLA. The statistics obtained are presented in table 6. Starting from the data presented in table 6, our method of alignment is better compared to method OLA. Indeed, our method of alignment provides measurements of more powerful qualities on almost the majority of the tests. These best results are explained by the two following aspects. The first is the fact that "our method" carries out a propagation of similarity definitely better than that of OLA. The second aspect is that our method, contrary to OLA, is not based on the stability of the measurement of similarity by using a threshold ε define by the user. The default value of this threshold is fixed to 0,01 in OLA.

5. Conclusion

In this paper, we presented our method for aligning ontologies OWL-Lite. Alignment method performed to search the best matching pairs by exploiting their respective graphs OWL-Graph. The results obtained by the alignment module are satisfactory compared with results obtained by other methods of alignment. In addition, the proposed method provides better results on most tests compared to the OLA method. A comparison of the execution time of both methods will be considered to study the scalability of real and complex ontologies. Several improvements are possible on the proposed alignment method to make it more relevant. These improvements include: the calculation richer and fuller of the similarity of terminology, the calculation of inter-category similarity and alignment of ontologies more complex. Finally this method will be integrated into a system of perception of learning activity by a tutor via e-learning platform.

6. References

Aleksovski Z., Klein M., ten Kate W., van Harmelen F., « Matching Unstructured Vocabularies using a Background Ontology », *Proceedings of the 15th International Conference on Knowledge Engineering and Knowledge Management*, Hong Kong, p. 182-197, 2006.

Bach T. L., Dien-Kuntz R., Gandon F., « On Ontology Matching Problems - for Building a Corporate Semantic Web in a Multi-Communities Organization », *Proceedings of ICEIS (4)*, Porto, Portugal, p. 236-243, 2004.

Berners-Lee T., Hendler J., Lassila O., « The semantic Web », *Scientific American*, 2001.

Charlet J., Bachimont B., Troncy R., « Ontologies pour leWeb Sémantique », *Revue I3, numéro Hors Série «Web sémantique»*p. 43-63, 2004.

Connolly D., Harmelen F. V., Horrocks I., McGuinness D. L., Patel-Schneider P. F., Stein L. A., DAML+OIL: Reference Description, Technical report, W3C: Word Wide Web Consortuim, http://www.w3.org/TR/2001/NOTE-daml+oil-reference-20011218, December, 2001.

Do H., Melnik S., Rahm E., « Comparison of schema matching evaluations », *Proceedings of the 2nd Int. Workshop on Web Databasess*, German Informatics Society, Erfurt, 2002.

Doan A. H., Madhavan J., Domingos P., Halevy A., *Handbook of Ontologies : International Handbooks on Information Systems*, Springer Verlag, Berlin, chapter 18 "Ontology Matching : a Machine Learning Approach", p. 385-404, 2004.

Ehrig M., Staab S., « QOM : Quick Ontology Mapping », *Proceedings of The 3rd ISWC, GI Jahrestagung (1)*, Hiroshima, Japon, p. 356-361, November, 2004a.

Ehrig M., Sure Y., « Ontology Mapping - An Integrated Approach », *in* , C. Bussler, , J. Davis, , D. Fensel, , R. Studer (eds), *Proceedings of the 1st ESWS*, vol. 3053, Springer Verlag, Hersounious, p. 76-91, 2004b.

EONW., « EON : Ontology Alignment Contest », *Proceedings of the 3rd Workshop Evaluation of Ontology-based Tools (EON)*, 2004.

Gruber T., « A translation approach to portable ontology specifications », *Knowledge Acquisition*, vol. 5, n" 2, p. 199-220, 1993.

Kalfoglou Y., Schorlemmer M., « IF-Map : an ontology mapping method based on information flow theory », *Journal of data semantics*, vol. 1, n" 1, p. 98-127, 2003.

Klyne G., Carroll J. J., Resource Description Framework (RDF) : Concepts and Abstract Syntax, Technical report, W3C : Word Wide Web Consortuim, http ://www.w3.org/TR/2004/REC-rdf-concepts-20040210/, February, 2004.

Smith M. K., Welty C., Mcguinness D. L., OWL : Ontology Web Language Guide, Technical report, W3C :WordWideWeb Consortium, http ://www.w3.org/TR/2004/REC-owl-guide-20040210/, February, 2004.

Noy N. F., Musen M. A., « Anchor-PROMPT : Using Non-Local Context for Semantic Matching », *Proceedings of the Workshop on Ontologies and Information Sharing at the Seventeenth International Joint Conference on Artificial Intelligence*, Seattle, WA, August, 2001.

Welty C., Guarino N., « Supporting ontological analysis of taxonomic relationships », *Data and Knowledge Engineering*, vol. 1, n" 39, p. 51-74, 2001.

Part 4

Application

11

Developing an Online/Onsite Community of Practice to Support K-8 Teachers' Improvement in Nature of Science Conceptions

Valarie L. Akerson[1], J. Scott Townsend[2], Ingrid S. Weiland[3] and Vanashri Nargund-Joshi[1]
[1]*Indiana University*
[2]*Eastern Kentucky University*
[3]*University of Louisville*
USA

1. Introduction

Research shows that teachers do not have adequate conceptions of science as inquiry and must be exposed to both content and pedagogical demands of inquiry to effectively teach using inquiry (Anderson, 2002). These results are especially unfortunate for the teacher and the learner because understanding of science as inquiry is reciprocally related to understanding important aspects of the nature of science (NOS) (Akerson, et al., 2008). This problem is coupled with the need to teach NOS and inquiry throughout all elementary grades (NSTA, 2000). Most elementary teacher preparation programs do not include specific courses on NOS or inquiry, and what teachers learn is usually embedded in a science methods course (Backus & Thompson, 2006). Certainly teachers can conceptualize and teach NOS once they understand it, are convinced of its importance, and have strategies to teach it to their own students. Professional development programs can help teachers attain these goals. We have found communities of practice (CoP) (Wenger, 1998) especially useful when working with inservice teachers in terms of helping them conceptualize and to teach NOS when used in an on-site professional development program (Akerson et al, 2009; Wenger, 2002). The CoP enabled the teachers to be committed to a vision of reform in their teaching, and to share ideas and provide peer feedback. To develop a COP there must be *mutual engagement* around a shared theme in which participants are engaged with colleagues, and share and respond to ideas in the context of the theme (in our case, NOS). In addition, a CoP should have a shared mission *(joint enterprise)* in which the community works toward a common purpose (for us, improving science teaching). Also, a CoP must include a *shared repertoire* of ideas, techniques, practices, terminology, as a needed outcome for the CoP and its participants (for us, shared strategies for NOS instruction) (Kerwald, 2008; Wenger, 1998; Wenger, 2006).

CoPs are useful in improving NOS conceptions and practice for inservice teachers (Akerson, et al., 2009). However, inservice elementary and middle school teachers may have difficulty attending traditional university science education courses or professional development programs meant to serve as CoPs due to their proximity to universities, work constraints, families and other various responsibilities, which may limit their participation in a NOS CoP. Research shows that teachers do not have adequate conceptions of NOS that would allow them to teach NOS to their students (Akerson, et al 2009), therefore it is vital to explore alternative communities that can support teachers in developing their views and practices. We created and tested the influence of a online/onsite CoP on teachers' NOS conceptions by means of a master's-level graduate course that included inservice and preservice teachers. With the benefits of integrating online coursework and face-to-face discourse, interaction, and hands-on activities, the teachers had opportunities to explicitly reflect on NOS conceptions online and receive feedback from their peers, as well as interact face to face to receive professional development and share ideas. Our research questions were (1) how can we develop a on-site/on-line online/on site CoP to improve K-8 teachers' NOS conceptions and (2) what is the influence of this CoP on teachers' conceptions of NOS?

2. Theoretical framework

We view learning as social in nature that encompasses teacher learning recommendations as forwarded by Putnam and Borko (2000) such as learning being situated in social contexts, takes place by the individual, with other persons, and through the use of tools. We agree with Putnam and Borko that learning takes place through interactions with others, which can be accomplished through a community of practice (CoP). Wegner et al. (2002) define CoPs as "groups of people who share concern, a set of problems, or a passion about a topic, and who deepen their knowledge and expertise in this area by interacting on an ongoing basis (p. 4)." In our study teachers were involved with refining their science teaching and knowledge of NOS, through interacting in an on-line and on-site forum in an ongoing basis. CoPs have been noted to have many common characteristics. Some important aspects of a learning community include (1) Commonality, which includes participants' shared beliefs, interests, and purposes, (2) Interdependence, which is supported when there is a need and opportunity for a community to interconnect, and (3) Infrastructure, which are the tools, support, and the opportunity for the community of practice to be facilitated (Barab & Duffy, 2000; Barab, Kling, & Gray, 2004; Hung & Chen, 2001; Reil & Polin, 2004). We used this structure of commonality, interdependence and infrastructure to design our CoP as well as to assess how well teachers were interacting in the CoP. Commonality was used through the teachers' interest in improving their teaching of science by taking this course. Interdependence was supported by the on-site discussions and supports provided by peers as well as the on line discussions surrounding science teaching issues. The infrastructure was the on line community that enabled teachers from remote locations to interact with peers, as well as the on site component that allowed for face to face interactions and explorations.

While we know that a solely face to face CoP has been effective for inservice (Akerson, Cullen, & Hanson, 2009) and preservice teachers (Akerson, Donnelly, Riggs, & Eastwood, in press), we acknowledge that other models of developing a CoP may be as effective with the ability to support and provide outreach to a larger number of teachers. One such model could be a on-site/on-line model that could integrate face-to-face as well as on-line communities to allow teachers from remote areas to interact with teachers who may be fortunate enough to be close to on site professional development opportunities. The on-site/on-line model we explored had an in-depth and reflective on-line component, as well as an on-site face-to-face component that enabled teachers to interact with instructors through inquiry activities that supported their NOS learning as well as share ideas and feedback on site.

3. Literature review

In this section we describe the literature that informed our development of the on-site/on-line course for NOS instruction. We explore literature related to on-line communities as professional development, improving teachers' conceptions of NOS and how CoPs have been used as to improve teacher knowledge and practice.

3.1 On-line communities

Research has shown that on-line communities have been successfully developed through the use of various tools. Vavasseur and MacGregor (2008) found that opportunities to engage in online communities have increased teachers' self-efficacy through the sharing of ideas, discussion of issues, and the making of connections with colleagues and principals. They also found that online discussion allowed teachers to communicate more frequently than in face-to-face only courses. Stagg, Peterson and Slotta (2009) noted that reserved teachers who may not have participated in face-to-face activities were very engaged in online communication. Online forums allow the instructor and students to think about the discussion topic and respond to one another directly. Additionally, Stagg Peterson and Slotta found that the "lasting aspect of written ideas allows students to more easily respond to and build on contributions of others, leading to a more resonant development of ideas" (p.122).

3.2 Communities of practice

Of course, "creating a CoP" cannot be solely the responsibility of the professional developers. That would be imposing a community on others. Therefore the learning experiences must be open and flexible, and facilitators need to be willing to personalize the CoP for the participants. We endeavored to connect teachers from different types of school communities as well as two different states together and to provide them with supports to enable them to engage and communicate with one another. We used Robertson's (2007) recommendations for building a CoP: (a) fostering dedication of the teachers to the program and the process, (b) holding open communication between all participants, including facilitators, (c) respecting and striving to understand different perspectives, (d) motivating and developing ownership toward a shared vision, and (e) establishing a positive collaborative environment.

Leite (2006) has found that teachers want to be part of a CoP. Teachers enjoy and appreciate the community they find even if they are isolated in their own school settings. Within a CoP teachers need to be free to raise and discuss issues (Leite, 2006) and provide feedback to one another (Shen, Zhen, & Poppink, 2007). Multiple voices of teachers should be heard and encouraged in the CoP. This encouragement should take the form of the facilitators structuring "good conversations" that trigger teachers to take perspectives, develop personal and professional authority, as well as helping teachers learn to engage with students (Snow-Gerano, 2005).

3.3 Nature of science

We recognize that there are components of NOS that are not applicable to K-8 classrooms, and have decided to use the NSTA Position Statement for K-12 students and National Science Education Standards requirements for K-4 and 5-8 because they are what teachers will be responsible for teaching (NRC, 1996; NSTA, 2000). Though our teachers who participated in this program were not high school teachers, we believed it important that they understand all NOS aspects that twelfth grade students should understand upon graduation. These aspects are (a) scientific knowledge is reliable and tentative, (b) no single scientific method exists, though there are shared characteristics of scientific approaches (e.g. inquiry approaches that require empirical data), (c) imagination and creativity play a role in the development of scientific knowledge, (d) there is a crucial distinction between observations and inferences, (e) though science strives for objectivity there is always an element of subjectivity in the development of scientific knowledge, and (f) social and cultural contexts play a role in the development of scientific knowledge (NRC, 1996; NSTA, 2000).

For teachers to be able to include NOS in their instruction, they need to understand the elements above, as well as conceptualize ways to teach NOS to their own students. Prior research has shown that professional development programs can be successful in preparing elementary teachers to conceptualize NOS (e.g. Akerson et al, 2007; 2009) as well as teach NOS (Akerson & Hanuscin, 2007; Akerson & Buzzelli, & Donnelly, 2010). In a previous study we have found that teachers who engaged in a professional development program that took place through a CoP framework improved their NOS conceptions and their teaching practice. The teachers' conceptions of NOS improved substantially as they grappled with ways of thinking about teaching these ideas to their own students. Sharing their ideas with their peers that were members of this CoP enabled them to try strategies and gain feedback in a safe setting. We believe that this kind of CoP, that enables teachers to discuss NOS ideas and teaching practice from their own contexts, can be further enhanced by including teachers that may have even more diverse contexts. In fact, these contexts can be so diverse that it may be difficult for them to attend an on-site class meeting on a regular basis. Therefore, using an online format through which teachers can discuss NOS ideas as well as ways to teach NOS to their own students in their own contexts could prove fruitful for all teachers who are members of this CoP.

4. Context

This CoP included teachers who had registered for an on-line on-site advanced science methods course. We believed that a CoP would benefit most teachers in terms of enabling them to develop their conceptions of NOS and of teaching NOS. The participants represented teachers from areas that were close to the universities and teachers from remote rural districts who were driving long distances due to their lack of proximity to the onsite locations.

4.1 The participants

This master's-level course consisted of seventeen teachers (9 middle school and 8 elementary). Fifteen of the teachers were inservice teachers ranging between 1-20 years of experience. Two of the participants were preservice middle school teachers newly enrolled in a MAT (Master of Arts in Teaching) transition to teaching program.

Of the eight elementary teachers in the class, two taught solely as fourth grade science teachers in which they taught three fourth grade science courses each day. The remaining elementary teachers in the program stated they did teach science in some form during the school year, although it was reported in different amounts ranging from 20-40 minutes every day to teaching it in six week spurts alternating with social studies. Of the nine middle school teachers, at least four of them taught science in the seventh grade. This is of significance because science is tested as part of the statewide accountability testing system in the fourth, seventh, and eleventh grades. Two of the middle school teachers taught ninth grade physical science courses and were allowed to register for the course due to their desire for more professional development in pedagogy and the implementation of various aspects of NOS into their classrooms. Both ninth grade teachers were finishing up the MAT (transition to teaching) program and had just completed their first year of teaching.

At least five participants were from in-state elementary or middle schools, but lived and taught in remote areas of rural Central Appalachia. Due to the distance and type of driving the teachers had to do, some drove 2-3 hours one way each Friday to attend the class. The remaining in-state participants lived closer and driving time and distance were somewhat less of a concern. Two of the teacher participants were from another state and met with one of the two science education professors at their local university for the onsite meetings. They participated in basically the same professional development activities and participated completely in the online aspects of the course. This on-site/on-line onsite/online course model was developed to help provide outreach to teachers who might not otherwise be able to travel or have the time to participate in such a science education professional development or MA-level course.

This course was taught onsite at two different universities by two different science education professors collaborating on the project. They worked closely to ensure the same topics and concepts were covered weekly for the participants at the two different on-campus sites. However, the experiences were the same for all participants for the online aspect of the course because the instructors combined both classes on the same Blackboard course site. We endeavored to develop a CoP for our professional development program to capitalize on the strengths of social interaction. We developed a on-site/on-line model so teachers from two different geographical locations (i.e., Kentucky and Indiana), as well as distances across locations, could interact with one another, share ideas, and provide feedback. Our CoP developed over the term of our course, and used features that are common to CoPs. For example, though we had two different states represented in the community, this allowed us to have both opportunities that are relevant to the local communities, as well as a more global community (Wenger, 1998). Therefore there was a local community at each university site, as well as a larger community that included teachers from both sites. However, teachers at each site were also part of larger communities in their own areas. We sought to create mutual engagement in these communities through the unifying theme (nature of science), shared mission (improving science teaching), and fostering a shared repertoire by providing opportunities to share ideas and strategies for teaching science. These are the components of CoP that are deemed important by Wenger (1998).

4.2 The intervention

The course was designed to introduce concepts of NOS by creating a space through which teachers could interact in a university onsite summer course that was supplemented with online readings, professional development videos, reflection assignments, and discussion board postings that followed and expanded upon the in-class experiences. Appendix A describes the structure and concepts for both the weekly onsite and online experiences and provides a listing of the prompts. The course met during the summer for 4.5 hours on six consecutive Fridays. The onsite aspect of the course used explicit reflective NOS instruction that has been previously shown to be effective in changing teachers' NOS views (Akerson, Townsend, Donnelly, Hanson, Tira, & White, 2008), but extended it by including the on-site/on-line on-line CoP aspect. Teachers were placed in online forum groups based on the grade level they taught (two middle school and two elementary groups) and participated in several weekly activities that involved them implicitly in various aspects of inquiry and NOS. Teachers were encouraged to participate in the activities and reflect on how the various activities related to concepts, their required standards, their classrooms, and their overall philosophy of science teaching. After participating in each activity, aspects of inquiry and NOS were explicitly addressed, usually through group and class discussions, in ways that promoted teacher understanding of science as aspects of content/concept, process, and habit of mind. Also, specific aspects of inquiry such as process skills, essential elements of inquiry (NSES, 1996), and aspects of NOS involving specific values and epistemological assumptions underlying these activities (Lederman, Abd-El-Khalick, Bell, & Schwartz, 2002) were explicitly addressed by participant reflection and class discussion.

The weekly onsite course sessions were supplemented with online components following each of the first five Friday class meetings. The weekly online supplemental components involved 2-3 assigned readings relating to inquiry and NOS from various sources, two professional development videos (from Annenberg Media) illustrating various aspects of inquiry teaching (pertaining to the previous week's onsite course activities), reflection questions for each video that allowed teachers to relate the video to various aspects of inquiry or NOS, and one or two discussion board prompts, such as "What common themes do you see between science as inquiry and the nature of science (NOS) at this point?" that encouraged participants to synthesize ideas from both the onsite and online aspects of class and post them to the discussion board for weekly interactions. The discussion board prompts were used as culminating assignments each week as a means to allow teachers to synthesize concepts based on the previous onsite and online experiences. Participants were given a multi-part question or statement and were asked to respond in full and post their responses on the discussion board. Finally, each participant was required to reply to a minimum of three other participants regarding the others' initial responses to the prompt and respond to questions posed to them by others. Course instructors found that this created much interaction in which teachers made statements of support, asked questions of one another and the course instructors, asked for peer clarification, and exchanged ideas about classroom implementation of inquiry and NOS instruction. To promote higher-level discourse, instructors often participated in discussion board interactions by asking participants for clarification and identifying possible misconceptions, much like they did in the onsite classroom meetings. The numbers of initial postings, along with responses to other members, were tallied each week by the instructors as a means to ensure full online participation in the learning community. Participants nearly always made far more online forum postings and responses than the minimum of three responses required each week.

5. Methods

The study adopted an interpretive stance (Bogdan & Biklen, 2003) and focused on exploring teachers' conceptions of NOS as well as their conversations through the on-site/on-line community regarding teaching NOS through inquiry. We collected a variety of data through interviews, bulletin board discussions, and teacher reflections that enabled us to develop themes related to learning about and teaching NOS. These methods will be described in the sections below.

5.1 Data collection

The study used a combination of methods to track the progress of the on-site/on-line course on teachers' views of NOS. Qualitative data included pre and post surveys of teachers' conceptions of NOS, one-on-one interviews to enable teachers to elaborate on their NOS conceptions, teacher reflections of NOS readings and viewings of instructional videos, and discussion board reflections and interactions.

Participants' conceptions of NOS were assessed before and after the summer class. Participants were sent an electronic copy of the *Views of Nature of Science Form B (VNOS-B)* (Lederman, Abd-El-Khalick, Bell, & Schwartz, 2002) prior to entering the course. They were instructed to complete the surveys without looking up outside information and to return them to the authors via email. Afterward, phone interviews were conducted with all teachers to allow them to elaborate on their written responses. Interviews lasted between thirty-five and sixty minutes. Teachers also responded to the VNOS-B after the course was completed, and follow-up interviews were conducted with each teacher by phone or on-site.

Each week, along with watching the weekly professional development videos, teachers were asked to respond to and submit (via Blackboard online social media) reflection questions that pertained to the video, their experiences in the previous class meeting, and their own experiences as teachers and students themselves. Weekly discussion board postings were also used as a data source. The primary uses of the discussion board were the analyses of teachers' responses to prompts and participant interaction with one another and the course instructors. The reflection responses and the progression of discussion board postings were both used to triangulate the findings from the pre and post VNOS-B interviews. Discussion board and reflection data were also used to identify emerging themes or patterns regarding teacher knowledge of NOS or teaching NOS, attitudes, or ideas in relation to the posted prompts as the course progressed.

5.2 Data analysis

Data analysis took place in two phases. The first phase included a review of the VNOS-B interviews regarding teachers' conceptions of NOS by two researchers reviewing the transcripts. Profiles of individual teachers' conceptions of NOS were developed first of pre instruction conceptions, and then of post instruction conceptions of NOS. We independently coded their responses to the questionnaire inadequate, adequate, and informed by NOS aspect, and then compared our analyses. Any differences, which were few, were resolved by discussion and further consultation of the data. The same procedure was followed for the post questionnaire VNOS-B data. We then independently compared the pre and post profiles to determine any change in NOS understandings. Changes in NOS conceptions were noted.

To determine the kinds of interactions that took place in the on-line community, two researchers reviewed all discussion board prompt conversations and teacher reflection responses that were archived through the Blackboard site. We used open-coding to search for themes related to conceptualizing NOS ideas as well as teaching NOS to K-8 students. We noted the kinds of conversations teachers engaged in with grade-level peers in the on-line community, searching for evidence of teachers sharing ideas, developing a repertoire for teaching NOS, and being mutually engaged in the content and conversation. The two researchers independently coded these conversations and teacher reflections and met to compare analyses. Any discrepancies were resolved through discussion and further consultation of the data.

6. Results

In this section we will share the teachers' pre instruction conceptions of NOS. We then share results regarding their participation in the on-line on-site CoP through the themes identified through weekly individual reflections pertaining to online professional development videos in addition to group online discussion board postings and interactions of the teachers as they progressed from the major topics as the class progressed. These themes were: (1) commonalities between NOS and scientific inquiry, (2) creating science lessons to better teach aspects of NOS, and (3) using aspects of NOS as a means of assessing children's understanding of science content. Finally, teachers' post-instruction NOS conceptions are shared to show the overall change in teacher' ideas over the span of the summer course.

6.1 Pre-instruction NOS conceptions

We had eight teachers for whom we had complete pre-instruction NOS conception data. This data was collected through the VNOS-B surveys as well as individual interviews. As expected, most teachers held inadequate with a few adequate views of the NOS aspects prior to participating in the on-line community. We will describe these views by NOS aspect in the sections below.

6.1.1 Tentative NOS

While all teachers believed that scientific theories could change, seven still held the misconception that these theories changed only due to adding new evidence, generally through technology, and one teacher held the idea that the scientific theory would change when it became a law. For instance, Melissa said "Theories change because new discoveries are made, especially through technology." Missing from her description of the tentative NOS is the idea that theories could change with reinterpretation of the evidence. Cynthia showed her belief that theories become laws, and included the element of technology when she stated "Everything starts with a theory and then it eventually becomes a law. It could change if we have new technology and have to re-experiment."

6.1.2 Observation and inference

There were a variety of conceptions related to the distinction between observation and inference, from those who thought scientists need to actually view something to make scientific claims, to a more adequate view that scientists make inferences about data. For example, one teacher (Sam) stated "They get really high-powered microscopes so they can see them, and then draw their models in the right way." [talking about scientists' development of models of the atom]. The remainder of the teachers (seven) all believed that scientists developed models of the atom through tests and observations of reactions. They were not clear about what kinds of tests they might have used, but these teachers realized that the scientists did not need to see the atoms to develop a model. Melissa stated "I don't think they are sure about what atoms look like. I think they are still inferring about them." However, Cynthia, who also stated they did not need to see atoms to make a model, stated "They probably saw them react like magnets and built their theory from there." It is clear that though the teachers generally recognize that scientists do not need to actually see an atom to infer their existence, they do not have adequate conceptions of how this inference takes place.

6.1.3 The relationship between theory and law

All eight teachers stated that theories were weaker forms of scientific knowledge that would eventually become laws when and if enough evidence could be found. They believed that laws were unchanging, and theories could change, mostly because they would become laws. For instance, Katy stated, "Theory attempts to explain occurrences and generally holds true, but a law is something that works all the time and there is no refutable evidence that it wouldn't work. A theory would become a law if there were enough evidence." Katy's response was typical of all teachers interviewed, and illustrates their inadequate conceptions of theory and law.

6.1.4 Empirical NOS

Regarding the empirical NOS, six teachers agreed that science has standardized procedures to guide inquiry. Sam stated "In science there are rules to follow. You have to go through a scientific method in order for people to accept what you come up with." Katy held a better conception of the role empirical data in developing scientific knowledge as evidenced in her statement "Science keeps raising new questions and uses evidence to answer them." Cynthia simply stated "Science is more tangible," which illustrates her confusion as to how scientific knowledge is developed.

6.1.5 Creative and imaginative NOS

While all eight teachers acknowledge that science is creative and imaginative, they have inadequate interpretations of how that creativity and imagination helps to build scientific knowledge. Three teachers stated that scientists cannot be creative or imaginative in collecting or interpreting data because "you have to accurately represent the data. You can't imagine it." Two teachers also spoke about removing creativity and imagination from scientific knowledge development in terms of leaving out subjectivity. Their belief was that science is objective, and if scientists used creativity or imagination they would be including subjectivity, as illustrated by Karen's statement "Things in science have to be very controlled. You have to maintain validity if you are doing research. You have to leave out subjectivity." Two other teachers stated that "they can be creative in how they present their scientific ideas, what kinds of graphs they use, appealing ways to display their data." In other words, they can create interesting ways to display their knowledge, but cannot use creativity or imagination in developing the knowledge. Tina held a more adequate view that creativity can help identify patterns in data as illustrated by her statement "Scientists use creativity before and after data collection. Outside the box thinkers may see patterns less creative people will not see."

6.1.6 Subjectivity

There was a range of inadequate and adequate conceptions of the subjective NOS. Sam's response illustrated his inadequate conceptions of the relationship of law and theory, and applied that to the role of subjectivity in developing scientific knowledge "Where there is no law in play then many theories can be made, and it is all based on how people perceive them."Three teachers believed that scientists intentionally looked at data in a way that supported their views, as is illustrated by Tina's statement "They can put a spin on the data to make it say what they want." Four teachers had more adequate views of the subjective NOS as illustrated by Karin's statement "scientists are creative in their interpretations of data, and come from different backgrounds, have different experiences, so look at the data differently and draw different conclusions."

6.2 Interactions in the online community of practice

Data were collected as part of the regular course assignments and progression during this six-week summer course. In addition to the five on-site class meetings, teachers interacted with one another and the course instructors in various ways in this on-site/on-line CoP. For instance, the culminating task each week was to respond to a discussion board prompt that promoted the teachers to synthesize ideas from the experiences, interactions, activities, and assignments from the previous onsite course meeting and the online assignments that occurred during the week after each onsite class meeting. These experiences and prompts ensured mutual engagement surrounding similar ideas and peer and instructor feedback enabled teachers to develop a shared repertoire of strategies for teaching and assessing NOS. Below are results regarding the online interactions to show participants' progression in understanding concepts as a result of the online aspects of the CoP. We provide representative quotes from these discussions to share the commonalities of teachers' interactions and the participants' interdependence within the learning community that helped them build understanding of NOS and of teaching NOS.

6.2.1 Common themes between inquiry and NOS

The first prompt (after the pre-interview and prior to the first onsite meeting) asked the teachers to reflect on their prior beliefs, their reading assignments and the professional development (PD) videos they watched. The discussion board posting for this week asked the teachers to post a response describing the commonalities they found, up to that point, between the nature of science and the practice of scientific inquiry. They were also asked to share any themes they noticed emerging from the two concepts. After teachers posted a response to the prompt, they were instructed to respond a minimum of three times to other teachers by asking questions, making comments and generally partaking in dialogue about the topic. In nearly every session of the online CoP teachers responded to one another well more than the minimum of three times on the weekly discussion board. This made for a rich interaction of dialogue for the duration of the class, and provided evidence of their mutual engagement in the topic

While all teachers showed initial signs of increase in understanding of both NOS and scientific inquiry in their interactions, there were many signs that the teachers had a difficult time conceptualizing the difference between NOS and inquiry. For instance, Tina said "One common idea is that students are actively exploring the world around them. Children are using their senses to make observations and change their thinking as new information becomes available. Both [NOS and inquiry] have children exploring, investigating, and discovering with their curiosity being the driving force. In each, teachers are facilitators instead of giving direct instruction." Although Tina uses ideas evidenced in the process of scientific inquiry, she simply inserts terminology from her reading to relate to the nature of science as a process of forming knowledge. Sam shares similar ideas in his initial posting:

> Commonalities and themes found between science as inquiry AND nature of science is that they rely on questioning and exploring the concepts introduced. Both questions and exploration are student led or initiated. This format gives more ownership for the learner and allows learning to occur at the pace best for students.

Although Sam does share some ideas that may be considered as best practices in science education, he is not yet able to distinguish between ideas relating to the process of science inquiry and the overall nature of science itself.

Cynthia posts a stronger statement during her initial posting that shows a connection, but leans more toward discussing inquiry in the end. She stated:

> NOS and inquiry have several common threads. One of these is the children are actively involved in their own learning. Exploration of the natural world is done actively through the senses. Thinking skills such as inferring are used regularly. Higher order thinking is a hallmark of both. Children change original inferences when knowledge is gained to do so. Inquiry and NOS are both curiosity driven and group interaction is at the center of learning. In both, the children design the method to acquire needed knowledge, and the teacher helps facilitate the learning...I am certainly going to evaluate my own teaching methods.

Although it is apparent that Cynthia is integrating characteristics of NOS such as science as being tentative but durable, observations and inferences, and somewhat implied, no single, rote scientific method, she is does still tend to focus on the pedagogical aspect of inquiry in comparing the two.

As the discussion board progressed during the first week of class, the majority of teachers responded in support of one another in feeling that they needed to rethink about how they teach or even perceive science in their own classrooms. In responding to Cynthia's response about the commonalities and her reflecting on her teaching practices, Amy replied:

> Cynthia, it caused me to think a lot about the way I did things this year too. I feel like after seeing the first grade classroom lesson [in the video] on sharks that I totally did my students a HUGE injustice this year. I think this class will definitely assist me with obtaining new ideas.

In an act of sharing empathy, Katy posted "I am almost wishing I could go back to the beginning of the school year and apologize to many of my students and parents....Man, I feel like the worst teacher ever." In response, the instructor replied to Katy's posting to share that it is very common for teachers (himself included) to feel that way about earlier teaching practices and he, himself, felt that way as he learned more about using aspects of inquiry and NOS in the classroom.

Based on the interactions on the discussion board for the first week, participants showed somewhat naïve views when comparing inquiry and NOS, but they readily shared teaching experiences, feelings of inadequacy, and readiness to learn more about the topics as the class continued. These kinds of interactions indicated the mutual engagement and joint enterprise components that were taking place in the on-line portion of the CoP.

6.2.2 Identifying aspects of NOS in instruction

After finishing the first week of the online CoP, the class met at the onsite locations for the first time. During the first class meeting, the participants were engaged in basic lessons regarding important aspects of NOS and inquiry and experiencing aspects of NOS for themselves both implicitly and explicitly. After the first class session, teachers each had reading assignments, two online PD videos from a series about inquiry, and online reflection questions pertaining to the videos and their own classroom experiences. The teachers were then asked to synthesize ideas from the onsite and online experiences by identifying three aspects of the implicit use of NOS from the video and/or the previous week's onsite meeting and sharing them in the discussion forum. This question asked them to focus on NOS from an inquiry-based perspective regarding their own learning or the classrooms shown in the video. This discussion board prompt was not related to NOS from a historical perspective.

The majority of initial postings regarding the aspects of NOS as identified by the teachers centered around the concepts of science being evidence-based (4), the presence of scientific creativity (7), the distinction between observations versus inferences (5), and science as being influenced by social and cultural factors (4). Although they were mentioned, there were fewer responses related to concepts of subjectivity (1), tentativeness (2), and the functions and relationships between theory and law (1). In referring to a video with kindergarteners observing earthworms, Haley describes an instance in which the students in a video were experiencing the empirical nature of science:

> This can be illustrated in the earthworm activity with kindergarteners. The children are each given their own earthworm and gummy worm to observe. They are able to collect evidence and make observations based on sight, touch, smell, etc. The children make observations such as, 'worms are wiggly, if feels squishy, etc.' This is a clear example of using one's senses to draw out empirical scientific evidence, even with young children.

Cynthia followed Haley's discussion about the children's experience with evidence (empirical nature of science) by furthering the post by relating evidence to observation and inference. She stated "The kindergarten clip I agree definitely shows the direct connection between observation and evidence. Their observations of the earthworms led to inferences about worms." Several other posts were made by teachers in the class about the simplicity and effectiveness of the inquiry activity portrayed in the video. Cynthia's post was followed by a post from one of the course instructors who was intentionally provoking ideas regarding the teaching of NOS both implicitly and explicitly:

> I love the discussions about observations and inferences and evidence. Even though the teachers in the videos did not generally use those terms, it seems that the students were implicitly getting those messages. I wonder how much more powerful the lessons would have been had the teachers actually used the terms 'observations, inferences, and evidence' even with very young children?

The online aspect of the CoP allowed the teachers to readily respond to one another and the course instructor to add to the dialogue and ask questions to further facilitate the conversation, providing further evidence of mutual engagement and joint enterprise.

It was common for teachers in the online community to exchange ideas both about what they saw in the PD videos and what they have experienced in their own classrooms. Although the time spent in the onsite aspect of this learning community was limited, the online aspect allowed the teachers to interact over the course of an entire week. For example, Katy, a fourth grade teacher who only taught science in a departmentalized setting, posted a strand on the discussion board regarding the use of creativity in the classroom, and it created an exchange among teachers that led to concerns about their own classrooms. Katy stated the following during a 9:45 PM posting:

> The first example of NOS this week that stood out in the videos is creativity. During the lesson on sound, there was one little boy who came up with his own investigation based on his teacher's presentation of the oscilloscope. Many students simply accept what the teacher says during a lesson, but it was evident that the students in this classroom feel very comfortable, and have no fear of giving input about their ideas. I thought it was great that the teacher followed up with his idea and took the class into the music room to investigate.

Amy, another fourth grade teacher who primarily taught science in a departmentalized setting, responded to Katy's initial strand post at 4:21 PM the next afternoon:

> Katy, do you feel like the creativity level that many of these students exhibited is at a much higher level than the students in your own classroom? I feel like many of my students lack a certain level of individual creativity therefore whenever anything is slightly creative is said I feel like it is wonderful. Is this 'lowering' expectations?

Even though Katy had responded to several other teachers in the classroom regarding various postings in different places, she replied to Amy's question:

> I agree that my students lack a certain degree of [scientific] creativity...but I think this is a result of many years of inquiry-deficient classrooms. In order for our students to rediscover their [scientifically] creative side, we will have to work extra hard to foster

> this skill! Once the students see how creative they can actually be, they will feel more comfortable to come out of their comfort zone that previous teachers have gotten them into!

Much like the abovementioned exchange between Katy and Amy, the other teachers began making important connections about regarding concepts and terminology they had not heard of or possibly thought about two weeks earlier. Based on the responses and interactive posts from all the teachers on this prompt, the community had quickly grown in both identifying and understanding aspects of NOS when seeing it taught in the context of inquiry-based lessons. Because of the joint enterprise developed through the CoP they were able to discuss issues regarding NOS teaching and enhanced their repertoire for teach NOS, further developing their shared repertoire through the CoP.

6.2.3 Creating lessons utilizing inquiry and nature of science

After finishing the third week of the online community and the second onsite meeting, teachers were asked to synthesize the ideas from the previous onsite meeting, the readings, and the PD video to reflect how they would take lessons from their classrooms, or future classrooms (for the participants in the transition to teaching program), and think about how they would change their science lessons to (1) be more inquiry-based and (2) purposefully integrate aspects of NOS explicitly in their own teaching.

This week the discussion board allowed the teachers to post their lesson ideas to the forum and receive feedback from their community of practice colleagues. The majority of the teachers chose to post units or lessons for which they had the most trouble in implementing in their classrooms, inviting feedback and advice from peers. For example, Sam, who teaches in a gifted program, shared about the unit he does with his fifth graders:

> A unit I struggle with is Force and Motion. This should naturally allow for hands-on inquiry, but it falls within a bad time during my county's curriculum framework. I am forced to either rush through it or drop it because it is in competition with testing. I can make it more inquiry-based by creating a challenge to solve a real-world problem… possibly by using historical evidence regarding the building of pyramids or other large structures locally (such as the capitol building and river transportation…maybe have the class design a system to move stones based on technology past civilizations had to use.

In his discussion board entry Sam further elaborated that he could implement aspects of NOS into the lesson by allowing the students to compare the various types of technology pertaining to force and motion at different times in order to make the connection to social/cultural context. He stated "The context of time affects the creation of both…for example, how would slides look if they were build 100 years ago or how long would it take to build similar structures today with current technology."

As the course progressed, the teachers became more comfortable in their online dialogue to the point of offering more critical suggestions to one another. In a sequence between Katy and Melissa, one challenged what the other posted and they constructively exchanged ideas about the aspect of time spent on inquiry in their own lessons. Katy made a posting about changes she plans on making with her fourth graders about sound. She said that she did not give them enough time to explore and she hoped to foster student creativity by allowing them to explore on their own for an extension aspect of the lesson. She further elaborated:

> While watching the video dealing with sound for this class, I realized that it is ok to let go of the reigns and let the children come up with different ways to explore sound and demonstrate the way sound behaves and travels. Next year, I may have one day dedicated to letting students be creative by thinking of various models that will demonstrate the vibrations created when sounds occurs.

Another teacher, Melissa, posted a response to Katy stating:

> A few red flags in your statements, "I may have one day dedicated..." Inquiry based learning takes a lot longer than lecturing and demonstrating. If your kids are not used to learning this way, it may take a while for them to grasp the concept...You will have to model and demonstrate the process and they will have to learn to work together in groups, and listen to and respect each other. This will take more than one day, but the time spent will result in the students understanding the material, instead of memorizing it.

Rather than getting upset with Melissa's response, Katy responded with agreement that it will take more than a day and that it would be a challenge, especially to stay on track with the other fourth grade teachers with whom she must team-plan. In furthering her concern for straying from the plan of her grade level team, she wrote "I will just have to help them see that using inquiry in their classrooms as well would be beneficial to us all."

Although this discussion board prompt encouraged the teachers to post their own lessons and provide constructive criticism to others' lessons, the majority of postings resulted in a chance for a group of teachers posting ideas and sharing lessons with one another in a true CoP teachers facilitated by their instructors. The slightly more critical postings about slight disagreements were found to be both respectful and constructive. There were elements of mutual engagement as they discussed ideas and provided feedback to one another, joint enterprise, as they sought to improve their teaching, and shared repertoire as they developed strategies for teaching NOS in collaboration with one another.

6.2.4 Assessing learning with aspects of NOS

We found throughout the course that teachers readily talked about and showed progression of the knowledge of implementing more inquiry in their classrooms and integrating NOS into those lessons. However, we found the teachers to have fewer ideas regarding how they could use aspects of NOS as a regular part of inquiry in the classroom. Although few comments were made on the nature of "implicitly and explicitly," many teachers did mention they would use end-of-lesson or unit NOS reflection as a form of assessment. When referring to using aspects of NOS at the end of a lesson, Karen wrote "I think this should be part of your closure, or you could even point them out during your activities at first until the students become more familiar with them. I like the idea of possibly making flash cards with aspects of NOS on them and using them throughout a lesson when the opportunity arose." In a response to Karen's discussion board response, Karen wrote:

> Karen, in looking with your ideas about NOS and assessment, I agree that it is ok to ask students whether they have used concepts in what they are doing. We saw this in the video of the first grade class doing inquiry. She asked the students "did we make comparisons today, did we make observations by looking closely at our data, did we communicate with others (little scientists) about what we found?" I think this is a good way to teach processes and to get into the habit of using NOS and inquiry as we go through investigations with our students and help them arrive at conclusions.

Based on teacher-teacher and teacher-student interactions through the discussion board, we see that teachers have progressively grown regarding their knowledge and connections made in the understanding of both NOS and inquiry.

6.3 Post-instruction NOS conceptions

In this section we will report on the post-CoP NOS conceptions held by the teachers. After participating in the CoP they had many improvements in their NOS ideas. After instruction, most teachers held adequate views of the NOS aspects. We will describe these views by NOS aspect in the sections below.

6.3.1 Tentative NOS

All eleven teachers believed that scientific theories could change, and nine believed these theories changed due to new evidence collected. For example Karen stated "Theories do change because the nature of science is tentative and subject to change when new evidence becomes available." The others simply stated that theories could change. Six teachers also described the role of technology in changing scientific claims, as illustrated by Melissa's statement "Yes theories change because technologies change as well as new discoveries are made."

6.3.2 Observation and inference

Post instruction all teachers realized that scientists do not need to actually see something to make inferences leading to a scientific claim. All teachers recognized that scientists are fairly certain about their claims, but not 100% sure due to the fact that they could collect more data, and because they do not necessarily see it through their senses they are making inferences. They stated that scientists developed a model of the atom, for instance, by using evidence of the behavior of "things around the atom." Melissa stated "they base the model on current evidence that they have, they are relatively certain about the structure of atoms. The specific kind of evidence I think scientists used to determine what an atom looks like is observations of behavior of atoms." Her response was typical of all teachers, and illustrates that the teachers also used the NOS terminology.

6.3.3 The relationship between theory and law

Eleven of the teachers stated that theories seek to explain why something occurs and laws describe how it occurs, which is an adequate conception of the relationship between theory and law. Teachers recognized that theories do not become laws, but in fact, are a different type of scientific knowledge. For example, Tina stated "Scientific theory is an attempt to explain why…scientific theories tend to be tentative and can change as new evidence comes to light. Scientific laws explain how something happens and usually has a mathematical equation to go along with it. Laws are universally accepted, but changes can be made." Indeed, teachers recognized that theories and laws could change if evidence, or interpretation of the evidence, warranted it. Only one teacher (Karen) retained the view that "laws are factual, and theories are what we believe."

6.3.4 Empircal NOS

Regarding the empirical NOS, all teachers agreed that science uses observations and inferences to make scientific claims. Indeed, they also described the need for collecting data, as well as conducting inquiries. Amy stated "scientists make observations and then inferences from those experiences." All teachers realized that scientific knowledge is based on empirical evidence. For example, Tina stated "Having scientific knowledge means that you can carry out a test, collect data, and realize when you have or haven't controlled all your variables." Karen shared her view by stating "Scientific knowledge is based on empirical evidence which involves observable phenomena either through the senses or technology" which also showed an adequate understanding of the inferential NOS.

6.3.5 Creative and imaginative NOS

All eleven teachers held adequate conceptions of the creative and imaginative NOS at the conclusion of instruction. Sam stated "Creativity in science comes from the questions that are asked and the investigations that are developed to answer questions." Karen agreed, and also noted that scientists "use creativity in looking for patterns, collecting, and analyzing data." Teachers also noted that scientists need to use creativity and imagination in order to develop scientific knowledge, as is illustrated by Melissa's statement "I think scientists use the data, evidence and observations to develop their theories." It is clear to see that no teachers retained the understanding that using creativity and imagination would cause scientists to develop incorrect knowledge, but rather that the use of creativity and imagination was a necessary component of the development of scientific knowledge, in terms of interpreting results, as well as raising questions and designing investigations from the outset.

6.3.6 Subjectivity

All eleven teachers recognized that though scientists strive for objectivity, there is an element of subjectivity inherent in the development of scientific knowledge. Teachers recognized the role of background knowledge and personal experience in the development of scientific knowledge, as illustrated by Jeremy's statement "The fact that individuals have different experiences, temperaments, and moral views create different interpretations. This allows for many different inferences to be made with the data that they have collected. None are necessarily correct or incorrect rather they are different conclusions that attempt to explain the data that is presented to them." Kent also reinforced the idea of the influence of the larger culture on scientific interpretations through his view that "part of the subjectivity is based on the social and cultural background of the scientist."

7. Discussion

In investigating our primary research question regarding the development of this on-site/on-line onsite/online CoP and teachers' conceptions of NOS, we found that teachers in the on-site/on-line onsite/online CoP improved their understanding of NOS and how to explicitly embed it into their classrooms. The majority of the teachers held inadequate conceptions of aspects of NOS prior to instruction. However, analysis of the ongoing discussion boards showed the teachers progressively changing in their ideas over time. Initial postings regarding common ideas between NOS and inquiry indicated the teachers could not yet distinguish between the various important aspects of NOS and the actual classroom practices of inquiry. As the course progressed through implementing onsite activities that modeled inquiry-based lessons that integrated aspects of NOS explicitly, the teachers began to readily recognize ways in which NOS was utilized in the various PD videos that were part of the online course assignments. Teachers shared a mutual goal, mutual engagement regarding teaching NOS, and developed a shared repertoire for teaching NOS (Wenger, 1998), by raising questions, discussing ideas, and providing feedback to one another through the on-line community discussions.

During the week following the third onsite course meeting, teachers were readily able to discuss ways in which they could improve their own lessons regarding the use of inquiry, and were able to specifically state how they could use NOS to supplement these lessons for better student understanding. By the last week of the online discussion forum, teachers were able to not only discuss how they could implement aspects of NOS in their inquiry-based lessons, they were also able to elaborate regarding several ways they could use NOS as a form of assessment. For example, one elementary teacher stated "We saw us some of the assessment pieces collected from 3rd graders this past year.. For example, she had done an observation and inference activity with them on solids and liquids where she created a written assessment where they noted their observations and their inferences. By doing this she was able to see which student had a clear understanding of the difference between the two. I think that you can choose to use the 7 concepts for pedagogical issue or assessment depending on the activity and any other assessment options you may already have for that activity. "

This ability to focus on NOS teaching as well as assessment is evident in the comparison of pre interview data, progression of dialogue during the weekly reflections and online discussion board postings, and the post interviews in which the majority of teachers were identified as having adequate views of NOS.

Onsite CoPs have been found to be influential in not only helping inservice teachers better conceptualize NOS, but to implement it in their teaching practices (Akerson, et al., 2009). The results of this online/onsite study indicate that teachers can effectively learn NOS through CoPs that are created by on-site/on-line (onsite/online) experiences. These on-line communities allow teachers to share ideas, raise questions, and ask for feedback regarding their ideas as well as their teaching strategies. Such communities, possibly most beneficial in areas in which teachers may live significant distances from campus, enable more teachers to fully participate in graduate coursework or professional development opportunities. This experience enabled teachers from around the state, and between states, to join the community and make significant growth regarding their understanding about NOS both contexts. Despite the limitations of being a single, MA-level graduate course, several important aspects of a CoP emerged. A practice of mutual engagement was obtained because all stakeholders, both instructors and participants, were immersed in the shared theme of NOS in the science classroom. Another important element of any CoP, a shared mission (joint enterprise), was practiced throughout as the teacher-participants continually worked, with the facilitation of the course instructors, towards learning more about major aspects of NOS and how to implement them into their classrooms. After participating in this CoP, the instructors feel the teachers improved in nearly all areas of their understanding of NOS and its implementation in the classroom. Finally, due to the group's shared growth regarding ideas, terminology, teaching techniques and practices, and overall knowledge and experiences regarding NOS, the group of teachers emerged with a shared repertoire they could implement in their own classrooms.

This on-site/on-line summer course created a CoP which helped resolve the issue of some teachers being reluctant to initially share their ideas with their peers. They were able to choose to share ideas in a written forum instead which may have led to their being more verbally involved in the onsite class meetings. Finally, instructors found this on-site/on-line model of teacher professional development to be beneficial because it allowed teachers from many different areas, backgrounds, and experiences to interact both online and onsite to improve their knowledge of science teaching. Many of the course participants made end-of-course evaluation requests suggesting a successful CoP. Teachers requested that the course Blackboard site be left open so they could continue to remain in contact with one another for ideas, post ongoing discussion forums, and upload documents and lessons for sharing. Also, several participants suggested that the instructors conduct one or two school-year follow up professional development workshops that focused on specific topics such as assessing content knowledge when content specific NOS and inquiry-based activities, which points further to the need for the on-site component of the CoP.

8. Implications and recommendations for professional development

We found that the use of a on-site/on-line online/onsite CoP is a beneficial and convenient method for providing necessary outreach to busy, practicing teachers, especially those who may be distant from professional development locations. It allowed participants, the overwhelming majority of whom had never previously heard the phrase, "nature of science," to discuss among peers on site as well as through a written format their ideas about the concepts as well as about teaching the concepts. Many of the participants had very few initial ideas of NOS or how it could effectively be used in teaching science. The evidence collected shows that participants grew in their understanding of NOS, and in ideas for including it in their classrooms. We believe that the mutual engagement teachers had toward this joint enterprise aided in their development of NOS conceptions as well as developing a shared repertoire for teaching NOS.

There were slight difficulties for the science education professors at each university to incorporate the same NOS activities during the same weeks. However, this was only a slight problem because both the overarching weekly and course-long themes were always the same. We plan to keep the same on-site/on-line model in which onsite meetings at the course locations are followed by combined online experiences. We plan to find ways to further expand this professional development experience for teachers further into isolated regions of Central Appalachia and rural areas of the Midwest. We also plan to align with science educators from other universities in the country in need of professional development outreach for teachers who have a difficult time attending the opportunities, training, or support they need. This model will allow the corresponding onsite workshops to take place in different geographic regions only to allow the teacher participants to come together in the online learning community to share knowledge, experiences, and growth. We think it would be beneficial to follow up the summer on-site/on-line experience with school-year follow-ups addressing teacher-requested topics such as planning and assessment. These follow-ups could be on-site once each semester, with on-line interactions throughout the semester. We feel such additions will allow participants to further their knowledge and share their experiences in implementing these changes, all with the support of the professional development coordinators. We recommend that the facilitators target NOS and scientific inquiry through context-appropriate activities that enable and encourage discussion amongst all teachers in the on-line community.

This CoP was well-supported due to its group of teachers with a common goal and shared resources, as well as their development of a shared repertoire for teaching NOS as part of scientific inquiry from participating in the same course. The onsite experiences which allowed the teachers to interact in face-to-face activities and discussion were supplemented by shared online resources and dialogue. Teachers benefited from both components of the CoP. Teachers who were more quiet during the on-site portion were verbally active in the on-line portion and were clearly developing their NOS ideas and strategies for teaching NOS. The primary difficulty of this CoP, however, was the situation itself. This professional development experience was based solely on two master's level courses in two states. Although it did allow teachers from rural areas of Central Appalachia and the Midwest to participate in a on-site/on-line CoP in two distinct geographic locations to be supplemented by a single online community, it lasted only a short amount of time after the six-week course was completed. It is our intention to create a more independent and longer-lasting CoP by including more participants in more onsite locations while maintaining the shared online community.

Despite the limitations of using a master's level course as a foundation for this CoP, we found the teachers showed significant amounts of growth in conceptualizing several aspects of NOS without having to meet onsite numerous times to participate in the professional development community In addition, the teachers were able to participate in an online community where they could more comfortably interact with one another, share ideas, ask questions, and allow important concepts to resonate throughout the community. It is our intention to use the short-term success of this CoP to expand both in terms of region and sustainability. Therefore we believe that an on-site/on-line approach for developing a NOS CoP is at least as effective as a solely on-site approach to professional development. More research is needed to explore variations of the amount of time spent in each component. We are curious whether an entirely on-line CoP could help teachers achieve the same results in terms of being able to develop strategies for teaching NOS to elementary students. Indeed, could a solely on-line course develop into a CoP?

9. Appendix A

Course Outline:

Week 1 (No Formal Course Meeting):

Pre-Interview (Written and Oral):

Main Topic: *What is Inquiry and Why Do It?*

- Watch Workshop Video #1 (www.learner.org k-8 inquiry)
- Chapters #1 & #2 Llewellyn
    - Upload Video #1 Reflection Questions to Bb (Word Document)

Discussion board prompt & responses (post video & chapter readings) Week One:

There were some common themes in this introductory week in the readings (Ch's 1 & 2 from Llewellyn and the NOS and Science Process Skills chapter) and in Workshop Video #1.

- The NOS and inquiry concepts
    - We'll get into this much deeper (especially when we start meeting face-to-face), but what commonalities/themes do you see between "science as inquiry" and the "nature of Science (NOS) at this point?
- Student learning
    - What themes do you see emerging from concepts of "scientific inquiry" and the "nature of science" that make you think about regarding the process(es)/sequence(s) of the **way students in grades k-8 may learn?**

***All discussion board threads required one initial response posting and three meaningful responses.*

Week 2

Main Topics: *Creating a Learning Community and Getting Started with Prior Knowledge*

1. NOS Activities (Observation/Inference)
2. Inquiry Activity for ELE and MS

After Week 2 Class Meeting:

- Inquiry Workshop Videos #2 & #3
- Chapters #4 & #5 Llewellyn Text
- Nature of Science (NOS) Science Process Skills (SPS) Reading→
    - Upload Reflection Questions for Video #2 and Video #3 (a different set for each video) to Bb

Discussion Board Prompts Week Two:

Your videos this week (#2: Establishing a Learning Community and #3: Launching the Inquiry Exploration) are based on getting things started in the inquiry classroom. As we are getting started in this process known as inquiry, let's reflect about a concept/philosophy that is probably pretty new (at least to some degree) to most of us-- the Nature of Science (NOS).

Think about the two videos and the students you observed in the early stages of inquiry in various content areas, grade levels, and contexts. Now think of your "7 Aspects of Nature of Science We can Reasonably Teach" sheet and any information you have that can go with that (national standards information, etc).

Pick Three of the NOS concepts that really stood out to you based on what you noticedin the videos when the students were participating in the early stages of inquiry. List each concept in your opening strand, what you observed the teachers/students doing that modeled this NOS concept, and *elaborate* on how what you observed in the video modeled each concept so well. Of course, you don't have to limit yourself to one activity…it is recommended that you choose different activities for your different NOS concepts—it is up to you. You'll want to list each NOS concept and explanation separately, however.

If you would like, your third listing cou7ld be something we did in class with the NOS activities for the little snippet of the sound lesson last week. The first two, however, need to be from Workshop Videos 2 and/or 3.

Once you create your own strand first, you can then do your minimum of three follow-ups by scouting out what others have said and engaging in conversation with their ideas. Do you agree/disagree? Have questions? Need further elaboration? Have any general comments? etc...

Week 3

Main Topics: *Inquiry Design, Collecting Data, and Drawing Conclusions*

In Class

1. NOS Activities (Creativity & Empirical)
2. Inquiry Activity for ELE and MS

After Week 3 Class Meeting:

- Inquiry Workshop videos #4 & #5
- Chapters #6 & #7 Llewellyn
  - Video Reflection Questions

Discussion Board Prompts for Week Three:

- Think of two lessons or units, either ones you do or want to do, and think about (1) what are the two lessons/activities (be specific), (2) what can you do to make them more inquiry-based (investigative of some type), and (3) how can you possibly implement some aspect(s) of NOS into each lesson that support(s) your "young scientists" doing real science like "professional scientists?"
- If you don't currently teach science (don't currently have your own classroom (you will soon!) or you teach math or language arts full time), then think about how you can integrate science and/or NOS/Inquiry into *specific* activities you do or will do.

Week 4

Student Processing and Interpretation; Teacher Assessment of Inquiry

In Class

1. NOS Activities (Subjectivity, Social/Cultural, Tentativeness)
2. Inquiry Activity for ELE and MS

After week 4:

- Inquiry Workshop Videos #6 & #7
- Chapters #9 & #10 Llewellyn
    - Video Reflection Questions (2 sets @ 20 points each)

Discussion Board Prompts Week Four:

- After having participated in class, doing the readings, watching the videos, and of course, your own life and teaching experiences, there are surely some questions, concerns, and excitement regarding the two major topics this week: student processing/interpreting of information (evidence) and assessing that entire learning process. Therefore this question has three different parts—they are big ideas and will require some elaboration.
    1. Processing Information: It can be very rewarding, but also a bit tricky, when giving students the opportunity to construct concepts for themselves rather than simply "telling" them someone else's conclusions written in a textbook (even though we know, in science, telling isn't really teaching). Once a teacher works hard to get students set up and to the point of allowing them to collect data and interpret their findings via inquiry (in order to begin constructing knowledge for themselves---how to think, not what to think), sometimes it can be tough to ensure they are constructing ideas that agree with the scientific community's ideas. What are some of the dangers you feel exist in allowing this and what can you do to ensure the students are processing information in a way that helps them build true conceptual understanding?
    2. Assessment: It seems obvious from the video that inquiry lends itself much more to formative assessment than more "traditional" lessons. What are some things you need to keep in mind—REALLY keep in mind—when assessing students to measure what they know, what they're learning, and how far they've come?
    3. NOS: Finally, given that you now know more about this huge concept of "nature of science" (how many teachers know as much about NOS as you now know?), how can you personally use ideas from the "7 Aspects of NOS You Can Reasonably Teach" for both formative and summative assessment in your current or future classroom? Really, how can we use those ideas to ensure students are learning content/concepts we all are required to teach using these seven big concepts? Can these NOS aspects help you assess more accurately? If so, how? If they are good for pedagogical issues, but not necessarily for assessment purposes, please elaborate why? Either way, please be specific.

Week 5

Professional Development/Guest Speaker:

Science as a Human Endeavor (NOS) and Inquiry: A Reciprocal Relationship

In Class

1. Inquiry Activity for ELE and MS

After Week 5:

- Inquiry Workshop Video #8
- Chapter #8 Llewellyn
- Free Book: Teaching NOS Through Science Process Skills (SPS): Grades 3-8
    - 1 Set of Video Reflection Questions
    - 1 Discussion Board (shorter)
    - Read (and enjoy) NOS & SPS text!

Week 6

No on site class for Week 6

Post-Interview

10. Acknowledgements

The authors would like to thank Center for Educational Research in Appalachia (CERA) of Eastern Kentucky University for their support of the project.

11. References

Akerson, V. L., Buzzelli, C. A., & Donnelly, L. A. (2010). On the nature of teaching nature of science: Preservice early childhood teachers' instruction in preschool and elementary settings. *Journal of Research in Science Teaching, 47,* 213-233.

Akerson, V. L., Cullen, T. A., & Hanson, D. L. (2009). Fostering a community of practice through a professional development program to improve elementary teachers' views of nature of science and teaching practice. *Journal of Research in Science Teaching.*

Akerson, V.L., Donnelly, L. A., Riggs, M. L., & Eastwood, J. (accepted) Supporting preservice elementary teachers' nature of science instruction through a community of practice. *International Journal of Science Education.*

Akerson, V. L., & Hanuscin, D. L. (2007). Teaching nature of science through inquiry: The results of a three-year professional development program. *Journal of Research in Science Teaching, 44,* 653-680.

Akerson, V.L., Townsend, J.S., Donnelly, L.A., Hanson, D.L., Tira, P., & White, O. (2008). Scientific modeling for inquiring teachers' network (SMIT'N): The influence on elementary teachers' views of nature of science, inquiry, and modeling, *Journal of Science Teacher Education,* 20(1): 21-40.

Anderson, R. (2002). Reforming science teaching: What research says about inquiry. *Journal of Science Teacher Education*. 13(1): 1-12.

Backus, D.A.,& Thompson,K.W. (2006). Addressing the nature of science in preservice science teacher preparation programs: Science educator perspectives. *Journal of Science Teacher Education, 17,* 65–81.

Barab, S. A., & Duffy, T. M. (2000). From practice fields to communities of practice. In D. H. Jonassen & S. M. Land (Eds.), *Theoretical foundations*

Barab, S. A., Kling, R., & Gray, J. H. (Eds.). (2004). *Designing for virtual communities in the service of learning*. Cambridge, UK: Cambridge University Press.

Bogdan, R. C & Biklen, S. K. (2003). Qualitative Research for Education: An introduction toTheories and Methods (4th ed.). New York: Pearson Education group

Hung, D. W. L., & Chen, D.-T. (2001). Situated cognition, Vygotskian thought and learning from the communities of practice perspective: Implications for the design of web-based e-learning. *Education Media International, 38*(1), 3-12.

Hung, D. W. L., & Chen, D.-T. (2002). Learning within the context of communities of practice: A reconceptualization of tools, rules and roles of the activity system. *Education Media International,39*(3&4), 247-255.

Kehrwald, B. (2008). Towards community based learner support: A case study. In Hello! Where are you in the landscape of educational technology? Proceedings ascilite Melbourne 2008.
http://www.ascilite.org.au/conferences/melbourne08/procs/kerwald.pdf

Lederman, N. G. (1992). Students' and teachers' conceptions about the nature of science: A review of the research. *Journal of Research in Science Teaching, 29,* 331-359.

Lederman, N. G., Abd-El-Khalick, F., Bell, R. L., & Schwartz, R. (2002). Views of nature of science questionnaire (VNOS): Toward valid and meaningful assessment of learners' conceptions of nature of science. *Journal of Research in Science Teaching, 39,* 497-521.

Learning Science Through Inquiry. (n.d.). Retreived June 30, 2009 from Annenberg Media website: http://www.learner.org/resources/series129.html

Leite, L. (2006). Prospective physical sciences teachers' willingness to engage in learning communities. *European Journal of Teacher Education, 29(*1), 3–22.

Merriam, S.B. (1998). *Qualitative research and case study applications in education.* San Francisco: Jossey-Bass Publishers.

National Research Council, (1996). National science education standards. Washington, DC: National Academy Press

National Science Teachers Association (2000). *NSTA position statement: The nature of science.* Document retrieved 12/08/08. http://www.nsta.org/159&psid=22

Putnam, R.T., & Borko, H. (2000). What do new views of knowledge and thinking have to say about research on teacher learning? *Educational Researcher, 29*(1), 4–15.

Reil, M., & Polin, L. (2004). Online learning communities: Common ground and critical differences in designing technical environments. In S. A. Barab, R. Kling & J. H. Gray (Eds.), *Designing for virtual communities in the service of learning* (pp. 16-50). Cambridge, UK: Cambridge University Press.

Robertson, A. (2007). Development of shared vision: Lessons from a science education community collaborative. *Journal of Research in Science Teaching, 44,* 681–705.

Shen, J., Zhen, J., & Poppink, S. (2007). Open lessons: A practice to develop a learning community for teachers. *Educational Horizons, 85*(3), 181–191.

Snow-Gerono, J.L. (2005). Professional development in a culture of inquiry: PDS teachers identify the benefits of professional learning communities. *Teaching and Teacher Education, 21,* 241–256.

Stagg Peterson, S., & Slotta, J. (2009). Saying yes to online learning: A first-time experience teaching an online graduate course in literacy education. *Literacy Research and Instruction, 48,* 120-136.

Vavasseur, C.B., & MacGregor, S.K. (2008). Extending content-focused professional development through online communities of practice. *Journal of Research on Technology in Education, 40*(4), 517-536.

Wenger, E. (1998) *Communities of practice: learning, meaning and identity.* New York, NY: Cambridge University Press.

Wenger, E. McDermott, R. & Snyder, W.M. (2002). *Cultivating Communities of Practice.* Cambridge, MA: Harvard Business School Press.

12

E-Learning in the Modern Curriculum Development

Robert Repnik, Branko Kaučič and Marjan Krašna
University of Maribor and University of Ljubljana, Faculty of Natural Sciences and Mathematics, Faculty of Education, Faculty of Arts
Slovenia

1. Introduction

In the evolution of web technology we have reached the level 3.0 (semantic web). But this does not mean that older technologies are extinct. They are still present and still flourish in some environments, especially Web 2.0 technology is regularly mentioned in the educational fields. In the scientific world only publications in "Web of science" are important, all the rest is meaningless. This concept gradually spread into the lower levels of education and the concept of information and resources quality was therefore set.

Today kids are digital natives or digi-kids. The concept "pencil and notebook" is strangest to them than the concept "computer and web". Doing homework mainly means copying and pasting topics from the web, while traditional writing is perceived as an extremely boring task. The speed of data manipulation have changed even the meaning of contemporary words. While we still use the concept of snail-mail for traditional post mail, contemporary kids use this expression for e-mail. Kids seem to be impatient; what takes more than few seconds for the response is useless. Even literacy has changed. There is no time to formulate proper linguistic sentences because of all the rush. Typing proper words in SMSs takes too much time and acronyms emerge daily (e.g. 4u = for you, tm1030bbbs = tomorrow at 10:30 bring basketball ball to school). Frustrated teachers observe that their students score less points every year and quality of study is going down. On the other hand, policy makers see only numbers and quality degradation is welcome excuse to decrease budgets and increase workload. Generalization as for example "lazy teachers who are overpaid and work nothing" is common.

Many authors agree that new generations of students can upgrade their competences with higher quality e-learning materials. In the past years the Ministry of Education of the Republic of Slovenia has funded many projects of e-learning materials production. As the result almost entire primary school curricula is covered. Along with the textual content, multimedia elements and interactivity was required in these projects. Most of e-learning materials are therefore Web 2.0 compliant. But we know that interactive multimedia e-learning materials do not guarantee quality. Perception of quality of web materials changes according to learner's age. In general primary school students do not discriminate web content (all materials are good for them), while the secondary school students begin to distinguish between good and bad web materials. At the university level understanding of web materials and multiple verifications of the acquired knowledge deepens. At that point students are aware that Wikipedia is definitely not the ultimate knowledge resource. The concept of verification of web contents mostly corresponds to the credibility of the author. If an author is well known and the contents are on renowned institution's web page it is considered to be valid.

How important are indeed the usage of Web 2.0 technology and the reputation of e-material's institution, we wanted to explore by preparing the quantification of narrow topics of physics history (Galileo's research) over major web sources. Research method was web survey of physics students and the research instrument was our e-material in relation with hard facts gathered from web sources. Results show that Web 2.0 technology is not mandatory to perceive e-material as credible. Implications from gathered results also show that curricula must not be fully complete but some time frame must be available for flexibility of contemporary topics that allow teachers to show interdisciplinary use of otherwise almost sterile clean scientific field.

2. E-learning materials in primary level education

There is a steadily growing production of web textbooks, workbooks and other e-materials, and the Web 2.0 technology seems to become mandatory in the production of new e-learning materials (Shneiderman, 2004) (Hofstetter, 2004) (Krašna, et al., 2005) (Smith-Atakan, 2006) (Repnik, et al., 2006) (Lau, 2008) (Krašna, et al., 2008) (Sandia National Laboratories, n.d.). Since there are several types of e-learning materials available on the web at the moment (for self- or blended learning, etc.), a question arises whether the demand for Web 2.0 technology is justified or not. Examples of non-fully-interactive e-learning materials that have been created recently are the materials for primary school including both natural and social science topics at the 3rd year primary school level (Ambrožič Dolinšek, et al., 2009).

Feedbacks from teachers in schools on using e-learning materials are different but they all join in one aspect. They never use the same learning materials from the start to the end. Students prefer changes of styles in learning materials but learning materials cannot change the style from one topic to another though. Such materials would be considered unprofessional and reviewers would grade them low.

Students use different types of e-learning materials and web contents. Even if we provide them high quality interactive multimedia e-learning materials they will still use Wikipedia for additional or complementary information. Wikipedia is not interactive and in most cases multimedia elements are limited to figures only. Despite media restrictions it is still an interesting source for students. Therefore we may rethink our strategies about interactive multimedia learning materials as contemporary pinnacle of e-learning material design.

3. E-materials in context of e-learning forms

There are many debates about e-learning effectiveness. Sometimes production cost may be really high due to multimedia material production but teachers do not like them. We discovered that we cannot prepare learning materials without active role of teachers in this learning process. Our first e-learning materials were very well accepted by students but not by teachers. Effectiveness of our first e-learning materials was low and especially we failed in the area of knowledge retention. Teachers delivered the students our e-learning materials without carefully defined pedagogical tasks. In short time we have learned the most important lesson: we need teachers in production of e-learning materials and e-learning materials are practically useless if teachers do not support and use them.

In the future development our effort was focused on teachers and their perspective of good e-learning materials. Consequently we included less electronics tests and provide more textual assignments. We did not force the use of LMS (Learning Management System, e.g. Moodle, Drupal etc.) in the education. Textual assignments can be submitted in the LMS, or send by e-mail or even printed out and handed to the teachers. Teachers have different ICT (Information-Communication Technology) and pedagogical skills, and should be autonomous in the classroom.

Autonomous competent teachers have higher quality learning outcomes. For knowledge evaluation tests are needed. Based on the previous research we can categorize tests according to complexity and openness (De Praetere, n.d.). Close and low complex tests are suitable for electronic knowledge evaluation. But higher level of complexity and openness require active involvement of intelligent reviewer – teacher. In our first attempts of e-learning material design we use low complexity and more closed tests: Select I, II, III; Identify I, II, III; Match I, II, II; Correct I, II, Complete I (see Fig. 1). Those tests are easy to implement and electronically assessed. In the next generation of e-learning materials production we use tests (assignments) from Project I, II, III, IV, V and Collaborate I, II, III, IV, V. Results of these type of tests force teacher to assume active role since these assignments still cannot be electronically assessed and verified.

Complexity →

Openness ↓

Action	I	II	III	IV	V
Select	True / False	Alternate choice	Multiple choice	Implicit answers	Certainty degree
Identify	Multiple True False	Yes/No with explanation	Multiple Answer	MA with images	Click on image zones
Match	Matching	Categorizing	Sequencing	Prioritizing	Assembling proof
Correct	Remove intruder from a list	Jumbled sentence	Detect wrong form filling	Click errors on an image	Problem solving
Complete	Fill-in blanks	Drop down fill-in blanks	Fill-in form	Calculated answer	Listening comprehension
Construct	Lab simulation	Analysed Open Answer	Link concepts on a map	Draw valid sequence	Delineate zone on an image
Project	Open answer / Essay	Word assignment	Spreadsheet assignment	Presentation assignment	Multimedia project
Collaborate	Forum discussion	Documents sharing + peer review	Group publication	Team blog with roles	Problem solving in team

Fig. 1. Complexity and openness in tests/assignments of knowledge assessment (De Praetere, n.d.).

Textual assignments as tests are suitable for higher knowledge retention since they require more mental effort to produce than just clicking right answer. Since we need to prevent copy/paste of text from other works we include the concept of citation. Namely, plagiarism is on a rise (Kaučič, et al., 2010) and we want our students to become aware of importance of citation and respect other's intellectual products. Good presentation can be seen in the figure (Fig. 2) where in a single page users see the use of multimedia materials, pictures and textual assignment. Additional issues that are also highly important in e-learning are navigation and position inside the materials. Therefore we provide global position and topic's navigation.

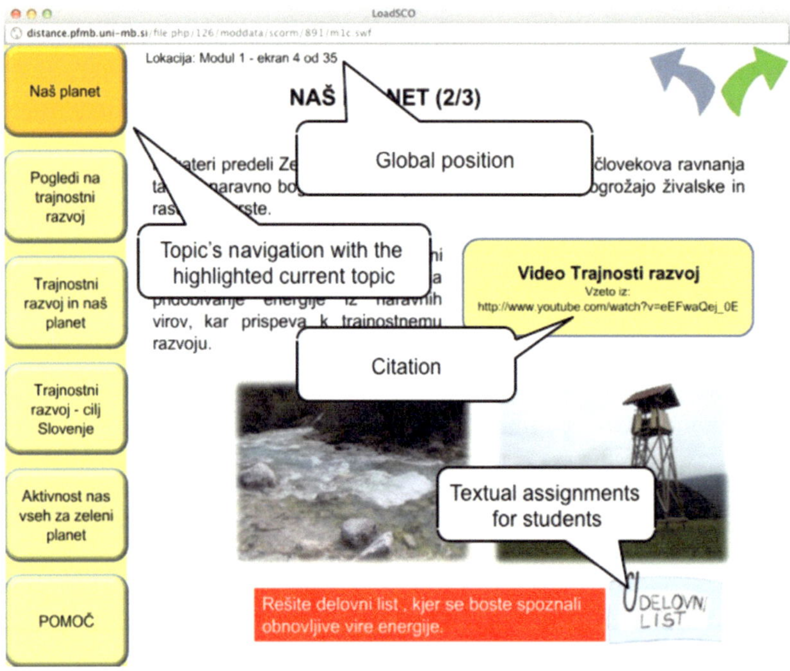

Fig. 2. Elements on the e-learning materials

Interestingly we have found that sometimes even simple web page (Web 1.0 technology) can significantly contribute to the understanding and enhance learning in schools. During the next few years we will gain better insights to the use of our web pages since we introduce the principles of citation into every seminar work and this would give us better insight than mere web hits.

In 2009 e-learning material about Galileo's life and work was prepared. It is suitable for higher classes of primary schools students as well as secondary school students (Repnik, et al., 2009). This interdisciplinary material (including topics from astronomy, physics, mathematics, technology and history of science) was developed for the occasion of the International Year of Astronomy 2009. Preliminary tests of its use in school practice were performed at the end of 2009 in the framework of the national project Development of Natural Science Competences (University of Maribor, Faculty of Natural Sciences and Mathematics, n.d.). In addition, we prepared the questionnaire for teachers and students about the use of e-learning materials.

In the continuation of this paper we describe the results of the school tests of the use of Galileo's web textbook and the results of the questionnaire. In addition, we compare the structure of our e-learning material and some similar e-learning materials on Galileo. Next, we discuss the question about the common demand for Web 2.0 in electronic education.

4. E-learning material about Galileo Galilei

The preparation of our web textbook (let us use the term *e-book* from now on for brevity, even for shorter e-learning materials) about Galileo was done mainly in March and April 2009. It was presented to students in April 2009 and after receiving their comments it was upgraded in summer months. We have divided the e-book into the following sections with subsections (Ambrožič, et al., 2009):

- Home page with short introduction
- Biography
    - Scientific work
    - Galileo's teachers, coworkers and students
    - Publications
    - »De motu« (about movement)
    - Writers about Galileo
- Development of Astronomy
- Technology
    - Telescope
    - Pendulum
    - Sector
    - Thermometer
    - Pump and hydrostatic balance
- Observations
    - Moon
    - Phases of Venus
    - Sunspots
    - Saturn
    - Jupiter's satellites
- Theory of tides
- Mechanics

This e-book was developed with the help of our students of educational physics. As mentioned above, they tested the material and gave useful comments about it. Even more, some students cooperated in the preparation of the book: they prepared the initial interface and design of it. They also prepared a few topics (which were subsequently reviewed before inserting in the main text), but professors of physics and astronomy wrote the largest part of the e-book. The e-book is closed for users and only experts with the provided password may upgrade it. However, the authors are attentive to suggestions from users, so this material was presented to a couple astronomic associations for review and tested at a few schools.

Furthermore, there is a list of references in this e-book as well as the functionality for internal searching through the material by keywords.

5. The results of the school tests

Until now, the Galileo e-book was tested in one primary and two secondary schools in the north-eastern part of Slovenia. The testing procedure was the following. One of the pupils/students read the part of the e-book, prepared the seminar about it and presented the material to his/her schoolmates. The focus of this seminar was on promotion of astronomy and other natural sciences. Then, students answered the questionnaire (test) with 7 questions about astronomy and science in general, which required some level of understanding and not just reproduction of facts. For example, one of the questions (the fourth one) was the following:

> *4) Why are we convinced that the Sun will rise tomorrow? Is this 100% certain? What is the difference between the proof in physics (and biology) and the mathematical proof? (Think about observations of nature, experiments and pure logical reasoning.)*

The goal of answers on such questions was not merely checking the knowledge but revealing the students' wider competencies as are ability of reasoning and imagination. The tests were done within the framework of the national project Development of natural science competences (University of Maribor, Faculty of Natural Sciences and Mathematics, n.d.). In the project, 14 so called *generic competences* (connected with natural sciences as declared in the project) were stressed, among others (key competences, subject-specific competences, etc.). Some of them, such as ability of collecting information, ability of analyzing and organization of information, ability of interpretation, etc., were definitely tested in these school experiments on Galileo e-book. The feedback of these tests was briefly the following. The materials were fine to teachers and most students, but they should have more animations then text explanations. The qualitative results (there was no quantitative marking) of tests were, however, concerning: most answers were bad, from a few words to a sentence or two for each questions. Students showed very poor imagination and ability of reasoning even in the 2nd year of secondary school. Despite several advantages of ICT, the conclusion of these preliminary tests may be taken as a kind of warning against (too) exclusive use of "user friendly" ICT (neglecting other means, such as speech, listening to each other, deep reasoning and thinking effort, handwork and true experiments, etc.).

6. The results of questionnaire for teachers and students

The questionnaire consists of two parts (each of them containing 10 questions) with different number of answers of selection type; in some cases only one answer has to be selected and in other cases more answers can be chosen. The first part of the survey is about e-books in general while the second part is about our Galileo e-book. Only teachers who performed school test on Galileo material answered this part. Since this means only a few teachers the presentation of their opinions in this paper would be irrelevant. We thus focus on the first 10 questions about the use of e-books in general. Maybe two most interesting (important) questions with the corresponding "single-choice" answers are the following (translation from Slovene):

1. *Compare web textbook with the printed one (in regard to its advantages and disadvantages). What do you think about its use in future?*
    a. *Web textbook has predominantly advantages in comparison to printed textbook, thus it should completely supplant it in future.*

b. *Web textbook should predominantly supplement the printed one, however, because of the knowledge protection copies of printed textbooks must remain.*
c. *Web textbook has, in my opinion, as many advantages as disadvantages, so it should be used in the same proportion as the printed one.*
d. *Web textbook could never supplement the printed one, e.g., because of tradition, that's why it should be used only to a minor extent in future.*

2. *If you decided for a frequent use of some web textbook, what would you prefer?*

   a. *Reliability of information, therefore the book should be of closed type, and only experts could supplement it. Expert review slows down the revision/supplementation of the book.*
   b. *Full access, also in regard to supplementation by non-experts, even if the information is consequently less reliable. It enables quick extension of the contents.*

The statistics of the answers on these questions is interesting. We received answers from 52 teachers and students altogether. In more than half of answers on first question the choice was the answer (c) - frequency: 30 times from 52 possible, i.e., the web and printed materials should be used in equal proportions in future. In regard to 2th question, the far most frequent choice was the answer (a) - frequency 41 (!), i.e., students and teachers prefer reliability of information as compared to full access for users. Three questions were about various advantages and disadvantages of e-books as compared to printed material with more than one possible choices; multimedia diversity in material presentation was chosen as the most common advantage while burdening the eyes was selected most frequently as one of main disadvantages. There was also a question of when (what age, level?) the pupils/students should start using e-books: the most frequent opinion was - in the third triad of 9-year primary school (frequency 27). On the contrary, opinions about connection of pure scientific vs. interdisciplinary approach and age span (one narrow age group vs. wider age span) were almost the same. In the last two questions, the opinion about connection of using the e-book for seminar preparation (by pupil or student) with general and key competences (as declared in our national project according to international some conventions) was searched. Three most frequently chosen *generic competences* (from the list of several competences in connection with natural sciences) were 1) ability of collecting information, 2) ability of literature analysis and organization of information, and 3) ability of interpretation. From the 8 *key competences* declared by EU that are essentially very general and should be developed for any person:

1. Mathematical competence and basic competences in science and technology.
2. Digital literacy.
3. Communication in native language in the area of natural sciences.
4. Learning of learning.
5. Communication in foreign languages.
6. Social and citizen competences.
7. Self-initiation and activity.
8. *Cultural consciousness and expression.*

Among them, the second one has been selected most frequently, but also the 1st, 4th and 5th seem to be important, in teachers'/students' opinion. And finally one of the questions was about the frequency of using web textbooks. Teachers and students had different questions about this topic. Teachers assessed the usability of e-books from their pupils and students perspective. Since in this relatively short period we have only the results from primary schools. As expected almost no pupils in primary school in the sample have already used the e-books (when they are not forced to). Students mostly used e-books on their own initiative.

7. Comparison of our e-material with other available e-books on Galileo

Finally, a qualitative and quantitative comparison between our e-book (Ambrožič, et al., 2009) and four others on Galileo (two in Slovene and two in English) (Rice University) (Wikipedia) (Dolenc) was done, in regard to the number of key words, sections, figures, etc. The free software package AntConc 3.2.1w was used to count keywords and analyze their network in textual documents. In the continuation, we will use the following abbreviations for the five e-books in comparison: *FNM* (Faculty of Natural Sciences and Mathematics) (Ambrožič, et al., 2009), *Rice* (material form Rice University), *Wiki-eng* (Wikipedia - English version), *Wiki-slo* (Wikipedia - Slovene version), and *Quark* (Kvarkadabra, eng. "Quarkadabra" after *quarks* and *abracadabra*) (Dolenc). Home pages of two of them (*FNM* and *Rice*) are shown in Fig. 3 and Fig. 4. The most important information source and sample for *FNM* was the material *Rice* since it is more extensive than other sources. Nevertheless, we used our own ideas in supplementation the contents of the material. First, we present some qualitative similarities and differences between the 5 materials. The structure of *Wiki-eng*, *Wiki-slo* and *Quark* is very simple: they are presented on a single (elongated) page, but *Wiki-slo* is much shorter than the other two. Menu bars in both Wikipedia materials just enable quick access (jump) on the desired topic on the same page. *FNM* and *Rice* have slightly more complex structure: its section (subsection) has its own page and is accessed by menu bar. The index menu in *FNM* works in a slightly different way as compared to *Rice*: when the subsection is chosen the bars for other subsections are still visible, contrary to the *Rice* system (Fig. 4). The depth level in *Quark* is 1: this material has only sections indicated by addresses in bold letters, but not enumerated. *Wiki-eng* has 2 levels of depths: there are enumerated sections and only the 3rd section - Astronomy is further divided into 3 subsections. Slovene version *Wiki-slo* is much simplified: there are no subsections at all, so the depth of levels is 1. *FNM* has two levels: sections and subsections although not all the sections are divided into subsections (see the structure above). *Rice* has the depth 2 or 3 (this is a matter of interpretation): there are usually sections and subsections, as in our e-book, but the section Science in divided into groups of subsections.

Some quantitative comparison of the e-books is presented in Table 1: number of words, figures, external links, and number of subsections. 15 most frequent keywords relevant for astronomy and science in general presented in all 5 materials are counted and shown in Table 2.

Some comments to Table 1 are the following. Subsections are counted in all sections together in the first row. The (horizontal) width is the largest number of subsections in any of the sections, or respectively, the number of sections if this exceeds the former value. Only the sections with actual contents are included in this counting: Notes, References, etc., are excluded from this counting. The same holds for counting words through the e-materials. The row labeled *Words* shows the total number of words, without those in Notes, References, etc. The depth and width in *Rice* depends on how we count levels as mentioned above (do we take the grouping of subsections in the sections Science as an intermediate level or not). Finally we note, that in contrast to other e-materials in our material *FNM* each section starts with some text before it is split into subsections, thus we have added the number of sections to the number of all subsections just in our case (first data row in table).

Number Of	**FNM**	**Rice**	**Wiki-eng**	**Wiki-slo**	**Quark**
All sub-sections	20	64	11	1	10
Words	18500	57634	8106	819	3326
Figures	59	176	13	2	6
Links	139	19	333	111	2
References	14	185	89	1	0
Width	6	43 (21)	9	1	10
Depth	2	2 (3)	2	1	1

Table 1. Number of different elements in five e-books.

WORD	FNM	Rice	Wiki-eng	Wiki-slo	Quark
Galileo	214	646	205	34	77
Observation	92	175	48	8	7
Publish	8	153	20	2	2
Telescope	73	142	37	0	3
Copernican	17	139	16	2	22
Moon	109	128	8	4	4
Motion	91	125	15	6	10
Earth	125	123	27	4	9
System	27	103	19	8	13
Kepler	14	98	11	0	5
Theory	31	95	25	0	4
Sun	38	93	21	4	8
University	15	92	6	3	7
Jupiter	45	85	14	2	2
Satellites	27	74	8	2	1

Table 2. Number of 15 most frequent keywords connected with astronomy and science in the five (5) e-books. The words are sorted by their frequency in the material *Rice*.

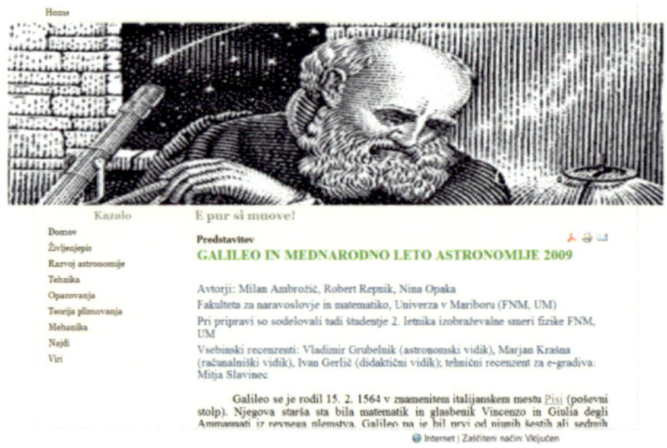

Fig. 3. The structure of *FNM's* (Faculty of Natural sciences and Mathematics) web portal about Galileo.

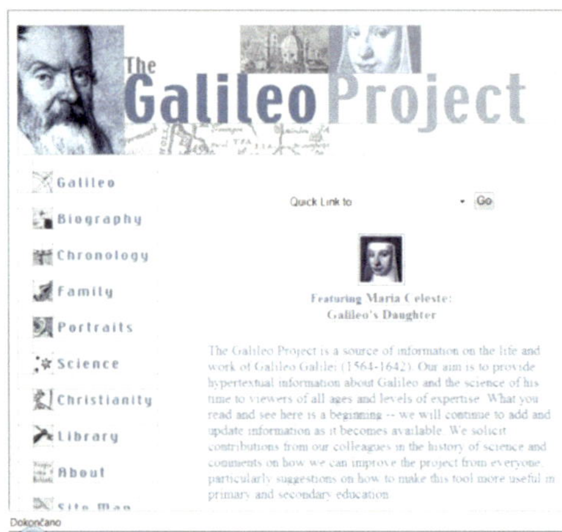

Fig. 4. The structure of *Rice* e-books about Galileo

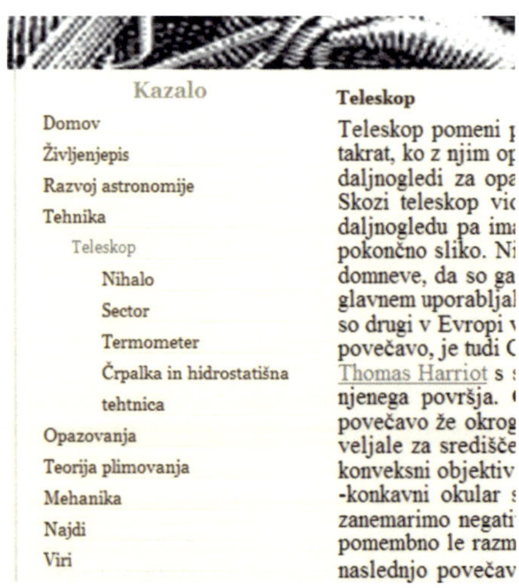

Fig. 5. Open subsection Telescope in *FNM*

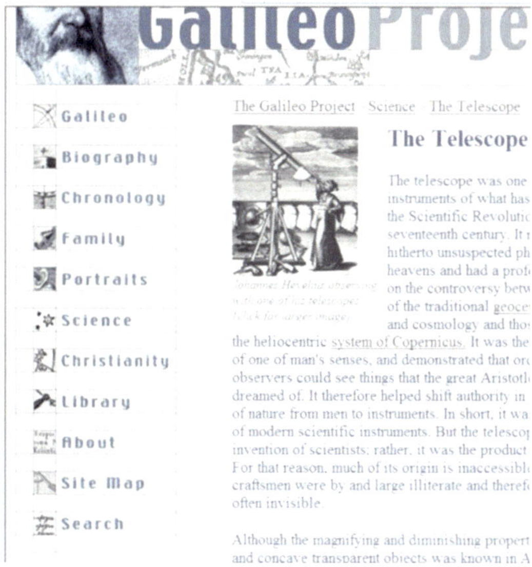

Fig. 6. Open subsection Telescope in *Rice*

8. Discussion

The preliminary results of testing our e-book on Galileo at schools and the results of the survey on e-books in general indicate some important conclusions. Teachers, pupils and students (but certainly not all of them) are prone to using e-books for teaching and learning. Most pupils in primary school have not used them yet. By teachers' opinion pupils ought to start using the e-books in the third triad of primary school. On the other hand, the majority of students at high school (at least in the educational physics) have already used e-books on their own initiative. We are going to encourage the teachers from secondary school to participate in this survey and we expect the results about the using of e-materials by students will be interesting and instructive. At the time being, they generally consider printed books and e-books as equally important. Another very significant observation in this small research of respondents' opinion was the user's preference to the information reliability over the fully open access to e-books.

The size of our e-book on Galileo is about one third of the corresponding material by Rice: this is roughly seen in number of words, figures and subsections. However, many professors from different universities in USA cooperated in the creation of the *Rice* e-book, while only a few people worked on our e-book for a couple of months. Nevertheless, the stuff and presentation of it in Rice gave us several useful ideas for our e-book. In the second part of our survey we also collect the opinions whether to extend our material further or not. Nevertheless, the extensiveness of our e-book (see FNM in Tables 1 and 2) is much larger than for other materials in Slovene language. What has become more evident in others' opinion is that the e-book should include more multimedia elements. Therefore, the preparation of videos of experiments and also some animations (connected with Galileo's work) is in progress. Our students will do this work and their products will extend the Galileo e-book.

Comparison of a few numbers in the two e-books in English in Table 1 (Rice and Wiki-eng), particularly the number of links and references, illuminates two opposite philosophies in the creation of e-books. Rice has very few external links and this material relies much more on references (which are mostly books and articles in scientific journals). The meaning of this is obvious: the Rice material puts the reliability of information on first place. It is difficult to imagine how much time it took for the authors to go through all the literature and crosscheck the sources (185 references!). On the other hand, Wikipedia relies on the broad audience and openness of the materials that is evident in many links. In regard to both the number of links and openness our e-book is between those of Rice and Wikipedia. We have directed many links to Wikipedia pages, where the information is not 100% reliable, but nevertheless we have read carefully the corresponding Wikipedia pages to see if information there is satisfactory. Many natural phenomena that were part of our web-book were tested this way but it is not the topic of this article to explain them in details.

The authors have decided that our e-book is going to be closed for editing. New topics will be collected and moderated and only if sufficient quality of the proposed topics could be achieved we are going to add them to the e-book. The proposals for new topics are not a part of our e-book. A news form is added where even anonymous users can post the requests and ideas. The changes and addition to the e-book is subjected mainly to the spare time of our authors who review and verify articles and then add them.

E-learning materials are not snapshots in the time. They change, evolve and mature. We will continue with our effort to improve the materials and customize them to the customers' wishes and preferences. Recently, (Kaučič, et al., 2011) showed that narrated e-learning materials have potential to improve learning experience.

9. The curricula changes

It is evident that "*e*" in e-learning means just tools and learning means goals (De Praetere, n.d.). Therefore it is necessary to incorporate ICT into the learning processes. We have changed our learning programs at the university levels according to the Bologna declaration. Accompanying these changes the system was established that enables changes of study programs faster and more suitable to the contemporary educational needs (Government of Republic of Slovenia, n.d.). In the lower levels of education we have project of changing perspective of learning. We need to give competences to the student and not just knowledge. A large project "Development of natural science competences" is at the end and we have prepared basic blocks for future curricula changes (University of Maribor, Faculty of Natural Sciences and Mathematics, n.d.).

At the university level we come to the evaluation period. Changes are necessary and more ICT topics need to be included into study programs. Lecturers who were authors of first changes in study programs discovered they are not ICT literate enough to follow the development in ICT and students were not advancing. Therefore new study courses emerge where e-learning; web technologies; and digital security are taught for pedagogical students (future teachers). What we take for granted has proven wrong. Our students have huge ICT knowledge but this is not deep knowledge at the same time. Shallow knowledge is not sufficient for them to use it effectively in school – either for study purposes or for teaching purposes. Old wisdom is correct again. We need deep and thorough understanding of the topic we want to teach competently.

Changes are inevitable in the curricula for primary schools too. Current curricula for natural science courses in primary schools are very detailed and do not allow teachers to insert any additional topics into the learning process. Only physics allows teachers to apply knowledge of physics on current events (Ministry of Education, Republic of Slovenia). One of such events was tsunami in Japan and nuclear power plant disaster. Such topics are known to boost retention level of students by magnitude and not just mere percentages. Even after years they will know how nuclear power plant works and how dangerous is radiation.

In the following years the curricula will change and acquiring competences will be the focus of learning objectives. ICT will become a second hand in such processes. But changes in the school are not rapid. Schools always have financial problems and new technology takes time to become effective. It is not unusual that schools were equipped with one technology that later proved to be unsuccessful and was replaced with more appropriated. Was money thrown away? Not at all, teachers have ability to experience, use and evaluate the technology and decide that it is not good. Such process is now in the area of interactive boards and tablet computers. Software technology that proves to be effective on traditional computers and interactive tablets - Flash is not suitable for low powered tablet computers. Transformation is costly and who knows if necessary. In year or two tablet computers will be powerful enough to play SWF files without glitches.

10. Conclusion

E-materials are here, with all their advantages and disadvantages (like burdening the eyes). Technology helps in the production of better and more capable e-learning materials but there remains an open question: reliability of information or full openness? Guarantee of quality is something that students are beginning to understand and in this respect we have compared our own e-learning material about Galileo with four other materials. Even a very simple quantitative analysis, such as counting the links and references, illustrates very different approaches in the creation of such materials. It is true that students like attractive e-learning materials but rarely participate in the e-learning material production. In their life they use interactive technology but when the same is applied in the school environment they become much more traditional. Different web technologies are going to coexist and flourish for foreseeable future. Quality of e-learning materials is not measured only with the number of interactive elements and can be achieved even with traditional web pages. Smart use and not extensive use of appropriate technology is the key for the success.

11. References

Ambrožič Dolinšek, J., Duh, M., Fošnarič, S., Golob, N., Grubelnik, V., Hus, V., et al. (2009). E-learning materials for subject Environmental education. Retrieved from University of Maribor, Faculty of Education: http://distance.pfmb.uni-mb.si/course/view.php?id=39

Ambrožič, M., Repnik, R., & Opaka, N. (2009). Galileo and International Year of Astronomiy 2009. Retrieved from http://fizika.dssl.si/Galileo/

De Praetere, T. (n.d.). E-Learning: Learning throught the use of devices. Retrieved 01 17, 2012, from KNOL - A unit of knowledge: http://knol.google.com/k/e-learning#

Dolenc, S. (n.d.). Galileo Galilei - med mitom in zgodovino. Retrieved October 1, 2011, from Kvarkadabra: http://www.kvarkadabra.net/article.php/Galileo-Galilei

Government of Republic of Slovenia. (n.d.). NAKVIS. Retrieved October 2, 2011, from SLOVENIAN QUALITY ASSURANCE AGENCY FOR HIGHER EDUCATION: http://www.nakvis.si/

Hofstetter, F. T. (2004). Internet technologies at work. Chicago: Irwin Professional Publications.

Kaučič, B., Ramšak, M., & Krašna, M. (2011). Rich media presentations in blended learning. Society and technology. Lovran.

Kaučič, B., Sraka, D., & Ramšak, M. (2010). Observations on plagiarism in programming courses. 2nd International Conference on Computer Supported Education (pp. 181-184). Valencia: INSTICC.

Krašna, M., & Bratina, T. (2008). Trends of e-learning in the education of teachers. The Fifth International Conference on Informatics, Educational Technology and New Media in Education (pp. 65-69). Sombor: University of Novi Sad, Faculty of Education Sombor.

Krašna, M., Gerlič, I., Skala, K., & Skala, T. (2005). Intelligent graphics interfaces in the distance education. MIPRO 2005: 28th international convention (pp. 291-294). Opatija: MIPRO.

Lau, J. (2008). Students' experience of using electronic textbooks in different levels of education. Retrieved April 20, 2009, from University of Toronto: http://jps.library.utoronto.ca/index.php/fdt/article/viewArticle/4907/1768

Ministry of Education, Republic of Slovenia. (n.d.). Posodobljeni učni načrti obveznih predmetov v osnovni šoli. Retrieved October 2, 2011, from Republika Slovenija, Ministrstvo za šolstvo in šport: http://www.mss.gov.si/si/solstvo/osnovnosolsko_izobrazevanje/ucni_nacrti/posodobljeni_ucni_nacrti_za_obvezne_predmete/

Repnik, R., & Ambrožič, M. (2009). Galileo on our web textbook on behalf of International Year of Astronomy. 20th International Conference CECIIS 2009 (pp. 29-33). Varaždin: Unviersity of Zagreb, Faculty of Organization and Informatics Varaždin.

Repnik, R., Vajngerl, V., & Krašna, M. (2006). Virtual learning environments. MIPRO 2006: 29th international convention (pp. 92-94). Opatija: MIPRO.

Rice University. (n.d.). The Galileo project. Retrieved Januar 2009, from Rice University - Galileo: http://galileo.rice.edu/

Sandia National Laboratories. (n.d.). Sandian's Web-based computational science textbook used in 100 schools. Retrieved April 20, 2009, from Sandia National Laboratories: http://www.sandia.gov/media/webtext.htm

Shneiderman, B. (2004). Designing the User Interface: Strategies for Effective Human-Computer Interaction (3 ed.). Addison-Wesley.

Smith-Atakan, S. (2006). Human-Computer Interaction. Thomson.

University of Maribor, Faculty of Natural Sciences and Mathematics. (n.d.). Development of Natural Science Competences. Maribor: University of Maribor, Faculty of Natural Sciences and Mathematics.

Wikipedia. (n.d.). Galileo Galilei. Retrieved October 1, 2011, from Wikipedia: http://en.wikipedia.org/wiki/Galileo_Galilei

13

Open Web-Based Virtual Lab for Experimental Enhanced Educational Environment

Fuan Wen
Beijing University of Posts and Telecommunications
China

1. Introduction

Nowadays, there exists a common problem that science and engineering students lack professional knowledge and skills. Students lack the ability that can guide them to practice with the theory and research methods. These problems are becoming more prominent among some poor condition schools.

Adams, Raymond K. introduced the virtual oscilloscope which was built aiming at the students who were majored in electrical and computer engineering in the University of Tennessee in the summer of 1988 (Adams & Raymond, 1989).

In 1990, Mercer, Lynn etc. from Canada University of Regina proposed the concept of the Virtual Lab and built a simple one (Mercer et al., 1990). During the next 20 years, a lot of researchers further built and enriched the concept of Virtual Lab (Hai Lin & Lin, 2005).

Educational environment means all the environments, places and conditions that can carry out learning and training activities, such as schools and training institutions. Learning environment means all the environments for learning. Chu-Ting Zhang considered that learning environment is composed of the factors that can affect people, which include the natural environment, the physical environment, the interpersonal environment and the educational concept environment (Zhang, 1999).

From the geographical point of view, the learning or educational environment can be divided into the classroom environment, the lab environment, the campus environment and the social environment. The specific learning environments correspond to the virtual learning environments. As shown in Fig. 1.

The most common modern classroom environment is the multimedia classroom which includes: projectors and large screens, object display platform, DVD player and computers. Among them, computer is increasingly becoming the centre of multimedia classrooms. Due to the lively features of having the image of specific and providing activities that students can personally involved in, modern curriculum resources provide students with a wide range of information stimulation and arouse students' sense and interests to participate in activities which seems like a real scene so that students can increase their knowledge pleasantly and develop their own capacity, which cannot be replaced by the traditional teaching.

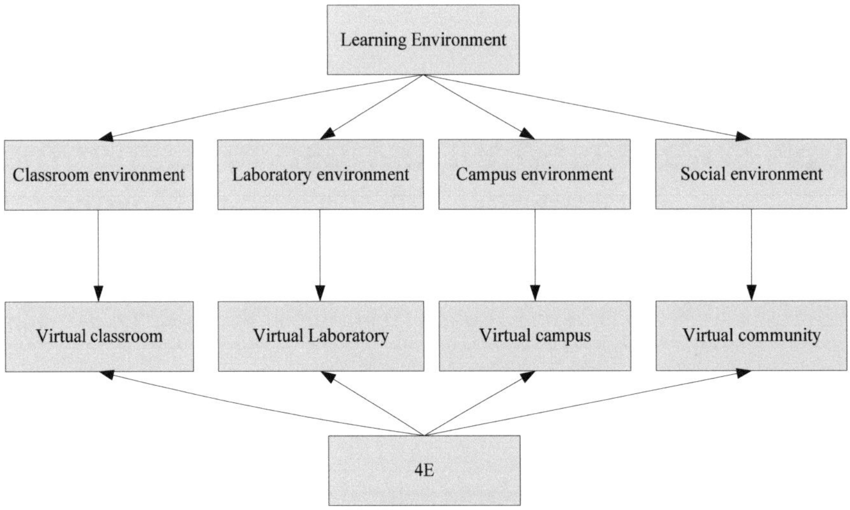

Fig. 1. The Learning Environment and Virtual Learning Environment

Laboratory environment refers to the laboratory which schools and training institutions build for teaching students. School laboratory is an essential part of teaching and learning environment. It provides students with convenient, safe and intuitive place to do scientific experiments. The experiment can stimulate interest in learning, experience the fun of exploration, improve the existing structure of knowledge and enhance the abilities of operating, diagnosis, analysis, design and innovation.

Campus environment refers to all the inside school learning environment except the classrooms and laboratories which includes the educational environment provided by the library, lecture hall, offices, communication rooms and other facilities.

Social environment refers to the learning environment except classrooms, laboratories and the campus environment that offered by the community such as science museum and internship department.

With the rapid development of information technology, the digitization and virtualization of the learning environment has become the future development trend. People construct virtualized learning environment through web technology and computer communication technology. This environment is widely used in distance education and Television University in China.

The virtual classroom is also called live classroom, which can provide real-time teaching function through web technology. Teachers can use texts, images, handwritings, voices, videos and other forms of media to teach students with theoretical knowledge. Students can use texts, voices and other forms of media to ask questions at anytime. The learning process is similar to the traditional classroom environment.

Virtual lab is an online virtual experiment system which is based on web technology and virtual reality technology. It is the digitization and virtualization of laboratories on campus. Virtual lab consists of a virtual laboratory bench, a virtual equipment cabinet and the web-based software for laboratory management. Virtual lab provides a bran-new learning and training environment for experimental courses. The virtual laboratory bench is similar with the real laboratory bench. Students can configure, connect, debug and operate the virtual experimental equipment by themselves. Teachers can use the equipment in the virtual equipment cabinets to set up any reasonable typical experiment or experiment cases. This is an important feature that is different from general experimental courseware.

It is indicated in the psychology research, the closer between content in the study with the life background for student, the stronger the awareness in the study become. On the contrary, it is difficult for the student to accept the very abstract content. For Analogue Circuit Curriculum in the field of electronic, for instance, the theoretical arithmetic is over emphasized in the current teaching material while such theoretical arithmetic model cannot reflect the real circuit system exactly in many cases. As the students get confused and bored easily the course has been nicknamed the "devil course" among many students in China. Even though they strive to acquire the calculation methods from the course, these given methods rarely play a role in the science and production practice. Circuit simulation system could get the circuit parameter faster and more precisely than manual calculation, in addition, it is economic and feasible. The virtual experiments provide the teachers and students a more direct and convenient simulation experiment environment. We can get rid of the constraint of complex and inefficient theoretical arithmetic in teaching process by using simulation technology.

Virtual campus presents the campus environment to students in term of web technology and virtual reality technology. The official website of school shows all the detailed information to the visitors. The content of website includes department introduction, service organization, specialized subjects, curriculum, scientific research, social service, recruitment, employment and so on. Students can browse on it and join the virtual library, the lecture hall, Q&A room or online BBS.

"Virtual communities are social aggregations that emerge from the Net when enough people carry on those public discussions long enough, with sufficient human feeling, to form webs of personal relationships in cyberspace." Virtual community was defined by Howard Rheingold (Rheingold, 1993). Types of virtual communities include Internet message boards, online chat rooms, virtual worlds and social network services. Here, we take virtual community as virtual educational environment corresponding to the social educational environment.

The virtual classrooms, virtual labs, virtual campus and virtual communities play an essential role in building the virtual educational environment. However, the progress of such technology does not fundamentally change the effect of teaching and learning. The main reason is that they are only a mapping for real educational environment. Therefore, it is difficult to go beyond and completely change the existing educational environment. However, it is already under ripe condition for the integration and innovation on this basis, so we can expect a courageous challenge for education innovation caused by information technology.

2. Experimental enhanced educational environment

Experimental Enhanced Educational Environment (4E) refers to a virtual learning environment focused on experiment simulation that is built by information technology. The

4E centres on virtual lab and supplements related functions of the virtual classroom, virtual campus and virtual community. Breaking the natural barrier among the classroom, the laboratory, school, and the outside community, the 4E puts theoretical study, experimental operation, collaboration, communication and social practice together as a whole. It allows education open to real application at a lower cost and enables students to adapt to future development in a more efficient way.

In the opinion of constructivists, if learners want to complete the construction of the meaning of the knowledge, in other words, to understand the nature and laws of the reflected things and to appreciate the links between things and others, the best way is to let learners feel and experience the real-world rather than just listening to people who introduce and explain this experience. Within the 4E, it will be quick and convenient to create an environment similar with the real teaching situation. The 4E is more suitable for the learning mode such as Self-learning - remedial learning, Inquiry-based instruction, Anchored instruction, Analyze the phenomena of learning, Discovery learning and other learning model, even effective to Transfer–to accept learning and Butler's self learning mode.

Using different educational environment and facilities to carry out teaching, students' knowledge acquisition, active participation, practical ability and intuitive feeling is different, see Table 1.

Educational Environment	Classroom	4E	Laboratory	Society
Knowledge Acquisition	Easy	Easy	Difficult	Most difficult
Active participation	Negative	Positive	Positive	Positive
Practical ability	Bad	Good	Better	Best
Intuitive feeling	Bad	Good	Better	Best
Cost	Lower	Low	High	Superior

Table 1. Comparison of the 4E and the traditional educational environment

By means of simulating the cognitive objects in the real world, the 4E provides a vivid operating environment, which makes the students be willing to approach, understand, like and thus be motivated to learn and explore actively. The 4E can arouse the students' happiness of exploring and creating, and stimulate their cognitive interest and learning motivation. The students will have a more perfect understanding of the knowledge structure and their abilities will improve more effectively.

The students perform an experiment provided by the virtual environment. In that the experimental models are created by the students, and the experimental data is also collected by the students, they will become more interested in the experimental model, design and results. They can acquire more knowledge than that got from books and multimedia CD for learns. This method will also improve student's hands-on training, observation, analysis, diagnosis, design and innovation capability. The interest is the best teacher and the strong driving force for students to learn actively, think positively and explore bravely. So using the 4E in learning tasks will promote the students to throw themselves to learning activities, and play a multiplier role.

The 4E is a new kind of educational environment, but it is not a mature of the pedagogy. Along with the establishment of the 4E, a new pedagogy will appear in the future. The characteristics of the new pedagogy is predicted as following

1. Attach importance to the construction of virtual environment and information resources, and provide more intuitive knowledge
2. Virtual labs are the most important learning environment for students, especially for students of science and technology
3. Cultivation of students' creative potential to enable students to explore on a large scale;
4. Stimulate the students' motivation
5. Create the environment to share knowledge and experience, and let student study collaboratively
6. Enhance the guidance to students by means of automation and intelligent
7. Every student can create their own knowledge structure and design their cognitive objects
8. Restore every student's learning process and result
9. More precise individualized teaching, all students have their own private roles and learning space
10. Maximize the student-centred teaching philosophy

3. Demands on the environment building

3.1 A variety of learning resources

Digital resources are the information resources available for education which are released, accessed and used in digital form. Rich resources are helpful to build a good learning environment. The resources required in the construction of the 4E are mainly included:

1. Providing virtual instruments, devices and other equipment in virtual experimental platform;
2. The learning objectives and the experiment instructions which created in the 4E by the instructional designing experts;
3. Learning guidance document;
4. Knowledge database;
5. Question& Answer database;

Rich digital resources provide a strong guarantee for designs in the learning process. They are presented to the learner in a variety of forms at anytime. The construction work of digital resources should start earlier and keep improving and supplementing constantly according to the feedback during the teaching process.

3.2 Completely and orderly learning process

The learning activity should be a process which is lively, active and full of personality. The proper design for the learning process can ensure that learners not only have an order which can be followed in the learning activities, but also are free and independent enough to perform themselves. The learning process includes instructional design and events which are completed by the teacher; the background study, test, experimental observation, explore & design, discussion and experience summary which are the student centred; the evaluation, display, statistical analysis of study files, archive report which is teacher-led.

3.3 Timely and effective instruction

Guidance for students should reflect the concept of student-centred. Instruction should be accurate, timely and effective. The teacher acts as an organiser, director, guider and partner, whose position in the instruction should not be doubted. But because of the constraints of some factors, such as time, energy and memory, teachers need help from the guidance system which is based on artificial intelligence, information retrieval and multimedia knowledge base (Wang, 2010). It is possible to guarantee the timely and effective instruction by the system.

Firstly the guidance system should have a strong ability to understand and perceive students, on this basis, which can provide learners with a variety of guidance and help. In terms of the perspective of the subjective will of the students, learning guide can be divided into two types: Searching for Help and the Director. The Searching for Help means that the students take the initiative to request system to give tips, guidance and help when they are confused. The Director means that the guidance system prompts and guides students without the students' requests according to the status and situation of the students. From the view of feedback time, learning guide is divided into two kinds: real-time guidance and non-real-time guidance. The real-time guidance means that the system immediately responds when the students seek help or some kind of system considers that in the case should be prompted, no matter where the response comes, which also is known as synchronous real-time guidance. Conversely, non-real-time guidance means that the system can not immediately respond after the student seek help or some kind of system considers that the prompt should be put forward in the case, then the students need to wait a long time to get feedback, so it also known as asynchronous guidance. In general, the cost of real-time guidance is relatively high, so the intelligent guidance and answering system based on expert system and knowledge database will greatly reduce the repeated work of teachers.

Like a virtual teacher, instruction system is the most humane part of the 4E.The instruction should be accurate, timely and enlightening, and also should be designed user-friendly to establish a strong feeling with students in the learning process.

3.4 Learning environment in harmony

The reform and development of learning environment is primarily the combination between real learning environment and virtual technology environment. There exits real environment, physical environment, interpersonal environment and ideal environment in the natural environment (Zhang, 1999). Learning environment is a real atmosphere, and the school has its own tacit culture which is difficult to create by any technology environment. Therefore, the virtual technology environment must be consistent with the existing learning philosophy and learning order. With the smooth transition and improving, we should gradually expand the proportion of virtual technology environment in the existing of learning environment in practice. Any attempt to completely replace the traditional learning environment may be counter-productive.

The learner is the centre of whole service of the system. Experience of learners should be concerned, including learners' study experiences, learning effect, enthusiasm of participation and initiative, the upgrading of skills, evaluation to the learning environment and teacher. Only those can truly make a positive or negative answer to a learning environment.

4. Technology solution

The 4E can be built on campus network. The technology of the 4E is based on the educational technology. The virtual classroom environment can be built on the basis of the electronic classroom, the examination system (including the student's psychological test system) and Course On Demand (COD). Virtual lab environment can be built on the basis of virtual laboratory, educational games and academic tools. Virtual campus environment can build on the basis of question and answer system (including instant messaging systems), electronic reading room, educational administration (including the enrollment application, course scheduling, teaching quality assessment and performance management, Office Automation (OA) of school). Virtual communities environment can be built on the basis of open forum, chat rooms, Social Networking Sites (SNS).

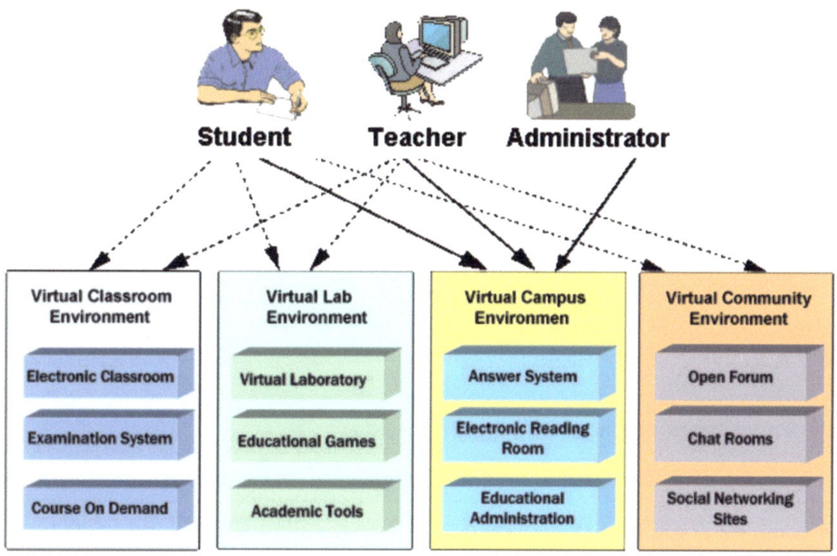

Fig. 2. Software functions included in the 4E

We will supplement related functions and strengthen the connections between systems based on the 4E idea. These systems get integrated through Web Service and realize single sign on that the user only need log on once during the process.

4.1 System architecture

The 4E software system uses three-tier system architecture: Client Tier, Server Tier and Data Tier. Client Tier is mainly about the user's Web Browser and Smart Client. Server Tier is mainly composed of Web Server and Application Server. The common Web Server has Apache, Nginx and Lighttpd. The main function is receiving the requests of the user, handling the request of static file download and forward dynamic process, it also can provide load balancing. There are some common application servers, such as Tomcat, Jetty and Weblogic, etc. It mainly used to handle the dynamic forwards request of Web Server. Data Tier mainly is the Database Server, File System Server and other external systems, Database Server is mainly used to store relational data. File System Server is mainly used to store pictures, documents and other non-relational data. Other external systems is a kind of system which exchange and transmit data with the 4E. Application Server could access to hardware which is connected to the server, so the experiment device could be controlled remotely.

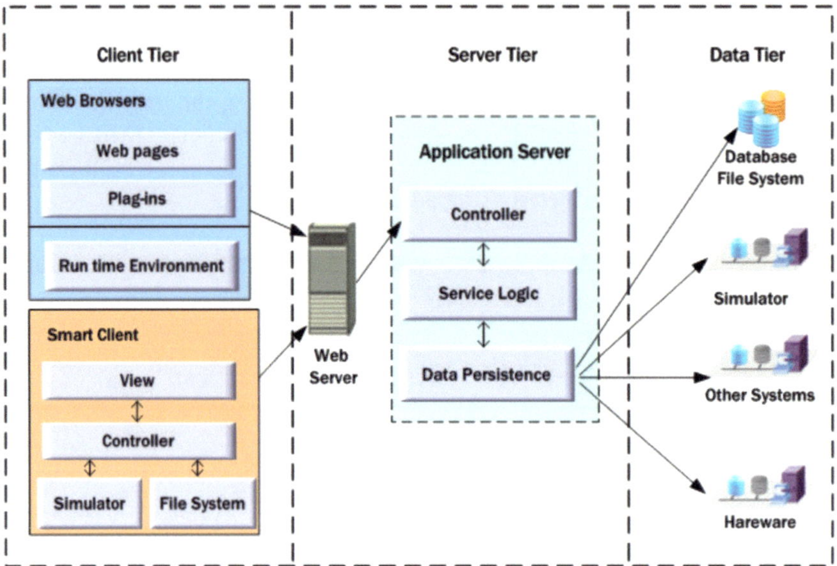

Fig. 3. System Architecture of the 4E

4.2 Development technology of information system

To build the 4E information system, there are an army of technological options to choose.

C/S is referred to Client/Server architecture which is called Rich Client (also called heavy, fat, or thick client). C/S is often characterised by the ability to perform many functions without connection to the network or the central server in order to reduce the pressure on the server. This architecture allows the user to work offline at most of the time, but it's complicated to deploy and update the client software and corresponding infrastructure software.

B/S is referred to Browser/Server architecture which is called Thin Client. The clients of B/S generally run application software in a browser. This architecture is easy to deploy, update and maintain. In addition, the server could take advantage of the cluster technology to improve its performance. B/S is a widely adopting architecture now, but it needs the real-time network connection when it is applied.

Smart Client combines the function and flexibility of Rich Client and deployment easily and stability which is belongs to Thin Client organically. It abandons the shortcomings of Thin Client and Rich Client, so it has certain advantages for developing the 4E.

There are many alternative technologies for B/S and C/S, such as Java, PHP, Python, Ruby and so on. Popular programming languages being adopted released on the form named TIOBE programming Community Index for October 2011. The rating of Java is 17.913%, in comparison, PHP is 6.818% and C# is 6.723%. The ratings are calculated by counting hits of the most popular search engines (TIOBE Software, 2011). These figures illustrate that the three language or namely called platform, such as JEE/Java, PHP, .NET, account for most of share in the field of web nowadays.

JEE/Java source file should be compiled to .class byte-code file firstly, and then the byte-code file would be interpreted and executed in the java virtual machine. Java has abundant functions and great resource utilization in server, so it's widely used in enterprise or large system though it has a great resource overhead. Java platform is open and stable enough. It has a great number of high-quality open-source frameworks and libraries, so it is also suitable for small or medium-sized applications.

PHP is a scripting language interpreted in the server. It's easy to learn. The grammar of PHP is similar with C. PHP is more widely used in small and medium applications on the Internet. Thinkphp or CakePHP MVC framework is widely used. However, PHP's prospects are not promising, because its design is too simple. There shows a downward trend of usage in the future.

Microsoft's C# combines the advantages of the Visual Basic, Java and PHP and other languages with the power of Java, the briefness of Visual Basic, and the easy-to-start of PHP. Consider that it is relatively closed platform only for Windows, not opened for other platforms, with the high licensing fees for the supporting software. It is worried about the prospects in the education industry.

There are also ROR, Python, Node, JavaScript and other Web development technologies, but these techniques are generally applied to specific areas, not the mainstream of the software technology for information systems.

In comparison, JEE/Java is more preferred because the Java platform is more open, and there are lots of open source frameworks such as Struts2, Spring, Hibernate, Wicket, Spring MVC, JSF, Guice, Ibatis. There are several combinations of the framework to develop B/S application. It is recommended to use the combination of the most common framework SSH, which is Struts2, Spring and Hibernate.

4.3 Simulator platform technology

Simulator platform is an essential part of the 4E, which provides the main interface for experimental operation. The human-machine interface is generally coded by the form of plug-ins within a browser. The simulator can be realized in the plug-ins, also can be implemented as an application programme in a client or servers. There are several common technologies to implementing the platform:

ActiveX has been used for a long time because of its flexibility and strong function, such as operating on the local file system; accessing the external network connection and so on. But the security problem is also appeared at the same time. Besides that, the compatibility between the browser and the platform based on ActiveX is poor. ActiveX can just run in the browser of Internet Explorer based on the Windows platform. Because of its security problem, ActiveX has been used less.

Flash has a variety of platform version, high installed rate and better browser compatibility. In addition to these, it is safer than ActiveX, and has a strong function include connecting the network and playing audio and video, so Flash has a strong expression for education. Flash mainly uses Action Script language and has a powerful Integrated Development Environment (IDE). Currently as a common element in the web page, it is widely used to increase the dynamic effects of the web page and even to be the main expressive form of the application system report and user interface. Its principal flaw is not open as a standard.

Applet/JavaFx use Java language as the language of development. It needs to download and install a relatively large Java Runtime Environment (JRE) to be able to run. It runs in the default sand box, so that the security is better. The Applet has an advantage of cross-platforms which means that it can run in all kinds of operating system and browsers.

JavaScript language is mainly used in the development of HTML5, which adds the "canvas" element and integrates SVG content. Besides that, it has powerful drawing functions and a part of the Rich Client functions. But its standard has not yet fully formed, and its function is not in full. On the other hand, it has not supported for old versions of the browser.

Comparing with the above four techniques, ActiveX has trouble in security and cross-platform supporting. The standard for HTML5 is not yet mature. Considering the fact that a large number of instruments' internal logic needs to be programming in the simulation platform, rigorous static language is more suitable than the script language. So Applet is preferred for the simulation platform.

5. An Open Web-based Virtual Lab

With the effort to design, realize and apply on educational environment based on the virtual experiments, this paper reports an Open Web-based Virtual Lab (OWVLab) for colleges on engineering experiment. The OWVLab is a real digital lab, which can be used by students, teachers and lab technician through Internet anywhere at any time. The service capability of the lab could be enlarged infinitely by Cloud Computing Service or Computer Cluster technology. It is the simulation of a real lab. Surrounding with the virtual entrance, information desk, the classroom, chat room, the instructor and the evaluator, the virtual devices, instruments and elements can be moved from the equipment cabinet to compose various trial and errors for the experiments in different disciplines and explore on the virtual laboratory bench just like in a real lab. An experimental enhanced educational environment with open web-based virtual lab has been set up for colleges [Fuan Wen, 2010].

5.1 Experiment enhanced learning management

For the requirement of learning in schools, OWVLab provides an integrated management solution. There are an army of useful functions such as curriculum management, academic programs management, course selection management, laboratory management, learning resources, learning activities management, knowledge learning, attendance management, virtual laboratory management, intelligent guidance, automatic correcting experimental records, laboratory reports management, the learning process monitoring, evaluation of the learning effectiveness, file management and etc.

System is divided into five roles such as system administrators, teachers and students and faculties for school governor, laboratory staff, different roles have their own permissions. The system is built by modules to make sure that the functions are easy to expand. With the ongoing of the application of experimental learning, the system can be customized to the actual requirement for different types of schools.

With the application of the system, we can promote that the laboratory will be more and more informationized and regulated. The threshold of the laboratory will be lower for students. The pedagogy of experimental learning will be improved greatly. Achievements of experimental learning will be accumulated.

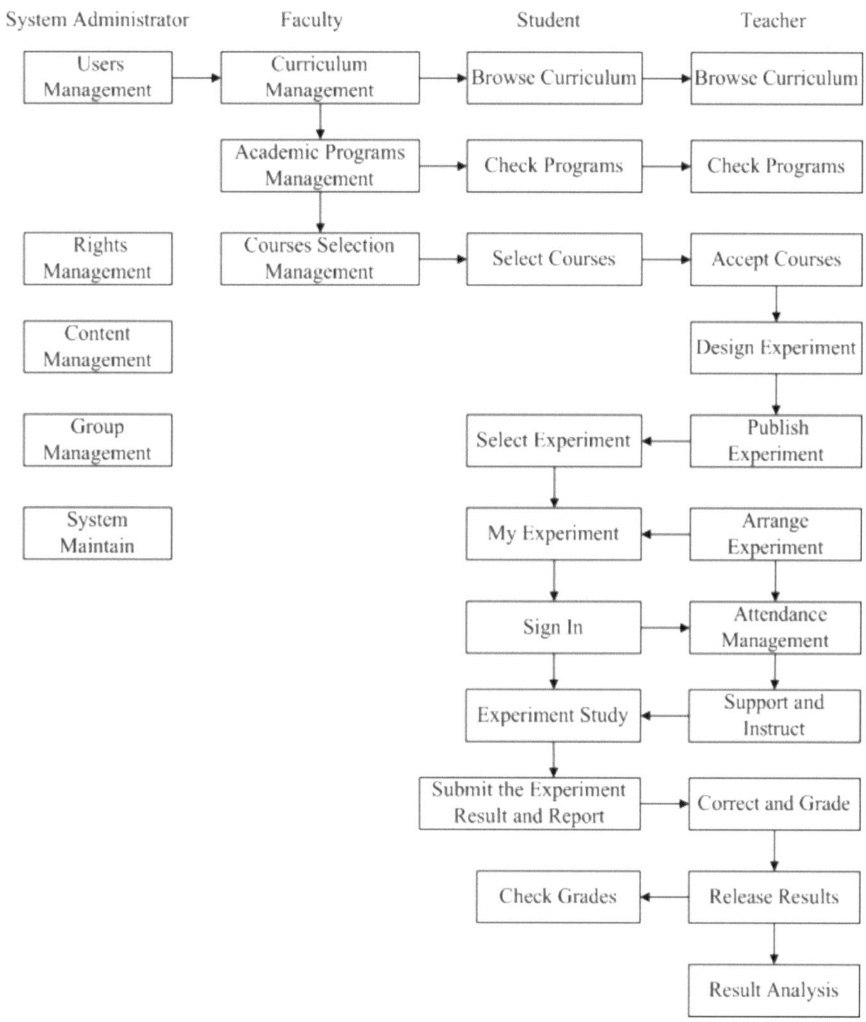

Fig. 4. The main working flow in OWVLab

5.2 Features of OWVLab

1. A set of effective virtual experiment management system has been provided and it is easy to integrate with other learning and instructional system.
2. Adopting multimedia technology, abundant experimental learning resources are offered for students.

3. Intellect and one-to-one real time guidance are provided on emphasis and difficult problems during the process of experiment for students.
4. Automatic correcting functions are provided to the experiment result thus to reduce teacher's duplicate work.
5. Adequate experiments models are designed by experts to enhance the abilities of operation, design and innovation to students.
6. The knowledge learning and operating ability cultivation are combined to form a complete experimental learning system.
7. The virtual instruments can present an experimental phenomenon that the real devices cannot reflect.
8. With direct and user-friendly interface all the virtual equipment is easy to operate and more similar to real equipment.
9. With strong extensibility and flexibility users can add experimental equipment and experiment model according to specific requirements which is individual customization service.
10. The standards such as SPICE (Simulation Program with Integrated Circuit Emphasis) are abided by the system.

6. Use case and simulation

6.1 Use case

There is a Use Case describing how the OWVLab is used by all kinds of users. When a student sit in front of a computer at home and log into a web site, a virtual lab will appear on the screen. She/he will find messages listed on the information desk, enter in a virtual classroom and listen to the teacher in class, and has a test on related knowledge. She/he may take a rest with music and beautiful pictures, go into a chat room has a talk with classmate, send message to teachers when they are absent. The virtual instructor may guide the student visit in a lab. A lab technician may show the intent of the experiment today. The student will drag the appropriate equipment to a laboratory bench, connect them together, manipulate the instruments, observe, ponder over and record the result. In case the study on the experiment has been finished, fill in report, save and submit all experiment record to his teacher. The teacher will retrieve and correct the experiments and grade the student at home. All the people active in virtual lab are monitored by the laboratory staff and school governors.

6.2 Simulator platform for the circuits, computers and communications

Simulator platform includes a virtual equipment cabinet in which there are about a hundred types of electronic component and popular instruments. It also include a virtual experimental platform for circuit design. Students can connect, configure and test the circuit.

6.2.1 Virtual components and Instrument

(1) Virtual Electronic Components

1. Resistor: 57 common value resistors, one custom value resistor and one sliding rheostat
2. Capacitor: 9 common value capacitors and one custom value capacitor

3. Inductor meter: 2 common value inductor meters and one custom value inductor meter
4. Transformer: Along the string transformer and Playing transformer, Parity four-terminal transformer, Ectopic four-terminal transformer
5. Diode: 6 general diode and 2 voltage regulator tubes
6. JFET: 2 JFET-NJF and 2 JFET-PJF
7. BJT: 7 BJT-PNP and 3 BJT-NPN
8. Integrated operational amplifier: μA741, OP37AJ, 741
9. Multiplier: Analog multiplier
10. Three terminal regulator: LM7805CT
11. Linear transformer: TS_PQ4_10
12. Bridge Rectifiers: 1B4B42
13. Quartz crystal oscillator: HC-49U_3MHZ
14. Source: AM signal, FM signal source
15. Three-phase Power: Star and triangular three-phase power
16. Switch: SPST switch, SPDT Switch
17. CC series: CC4001, CC4012, CC4071
18. 74series chips: 74LS00, 74LS03, 74LS04, 74LS08, 74LS20, 74LS21, 74LS32, 74LS48, 74LS74, 74LS85, 74LS86, 74LS90, 74LS112, 74LS125, 74LS138, 74LS148, 74LS151, 74LS153, 74LS160, 74LS161, 74LS164, 74LS169, 74LS175, 74LS183, 74LS192, 74LS194, 74LS244, 74LS283, 74LS373
19. Load: Lamp, fluorescent lamp, ballast
20. Others: Connectivity board, potentiometer

Note: The above parameters of the components can be edited as needed, types of component can be expanding

(2) Virtual Electronic Instruments:

Digital DC ammeter, digital DC voltmeter, digital AC ammeter, digital AC voltmeter, DC milliammeter, a multimeter, signal generator, oscilloscope, DC power supply, pulse pen, pulse signal, high and low end, cycle counter, logic analysis unit, power meter. Some new equipment or model may continue to be added.

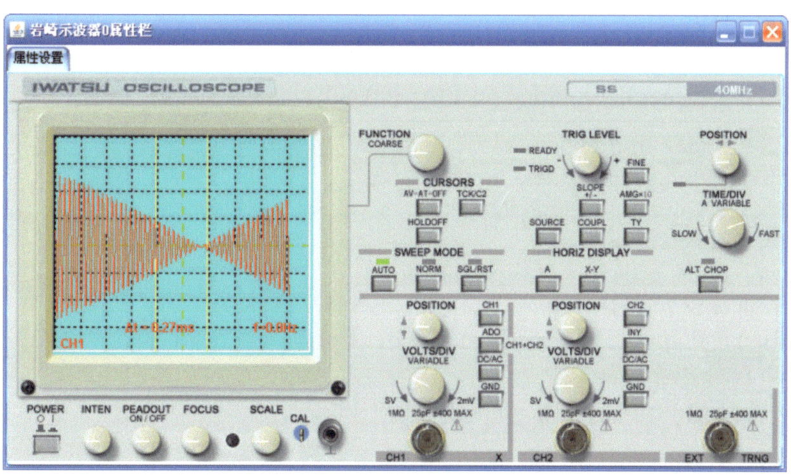

Fig. 5. Virtual Oscilloscope SS7802A Iwasaki

(3) Virtual Network Equipments

1. **Computer:** Windows PC, Linux PC
2. **Routers:**
   Cisco: Seven kinds of 2500 Serials, Four kinds of 2600 Serials, Two kinds of 3600 Serials, 4500 Serials
   Ruijie: RSR20-40
   Digital China: DCR-2626
   HuaWei: AR18-22-24, AR46-40

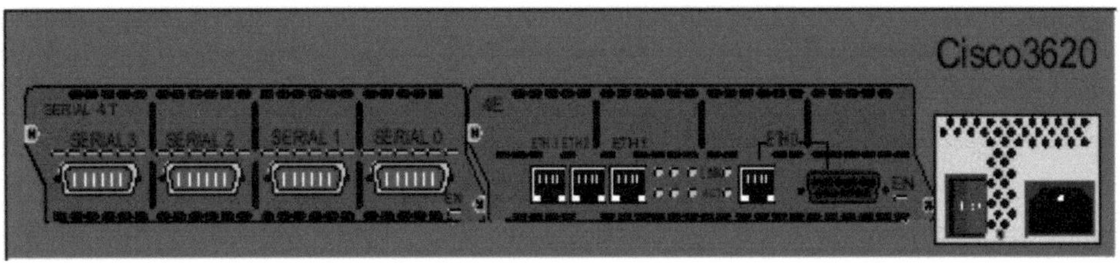

Fig. 6. A Virtual Cisco Router

3. **Switches:**
   Cisco: 2950, 3550, 1900
   Ruijie: RG-S3760-24
   Digital China: DCRS-5650-28
   HuaWei: S3928
4. **Hubs:** Hub of 8 ports , Hub of 12 ports

6.2.2 Typical experience cases

Experimental teaching experts build a large number of typical virtual experience cases on the virtual lab platform according to different learning goals. Most of the cases are similar with traditional physical case. Every typical case includes experimental name, goals, equipment, steps and report formats. The experiment platform build the initial system previously in some typical cases, and student could design and build on a virtual laboratory bench according to schematic diagram in some other cases.

(1) 16 typical experiments provided on Circuit Analysis (OWVLab CAS)

1. Use of the digital multimeter
2. Use of the signal generator and oscilloscope
3. Measurment volt-ampere characteristics
4. Validation of Kirchhoff's law
5. Validation of the principle of superposition
6. Validation of Several theorems of linear network
7. Validation and application of Thevenin's theorem
8. Study of resonant circuit
9. Performance of the PLC component in the Sinusoidal AC circuits
10. Response test of First-order RC circuit
11. Study of the transition process of first-order
12. Second-order circuit response and its state trajectory

13. The research of the controlled source's characteristics
14. Sine steady-state ac circuits phasor research
15. Voltage source, a current source and its power equivalent conversion
16. The flow of current and voltage in three-phase AC circuit

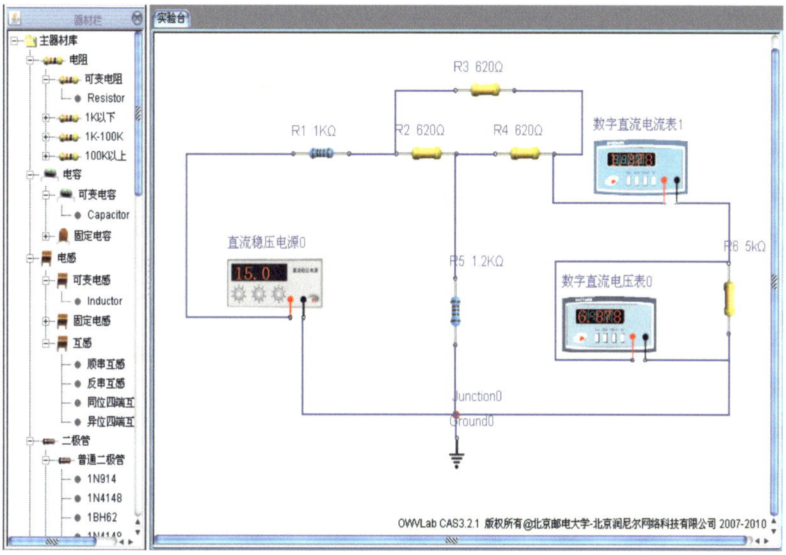

Fig. 7. A Circuit Analysis Simulation Platform

(2) 19 typical experiments provided on Analog Circuits (OWVLab ACS)

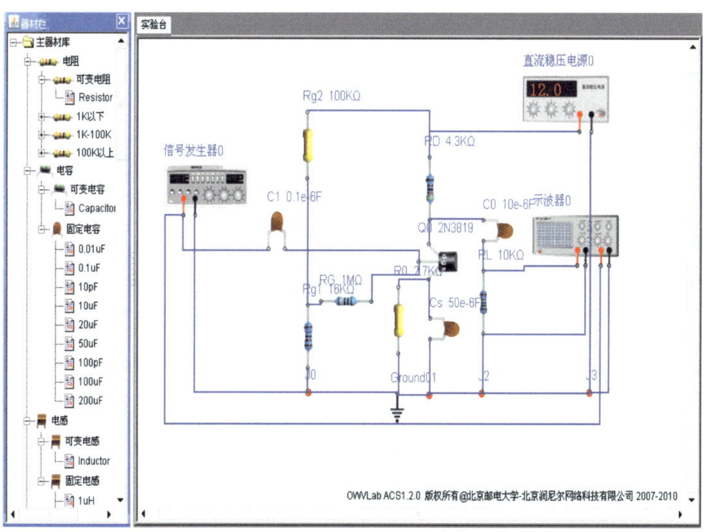

Fig. 8. An Analog Circuits Simulation Platform

1. Single-tube AC amplifier
2. Negative feedback amplifier

3. FET amplifier
4. Differential amplifier circuit
5. Two AC amplifier
6. Emitter follower
7. RC sinusoidal oscillator
8. LC and LC selected frequency sine wave oscillator circuit to enlarge
9. Low-frequency amplifier-OTL power amplifier
10. Integral and differential circuit
11. Testing integrated operational amplifier indicators
12. The basic application of integrated operational amplifier—Active filter
13. Oscillator controlling pressure
14. The basic application of integrated operational amplifier—Analog computing circuits
15. Waveform converting circuit
16. The basic application of integrated operational amplifier—Voltage comparator
17. Complementary symmetry power amplifier
18. The basic application of integrated operational amplifier—Waveform generator
19. Single-tube transistor common emitter amplifier circuit

(3) 20 typical experiments provided on Digital Circuits (OWVLab DCS)

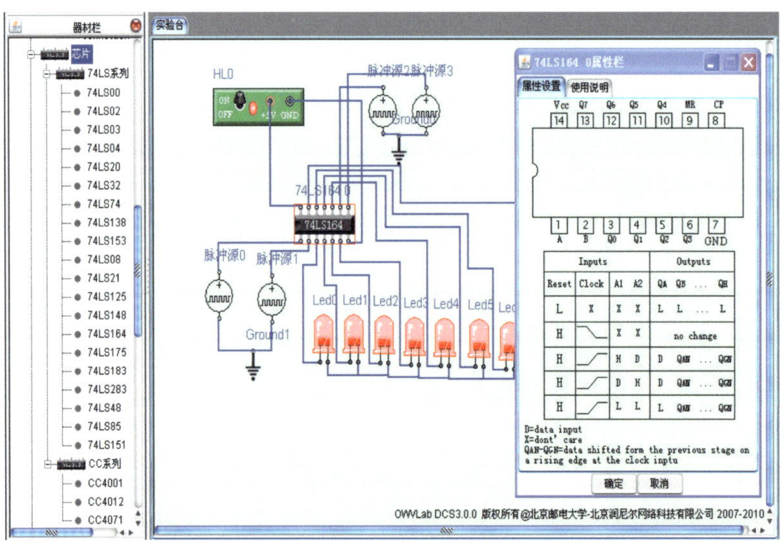

Fig. 9. A Digital Circuits Simulation Platform

1. The test of the performance parameters of TTL integrated logic gate
2. The application test of TTL OC tri-state logic gate and door
3. Characteristics of CMOS integrated logic gates' performances
4. Constitute the counter by the JK flip-flop
5. Basic logic operations and circuits
6. The design of Serial Signal Generator
7. The basic logic function of the trigger
8. D flip-flop formed by the twisted ring counter

9. The design of Pulse distributor
10. Asynchronous Counter
11. Small-scale combinational logic circuit experiments1: majority voting circuit
12. Small-scale combinational logic circuit experiments 2: Water-level shown control circuit
13. Mid-scale combinational logic circuit experiments 1: Comparator and its application
14. Mid-scale combinational logic circuit experiments 2: Decoder and its application;
15. Mid-scale combinational logic circuit experiment 3: Selection and its application
16. Mid-scale combinational logic circuit experiments 4: Adder and its application
17. Mid-scale timing integrated circuits - the second application of the counter
18. Mid-scale timing integrated circuits -The application of the shift register
19. Mid-scale timing integrated circuits - the first application of the counter
20. Mid-scale timing integrated circuits -Cascaded counter

(4) 17 typical experiments provided on High-frequency Circuits (OWVLab HFCS)

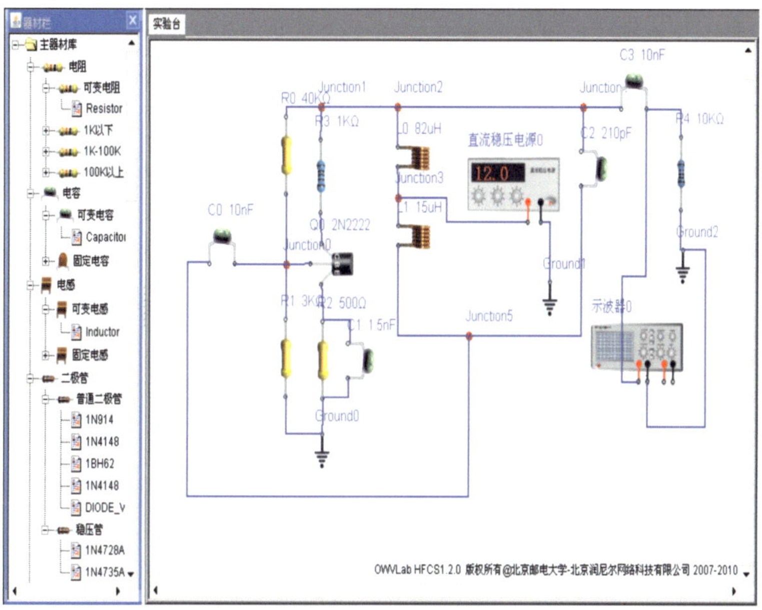

Fig. 10. A High-frequency Circuits Simulation Platform

1. Single-tuned circuit small-signal frequency-selective amplifier
2. Double-tuned circuit small-signal frequency-selective amplifier
3. C-Class amplifier
4. Inductance three-end oscillator
5. Capacitance three-end oscillator
6. Carat dial oscillation circuit
7. Syracuse oscillation circuit
8. RC sinusoidal oscillator
9. Differential amplitude modulation circuit
10. Multiplier AM circuit
11. Differential transistor mixer circuit

12. Demodulation of AM signal- Multiplier demodulation circuit
13. Multiplier mixer circuit
14. VCO transistor circuit
15. FET mixer circuit
16. Demodulation of AM signal- Diode envelope detector circuit
17. Multiplier phase discriminator circuit

(5) Linux experiment simulation platform provides 11 experiments of 2 categories

Linux System Management Experiment:

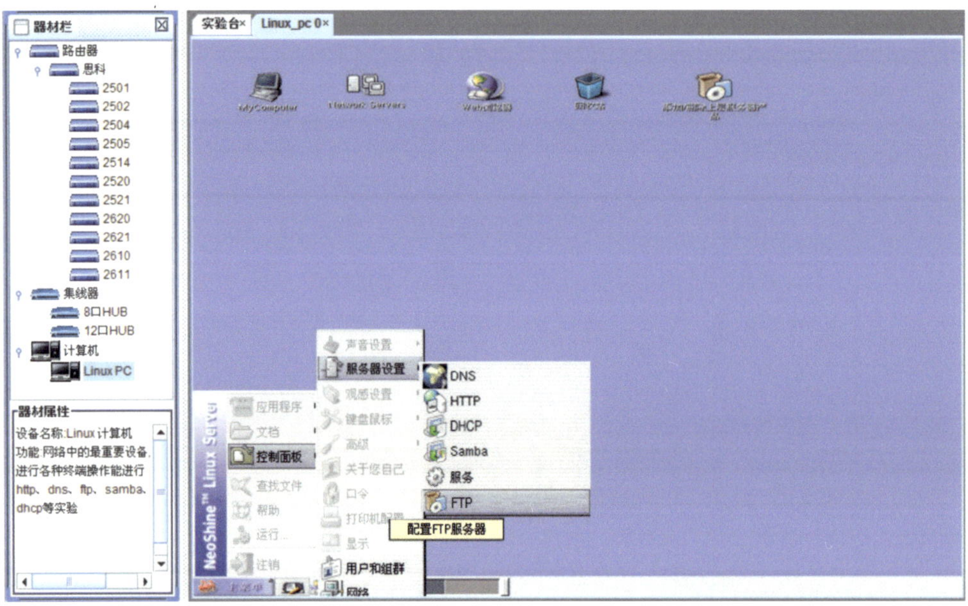

Fig. 11. A Linux System Simulation Platform

1. Linux Commands Experiment
2. Linux Files Management Experiment
3. Linux Process Experiment
4. VI Text Editor Useage Experiment
5. Linux User Management Experiment

Linux Network Experiment:

1. Linux NIC Configuration Experiment
2. Linux DHCP Server Configuration Experiment
3. Linux HTTP Server Configuration Experiment
4. Linux FTP Server Configuration Experiment
5. Linux DNS Server Configuration Experiment
6. Linux Samba Server Configuration Experiment

(6) Computer Network provides 33 typical experiments as 3 categories

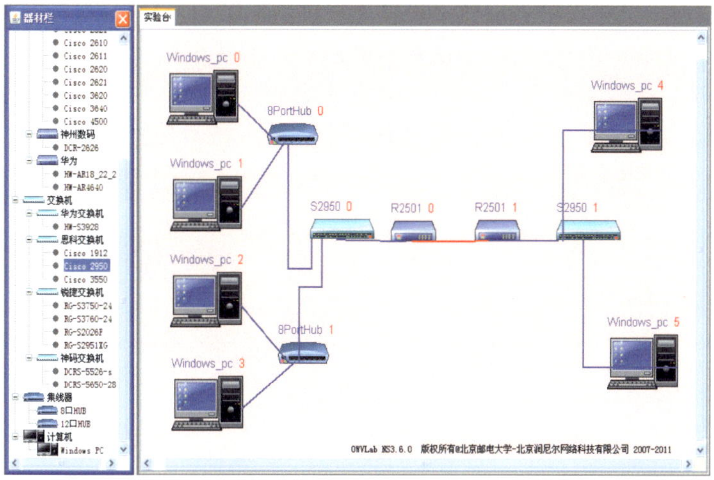

Fig. 12. A Computer Network Simulation Platform

(1 Windows Network Experiment:

1. Windows LAN Configuration
2. Windows WEB Server Configuration
3. Windows FTP Server Configuration
4. Windows DNS Server Configuration
5. Windows DHCP Server Configuration

(2 Routers Configuration Operation Experiment:

1. Routers Basic Configuration
2. Routers IP Configuration
3. Routers Static Routing Configuration
4. Routers Default Routing Configuration
5. Routers Configuration Copy Operation
6. Routers ARP Operation
7. Routers RIP Configuration I
8. Routers RIP Configuration II
9. Routers IGRP Configuration
10. Routers EIGRP Configuration
11. Routers OSPF Protocol
12. Create HOST Watches
13. Routers TELNET

(3 Switches Configuration Operation Experiment:

1. Switches IP Configuration
2. Switches Ports Configuration
3. Switches TRUNK Configuration
4. Switches VLAN Configuration I

5. Switches VLAN Configuration II
6. Switches VTP Configuration
7. Switches VTP Client Model Configuration

(7) 15 typical experiments provided on Signal and System (OWVLab SSS)

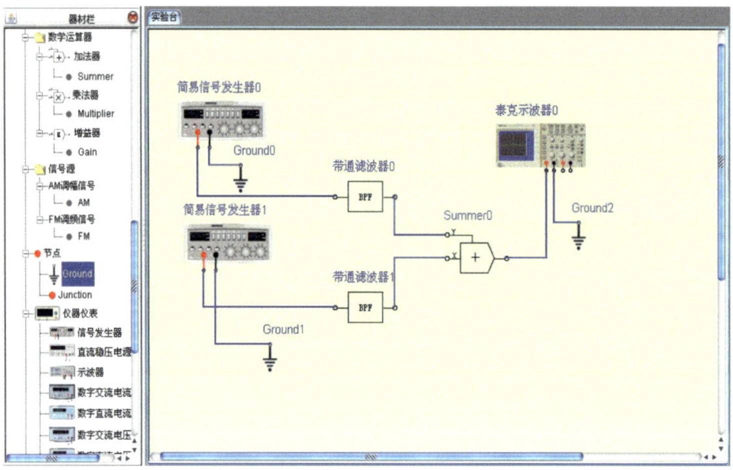

Fig. 13. A Signal and System Simulation Platform

1. Zero input, zero state and the complete response
2. Decomposition and synthesis of signal
3. Lossless transmission system
4. Analysis of analog filters
5. Passive filters and active filters
6. Transmission characteristics of second-order circuit
7. Simulation of continuous-time systems
8. Transient response of second-order circuit
9. AM Amplitude's modulation and demodulation
10. The analog of Second-order function network
11. The test of RC frequency selection circuit
12. The realization of single-sideband modulation signal
13. Common signal's classification and observation
14. Linear time-invariant system
15. Signal frequency-domain analysis

In addition to these experiments, users can also use the equipment provided to design experiments on the platform.

7. Application practice in China

The research results have been used in Beijing University of Posts and Telecommunications, China University of Petroleum, Dalian University of Technology, PLA University of Science and Technology and other twenty universities. The system has won the praises from teachers who are responsible for guiding the experimental learning, college students, national experts in the field of educational technology, experts on electronic electrical, computer science and communications.

8. Conclusion

Paving the way for carrying out large scale distance experimental learning, virtual lab is the future trend in the construction of laboratories and training rooms in all kinds of colleges and continuing education institutions. In terms of the change in the educational model, the system has filled the insurmountable gap between the lab and the classroom. Open virtual lab has broken boundaries of the labs and classrooms ever. Blending the knowledge study within an experiment, there shall be a historic opportunity for the real integration of experimental and theoretical learning. OWVLab will become an essential equipment of experimental learning in school, and it will stimulate the next wave of educational innovation.

OWVLab can promote the students to combine their study with application, plan the flexible experiments without the limit of time and space. Where the Internet is connected, the experiment can be conducted, so the open lab in the real sense is achieved. Virtual experiments can reduce the intensity of maintaining the experimental equipment and alleviate the current shortage of lab equipment. With the supporting of the abundant learning resources, the corresponding intelligent tutor for the experimental process and automatic correction for the virtual experiment results, virtual experiment can achieve the organic integration of the theoretical and practical learning, cultivate the students' ability to design, diagnose and innovate. The 4E blaze a promising way to solve the problem occurred in a classroom. It let us to avoid facing the embarrassed when we lack of audiovisual aids. The existing experimental learning system on computer science, electronics, telecommunication would be improved with the establishment of the virtual lab.

9. Acknowledgment

This paper is supported by the Key Project in the National Science & Technology Pillar Program of China under the grant No.2008BAH29B00.

10. References

Adams, R. K. (1989). The virtual scope: an impedance match to the beginning ECE student, *Proceedings of Energy and Information Technologies in the Southeast,* Digital Object Identifier: 10.1109/SECON.1989.132655, Columbia, USA, April 1989

Zhang, C. T. (1999). Thinking in Learning Environment and Curriculum, *Journal of Social Science of Hunan Normal University,*Vol. 01, Jan 1999, pp. ISSN 1000-2529

Wen, F., Suo, D., Chen, M., &Li, J.(2010) An OpenLab Platform with Virtual Experiment Learning System, *2010 2nd International Conference on Network Infrastructure and Digital Content (IEEE IC-INIDC 2010),* 0170-303 P839-P843, Beijing, China, September 2010

Rheingold, H.(1993). The Virtual Community : Homesteading on the Electronic Frontier, Addison-Wesley, ISBN: 9780262681216, MA

Mercer, L., Prusinkiewicz, P., &Hanan J. (1990). Concept and design of a virtual laboratory, Source, *Graphics Interface,* ISSN: 07135424, Nova Scotia, Canada, May 1990

Hai Lin, P., Lin, M. (2005). Design and implementation of an Internet-based virtual lab system for e-learning support, *Fifth IEEE International Conference on Advanced Learning Technologies*, New York, NY, USA, July 2005

Wang, Z., Wen, F., Chen, M., Sun, Y., (2010) The Design and Implement ion of General marking System for Circuit-Based virtual Experiment, *2010 3rd International Conference on Advanced Computer Theory and Engineering,* ISSN: 2154-7491, Chengdu, China, August 2010

TIOBE Software, TIOBE programming Community Index for October 2011, In: *Java is losing ground despite its new version 7 release,* October 2011, Available from: http://www.tiobe.com/index.php/content/paperinfo/tpci/index.html